AMERICA'S FAVORITES™

Bake Sale

pil

Publications International, Ltd.
Favorite Brand Name Recipes at www.fbnr.com

Pictured on the front cover: Mandarin Orange Tea Cake *(page 49).*

Pictured on the back cover *(left to right):* Raspberry Bars *(page 122)* and Original Nestle® Toll House® Chocolate Chip Cookies *(page 92).*

ISBN: 1-4127-2239-X

Library of Congress Control Number: 2005926107

Manufactured in China.

8 7 6 5 4 3 2 1

Microwave Cooking: Microwave ovens vary in wattage. Use the cooking times as guidelines and check for doneness before adding more time.

Preparation/Cooking Times: Preparation times are based on the approximate amount of time required to assemble the recipe before cooking, baking, chilling or serving. These times include preparation steps such as measuring, chopping and mixing. The fact that some preparations and cooking can be done simultaneously is taken into account. Preparation of optional ingredients and serving suggestions is not included.

Contents

Strawberry Muffins

1 ¼ cups all-purpose flour

2 ½ teaspoons baking powder

½ teaspoon salt

1 cup uncooked old-fashioned oats

½ cup sugar

1 cup milk

½ cup (1 stick) butter, melted

1 egg, beaten

1 teaspoon vanilla

1 cup chopped fresh strawberries

1. Preheat oven to 425°F. Grease bottoms only of 12 standard (2½-inch) muffin pan cups or line with paper liners; set aside.

2. Combine flour, baking powder and salt in large bowl. Stir in oats and sugar. Combine milk, butter, egg and vanilla in small bowl until well blended; stir into flour mixture just until moistened. Fold in strawberries. Spoon into prepared muffin cups, filling about ⅔ full.

3. Bake 15 to 18 minutes or until lightly browned and toothpick inserted into centers comes out clean. Remove from pan. Cool on wire rack 10 minutes. Serve warm or cool completely.

Makes 12 muffins

Strawberry Muffins

Chocolate Chip Coffeecake

- **3 cups all-purpose flour, divided**
- **¹/₃ cup sugar**
- **2 envelopes FLEISCHMANN'S® RapidRise™ Yeast**
- **1 teaspoon salt**
- **¹/₂ cup milk**
- **¹/₂ cup water**
- **¹/₂ cup butter or margarine**
- **2 large eggs**
- **³/₄ cup semi-sweet chocolate morsels**
- **Chocolate Nut Topping (recipe follows)**

In large bowl, combine 1 cup flour, sugar, undissolved yeast and salt. Heat milk, water and butter until very warm (120° to 130°F). Gradually add to dry ingredients. Beat 2 minutes at medium speed of electric mixer, scraping bowl occasionally. Add eggs and 1 cup flour; beat 2 minutes at high speed, scraping bowl occasionally. Stir in chocolate morsels and remaining flour to make a soft batter. Turn into greased 13×9×2-inch baking pan. Cover; let rise in warm, draft-free place until doubled in size, about 1 hour.

Bake at 400°F for 15 minutes; remove from oven and sprinkle with Chocolate Nut Topping. Return to oven and bake additional 10 minutes or until done. Cool in pan for 10 minutes. Remove from pan; cool on wire rack.   *Makes 1 cake*

Chocolate Nut Topping: In medium bowl, cut ½ cup butter into ⅔ cup all-purpose flour until crumbly. Stir in ⅔ cup sugar, 2 teaspoons ground cinnamon, 1 cup semi-sweet chocolate morsels and 1 cup chopped pecans.

Chocolate Chip Coffeecake

Cinnamini Buns

2 tablespoons packed brown sugar
½ teaspoon ground cinnamon
1 can (8 ounces) refrigerated crescent roll dough
1 tablespoon butter, melted
½ cup powdered sugar
1 tablespoon milk

1. Preheat oven to 375°F. Generously grease large baking sheet. Combine brown sugar and cinnamon in small bowl; mix well.

2. Unroll dough and separate into two long (12×4-inch) rectangles; firmly press perforations to seal. Brush dough with melted butter; sprinkle with brown sugar mixture. Roll up each rectangle tightly starting from long side; pinch edges to seal. Cut each roll into 12 (1-inch) slices with serrated knife. Place slices, cut sides up, about 1½ inches apart on prepared baking sheet.

3. Bake about 10 minutes or until golden brown. Remove to wire rack. Blend powdered sugar and milk in small bowl until smooth; add additional milk, if necessary, to reach desired consistency. Drizzle glaze over cinnamon buns.

Makes 2 dozen mini cinnamon buns

Tip

To make sure your glaze has a smooth consistency without any lumps, sift the powdered sugar before stirring in the milk.

Cinnamini Buns

Apricot-Peanut Butter Muffins

1 3/4 cups all-purpose flour

2 1/2 tablespoons sugar

2 1/2 teaspoons baking powder

3/4 teaspoon salt

1/4 cup **CRISCO®** all-vegetable shortening

1/4 cup **JIF®** Creamy Peanut Butter

3/4 cup milk

2 eggs

2 tablespoons **SMUCKER'S®** Apricot Preserves

Preheat oven to 400°F. Grease 10 large muffin cups.

Combine flour, sugar, baking powder and salt; cut in shortening and peanut butter.

Mix milk and eggs together; add all at once to dry ingredients. Stir only until dry ingredients are moistened.

Fill muffin cups 2/3 full. Spoon about 1/2 teaspoon preserves in center of each muffin.

Bake for 25 minutes or until done.   *Makes 10 muffins*

Variation: Substitute your favorite SMUCKER'S® flavors in place of the apricot preserves in the above recipe. Experiment with strawberry or blackberry preserves or even apple butter.

10

Apricot-Peanut Butter Muffins

Aloha Bread

  1 (10-ounce) jar maraschino cherries
1 ¾ cups all-purpose flour
  2 teaspoons baking powder
  ½ teaspoon salt
  ⅔ cup firmly packed brown sugar
  ⅓ cup butter or margarine, softened
  2 eggs
  1 cup mashed ripe bananas
  ½ cup chopped macadamia nuts or walnuts

Drain maraschino cherries, reserving 2 tablespoons juice. Cut cherries into quarters; set aside.

Combine flour, baking powder and salt in small bowl; set aside.

In medium bowl, combine brown sugar, butter, eggs and reserved cherry juice; mix at medium speed of electric mixer until ingredients are thoroughly combined. Add flour mixture alternately with mashed bananas, beginning and ending with flour mixture. Stir in cherries and nuts. Lightly spray 9×5×3-inch loaf pan with nonstick cooking spray. Spread batter evenly in pan.

Bake in preheated 350°F oven 1 hour or until loaf is golden brown and wooden pick inserted near center comes out clean. Remove from pan and cool on wire rack. Store in tightly covered container or wrapped in foil.   *Makes 1 loaf (about 16 slices)*

Favorite recipe from **Cherry Marketing Institute**

12

Aloha Bread

Peachy Cinnamon Coffeecake

1 can (8 ¼ ounces) juice packed sliced yellow cling peaches
1 package DUNCAN HINES® Bakery-Style Cinnamon Swirl Muffin Mix
1 egg

1. Preheat oven to 400°F. Grease 8-inch square or 9-inch round pan.

2. Drain peaches, reserving juice. Add water to reserved juice to equal ¾ cup liquid. Chop peaches.

3. Combine muffin mix, egg and ¾ cup peach liquid in medium bowl; fold in peaches. Pour batter into prepared pan. Knead swirl packet 10 seconds before opening. Squeeze contents onto top of batter and swirl with knife. Sprinkle topping over batter. Bake at 400°F for 28 to 33 minutes for 8-inch pan (or 20 to 25 minutes for 9-inch pan) or until golden. Serve warm.   *Makes 9 servings*

Cheddar and Apple Muffins

2 cups buttermilk baking mix
½ to 1 teaspoon ground red pepper
½ teaspoon salt
⅔ cup milk
1 egg, lightly beaten
1 medium apple, peeled, cored and grated
1 cup (4 ounces) shredded sharp Cheddar cheese

1. Preheat oven to 375°F. Spray 12 standard (2½-inch) muffin pan cups with nonstick cooking spray.

2. Combine baking mix, red pepper and salt in large bowl. Add milk and egg; mix until just moistened. *Do not overmix.* Fold in apple and cheese. Spoon batter into prepared muffin cups filling ¾ full.

3. Bake 20 to 25 minutes or until golden brown. Cool 5 minutes in pan. Loosen sides of muffins with knife; remove from pan to wire rack. Serve warm.

Makes 12 muffins

Peachy Cinnamon Coffeecake

Banana Brunch Coffeecake

2 ripe, medium DOLE® Bananas
1 package (18.25 ounces) yellow cake mix
1 package (3.4 ounces) instant vanilla pudding mix (4 servings)
4 eggs
1/2 cup vegetable oil
1 teaspoon vanilla extract
1/2 cup chopped almonds
1/3 cup packed brown sugar
1 teaspoon ground cinnamon
1/2 teaspoon ground nutmeg

✦ Purée bananas in blender (about 1 cup). Combine bananas, cake mix, pudding mix, eggs, oil and vanilla in large mixing bowl. Mix well and beat at medium speed 8 minutes, scraping side of bowl occasionally.

✦ Combine almonds, brown sugar, cinnamon and nutmeg. Pour one-half cake batter into greased 3-quart Bundt pan. Sprinkle with almond mixture. Cover with remaining batter. Insert knife in batter and swirl in figure eight patterns through layers. (Be sure not to overmix layers.)

✦ Bake at 325°F 60 to 65 minutes. Cool in pan on wire rack 10 minutes. Invert onto rack to complete cooling. Dust with powdered sugar when cool, if desired. Garnish with sliced bananas and fresh mint, if desired. *Makes 12 servings*

Prep Time: 15 minutes ✦ Bake Time: 60 minutes

Cranberry Oat Bread

¾ cup honey

2 eggs

½ cup milk

⅓ cup vegetable oil

2½ cups all-purpose flour

1 cup quick-cooking rolled oats

1 teaspoon baking soda

1 teaspoon baking powder

½ teaspoon salt

½ teaspoon ground cinnamon

2 cups fresh or frozen cranberries

1 cup chopped nuts

Combine honey, eggs, milk and oil in large bowl; mix well. Combine flour, oats, baking soda, baking powder, salt and cinnamon in medium bowl; mix well. Stir into honey mixture. Fold in cranberries and nuts. Spoon into 2 greased and floured 8½×4½×2½-inch loaf pans.

Bake in preheated 350°F oven 40 to 45 minutes or until wooden toothpick inserted near centers comes out clean. Cool in pans on wire racks 15 minutes. Remove from pans; cool completely on wire racks.   *Makes 2 loaves*

Favorite recipe from **National Honey Board**

Blueberry Orange Muffins

1 ¾ cups all-purpose flour

⅓ cup sugar

2 ½ teaspoons baking powder

½ teaspoon baking soda

½ teaspoon salt

½ teaspoon ground cinnamon

¾ cup milk

1 egg, lightly beaten

¼ cup (½ stick) butter, melted and slightly cooled

3 tablespoons orange juice concentrate, thawed

1 teaspoon vanilla

¾ cup fresh or frozen blueberries, thawed

1. Preheat oven to 400°F. Grease 12 standard (2½-inch) muffin pan cups or line with paper liners.

2. Combine flour, sugar, baking powder, baking soda, salt and cinnamon in large bowl. Beat milk, egg, butter, orange juice concentrate and vanilla in medium bowl with electric mixer at medium speed until well combined. Add milk mixture to dry ingredients. Mix lightly until dry ingredients are barely moistened (mixture will be lumpy). Add blueberries; stir gently just until berries are evenly distributed. Spoon batter into prepared muffin cups filling ¾ full.

3. Bake 20 to 25 minutes (25 to 30 minutes if using frozen berries) or until toothpick inserted into centers comes out clean. Cool 5 minutes in pan; remove from pan to wire rack. Serve warm.   *Makes 12 servings*

Blueberry Orange Muffins

Peanut Butter Coffee Cake

1 ½ cups packed brown sugar, divided
2 ½ cups all-purpose flour, divided
¾ cup JIF® Creamy Peanut Butter, divided
2 tablespoons butter or margarine, melted
¼ cup CRISCO® all-vegetable shortening
2 eggs
2 teaspoons baking powder
½ teaspoon salt
½ teaspoon baking soda
1 cup milk
Powdered sugar icing (optional)

1. Preheat oven to 375°F.

2. Combine ½ cup brown sugar, ½ cup flour, ¼ cup peanut butter and melted butter until crumbly; set aside.

3. Cream remaining ½ cup peanut butter and shortening. Slowly beat in remaining 1 cup brown sugar. Add eggs, 1 at a time, beating until fluffy.

4. Combine remaining 2 cups flour, baking powder, salt and baking soda; mix well. Add flour mixture alternately with milk to creamed mixture, beating after each addition.

5. Spread batter in greased 13×9×2-inch baking pan. Top with reserved crumbly mixture. Bake for 30 to 35 minutes or until toothpick inserted into center comes out clean. Cool completely. Drizzle with icing, if desired.   *Makes 16 to 18 servings*

Peanut Butter Coffee Cake

Walnut-Chocolate Quick Bread

1 ½ cups milk

1 cup sugar

⅓ cup vegetable oil

1 egg, beaten

1 tablespoon molasses

1 teaspoon vanilla

3 cups all-purpose flour

3 tablespoons unsweetened cocoa powder

2 teaspoons baking soda

2 teaspoons baking powder

1 teaspoon salt

1 cup chocolate chips

½ cup walnuts, coarsely chopped

1. Preheat oven to 350°F. Grease four 5×3-inch loaf pans; set aside.

2. Combine milk, sugar, oil, egg, molasses and vanilla in medium bowl. Stir until sugar is dissolved.

3. Combine flour, cocoa, baking soda, baking powder and salt in large bowl. Add chocolate chips, walnuts and milk mixture; stir just until combined. Pour into prepared pans.

4. Bake 30 minutes or until toothpick inserted into centers of loaves comes out clean. Cool in pans 15 minutes. Remove from pans and cool on wire racks.

Makes 4 small loaves

Muffin Variation: Preheat oven to 375°F. Spoon batter into 12 standard (2½-inch) greased muffin pan cups. Bake 20 minutes or until toothpick inserted into centers comes out clean.

22

Orange Streusel Coffeecake

Cocoa Streusel (recipe follows)
³⁄₄ **cup (1 ¹⁄₂ sticks) butter or margarine, softened**
 1 **cup sugar**
 3 **eggs**
 1 **teaspoon vanilla extract**
¹⁄₂ **cup dairy sour cream**
 3 **cups all-purpose flour**
 2 **teaspoons baking powder**
 1 **teaspoon baking soda**
 1 **cup orange juice**
 2 **teaspoons grated orange peel**
¹⁄₂ **cup orange marmalade or apple jelly**

1. Prepare Cocoa Streusel. Heat oven to 350°F. Generously grease 12-cup fluted tube pan.

2. Beat butter and sugar in large bowl until well blended. Add eggs and vanilla; beat well. Add sour cream; beat until blended. Stir together flour, baking powder and baking soda; add alternately with orange juice to butter mixture, beating until well blended. Stir in orange peel.

3. Spread marmalade in bottom of prepared pan; sprinkle half of streusel over marmalade. Pour half of batter into pan, spreading evenly. Sprinkle remaining streusel over batter; spread remaining batter evenly over streusel.

4. Bake about 1 hour or until toothpick inserted near center of cake comes out clean. Loosen cake from side of pan with metal spatula; immediately invert onto serving plate.   *Makes 12 servings*

Cocoa Streusel: Stir together ²⁄₃ cup packed light brown sugar, ¹⁄₂ cup chopped walnuts, ¹⁄₄ cup HERSHEY'S Cocoa and ¹⁄₂ cup MOUNDS® Sweetened Coconut Flakes, if desired.

Coconut Chocolate Chip Loaf

1 package DUNCAN HINES® Bakery-Style Chocolate Chip Muffin Mix
1 1/3 cups toasted flaked coconut (see Tip)
3/4 cup water
1 egg
1/2 teaspoon vanilla extract
Confectioners' sugar for garnish (optional)

1. Preheat oven to 350°F. Grease and flour 9×5×3-inch loaf pan.

2. Empty muffin mix into medium bowl. Break up any lumps. Add coconut, water, egg and vanilla extract. Stir until moistened, about 50 strokes. Pour into prepared pan. Bake at 350°F for 45 to 50 minutes or until toothpick inserted in center comes out clean. Cool in pan 15 minutes. Invert onto cooling rack. Turn right side up. Cool completely. Dust with confectioners' sugar, if desired.   *Makes 1 loaf (12 slices)*

Tip

To toast coconut, spread evenly on a baking sheet. Bake at 350°F for 5 minutes. Stir and bake 1 to 2 minutes longer or until light golden brown.

Coconut Chocolate Chip Loaf

Lemon Poppy Seed Muffins

3 cups all-purpose flour

1 cup sugar

3 tablespoons poppy seeds

1 tablespoon grated lemon peel

2 teaspoons baking powder

1 teaspoon baking soda

$\frac{1}{2}$ teaspoon salt

1 container (16 ounces) plain low-fat yogurt

$\frac{1}{2}$ cup fresh lemon juice

2 eggs, beaten

$\frac{1}{4}$ cup vegetable oil

1 $\frac{1}{2}$ teaspoons vanilla

1. Preheat oven to 400°F. Lightly grease 12 large (3$\frac{1}{2}$-inch) muffin pan cups or line with paper liners.

2. Combine flour, sugar, poppy seeds, lemon peel, baking powder, baking soda and salt in large bowl; stir until blended. Combine yogurt, lemon juice, eggs, oil and vanilla in small bowl; stir until well blended. Stir yogurt mixture into flour mixture just until moistened. Spoon batter into prepared muffin cups, filling $\frac{2}{3}$ full.

3. Bake 25 to 30 minutes or until toothpick inserted into centers comes out clean. Cool in pans on wire racks 5 minutes. Remove from pans. Cool on wire racks 10 minutes. Serve warm or cool completely.

Makes 12 large muffins

27

Lemon Poppy Seed Muffins

Pumpkin Bread

- 1 package (about 18 ounces) yellow cake mix
- 1 can (16 ounces) solid pack pumpkin
- 4 eggs
- 1/3 cup GRANDMA'S® Molasses
- 1 teaspoon cinnamon
- 1 teaspoon nutmeg
- 1/3 cup nuts, chopped (optional)
- 1/3 cup raisins (optional)

Preheat oven to 350°F. Grease two 9×5-inch loaf pans.

Combine all ingredients in large bowl and mix well. Beat at medium speed 2 minutes. Pour into prepared pans. Bake 60 minutes or until toothpick inserted into center comes out clean.   *Makes 2 loaves*

Hint: Serve with cream cheese or preserves, or top with cream cheese frosting or ice cream.

 Tip

Before measuring molasses, lightly coat a measuring cup with nonstick cooking spray so the molasses will slide out easily instead of clinging to the cup.

Pumpkin Bread

Mini Chocolate Cheesecakes

- **3 packages (8 ounces each) cream cheese, softened**
- **1/2 cup sugar**
- **3 eggs**
- **1 teaspoon vanilla**
- **8 squares (1 ounce each) semisweet baking chocolate, chopped**

1. Preheat oven to 325°F. Lightly grease 12 standard (2¾-inch) muffin pan cups or line with foil liners; set aside.

2. Beat cream cheese and sugar in large bowl with electric mixer at medium speed about 2 minutes or until light and fluffy. Add eggs and vanilla; beat about 2 minutes or until well blended.

3. Place chocolate in microwavable bowl. Microwave at HIGH 1 to 1½ minutes or until chocolate is melted, stirring after 1 minute. Beat melted chocolate into cream cheese mixture until well blended.

4. Divide mixture evenly among prepared muffin cups. Place muffin pan in larger baking pan; place on oven rack. Pour warm water into larger pan to depth of ½ to 1 inch. Bake cheesecakes 30 minutes or until edges are dry and centers are almost set. Remove muffin pan from water. Cool cheesecakes completely in muffin pan on wire rack.

Makes 12 cheesecakes

Mini Swirl Cheesecakes: Before adding melted chocolate to batter, place about 2 tablespoons of batter into each muffin cup. Add chocolate to remaining batter and beat to combine. Spoon chocolate batter over plain batter in muffin cups. Swirl with knife before baking.

Mini Swirl Cheesecakes

Toll House® Crumbcake

Topping
- ⅓ cup packed brown sugar
- 1 tablespoon all-purpose flour
- 2 tablespoons butter or margarine, softened
- ½ cup chopped nuts
- 2 cups (12-ounce package) **NESTLÉ® TOLL HOUSE®** Semi-Sweet Chocolate Mini Morsels, *divided*

Cake
- 1 ¾ cups all-purpose flour
- 1 teaspoon baking powder
- 1 teaspoon baking soda
- ¼ teaspoon salt
- ¾ cup granulated sugar
- ½ cup (1 stick) butter or margarine, softened
- 1 teaspoon vanilla extract
- 3 large eggs
- 1 cup sour cream

PREHEAT oven to 350°F. Grease 13×9-inch baking pan.

For Topping
COMBINE brown sugar, flour and butter in small bowl with pastry blender or two knives until crumbly. Stir in nuts and *½ cup* morsels.

For Cake
COMBINE flour, baking powder, baking soda and salt in small bowl. Beat granulated sugar, butter and vanilla extract in large mixer bowl until creamy. Add eggs, one at a time, beating well after each addition. Gradually add flour mixture alternately with sour cream. Fold in *remaining 1 ½ cups* morsels. Spread into prepared baking pan; sprinkle with topping.

BAKE for 25 to 35 minutes or until wooden pick inserted in center comes out clean. Cool in pan on wire rack.

Makes 12 servings

Toll House® Crumbcake

Pumpkin Chiffon Cake

Cake

- 1 package DUNCAN HINES® Moist Deluxe® Spice Cake Mix
- 3 eggs
- 1 cup water
- 1 tablespoon vegetable oil plus additional for greasing
- 1 ½ cups solid pack pumpkin, divided

Filling

- 2 cups whipping cream, chilled
- ½ cup sugar
- 1 cup Sugared Pecans, chopped (recipe follows)
- Sugared Pecan halves for garnish

1. Preheat oven to 350°F. Grease and flour two 8-inch round cake pans.

2. For cake, combine cake mix, eggs, water and oil in large bowl. Beat at low speed with electric mixer until moistened. Beat at medium speed for 2 minutes. Fold in 1 cup pumpkin. Pour batter into pans. Bake and cool cake following package directions.

3. For filling, place whipping cream and sugar in large bowl. Beat at high speed with electric mixer until stiff peaks form. Fold in remaining ½ cup pumpkin and chopped Sugared Pecans.

4. To assemble, level cake layers. Split each cake layer in half horizontally. Place 1 cake layer on serving plate. Spread with one-fourth the filling. Repeat layering 3 more times. Garnish with Sugared Pecan halves. *Makes 12 to 16 servings*

Sugared Pecans: Preheat oven to 300°F. Combine 1 cup sugar, 1 tablespoon ground cinnamon and 1 teaspoon salt in small bowl; set aside. Beat 1 egg white and 1 tablespoon water in medium bowl with electric mixer at medium speed until frothy but not stiff. Pour 1 pound pecan halves into egg white mixture; stir until coated. Add sugar mixture; stir until evenly coated. Spread on cookie sheet. Bake at 300°F for 45 minutes, stirring every 15 minutes. Cool completely.

Pumpkin Chiffon Cake

Butterscotch Bundt Cake

- **1 package (about 18 ounces) yellow cake mix *without* pudding in the mix**
- **1 package (4-serving size) butterscotch-flavored instant pudding and pie filling mix**
- **1 cup water**
- **3 eggs**
- **2 teaspoons ground cinnamon**
- **1/2 cup chopped pecans**
- **Powdered sugar (optional)**

Preheat oven to 325°F. Spray 12-cup bundt pan with nonstick cooking spray. Beat cake mix, pudding mix, water, eggs and cinnamon in large bowl with electric mixer at medium-high speed 2 minutes or until blended. Stir in pecans. Pour into prepared pan. Bake 40 to 50 minutes or until cake springs back when lightly touched. Cool on wire rack 10 minutes. Invert cake onto serving plate; cool completely. Sprinkle with powdered sugar, if desired.

Makes 12 to 16 servings

Pistachio-Walnut Bundt Cake: Substitute white cake mix for yellow cake mix, pistachio-flavored pudding mix for butterscotch and walnuts for pecans.

Tip

For the best results when baking a cake, avoid opening the oven door during the first half of the baking time. The oven temperature must remain constant in order for the cake to rise properly.

Butterscotch Bundt Cake

Dump Cake

   1 can (20 ounces) crushed pineapple with juice, undrained
   1 can (21 ounces) cherry pie filling
   1 package DUNCAN HINES® Moist Deluxe® Yellow Cake Mix
   1 cup chopped pecans or walnuts
   ½ cup butter or margarine, cut into thin slices

1. Preheat oven to 350°F. Grease 13×9-inch pan.

2. Dump pineapple with juice into prepared pan. Spread evenly. Dump in pie filling. Spread evenly. Sprinkle cake mix evenly over cherry layer. Sprinkle pecans over cake mix. Dot with butter. Bake at 350°F for 50 minutes or until top is lightly browned. Serve warm or at room temperature. *Makes 12 to 16 servings*

Tip: You can use Duncan Hines® Moist Deluxe® Pineapple Supreme Cake Mix in place of Moist Deluxe® Yellow Cake Mix.

38

Apple-Pecan Cheesecake

   2 packages (8 ounces each) cream cheese, softened
   ⅔ cup sugar, divided
   2 eggs
   ½ teaspoon vanilla
   1 (9-inch) prepared graham cracker crust
   ½ teaspoon ground cinnamon
   4 cups Golden Delicious apples, peeled, cored and thinly sliced (about
      2½ pounds)
   ½ cup chopped pecans

Preheat oven to 350°F. Beat cream cheese and ⅓ cup sugar in large bowl until well blended. Beat in eggs, 1 at a time. Blend in vanilla; pour into crust. Combine remaining ⅓ cup sugar and cinnamon in large bowl. Add apples; toss gently to coat. Spoon or arrange apple mixture over cream cheese mixture. Sprinkle with pecans. Bake 1 hour and 10 minutes or until set. Cool completely. *Makes one 9-inch cheesecake*

Dump Cake

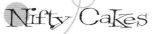

Fresh Lemon Sunshine Cake

1 ½ **cups sifted cake flour**
¼ **teaspoon salt**
6 **eggs, separated**
¼ **teaspoon cream of tartar**
1 ½ **cups sugar, divided**
5 **tablespoons water**
Grated peel and juice of 1 SUNKIST® lemon (3 tablespoons juice)
Hint O' Lemon Glaze (recipe follows)

Sift together flour and salt. In large bowl with electric mixer, beat egg whites and cream of tartar at high speed until soft peaks form. Gradually add ½ cup sugar, beating until medium-stiff peaks form; set aside. With same beaters, in medium bowl, beat egg yolks 2 minutes. Gradually add remaining 1 cup sugar, beating at high speed until egg yolk mixture is very thick. Beat in water and lemon juice; stir in lemon peel. Add flour mixture all at once; gently fold, then lightly stir until well blended. Carefully fold yolk mixture into beaten egg whites. Pour batter into *ungreased* 10-inch tube pan with removable bottom. Smooth top and cut through batter with table knife to remove any large air bubbles. Bake at 325°F for 45 to 55 minutes or until cake springs back when lightly touched. Immediately invert onto neck of bottle or wire rack; cool completely upside-down. With narrow spatula or knife, loosen around tube and side. Lift out tube and cake; loosen cake around bottom. Invert onto cake plate. Glaze top with Hint O' Lemon Glaze, allowing some to drizzle over side.* Garnish each serving with lemon cartwheel twists, fresh berries and fresh mint leaves, if desired.

Makes 16 servings

Or, cover top of cake with thin layer of Hint O' Lemon Glaze; let dry. Cover remaining glaze with damp paper towels and plastic wrap. When top of cake is dry, drizzle or pipe remaining glaze (thinned with a few drops of lemon juice, if necessary) over top of cake in decorative pattern.

Hint O' Lemon Glaze: In small bowl combine 1 ½ cups sifted confectioners' sugar and 1 ½ to 2 tablespoons fresh squeezed SUNKIST® lemon juice; stir until smooth.

Banana Split Cake

1 1/4 cups sugar, divided
1/2 cup (1 stick) butter, softened
1 package graham crackers (about 20)
2 packages (8 ounces each) cream cheese, softened
4 to 5 bananas
1 can (20 ounces) crushed pineapple, drained
1 container (12 ounces) frozen whipped topping, thawed
1/4 cup chopped pecans or walnuts

1. Beat 1/4 cup sugar and butter in medium bowl with electric mixer at medium speed until creamy. Finely crush graham crackers in resealable plastic food storage bag with rolling pin. Add to butter mixture. Press into bottom of well-greased 13×9-inch baking dish.

2. Beat cream cheese and remaining 1 cup sugar in medium bowl with electric mixer at medium speed 2 minutes or until creamy. Spread over crust. Slice bananas and layer over cream cheese mixture. Spread pineapple over bananas. Spread whipped topping over pineapple; sprinkle with pecans. Cover and chill 4 to 6 hours.

Makes 8 servings

Tip

To soften cream cheese quickly, remove it from the wrapper and place it in a microwavable bowl. Microwave at Medium (50% power) 15 to 20 seconds or until slightly softened. Add 15 seconds for each additional package of cream cheese.

Chocolate Chip Cheesecake

Crust

1 1/2 cups (about 15) crushed chocolate sandwich cookies

2 tablespoons butter or margarine, melted

2 cups (12-ounce package) NESTLÉ® TOLL HOUSE® Semi-Sweet Chocolate Mini Morsels, *divided*

Filling

2 packages (8 ounces *each*) cream cheese, softened

1/2 cup granulated sugar

1 tablespoon vanilla extract

2 large eggs

2 tablespoons all-purpose flour

3/4 cup NESTLÉ® CARNATION® Evaporated Milk

1/2 cup sour cream

For Crust

PREHEAT oven to 300°F.

COMBINE cookie crumbs with butter in medium bowl until moistened; press onto bottom of ungreased 9-inch springform pan. Sprinkle with *1 cup* morsels.

For Filling

BEAT cream cheese, sugar and vanilla extract in large mixer bowl until smooth. Beat in eggs and flour. Gradually beat in evaporated milk and sour cream. Pour over crust. Sprinkle with *remaining* morsels.

BAKE for 25 minutes. Cover loosely with aluminum foil. Bake for additional 30 to 40 minutes or until edge is set but center still moves slightly. Place in refrigerator immediately; refrigerate for 2 hours or until firm. Remove side of springform pan.

Makes 12 to 14 servings

Note: Cheesecake may be baked in 13×9-inch pan. Prepare as above. Bake in preheated 300°F. oven for 20 minutes. Cover loosely with aluminum foil. Bake for additional 20 to 30 minutes.

Chocolate Chip Cheesecake

Lemon Pound Cake with Strawberries

2 cups all-purpose flour

1 teaspoon baking powder

1 teaspoon baking soda

$\frac{1}{2}$ teaspoon salt

$\frac{1}{2}$ cup sour cream

$\frac{1}{2}$ cup milk

$\frac{1}{3}$ cup sugar

$\frac{1}{4}$ cup vegetable oil

1 egg

2 tablespoons lemon juice

1 teaspoon grated lemon peel

3 pints strawberries

Additional sugar (optional)

1. Preheat oven to 350°F. Coat 8×4-inch loaf pan with nonstick cooking spray. Combine flour, baking powder, baking soda and salt in large bowl.

2. Combine sour cream, milk, sugar, oil, egg, lemon juice and lemon peel in medium bowl. Stir sour cream mixture into flour mixture until well combined; pour batter into prepared pan. Bake 45 to 50 minutes or until toothpick inserted into center comes out clean.

3. Let cake cool in pan on wire rack 20 minutes; remove from pan and cool completely on wire rack. Meanwhile, slice strawberries and sprinkle to taste with additional sugar, if desired. Slice cake and serve with strawberries. *Makes 16 servings*

44

Lemon Pound Cake with Strawberries

Hershey's Red Velvet Cake

½ cup (1 stick) butter or margarine, softened
1 ½ cups sugar
2 eggs
1 teaspoon vanilla extract
1 cup buttermilk or sour milk*
2 tablespoons (1-ounce bottle) red food color
2 cups all-purpose flour
⅓ cup HERSHEY'S Cocoa
1 teaspoon salt
1 ½ teaspoons baking soda
1 tablespoon white vinegar
1 can (16 ounces) ready-to-spread vanilla frosting
HERSHEY'S MINI CHIPS™ Semi-Sweet Chocolate Chips or
HERSHEY'S Milk Chocolate Chips (optional)

*To sour milk: Use 1 tablespoon white vinegar plus milk to equal 1 cup.

1. Heat oven to 350°F. Grease and flour 13×9×2-inch baking pan.**

2. Beat butter and sugar in large bowl; add eggs and vanilla, beating well. Stir together buttermilk and food color. Stir together flour, cocoa and salt; add alternately to butter mixture with buttermilk mixture, mixing well. Stir in baking soda and vinegar. Pour into prepared pan.

3. Bake 30 to 35 minutes or until wooden pick inserted in center comes out clean. Cool completely in pan on wire rack. Frost; garnish with chocolate chips, if desired.   *Makes about 15 servings*

**This recipe can be made in 2 (9-inch) cake pans. Bake at 350°F for 30 to 35 minutes.

Hershey's Red Velvet Cake

Moist and Tender Carrot Cake

  2 cups granulated sugar
1 ½ cups vegetable oil
  1 teaspoon vanilla
2 ½ cups all-purpose flour
  2 tablespoons ground cinnamon, divided
  1 teaspoon baking soda
  1 teaspoon salt
  ½ teaspoon ground ginger
  4 eggs
  2 cups grated carrots
  1 cup canned crushed pineapple, drained and juice reserved
  ¾ cup chopped pecans
  ½ cup golden raisins
    Pineapple juice
    Cream Cheese Frosting (page 49)

1. Preheat oven to 350°F. Grease and flour two 8-inch round cake pans.

2. Combine sugar, oil and vanilla in large bowl. Sift flour, 1 tablespoon cinnamon, baking soda, salt and ginger into medium bowl. Add flour mixture to sugar mixture, alternating with eggs. Add carrots, pineapple, pecans and raisins; mix well. Pour evenly into prepared pans.

3. Bake 45 to 50 minutes or until toothpick inserted into centers comes out clean. Poke holes in warm cakes with wooden skewer. Combine reserved canned pineapple juice with enough pineapple juice to equal 2 cups. Pour 1 cup over each cake. Allow cakes to soak up juice and cool in pans.

4. Prepare Cream Cheese Frosting.

5. Invert one cake layer onto serving plate; frost top of cake. Top with second cake layer. Frost top and side of cake. Decorate cake by using icing spreader to make peaks with frosting. Sprinkle remaining 1 tablespoon cinnamon over frosting. Store cake in refrigerator.   *Makes 10 to 12 servings*

Cream Cheese Frosting

2 cups (4 sticks) butter, softened
1 package (8 ounces) cream cheese, softened
2 tablespoons vanilla
2 cups powdered sugar
   Whipping cream

Beat butter, cream cheese and vanilla in large bowl with electric mixer until light and fluffy. Add powdered sugar until completely combined. If frosting is too thick, add whipping cream, 1 tablespoon at a time, until desired consistency.

Mandarin Orange Tea Cake

1 package (16 ounces) pound cake mix
$^1/_2$ cup plus 2 tablespoons orange juice, divided
2 eggs
$^1/_4$ cup milk
1 can (15 ounces) mandarin orange segments in light syrup, drained
$^3/_4$ cup powdered sugar
   Grated peel of 1 orange

1. Preheat oven to 350°F. Grease 9-inch bundt pan.

2. Beat cake mix, $^1/_2$ cup orange juice, eggs and milk in large bowl with electric mixer at medium speed 2 minutes or until light and fluffy. Fold in orange segments; pour batter into prepared pan.

3. Bake 45 minutes or until golden brown and toothpick inserted near center comes out clean. Cool in pan on wire rack 15 minutes. Invert cake onto wire rack; cool completely.

4. To prepare glaze, combine sugar, orange peel and remaining 2 tablespoons orange juice in small bowl; beat until smooth. Drizzle glaze over cake. Allow glaze to set about 5 minutes before serving.   *Makes 16 servings*

Banana-Coconut Crunch Cake

Cake

 1 package DUNCAN HINES® Moist Deluxe® Banana Supreme Cake Mix

 1 package (4-serving size) banana-flavor instant pudding and pie filling mix

 1 can (16 ounces) fruit cocktail, in juice, undrained

 4 eggs

 1/4 cup vegetable oil

 1 cup flaked coconut

 1/2 cup chopped pecans

 1/2 cup firmly packed brown sugar

Glaze

 3/4 cup granulated sugar

 1/2 cup butter or margarine

 1/2 cup evaporated milk

 1 1/3 cups flaked coconut

1. Preheat oven to 350°F. Grease and flour 13×9×2-inch pan.

2. For cake, combine cake mix, pudding mix, fruit cocktail with juice, eggs and oil in large bowl. Beat at medium speed with electric mixer for 4 minutes. Stir in 1 cup coconut. Pour into prepared pan. Combine pecans and brown sugar in small bowl. Stir until well mixed. Sprinkle over batter. Bake at 350°F for 45 to 50 minutes or until toothpick inserted in center comes out clean.

3. For glaze, combine granulated sugar, butter and evaporated milk in medium saucepan. Bring to a boil. Cook for 2 minutes, stirring occasionally. Remove from heat. Stir in 1 1/3 cups coconut. Pour over warm cake. Serve warm or at room temperature.

Makes 12 to 16 servings

Tip: Assemble all ingredients and utensils together before beginning the recipe.

Banana-Coconut Crunch Cake

Cookies 'n' Cream Cake

- 1 package (about 18 ounces) white cake mix *without* pudding in the mix
- 1 package (4-serving size) instant white chocolate-flavor pudding and pie filling mix
- 1 cup vegetable oil
- 4 egg whites
- 1/2 cup milk
- 20 chocolate sandwich cookies, coarsely chopped
- 1/2 cup semisweet chocolate chips
- 1 teaspoon shortening
- 4 chocolate sandwich cookies, cut into quarters for garnish

1. Preheat oven to 350°F. Spray 12-cup bundt pan with nonstick cooking spray.

2. Beat cake mix, pudding mix, oil, egg whites and milk in large bowl with electric mixer at medium speed 2 minutes or until ingredients are well blended. Stir in chopped cookies; spread in prepared pan.

3. Bake 50 to 60 minutes or until cake springs back when lightly touched. Cool 1 hour in pan on wire rack. Invert cake onto serving plate; cool completely.

4. Combine chocolate chips and shortening in small microwavable bowl. Microwave at HIGH (100% power) 1 minute; stir. Microwave at 15-second intervals, as necessary, stirring until melted and smooth. Drizzle glaze over cake and garnish with quartered cookies. *Makes 10 to 12 servings*

Cookies 'n' Cream Cake

Pineapple Upside-Down Cake

Topping

1/2 cup butter or margarine

1 cup firmly packed brown sugar

1 can (20 ounces) pineapple slices, well drained

Maraschino cherries, drained and halved

Walnut halves

Cake

1 package DUNCAN HINES® Moist Deluxe® Pineapple Supreme Cake Mix

1 package (4-serving size) vanilla-flavor instant pudding and pie filling mix

4 eggs

1 cup water

1/2 cup oil

1. Preheat oven to 350°F.

2. For topping, melt butter over low heat in 12-inch cast-iron skillet or skillet with ovenproof handle. Remove from heat. Stir in brown sugar. Spread to cover bottom of skillet. Arrange pineapple slices, maraschino cherries and walnut halves in skillet. Set aside.

3. For cake, combine cake mix, pudding mix, eggs, water and oil in large mixing bowl. Beat at medium speed with electric mixer for 2 minutes. Pour batter evenly over fruit in skillet. Bake at 350°F for 1 hour or until toothpick inserted in center comes out clean. Invert onto serving plate.   *Makes 16 to 20 servings*

Tip: Cake can be made in a 13×9×2-inch pan. Bake at 350°F for 45 to 55 minutes or until toothpick inserted in center comes out clean. Cake is also delicious using Duncan Hines® Moist Deluxe® Yellow Cake Mix.

Pineapple Upside-Down Cake

Groovy Pies

Red, White & Blueberry Cream Pie

1 1/4 cups fresh blueberries, rinsed, drained and divided
1 (6-ounce) READY CRUST® Graham Cracker Pie Crust
1 (8-ounce) package cream cheese, softened
1 (14-ounce) can sweetened condensed milk
1/3 cup lemon juice
1 teaspoon vanilla extract
   Sliced fresh strawberries

1. Place 3/4 cup blueberries on crust.

2. Beat cream cheese in large bowl until fluffy. Gradually beat in sweetened condensed milk until smooth. Stir in lemon juice and vanilla. Spread into crust.

3. Chill 3 hours or until set. Top with remaining 1/2 cup blueberries and strawberries. Refrigerate leftovers.

Makes 8 servings

Prep Time: 10 minutes ✦ Chill Time: 3 hours

Red, White & Blueberry Cream Pie

Nestlé® Toll House® Chocolate Chip Pie

2 large eggs

$^1/_2$ cup all-purpose flour

$^1/_2$ cup granulated sugar

$^1/_2$ cup packed brown sugar

$^3/_4$ cup (1 $^1/_2$ sticks) butter, softened

1 cup (6 ounces) NESTLÉ® TOLL HOUSE® Semi-Sweet Chocolate Morsels

1 cup chopped nuts

1 *unbaked* 9-inch (4-cup volume) deep-dish pie shell*

Sweetened whipped cream or ice cream (optional)

If using frozen pie shell, use deep-dish style, thawed completely. Bake on baking sheet; increase baking time slightly.

PREHEAT oven to 325°F.

BEAT eggs in large mixer bowl on high speed until foamy. Beat in flour, granulated sugar and brown sugar. Beat in butter. Stir in morsels and nuts. Spoon into pie shell.

BAKE for 55 to 60 minutes or until knife inserted halfway between outside edge and center comes out clean. Cool on wire rack. Serve warm with whipped cream.

Makes 8 servings

58

Tip

Store nuts in an airtight container in a cool place. They can also be refrigerated up to 4 months or frozen up to 8 months.

Nestlé® Toll House® Chocolate Chip Pie

Peanut Supreme Pie

Crust
   1 unbaked Classic Crisco® Single Crust (page 62)

Peanut Layer
   1/2 cup chopped peanuts
   1/2 cup JIF® Creamy Peanut Butter
   1/2 cup confectioners' sugar
   1/2 cup half-and-half

Filling
   1 can (14 ounces) sweetened condensed milk
   1/2 cup JIF® Creamy Peanut Butter
   1 cup milk
   1 package (6-serving size) vanilla flavor instant pudding and pie filling mix
     (not sugar-free)

Topping
   3/4 cup chopped peanuts

60

1. For crust, prepare as directed. Press dough into 9-inch pie pan. Do not bake. Heat oven to 400°F.

2. For peanut layer, combine 1/2 cup nuts, peanut butter, confectioners' sugar and half-and-half in medium bowl. Stir until well blended. Pour into unbaked pie crust.

3. Bake at 400°F for 20 to 25 minutes or until crust is golden brown. *Do not overbake.* Cool completely.

4. For filling, combine sweetened condensed milk and peanut butter in large bowl. Beat at low speed of electric mixer until well blended. Add milk slowly. Add pudding mix. Increase speed to medium. Beat 2 minutes. Pour over cooled peanut layer.

5. For topping, sprinkle 3/4 cup nuts over filling. Refrigerate 1 hour or more.

Makes 1 (9-inch) pie

Peanut Supreme Pie

Classic Crisco® Single Crust

1 ⅓ **cups all-purpose flour**
½ **teaspoon salt**
½ **CRISCO® Stick or** ½ **cup CRISCO® all-vegetable shortening**
3 **tablespoons cold water**

1. Spoon flour into measuring cup and level. Combine flour and salt in medium bowl.

2. Cut in ½ cup shortening using pastry blender or 2 knives until all flour is blended to form pea-size chunks.

3. Sprinkle with water, 1 tablespoon at a time. Toss lightly with fork until dough forms a ball.

4. Press dough between hands to form 5- to 6-inch "pancake." Flour rolling surface and rolling pin lightly. Roll dough into circle. Trim circle 1 inch larger than upside-down pie plate. Carefully remove trimmed dough. Set aside to reroll and use for pastry cutout garnish, if desired.

5. Fold dough into quarters. Unfold and press into pie plate. Fold edge under. Flute.

6. **For recipes using a baked pie crust,** heat oven to 425°F. Prick bottom and side thoroughly with fork (50 times) to prevent shrinkage. Bake at 425°F for 10 to 15 minutes or until lightly browned.

7. **For recipes using an unbaked pie crust,** follow directions given for that recipe.

Makes 1 (9-inch) single crust

62

Lemon Buttermilk Pie

1 (9-inch) unbaked pie crust*
1 1/2 cups sugar
1/2 cup (1 stick) butter, softened
3 eggs
1 cup buttermilk
1 tablespoon cornstarch
1 tablespoon fresh lemon juice
1/8 teaspoon salt

*If using a commercial frozen pie crust, purchase a deep-dish crust and thaw before using.

Heat oven to 350°F. Prick crust all over with fork. Bake until light golden brown, about 8 minutes; cool on wire rack. *Reduce oven temperature to 325°F.* In large bowl, beat sugar and butter until creamy. Add eggs, one at a time, beating well after each addition. Add buttermilk, cornstarch, lemon juice and salt; mix well. Pour filling into crust. Bake 55 to 60 minutes or just until knife inserted near center comes out clean. Cool; cover and chill. *Makes 8 servings*

Favorite recipe from **Southeast United Dairy Industry Association, Inc.**

Pineapple Cream Cheese Pie

1 package (8 ounces) cream cheese, softened
1 can (20 ounces) crushed pineapple, drained and juice reserved
2 cups cold milk
2 packages (4-serving size) vanilla instant pudding and pie filling mix
2 (9-inch) graham cracker crusts
Whipped topping

Beat cream cheese, reserved pineapple juice and milk in medium bowl with electric mixer on medium speed until well blended. Add pudding mix; beat until smooth. Stir in pineapple. Pour into crusts; refrigerate until set. Serve with whipped topping.
Makes 16 servings

Hershey's Cocoa Cream Pie

   1 baked 9-inch pie crust *or* graham cracker crumb crust
1 1/4 cups sugar
   1/2 cup **HERSHEY'S Cocoa**
   1/3 cup cornstarch
   1/4 teaspoon salt
   3 cups milk
   3 tablespoons butter or margarine
1 1/2 teaspoons vanilla extract
      Sweetened whipped cream

1. Prepare crust; cool.

2. Stir together sugar, cocoa, cornstarch and salt in medium saucepan. Gradually add milk, stirring until smooth. Cook over medium heat, stirring constantly, until mixture comes to a boil; boil 1 minute.

3. Remove from heat; stir in butter and vanilla. Pour into prepared crust. Press plastic wrap directly onto surface. Cool to room temperature. Refrigerate 6 to 8 hours. Serve with sweetened whipped cream. Garnish as desired. Cover; refrigerate leftover pie.

Makes 6 to 8 servings

64

Tip

In sweet sauces, pie fillings and puddings, mixing cornstarch with the granulated sugar in the recipe before adding cold liquid helps to prevent lumps

Hershey's Cocoa Cream Pie

Apple Crunch Pie

1 refrigerated pie crust (¹/₂ of 15-ounce package)
1 ¹/₄ cups all-purpose flour, divided
1 cup granulated sugar
6 tablespoons butter, melted and divided
1 ¹/₂ teaspoons ground cinnamon, divided
³/₄ teaspoon ground nutmeg, divided
¹/₂ teaspoon ground ginger
¹/₄ teaspoon salt
4 cups peeled, cored, diced apples
¹/₂ cup packed brown sugar
¹/₂ cup chopped walnuts

1. Preheat oven to 350°F. Place crust in 9-inch pie pan; flute edge as desired.

2. Combine ¹/₄ cup flour, granulated sugar, 2 tablespoons butter, 1 teaspoon cinnamon, ¹/₂ teaspoon nutmeg, ginger and salt; mix well. Add apples; toss to coat. Place apple mixture in crust.

3. Combine remaining 1 cup flour, 4 tablespoons butter, ¹/₂ teaspoon cinnamon, ¹/₄ teaspoon nutmeg, brown sugar and walnuts in small bowl. Sprinkle evenly over apple mixture.

4. Bake 45 to 55 minutes or until apples are tender. *Makes 8 servings*

Apple Crunch Pie

Grasshopper Mint Pie

- 1 (8-ounce) package cream cheese, softened
- 1/3 cup sugar
- 1 (8-ounce) tub frozen whipped topping, thawed
- 1 cup chopped KEEBLER® Fudge Shoppe® Grasshopper Cookies
- 3 drops green food coloring
- 1 (6-ounce) READY CRUST® Chocolate Pie Crust
  Additional KEEBLER® Fudge Shoppe® Grasshopper Cookies, halved, for garnish

1. Mix cream cheese and sugar with electric mixer until well blended. Fold in whipped topping, chopped cookies and green food coloring. Spoon into crust.

2. Refrigerate 3 hours or overnight.

3. Garnish with cookie halves. Refrigerate leftovers.   *Makes 8 servings*

Butter Pecan Pie

- 1 cup coarsely chopped pecans
- 1/4 cup butter or margarine
- 1 container DUNCAN HINES® Creamy Home-Style Vanilla Buttercream Frosting
- 1 package (8 ounces) cream cheese, softened
- 1 cup frozen non-dairy whipped topping, thawed
- 1 prepared 9-inch graham cracker crumb pie crust
  Pecan halves for garnish

1. Place pecans and butter in 10-inch skillet on medium heat. Cook, stirring constantly, until butter is lightly browned. Pour into heatproof large bowl. Add Buttercream frosting and cream cheese. Stir until thoroughly blended.

2. Fold in whipped topping. Pour into prepared crust. Garnish with pecan halves, if desired. Refrigerate for 4 hours or until firm.   *Makes 8 to 10 servings*

Groovy Pies

Grasshopper Mint Pie

Cherry-Topped Lemon Cheesecake Pie

- 1 (8-ounce) package cream cheese, softened
- 1 (14-ounce) can **EAGLE BRAND®** Sweetened Condensed Milk (**NOT** evaporated milk)
- 1/3 cup lemon juice from concentrate
- 1 teaspoon vanilla extract
- 1 (6-ounce) graham cracker crumb pie crust
- 1 (21-ounce) can cherry pie filling, chilled

1. In large mixing bowl, beat cream cheese until fluffy. Gradually beat in EAGLE BRAND® until smooth. Stir in lemon juice and vanilla. Pour into crust. Chill at least 3 hours.

2. To serve, top with cherry pie filling. Store covered in refrigerator.

Makes 6 to 8 servings

Note: For a firmer crust, brush crust with beaten egg white; bake in 375°F oven 5 minutes. Cool before pouring filling into crust.

Prep Time: 10 minutes ✦ Chill Time: 3 hours

Tip

Unopened cans of sweetened condensed milk can be stored at room temperature for up to 6 months.

Cherry-Topped Lemon Cheesecake Pie

Fresh Lemon Meringue Pie

1 1/2 cups sugar

1/4 cup plus 2 tablespoons cornstarch

1/2 teaspoon salt

1/2 cup cold water

1/2 cup freshly squeezed SUNKIST® lemon juice

3 egg yolks, well beaten

2 tablespoons butter or margarine

1 1/2 cups boiling water

Grated peel of 1/2 SUNKIST® lemon

2 to 3 drops yellow food coloring (optional)

1 (9-inch) baked pie crust

Three-Egg Meringue (recipe follows)

In large saucepan, combine sugar, cornstarch and salt. Gradually blend in cold water and lemon juice. Stir in egg yolks. Add butter and boiling water. Bring to a boil over medium-high heat, stirring constantly. Reduce heat to medium and boil 1 minute. Remove from heat; stir in lemon peel and food coloring. Pour into baked pie crust. Top with Three-Egg Meringue, sealing well at edges. Bake at 350°F 12 to 15 minutes. Cool 2 hours before serving. *Makes 6 servings*

Three-Egg Meringue

3 egg whites

1/4 teaspoon cream of tartar

6 tablespoons sugar

In large bowl with electric mixer, beat egg whites with cream of tartar until foamy. Gradually add sugar and beat until stiff peaks form.

Fresh Lemon Meringue Pie

Sweet Potato Pecan Pie

1 can (16 ounces) sweet potatoes, drained and mashed

3 eggs, divided

3/4 cup sugar, divided

1 teaspoon cinnamon

1/2 teaspoon ground nutmeg

1/4 teaspoon ground ginger

Easy-As-Pie Crust (page 75) or 1 (9-inch) frozen deep-dish pie crust*

2/3 cup KARO® Light or Dark Corn Syrup

2 tablespoons margarine or butter, melted

1/2 teaspoon vanilla

1 cup chopped pecans

*To use prepared frozen pie crust: Use 9-inch deep-dish pie crust. Do not thaw. Preheat oven and a cookie sheet. Pour filling into frozen crust; bake on cookie sheet.

1. Preheat oven to 350°F.

2. In medium bowl combine sweet potatoes, 1 egg, 1/4 cup sugar, cinnamon, nutmeg and ginger; stir until well blended. Spread evenly in bottom of pie crust.

3. In same bowl combine remaining 2 eggs, 1/2 cup sugar, corn syrup, margarine and vanilla; stir until well combined. Stir in pecans. Spoon over sweet potato mixture.

4. Bake 60 minutes or until puffed and set. Cool completely on wire rack.

Makes 8 servings

Prep Time: 20 minutes ✦ Bake Time: 60 minutes, plus cooling

Easy-As-Pie Crust

1 ¼ cups unsifted flour
⅛ teaspoon salt
1 stick margarine or butter
2 to 3 tablespoons cold water

1. In medium bowl, combine flour and salt. With pastry blender or 2 knives, cut in margarine until mixture resembles fine crumbs.

2. Sprinkle water over mixture while tossing to blend well. Press dough firmly into ball.

3. On lightly floured surface, roll into 12-inch circle. Fit loosely into 9-inch pie plate. Trim and flute edge. Fill and bake according to recipe.   *Makes 1 (9-inch) crust*

Baked Pie Shell: Preheat oven to 450°F. Pierce pie crust thoroughly with fork. Bake 12 to 15 minutes or until light golden brown.

Caramel-Pecan Pie

3 eggs
⅔ cup sugar
1 cup (12-ounce jar) SMUCKER'S® Caramel Topping
¼ cup butter or margarine, melted
1 ½ cups pecan halves
1 (9-inch) unbaked pie shell

1. In mixing bowl, beat eggs slightly with fork. Add sugar, stirring until dissolved. Stir in caramel topping and butter; mix well. Stir in pecan halves. Pour filling into pie shell.

2. Bake at 350°F for 45 minutes or until knife inserted near center comes out clean. Cool completely on rack before serving. Cover and store in refrigerator.

Makes 6 to 8 servings

Easy Coconut Banana Cream Pie

- 1 *prebaked* 9-inch (4-cup volume) deep-dish pie shell
- 1 can (14 ounces) NESTLÉ® CARNATION® Sweetened Condensed Milk
- 1 cup cold water
- 1 package (3.4 ounces) vanilla or banana cream instant pudding and pie filling mix
- 1 cup flaked coconut
- 1 container (8 ounces) frozen whipped topping, thawed, *divided*
- 2 medium bananas, sliced, dipped in lemon juice
  Toasted or tinted flaked coconut (optional)

COMBINE sweetened condensed milk and water in large bowl. Add pudding mix and coconut; mix well. Fold in *1 ½ cups* whipped topping.

ARRANGE single layer of bananas on bottom of pie crust. Pour filling into crust. Top with *remaining* whipped topping. Refrigerate for 4 hours or until very set. Top with toasted or tinted coconut.   *Makes 8 servings*

Note: To make 2 pies, divide filling between 2 *prebaked* 9-inch (2-cup volume *each*) pie crusts. Top with *remaining* whipped topping.

Tip

Bananas begin to turn brown soon after they are peeled. Dipping banana slices in lemon juice helps to retain their creamy color and prevent browning.

76

Easy Coconut Banana Cream Pie

Chocolate Chiffon Pie

2 (1-ounce) squares unsweetened chocolate, chopped

1 (14-ounce) can **EAGLE BRAND®** Sweetened Condensed Milk (**NOT** evaporated milk)

1 envelope unflavored gelatin

1/3 cup water

1/2 teaspoon vanilla extract

1 cup (1/2 pint) whipping cream, whipped

1 (6-ounce) chocolate or graham cracker crumb pie crust

Additional whipped cream

1. In heavy saucepan over low heat, melt chocolate with EAGLE BRAND.® Remove from heat.

2. Meanwhile, in small saucepan, sprinkle gelatin over water; let stand 1 minute. Over low heat, stir until gelatin dissolves.

3. Stir gelatin into chocolate mixture. Add vanilla. Cool to room temperature. Fold in whipped cream. Spread into crust.

4. Chill 3 hours or until set. Garnish with additional whipped cream. Store covered in refrigerator.

Makes 1 pie

Prep Time: 20 minutes ✦ Chill Time: 3 hours

78

Chocolate Chiffon Pie

Pumpkin Spiced and Iced Cookies

2 1/4 cups all-purpose flour

1 1/2 teaspoons pumpkin pie spice

1 teaspoon baking powder

1/2 teaspoon baking soda

1/2 teaspoon salt

1 cup (2 sticks) butter or margarine, softened

1 cup granulated sugar

1 can (15 ounces) LIBBY'S® 100% Pure Pumpkin

2 eggs

1 teaspoon vanilla extract

2 cups (12-ounce package) NESTLÉ® TOLL HOUSE® Semi-Sweet Chocolate Morsels

1 cup chopped walnuts (optional)

Vanilla Glaze (recipe follows)

PREHEAT oven to 375°F. Grease baking sheets.

COMBINE flour, pumpkin pie spice, baking powder, baking soda and salt in medium bowl. Beat butter and granulated sugar in large mixer bowl until creamy. Beat in pumpkin, eggs and vanilla extract. Gradually beat in flour mixture. Stir in morsels and nuts. Drop by rounded tablespoon onto prepared baking sheets.

BAKE for 15 to 20 minutes or until edges are lightly browned. Cool on baking sheets for 2 minutes; remove to wire rack to cool completely. Spread or drizzle with Vanilla Glaze.

Makes about 5 1/2 dozen cookies

Vanilla Glaze: **COMBINE** 1 cup powdered sugar, 1 to 1 1/2 tablespoons milk and 1/2 teaspoon vanilla extract in small bowl; mix well.

Pumpkin Spiced and Iced Cookies

Lollipop Sugar Cookies

1 1/4 cups granulated sugar

1 Butter Flavor CRISCO® Stick or 1 cup Butter Flavor CRISCO®
    all-vegetable shortening

2 eggs

1/4 cup light corn syrup or regular pancake syrup

1 tablespoon vanilla

3 cups all-purpose flour

3/4 teaspoon baking powder

1/2 teaspoon baking soda

1/2 teaspoon salt

36 flat ice cream sticks

Any of the following: miniature baking chips, raisins, red hots, nonpareils,
    colored sugar or nuts

1. Combine sugar and 1 cup shortening in large bowl. Beat at medium speed of electric mixer until well blended. Add eggs, syrup and vanilla; beat until well blended and fluffy.

2. Combine flour, baking powder, baking soda and salt. Add gradually to creamed mixture at low speed until well blended. Wrap dough in plastic wrap. Refrigerate at least 1 hour.

3. Heat oven to 375°F. Place foil on countertop for cooling cookies.

4. Shape dough into 1 1/2-inch balls. Push ice cream stick into center of each ball. Place balls 3 inches apart on ungreased baking sheet. Flatten balls to 1/2-inch thickness with bottom of greased and floured glass. Decorate as desired; press decorations gently into dough.*

5. Bake at 375°F for 8 to 10 minutes. *Do not overbake.* Cool on baking sheet 2 minutes. Remove cookies to foil to cool completely.

Makes about 3 dozen cookies

Cookies can also be painted before baking. Mix 1 egg yolk and 1/4 teaspoon water. Divide into 3 small cups. Add 2 to 3 drops food color to each. Stir. Use clean watercolor brushes to paint designs on cookies.

Lollipop Sugar Cookies

Malted Milk Cookies

1 cup (2 sticks) butter

$^3/_4$ cup granulated sugar

$^3/_4$ cup packed brown sugar

1 teaspoon baking soda

2 eggs

2 squares (1 ounce each) unsweetened chocolate, melted and cooled
    to room temperature

1 teaspoon vanilla

2 $^1/_4$ cups all-purpose flour

$^1/_2$ cup malted milk powder

1 cup chopped malted milk balls

1. Preheat oven to 375°F.

2. Beat butter in large bowl with electric mixer at medium speed 30 seconds. Add granulated sugar, brown sugar and baking soda; beat until blended. Add eggs, chocolate and vanilla; beat until well blended.

3. Beat in as much flour as possible with mixer. Using spoon, stir in any remaining flour and malted milk powder. Stir in malted milk balls.

4. Drop dough by rounded teaspoonfuls 2½ inches apart onto ungreased cookie sheets. Bake about 10 minutes or until edges are firm. Cool on cookie sheets 1 minute. Remove to wire racks; cool completely.   *Makes about 3 dozen cookies*

Tip

Make sure cookies are completely cool before storing them, otherwise they will become soggy.

Malted Milk Cookies

Peanut Butter and Jelly Pinwheels

- 1 Butter Flavor CRISCO® Stick or 1 cup Butter Flavor CRISCO® all-vegetable shortening
- 1 cup JIF® Creamy Peanut Butter
- ¾ cup granulated sugar
- ¾ cup firmly packed light brown sugar
- 2 eggs
- 1 teaspoon vanilla
- 2½ cups all-purpose flour
- 1 teaspoon salt
- 1 teaspoon baking soda
- ½ cup SMUCKER'S® Seedless Red Raspberry Jam*
- ⅔ cup very finely chopped peanuts

*If desired, top with additional jam before serving.

Combine shortening, peanut butter, granulated sugar and brown sugar in large bowl. Beat at medium speed of electric mixer until well blended. Beat in eggs and vanilla.

Combine flour, salt and baking soda. Add gradually to creamed mixture at low speed. Beat until well blended.

Cut parchment paper to line 17×11-inch pan. Press dough out to edges of paper. Spread with jam to within ½ inch of edges.

Lift up long side of paper. Loosen dough with spatula. Roll up dough jelly-roll fashion; seal seam. Sprinkle nuts on paper; roll dough over nuts. Press any remaining nuts into dough. Wrap rolled-up dough in parchment paper; place in plastic bag. Refrigerate overnight.

Preheat oven to 375°F.

Line baking sheet with foil or parchment paper. Unwrap dough and cut into ½-inch slices. Place 2 inches apart on prepared baking sheet.

Bake for 10 to 12 minutes or until set. Cool about 5 minutes on baking sheet before removing to new foil to cool completely. *Makes 3 dozen cookies*

Peanut Butter and Jelly Pinwheels

Orange Pecan Refrigerator Cookies

2 1/3 cups all-purpose flour
1/2 teaspoon baking soda
1/4 teaspoon salt
1/2 cup (1 stick) butter or margarine, softened
1/2 cup packed brown sugar
1/2 cup granulated sugar
1 egg, lightly beaten
Grated peel of 1 SUNKIST® orange
3 tablespoons freshly squeezed SUNKIST® orange juice
3/4 cup pecan pieces

In bowl, stir together flour, baking soda and salt. In large bowl, blend together butter, brown sugar and granulated sugar. Add egg, orange peel and juice; beat well. Stir in pecans. Gradually beat in flour mixture. (Dough will be stiff.) Divide mixture in half and shape each half (on long piece of waxed paper) into roll about 1 1/4 inches in diameter and 12 inches long. Roll up tightly in waxed paper. Chill several hours or overnight.

Cut dough rolls into 1/4-inch slices and arrange on lightly greased cookie sheets. Bake at 350°F for 10 to 12 minutes or until lightly browned. Cool on wire racks.

Makes about 6 dozen cookies

Chocolate Filled Sandwich Cookies: Cut each roll into 1/8-inch slices and bake as directed above. When cool, to make each sandwich cookie, spread about 1 teaspoon canned chocolate fudge frosting on bottom side of 1 cookie; cover with second cookie of same shape. Makes about 4 dozen sandwich cookies.

Banana Sandies

2 ⅓ cups all-purpose flour

1 cup (2 sticks) butter, softened

¾ cup granulated sugar

¼ cup packed light brown sugar

½ cup ¼-inch banana slices (about 1 medium)

1 teaspoon vanilla

¼ teaspoon salt

⅔ cup chopped pecans

Prepared cream cheese frosting

Yellow food coloring (optional)

1. Preheat oven to 350°F. Grease cookie sheets.

2. Combine flour, butter, sugars, banana slices, vanilla and salt in large bowl. Beat 2 to 3 minutes, scraping bowl often, until well blended. Stir in pecans. Shape dough into 1-inch balls. Place 2 inches apart on prepared cookie sheets; flatten to ¼-inch thickness with bottom of glass dipped in sugar. Bake 12 to 15 minutes or until edges are lightly browned. Remove immediately to wire racks; cool completely.

3. Tint frosting with food coloring, if desired. Spread 1 tablespoon frosting over bottoms of half the cookies. Top with remaining cookies.

Makes about 2 dozen sandwich cookies

Tip

When a recipe calls for greasing the cookie sheets, don't grease them too heavily—it could cause the cookies to spread and overbrown on the bottoms.

Tea Cookies

- **3 cups granulated sugar**
- **2 cups shortening**
- **2 teaspoons vanilla**
- **4 eggs**
- **5 1/2 cups all-purpose flour**
- **4 teaspoons cream of tartar**
- **2 teaspoons baking soda**
- **1/2 teaspoon salt**
- **1 cup finely chopped almonds, walnuts or pecans (optional)**
- **Powdered sugar (optional)**

1. Preheat oven to 375°F.

2. Beat sugar, shortening and vanilla with electric mixer at medium speed until creamy. Add eggs, one at a time, beating well after each addition. Continue beating until mixture is smooth.

3. Sift flour, cream of tartar, baking soda and salt into separate large bowl. Add nuts, if desired. Stir into shortening mixture until well blended.

4. Shape dough into walnut-sized balls. Place 2 inches apart on ungreased cookie sheets. Bake 8 to 10 minutes.

5. Cool 2 hours on wire racks. Dust cookies with powdered sugar, if desired.

Makes 8 to 9 dozen cookies

Tea Cookies

Original Nestlé® Toll House® Chocolate Chip Cookies

2 ¼ cups all-purpose flour

1 teaspoon baking soda

1 teaspoon salt

1 cup (2 sticks) butter or margarine, softened

¾ cup granulated sugar

¾ cup packed brown sugar

1 teaspoon vanilla extract

2 large eggs

2 cups (12-ounce package) NESTLÉ® TOLL HOUSE® Semi-Sweet Chocolate Morsels

1 cup chopped nuts

PREHEAT oven to 375°F.

COMBINE flour, baking soda and salt in small bowl. Beat butter, granulated sugar, brown sugar and vanilla extract in large mixer bowl until creamy. Add eggs, one at a time, beating well after each addition. Gradually beat in flour mixture. Stir in morsels and nuts. Drop by rounded tablespoon onto ungreased baking sheets.

BAKE for 9 to 11 minutes or until golden brown. Cool on baking sheets for 2 minutes; remove to wire racks to cool completely.

Makes about 5 dozen cookies

Pan Cookie Variation: **GREASE** 15×10-inch jelly-roll pan. Prepare dough as above. Spread into prepared pan. Bake for 20 to 25 minutes or until golden brown. Cool in pan on wire rack. Makes 4 dozen bars.

Cool Cat Cookies

93

Original Nestlé® Toll House®
Chocolate Chip Cookies

Chewy Chocolate Macaroons

5 1/3 cups MOUNDS® Sweetened Coconut Flakes
1/2 cup HERSHEY'S Cocoa
1 can (14 ounces) sweetened condensed milk (not evaporated milk)
2 teaspoons vanilla extract
About 24 red candied cherries, halved (optional)

1. Heat oven to 350°F. Generously grease cookie sheet.

2. Stir together coconut and cocoa in large bowl; stir in sweetened condensed milk and vanilla until well blended. Drop by rounded teaspoons onto prepared cookie sheet. Press cherry half into center of each cookie, if desired.

3. Bake 8 to 10 minutes or until almost set. Immediately remove from cookie sheet to wire rack. Cool completely. *Makes about 4 dozen cookies*

Applesauce Raisin Chews

1 cup (2 sticks) margarine or butter, softened
1 cup firmly packed brown sugar
1 cup applesauce
1 egg
1 teaspoon vanilla
2 cups all-purpose flour
1 teaspoon baking soda
1 teaspoon ground cinnamon
1/2 teaspoon salt (optional)
2 1/2 cups QUAKER® Oats (quick or old fashioned, uncooked)
1 cup raisins

Heat oven to 350°F. Beat together margarine and sugar until creamy. Add applesauce, egg and vanilla; beat well. Add combined flour, baking soda, cinnamon and salt; mix well. Stir in oats and raisins. Drop by rounded tablespoonfuls onto ungreased cookie sheets. Bake 11 to 13 minutes or until light golden brown. Cool 1 minute on cookie sheets; remove to wire racks. Cool completely. *Makes about 4 dozen cookies*

Chewy Chocolate Macaroons

Mexican Wedding Cakes

1 1/3 cups Butter Flavor **CRISCO®** all-vegetable shortening

2/3 cup confectioners' sugar

1/2 teaspoon vanilla

1/2 teaspoon almond extract

2 1/4 cups all-purpose flour

1/8 teaspoon salt

1 cup finely chopped pecans

Additional confectioners' sugar

In large mixing bowl cream shortening, confectioners' sugar, vanilla and almond extract until light and fluffy. Add flour, salt and pecans; mix well. Cover and refrigerate for at least 2 hours.

Preheat oven to 325°F. Shape dough into 1- to 1 1/2-inch balls. Place 2 inches apart on ungreased baking sheet. Bake at 325°F for about 25 minutes, or until edges of cookies are light brown. Roll warm cookies in confectioners' sugar. Remove to cooling rack.

Makes 3 dozen cookies

Date Pinwheel Cookies

1 1/4 cups dates, pitted and finely chopped

3/4 cup orange juice

1/2 cup granulated sugar

1 tablespoon butter

3 cups plus 1 tablespoon all-purpose flour, divided

2 teaspoons vanilla, divided

1 cup packed brown sugar

4 ounces cream cheese

1/4 cup shortening

2 eggs

1 teaspoon baking soda

1/2 teaspoon salt

1. Heat dates, orange juice, granulated sugar, butter and 1 tablespoon flour in medium saucepan over medium heat. Cook 10 minutes or until thick, stirring frequently; remove from heat. Stir in 1 teaspoon vanilla; set aside to cool.

2. Beat brown sugar, cream cheese and shortening in large bowl with electric mixer about 3 minutes or until light and fluffy. Add eggs and remaining 1 teaspoon vanilla; beat 2 minutes longer.

3. Combine remaining 3 cups flour, baking soda and salt in medium bowl. Add to shortening mixture; stir just until blended. Divide dough in half. Roll one half of dough on lightly floured surface into 12×9-inch rectangle. Spread half of date mixture over dough. Spread evenly, leaving 1/4-inch border at top short edge. Starting at short side, tightly roll up dough jelly-roll style. Wrap in plastic wrap; freeze at least 1 hour. Repeat with remaining dough and date mixture.

4. Preheat oven to 350°F. Grease cookie sheets. Unwrap dough. Using heavy thread or unflavored dental floss, cut dough into 1/4-inch slices. Place slices 1 inch apart on prepared cookie sheets.

5. Bake 12 minutes or until lightly browned. Let cookies stand on cookie sheets 2 minutes. Remove cookies to wire racks; cool completely.

Makes 6 dozen cookies

Oatmeal Butterscotch Cookies

3/4 cup (1 1/2 sticks) butter or margarine, softened
3/4 cup granulated sugar
3/4 cup packed light brown sugar
2 eggs
1 teaspoon vanilla extract
1 1/4 cups all-purpose flour
1 teaspoon baking soda
1/2 teaspoon salt
1/2 teaspoon ground cinnamon
3 cups quick-cooking or regular rolled oats, uncooked
2 cups (12-ounce package) HERSHEY'S Butterscotch Chips

1. Heat oven to 375°F.

2. Beat butter, granulated sugar and brown sugar in large bowl until well blended. Add eggs and vanilla; blend thoroughly. Stir together flour, baking soda, salt and cinnamon; gradually add to butter mixture, beating until well blended. Stir in oats and butterscotch chips; mix well. Drop by teaspoons onto ungreased cookie sheet.

3. Bake 8 to 10 minutes or until golden brown. Cool slightly; remove from cookie sheet to wire rack. Cool completely.   *Makes about 4 dozen cookies*

Oatmeal Butterscotch Cookies

Cinnamon Roll Cookies

Cinnamon Mixture
   1/4 cup granulated sugar
   1 tablespoon ground cinnamon

Cookie Dough
   1 Butter Flavor CRISCO® Stick or 1 cup Butter Flavor CRISCO®
      all-vegetable shortening
   1 cup firmly packed light brown sugar
   2 large eggs
   1 teaspoon vanilla
   3 cups all-purpose flour
   2 teaspoons baking powder
   1 teaspoon ground cinnamon
   1/2 teaspoon salt

1. For cinnamon mixture, combine granulated sugar and 1 tablespoon cinnamon in small bowl; mix well. Set aside.

2. For cookie dough, beat 1 cup shortening and brown sugar in large bowl with electric mixer at medium speed until well blended. Beat in eggs and vanilla until well blended.

3. Combine flour, baking powder, 1 teaspoon cinnamon and salt in small bowl. Add to creamed mixture; mix well.

4. Turn dough onto sheet of waxed paper. Spread dough into 9×6-inch rectangle using rubber spatula. Sprinkle with 4 tablespoons cinnamon mixture to within 1 inch of edge. Roll up jelly-roll style into log. Dust log with remaining cinnamon mixture. Wrap tightly in plastic wrap; refrigerate 4 hours or overnight.

5. Heat oven to 350°F. Spray cookie sheets with CRISCO® No-Stick Cooking Spray.

6. Slice dough 1/4 inch thick. Place on prepared cookie sheets. Bake at 350°F for 8 minutes or until lightly browned on top. Cool on cookie sheets 4 minutes; transfer to cooling racks.   *Makes about 5 dozen cookies*

Kitchen Hint: Be careful when working with this dough. Since it is a stiff dough, it can crack easily when it is rolled. Roll the dough slowly and smooth any cracks with your finger as you go.

101

Cinnamon Roll Cookies

Orange-Almond Sables

1 1/2 cups powdered sugar

1 cup (2 sticks) butter, softened

1 tablespoon finely grated orange peel

1 tablespoon almond-flavored liqueur *or* 1 teaspoon almond extract

3/4 cup whole blanched almonds, toasted*

1 3/4 cups all-purpose flour

1/4 teaspoon salt

1 egg, beaten

To toast almonds, spread in single layer on baking sheet. Bake in preheated 350°F oven 8 to 10 minutes or until brown, stirring twice.

1. Preheat oven to 375°F.

2. Beat powdered sugar and butter in large bowl with electric mixer at medium speed until light and fluffy. Beat in orange peel and liqueur.

3. Reserve 24 whole almonds. Place remaining cooled almonds in food processor. Process using on/off pulsing action until almonds are ground but not pasty.

4. Combine ground almonds, flour and salt in medium bowl; stir. Gradually add to butter mixture. Beat with electric mixer at low speed until well blended.

5. Roll dough on lightly floured surface with lightly floured rolling pin to just under 1/4-inch thickness. Cut dough with floured 2 1/2-inch fluted or round cookie cutter. Place cutouts 2 inches apart on ungreased cookie sheets.

6. Lightly brush tops of cutouts with beaten egg. Press one whole reserved almond in center of each cutout. Brush almond lightly with beaten egg. Bake 10 to 12 minutes or until light golden brown.

7. Let cookies stand 1 minute on cookie sheets. Remove cookies with spatula to wire racks; cool completely. Store tightly covered at room temperature, or freeze up to 3 months.

Makes about 2 dozen cookies

Orange-Almond Sables

Chunky Chocolate Chip Peanut Butter Cookies

1 1/4 cups all-purpose flour

1/2 teaspoon baking soda

1/2 teaspoon ground cinnamon

1/2 teaspoon salt

3/4 cup (1 1/2 sticks) butter or margarine, softened

1/2 cup packed brown sugar

1/2 cup granulated sugar

1/2 cup creamy peanut butter

1 large egg

1 teaspoon vanilla extract

2 cups (12-ounce package) NESTLÉ® TOLL HOUSE® Semi-Sweet Chocolate Morsels

1/2 cup coarsely chopped peanuts

PREHEAT oven to 375°F.

COMBINE flour, baking soda, cinnamon and salt in small bowl. Beat butter, brown sugar, granulated sugar and peanut butter in large mixer bowl until creamy. Beat in egg and vanilla extract. Gradually beat in flour mixture. Stir in morsels and peanuts.

DROP dough by rounded tablespoon onto ungreased baking sheets. Press down slightly to flatten into 2-inch circles.

BAKE for 7 to 10 minutes or until edges are set but centers are still soft. Cool on baking sheets for 4 minutes; remove to wire racks to cool completely.

Makes about 3 dozen cookies

Chunky Chocolate Chip Peanut Butter Cookies

Rocky Road Brownies

1 ¼ cups miniature marshmallows

1 cup **HERSHEY'S** Semi-Sweet Chocolate Chips

½ cup chopped nuts

½ cup (1 stick) butter or margarine

1 cup sugar

2 eggs

1 teaspoon vanilla extract

½ cup all-purpose flour

⅓ cup **HERSHEY'S** Cocoa

½ teaspoon baking powder

½ teaspoon salt

1. Heat oven to 350°F. Grease 9-inch square baking pan.

2. Stir together marshmallows, chocolate chips and nuts; set aside. Place butter in large microwave-safe bowl. Microwave at HIGH (100% power) 1 to 1 ½ minutes or until melted. Add sugar, eggs and vanilla, beating with spoon until well blended. Add flour, cocoa, baking powder and salt; blend well. Spread batter in prepared pan.

3. Bake 22 minutes. Sprinkle chocolate chip mixture over top. Continue baking 5 minutes or until marshmallows have softened and puffed slightly. Cool completely. With wet knife, cut into squares.

Makes about 20 brownies

Rocky Road Brownies

Strawberry Oat Bars

1 cup (2 sticks) butter, softened
1 cup packed light brown sugar
2 cups uncooked quick oats
1 cup all-purpose flour
2 teaspoons baking soda
1/2 teaspoon ground cinnamon
1/4 teaspoon salt
1 can (21 ounces) strawberry pie filling
3/4 teaspoon almond extract

1. Preheat oven to 375°F. Beat butter in large bowl with electric mixer at medium speed until smooth. Add brown sugar; beat until well blended.

2. Combine oats, flour, baking soda, cinnamon and salt in large bowl; mix well. Add flour mixture to butter mixture, beating at low speed until well blended and crumbly.

3. Spread 2/3 of crumb mixture in bottom of ungreased 13×9-inch baking pan, pressing to form firm layer. Bake 15 minutes; let cool 5 minutes on wire rack.

4. Meanwhile, place strawberry filling in food processor or blender; process until smooth. Stir in almond extract.

5. Pour strawberry mixture over partially baked crust. Sprinkle remaining crumb mixture evenly over strawberry layer.

6. Return pan to oven; bake 20 to 25 minutes or until topping is golden brown and filling is slightly bubbly. Let cool completely on wire rack before cutting into bars.

Makes about 4 dozen bars

Strawberry Oat Bars

Butterscotch Blondies

¾ cup (1 ½ sticks) butter or margarine, softened

¾ cup packed light brown sugar

½ cup granulated sugar

 2 eggs

 2 cups all-purpose flour

 1 teaspoon baking soda

½ teaspoon salt

1 ⅔ cups (10-ounce package) or 2 cups (12-ounce package) HERSHEY'S Butterscotch Chips

 1 cup chopped nuts (optional)

1. Heat oven to 350°F. Grease 13×9×2-inch baking pan.

2. Beat butter, brown sugar and granulated sugar in large bowl until creamy. Add eggs; beat well. Stir together flour, baking soda and salt; gradually add to butter mixture, blending well. Stir in butterscotch chips and nuts, if desired. Spread into prepared pan.

3. Bake 30 to 35 minutes or until top is golden brown and center is set. Cool completely in pan on wire rack. Cut into bars.   *Makes about 36 bars*

Tip

Try cutting bar cookies into triangles or diamonds for a festive new shape. To make serving easy, remove a corner piece first, then remove the rest.

Butterscotch Blondies

Cocoa Bottom Banana Pecan Bars

1 cup sugar

1/2 cup (1 stick) butter, softened

1 egg

1 teaspoon vanilla

5 ripe bananas, mashed

1 1/2 cups all-purpose flour

1 teaspoon baking powder

1 teaspoon baking soda

1/2 teaspoon salt

1/2 cup chopped pecans

1/4 cup unsweetened cocoa powder

1. Preheat oven to 350°F. Grease 13×9-inch pan.

2. Beat sugar and butter in large bowl with electric mixer until creamy. Add egg and vanilla; beat until well combined. Beat in bananas. Combine flour, baking powder, baking soda and salt in medium bowl. Add to banana mixture; mix well. Add pecans; mix well.

3. Divide batter in half. Add cocoa to one half. Spread cocoa batter into prepared pan. Spread remaining batter over cocoa batter and swirl with knife.

4. Bake 30 to 35 minutes or until edges are lightly browned and toothpick inserted into center comes out clean.   *Makes 15 to 18 bars*

Cocoa Bottom Banana Pecan Bars

Blueberry Cheesecake Bars

1 package **DUNCAN HINES®** Bakery-Style Blueberry Streusel Muffin Mix

1/4 cup cold butter or margarine

1/3 cup finely chopped pecans

1 package **(8 ounces)** cream cheese, softened

1/2 cup sugar

1 egg

3 tablespoons lemon juice

1 teaspoon grated lemon peel

1. Preheat oven to 350°F. Grease 9-inch square baking pan.

2. Rinse blueberries from Mix with cold water and drain; set aside.

3. Place muffin mix in medium bowl; cut in butter with pastry blender or two knives. Stir in pecans. Press onto bottom of prepared pan. Bake at 350°F for 15 minutes or until set.

4. Combine cream cheese and sugar in medium bowl. Beat until smooth. Add egg, lemon juice and lemon peel. Beat well. Spread over baked crust. Sprinkle with blueberries. Sprinkle topping packet from Mix over blueberries. Return to oven. Bake at 350°F for 35 to 40 minutes or until filling is set. Cool completely. Refrigerate until ready to serve. Cut into bars. *Makes about 16 bars*

Blueberry Cheesecake Bars

Fruit and Nut Bars

- 1 cup unsifted all-purpose flour
- 1 cup uncooked quick oats
- 2/3 cup brown sugar
- 2 teaspoons baking soda
- 1/2 teaspoon salt
- 1/2 teaspoon ground cinnamon
- 2/3 cup buttermilk
- 3 tablespoons vegetable oil
- 2 egg whites, lightly beaten
- 1 Washington Golden Delicious apple, cored and chopped
- 1/2 cup dried cranberries or raisins, chopped
- 1/4 cup chopped nuts
- 2 tablespoons flaked coconut (optional)

1. Heat oven to 375°F. Lightly grease 9-inch square baking pan. In large mixing bowl, combine flour, oats, brown sugar, baking soda, salt and cinnamon; stir to blend.

2. Add buttermilk, oil and egg whites; beat with electric mixer just until mixed. Stir in apple, dried fruit and nuts; spread evenly in pan and top with coconut, if desired. Bake 20 to 25 minutes or until cake tester inserted in center comes out clean. Cool and cut into bars. *Makes 16 bars*

Favorite recipe from **Washington Apple Commission**

Marbled Cheesecake Bars

2 cups finely crushed crème-filled chocolate sandwich cookie crumbs
   (about 24 cookies)

3 tablespoons butter or margarine, melted

3 (8-ounce) packages cream cheese, softened

1 (14-ounce) can EAGLE BRAND® Sweetened Condensed Milk
   (NOT evaporated milk)

3 eggs

2 teaspoons vanilla extract

2 (1-ounce) squares unsweetened chocolate, melted

1. Preheat oven to 300°F. Line 13×9-inch baking pan with heavy foil; set aside.
In medium mixing bowl, combine cookie crumbs and butter; press firmly on bottom
of prepared pan.

2. In large mixing bowl, beat cream cheese until fluffy. Gradually beat in EAGLE
BRAND® until smooth. Add eggs and vanilla; mix well. Pour half the batter evenly
over prepared crust.

3. Stir melted chocolate into remaining batter; spoon over vanilla batter. With table
knife or metal spatula, gently swirl through batter to marble.

4. Bake 45 to 50 minutes or until set. Cool. Chill. Cut into bars. Store covered in
refrigerator.   *Makes 2 to 3 dozen bars*

Tip: For even marbling, do not oversoften or overbeat the cream cheese.

Prep Time: 20 minutes ✦ Bake Time: 45 to 50 minutes

Fudgy Brownie Bars

1 package (about 20 ounces) brownie mix
2 eggs
$^1/_3$ cup water
$^1/_3$ cup vegetable oil
1 package (6 ounces) semisweet chocolate chips
$^2/_3$ cup butterscotch chips
$^2/_3$ cup chopped pecans
$^3/_4$ cup flaked coconut
1 can (14 ounces) sweetened condensed milk

1. Preheat oven to 350°F. Grease 13×9-inch baking pan.

2. Combine brownie mix, eggs, water and oil in large bowl. Beat until well blended. Spread in prepared pan. Bake 18 minutes.

3. Sprinkle chocolate chips over partially baked brownie base; layer butterscotch chips, pecans and coconut over chocolate chips. Pour condensed milk over top. Bake 22 to 25 minutes or until light golden brown. Cool completely in pan on wire rack. Cut into bars. *Makes 2 dozen bars*

Tip

Peanut butter chips or white chocolate chips may be substituted for the butterscotch chips.

Fudgy Brownie Bars

Peanut Butter Marshmallow Bars

- ½ **Butter Flavored CRISCO® Stick** or ½ **cup Butter Flavor CRISCO®** all-vegetable shortening plus additional for greasing
- ½ **cup JIF® Extra Crunchy Peanut Butter**
- ¼ **cup firmly packed light brown sugar**
- ¼ **cup granulated sugar**
- 1 **egg**
- 1 ¼ **cups all-purpose flour**
- 1 **teaspoon baking powder**
- ¼ **teaspoon salt**
- ½ **cup JIF® Creamy Peanut Butter**
- 4 **cups miniature marshmallows**
- ½ **cup chocolate flavored syrup**

Preheat oven to 350°F. Grease 13×9×2-inch glass baking dish with shortening.

For cookie base, combine shortening, crunchy peanut butter, brown sugar, granulated sugar and egg in large bowl. Beat at medium speed of electric mixer until well blended.

Combine flour, baking powder and salt. Add gradually to creamed mixture at low speed. Beat until well blended. Cover and refrigerate 15 minutes. Press chilled cookie base into prepared dish. Bake for 20 minutes or until light brown. Do not overbake. Cool 2 to 3 minutes.

For topping, place creamy peanut butter in microwave-safe measuring cup. Microwave at HIGH for 1 minute. Pour over baked surface. Spread to cover. Top with marshmallows. Drizzle chocolate syrup over marshmallows. Return to oven. Bake 5 minutes or until marshmallows are light brown. Do not overbake. Loosen from sides of dish with knife. Remove dish to cooling rack. Cool completely. Cut with sharp greased knife into bars about 2×2 inches. *Makes 2 dozen bars*

Peanut Butter Marshmallow Bars

Raspberry Bars

1 ¼ cups all-purpose flour

¾ cup sugar, divided

½ cup (1 stick) butter, cut into ½-inch pieces

1 egg, beaten

2 egg whites

¾ cup chopped pecans

¾ cup raspberry jelly or jam

1. Preheat oven to 350°F. Grease 9-inch square baking pan.

2. Combine flour and ¼ cup sugar in medium bowl. Add butter; rub into flour mixture with fingers until fine crumbs form. Add egg; mix with fork until dough holds together. Pat into smooth ball. Firmly press dough evenly into bottom of prepared pan. Bake 20 to 25 minutes or until crust is lightly browned.

3. Meanwhile, beat egg whites in medium bowl with electric mixer at high speed until soft peaks form. Fold in remaining ½ cup sugar and pecans.

4. Spread jelly evenly over warm crust. Spread egg white mixture over jelly.

5. Bake 25 minutes more or until top is lightly browned. Cool in pan about 1 hour. Cut into bars. *Makes about 16 bars*

Raspberry Bars

Almond Chinese Chews

1 cup granulated sugar

3 eggs, lightly beaten

1 can SOLO® or 1 jar BAKER® Almond Filling

¾ cup all-purpose flour

1 teaspoon baking powder

¼ teaspoon salt

Powdered sugar

1. Preheat oven to 300°F. Grease 13×9-inch baking pan; set aside.

2. Beat granulated sugar and eggs in medium-size bowl with electric mixer until thoroughly blended. Add almond filling; beat until blended. Sift together flour, baking powder and salt; fold into almond mixture. Spread batter evenly in prepared pan.

3. Bake 40 to 45 minutes or until wooden toothpick inserted in center comes out clean. Cool completely in pan on wire rack. Cut into 2×1½-inch bars; dust with powdered sugar.   *Makes about 3 dozen bars*

Tip

For easy removal of brownies and bar cookies (and no cleanup!), line the baking pan with foil and leave at least 3 inches hanging over each end. Grease the foil if the recipe directs. After baking and cooling, use the foil to lift the bars onto a cutting board; remove the foil before cutting.

Almond Chinese Chews

Marshmallow Krispie Bars

1 (21-ounce) package DUNCAN HINES® Family-Style Chewy
  Fudge Brownie Mix
1 package (10½ ounces) miniature marshmallows
1½ cups semisweet chocolate chips
1 cup creamy peanut butter
1 tablespoon butter or margarine
1½ cups crisp rice cereal

1. Preheat oven to 350°F. Grease bottom only of 13×9-inch pan.

2. Prepare and bake brownies following package directions for cake-like recipe. Remove from oven. Sprinkle marshmallows on hot brownies. Return to oven. Bake for 3 minutes longer.

3. Place chocolate chips, peanut butter and butter in medium saucepan. Cook over low heat, stirring constantly, until chips are melted. Add rice cereal; mix well. Spread mixture over marshmallow layer. Refrigerate until chilled. Cut into bars.

Makes about 2 dozen bars

Oatmeal Toffee Bars

- **1 cup (2 sticks) butter or margarine, softened**
- **1 cup packed light brown sugar**
- **2 eggs**
- **1 teaspoon vanilla extract**
- **1 1/2 cups all-purpose flour**
- **1 teaspoon baking soda**
- **1/2 teaspoon ground cinnamon**
- **1/2 teaspoon salt**
- **1 1/3 cups (8-ounce package) HEATH® BITS 'O BRICKLE® Toffee Bits, divided**
- **3 cups quick-cooking or regular rolled oats**

1. Heat oven to 350°F. Grease 13×9×2-inch baking pan.

2. Beat butter and brown sugar in large bowl until well blended. Add eggs and vanilla; beat well. Stir together flour, baking soda, cinnamon and salt; gradually add to butter mixture, beating until well blended. Set aside 1/4 cup toffee bits. Stir remaining toffee bits and oats into batter (batter will be stiff). Spread batter in prepared pan; sprinkle reserved 1/4 cup toffee bits over surface.

3. Bake 25 minutes or until wooden pick inserted in center comes out clean. Cool completely in pan on wire rack. Cut into bars.   *Makes about 36 bars*

Tip: Bar cookies can be cut into different shapes for variety. To cut into triangles, cut cookie bars into 2- to 3-inch squares, then diagonally cut each square in half. To make diamond shapes, cut parallel lines 2 inches apart across the length of the pan, then cut diagonal lines 2 inches apart.

Magic Cookie Bars

¹/₂ cup (1 stick) butter or margarine

1 ¹/₂ cups graham cracker crumbs

1 (14-ounce) can **EAGLE BRAND®** Sweetened Condensed Milk (**NOT** evaporated milk)

2 cups (12 ounces) semi-sweet chocolate chips

1 ¹/₃ cups flaked coconut

1 cup chopped nuts

1. Preheat oven to 350°F (325°F for glass dish). In 13×9-inch baking pan, melt butter in oven.

2. Sprinkle graham cracker crumbs over butter; pour EAGLE BRAND® evenly over crumbs. Layer evenly with remaining ingredients; press down firmly.

3. Bake 25 minutes or until lightly browned. Cool. Cut into bars. Store loosely covered at room temperature.   *Makes 2 to 3 dozen bars*

7-Layer Magic Cookie Bars: Substitute 1 cup (6 ounces) butterscotch-flavored chips for 1 cup semi-sweet chocolate chips. (Peanut butter-flavored chips or white chocolate chips can be substituted for butterscotch-flavored chips.)

Magic Peanut Cookie Bars: Substitute 2 cups (about ³/₄ pound) chocolate-covered peanuts for semi-sweet chocolate chips and chopped nuts.

Magic Rainbow Cookie Bars: Substitute 2 cups plain candy-coated chocolate pieces for semi-sweet chocolate chips.

Prep Time: 10 minutes ✦ **Bake Time**: 25 minutes

Magic Cookie Bars

Easy Double Chocolate Chip Brownies

- **2 cups (12-ounce package) NESTLÉ® TOLL HOUSE® Semi-Sweet Chocolate Morsels,** *divided*
- **¹/₂ cup (1 stick) butter or margarine, cut into pieces**
- **3 large eggs**
- **1 ¹/₄ cups all-purpose flour**
- **1 cup granulated sugar**
- **1 teaspoon vanilla extract**
- **¹/₄ teaspoon baking soda**
- **¹/₂ cup chopped nuts**

PREHEAT oven to 350°F. Grease 13×9-inch baking pan.

MELT *1 cup* morsels and butter in large, *heavy-duty* saucepan over low heat; stir until smooth. Remove from heat. Stir in eggs. Stir in flour, sugar, vanilla extract and baking soda. Stir in *remaining* morsels and nuts. Spread into prepared baking pan.

BAKE for 18 to 22 minutes or until wooden pick inserted in center comes out slightly sticky. Cool completely in pan on wire rack.   *Makes 2 dozen brownies*

Easy Double Chocolate Chip Brownies

Swell Sweets

Pretty-in-Pink Peppermint Cupcakes

  1 package (about 18 ounces) white cake mix
1 1/3 cups water
  3 egg whites
  2 tablespoons vegetable oil or melted butter
  1/2 teaspoon peppermint extract
  3 to 4 drops red liquid food coloring *or* 1/4 teaspoon gel food coloring
  1 container (16 ounces) vanilla frosting
  1/2 cup crushed peppermint candies (about 16 candies)

1. Preheat oven to 350°F. Line 30 standard (2½-inch) muffin pan cups with pink or white paper liners.

2. Beat cake mix, water, egg whites, oil, peppermint extract and food coloring in large bowl with electric mixer at low speed 30 seconds. Beat at medium speed 2 minutes.

3. Spoon batter into prepared muffin cups filling ¾ full. Bake 20 to 22 minutes or until toothpick inserted into centers comes out clean. Cool in pans on wire racks 10 minutes. Remove from pans to wire racks; cool completely. (At this point, cupcakes may be frozen up to 3 months. Thaw at room temperature before frosting.)

4. Spread frosting over cooled cupcakes; sprinkle with crushed candies. Store at room temperature up to 24 hours or cover and refrigerate up to 3 days before serving.

Makes about 30 cupcakes

Pretty-in-Pink Peppermint Cupcakes

Foolproof Dark Chocolate Fudge

3 cups (18 ounces) semi-sweet chocolate chips

1 (14-ounce) can EAGLE BRAND® Sweetened Condensed Milk (NOT evaporated milk)

Dash salt

¹/₂ to 1 cup chopped nuts (optional)

1 ¹/₂ teaspoons vanilla extract

1. Line 8- or 9-inch square pan with waxed paper. Butter paper; set aside.

2. In heavy saucepan over low heat, melt chips with EAGLE BRAND® and salt. Remove from heat; stir in nuts, if desired, and vanilla. Spread evenly in prepared pan.

3. Chill 2 hours or until firm. Turn fudge onto cutting board; peel off paper and cut into squares. Store covered in refrigerator.   *Makes about 2 pounds fudge*

Marshmallow Fudge: Substitute 2 cups miniature marshmallows for nuts. Stir in 2 tablespoons butter with vanilla. Proceed as directed above.

Prep Time: 10 minutes ✦ *Chill Time:* 2 hours

Foolproof Dark Chocolate Fudge

Carrot Cream Cheese Cupcakes

1 package (8 ounces) cream cheese, softened

1/4 cup powdered sugar

1 package (18 1/4 ounces) spice cake mix, plus ingredients to prepare mix

2 cups grated carrots

2 tablespoons finely chopped candied ginger

1 container (16 ounces) cream cheese frosting

3 tablespoons maple syrup

Orange peel strips for garnish (optional)

1. Preheat oven to 350°F. Line 14 large (3 1/2-inch) muffin pan cups with paper or foil liners.

2. Beat cream cheese and powdered sugar in large bowl at medium speed of electric mixer 1 minute or until light and fluffy. Cover and refrigerate until needed.

3. Prepare cake mix according to package directions. Fold in carrots and ginger.

4. Fill muffin cups 1/3 full with batter (about 1/4 cup). Place 1 tablespoon cream cheese mixture in center of each cup. Fill with remaining batter (muffin cups should be 2/3 full).

5. Bake 25 to 28 minutes or until toothpick inserted into centers comes out clean. Cool in pan on wire rack 10 minutes. Remove from pan to wire rack; cool completely.

6. Mix frosting and maple syrup until well blended. Frost tops of cupcakes; decorate with orange peel, if desired. *Makes 14 cupcakes*

Carrot Cream Cheese Cupcakes

Touchdown Brownie Cups

1 cup (2 sticks) butter or margarine
½ cup HERSHEY'S Cocoa or HERSHEY'S Dutch Processed Cocoa
1 cup packed light brown sugar
½ cup granulated sugar
3 eggs
1 teaspoon vanilla extract
1 cup all-purpose flour
1 ⅓ cups chopped pecans, divided

1. Heat oven to 350°F. Line 2½-inch muffin cups with foil or paper bake cups.

2. Place butter in large microwave-safe bowl; cover. Microwave at HIGH (100%) 1½ minutes or until melted. Add cocoa; stir until smooth. Add brown sugar and granulated sugar; stir until well blended. Add eggs and vanilla; beat well. Add flour and 1 cup pecans; stir until well blended. Fill prepared muffin cups about ¾ full with batter; sprinkle about 1 teaspoon remaining pecans over top of each.

3. Bake 20 to 25 minutes or until tops are beginning to dry and crack. Cool completely in cups on wire rack.   *Makes about 17 cupcakes*

Tip

To fill muffin cups neatly and easily, place the batter in a 4-cup glass measure. Use a plastic spatula to control the flow of the batter.

Touchdown Brownie Cups

Peanut Butter Cereal Treats

MAZOLA NO STICK® Cooking Spray
4 cups crispy rice cereal or combination of ready-to-eat cereals*
¹/₂ cup KARO® Light or Dark Corn Syrup
¹/₂ cup sugar
¹/₂ cup chunk or creamy peanut butter

*If using flake cereal, increase amount to 5 cups.

1. Spray 8- or 9-inch square baking pan with cooking spray. Pour cereal into large bowl.

2. In medium saucepan combine corn syrup and sugar. Stirring occasionally, bring to boil over medium heat and boil 1 minute. Remove from heat.

3. Stir in peanut butter until smooth. Pour over cereal; stir to coat well.

4. Press evenly into prepared pan. Cool about 15 minutes. Invert onto cutting board. Cut into 1½-inch bars.   *Makes 36 bars*

Microwave Directions: Prepare pan as directed above. In 2-quart microwavable bowl combine corn syrup, sugar and peanut butter. Microwave on High (100%), stirring twice, 3½ to 4 minutes or until mixture is smooth and sugar is dissolved. Continue as directed in steps 3 and 4.

S'Mores Treats: Prepare Peanut Butter Cereal Treats as above; do not remove from pan. Melt 1 package (11½ ounces) milk chocolate chips; spread over top. Sprinkle with 2 cups miniature marshmallows. Broil a few seconds, just until golden brown. Cool.

Prep Time: 6 minutes, plus cooling

Rocky Road Clusters

2 cups (12-ounce package) NESTLÉ® TOLL HOUSE® Semi-Sweet Chocolate Morsels
1 can (14 ounces) NESTLÉ® CARNATION® Sweetened Condensed Milk
2 ½ cups miniature marshmallows
1 cup coarsely chopped nuts
1 teaspoon vanilla extract

LINE baking sheets with waxed paper.

COMBINE morsels and sweetened condensed milk in large, uncovered, microwave-safe bowl. Microwave on HIGH (100%) power for 1 minute. STIR. Morsels may retain some of their original shape. If necessary, microwave at additional 10- to 15-second intervals, stirring just until morsels are melted. Stir in marshmallows, nuts and vanilla extract.

DROP by heaping tablespoon in mounds onto prepared baking sheets. Refrigerate until firm.   *Makes about 2 dozen candies*

141

Tip

To prevent marshmallows from drying out, store them in a tightly sealed bag in the freezer.

Cookies & Cream Cupcakes

2 ¼ cups all-purpose flour

1 tablespoon baking powder

½ teaspoon salt

1 ⅔ cups sugar

1 cup milk

½ cup (1 stick) butter, softened

2 teaspoons vanilla

3 egg whites

1 cup crushed chocolate sandwich cookies (about 10 cookies) plus additional for garnish

1 container (16 ounces) vanilla frosting

1. Preheat oven to 350°F. Lightly grease 24 standard (2½-inch) muffin pan cups or line with paper liners.

2. Sift flour, baking powder and salt together in large bowl. Stir in sugar. Add milk, butter and vanilla; beat with electric mixer at low speed 30 seconds. Beat at medium speed 2 minutes. Add egg whites; beat 2 minutes. Stir in 1 cup crushed cookies.

3. Spoon batter evenly into prepared muffin cups. Bake 20 to 25 minutes or until toothpick inserted into centers comes out clean. Cool in pans on wire racks 10 minutes. Remove to wire racks; cool completely.

4. Frost cupcakes; garnish with additional crushed cookies.

Makes 24 cupcakes

Cookies & Cream Cupcakes

Butter Almond Crunch

I ½ cups **HERSHEY'S Semi-Sweet Chocolate Chips or HERSHEY'S MINI CHIPS™ Semi-Sweet Chocolate Chips, divided**

I ¾ cups **chopped almonds, divided**

I ½ cups **(3 sticks) butter or margarine**

I ¾ cups **sugar**

3 tablespoons **light corn syrup**

3 tablespoons **water**

1. Heat oven to 350°F. Line 13×9×2-inch pan with foil; butter foil.

2. Sprinkle 1 cup chocolate chips into pan; set aside. Spread chopped almonds in shallow baking dish. Bake about 7 minutes or until golden brown, stirring occasionally; set aside.

3. Melt butter in heavy 3-quart saucepan; stir in sugar, corn syrup and water. Cook over medium heat, stirring constantly, to 280°F on a candy thermometer or until mixture separates into hard, brittle threads when dropped into small amount of very cold water. (Bulb of candy thermometer should not rest on bottom of saucepan.)

4. Remove from heat; stir in 1 ½ cups toasted almonds. Immediately spread mixture evenly over chocolate chips in prepared pan; do not disturb chips. Sprinkle with remaining ¼ cup toasted almonds and remaining ½ cup chocolate chips; cool slightly.

5. Cool completely; remove from pan. Remove foil; break candy into small pieces. Store in airtight container in cool, dry place.   *Makes about 2 pounds candy*

144

Butter Almond Crunch

Mini Turtle Cupcakes

1 package (21 ½ ounces) brownie mix plus ingredients to prepare mix
½ cup chopped pecans
1 cup prepared or homemade dark chocolate frosting
½ cup coarsely chopped pecans, toasted
12 caramels
1 to 2 tablespoons whipping cream

1. Heat oven to 350°F. Line 54 mini (1 ½-inch) muffin cups with paper liners.

2. Prepare brownie batter as directed on package. Stir in chopped pecans.

3. Spoon batter into prepared muffin cups filling ⅔ full. Bake 18 minutes or until toothpick inserted into centers comes out clean. Cool in pans on wire racks 5 minutes. Remove cupcakes to racks; cool completely. (At this point, cupcakes may be frozen up to 3 months. Thaw at room temperature before frosting.)

4. Spread frosting over cooled cupcakes; top with toasted pecans.

5. Combine caramels and 1 tablespoon cream in small saucepan. Cook and stir over low heat until caramels are melted and mixture is smooth. Add additional 1 tablespoon cream if needed to thin mixture. Spoon caramel decoratively over cupcakes. Store at room temperature up to 24 hours or cover and refrigerate for up to 3 days before serving.
Makes 54 mini cupcakes

Tip

To toast nuts, spread them on a baking sheet and place in a 350°F oven for 6 to 8 minutes. Or, toast nuts in an ungreased skillet over medium heat until golden brown, stirring frequently.

Mini Turtle Cupcakes

Fudgey Cocoa No-Bake Treats

2 cups sugar
$\frac{1}{2}$ cup (1 stick) butter or margarine
$\frac{1}{2}$ cup milk
$\frac{1}{3}$ cup HERSHEY'S Cocoa
$\frac{2}{3}$ cup REESE'S® Crunchy Peanut Butter
3 cups quick-cooking rolled oats
$\frac{1}{2}$ cup chopped peanuts (optional)
2 teaspoons vanilla extract

1. Place piece of wax paper or foil on tray or cookie sheet. Combine sugar, butter, milk and cocoa in medium saucepan.

2. Cook over medium heat, stirring constantly, until mixture comes to a rolling boil.

3. Remove from heat; cool 1 minute.

4. Add peanut butter, oats, peanuts, if desired, and vanilla; stir to mix well. Quickly drop mixture by heaping teaspoons onto wax paper or foil. Cool completely. Store in cool, dry place.   *Makes about 4 dozen treats*

Brunchtime Sour Cream Cupcakes

 1 cup (2 sticks) butter, softened
 2 cups plus 4 teaspoons sugar, divided
 2 eggs
 1 cup sour cream
 1 teaspoon almond extract
 2 cups all-purpose flour
 1 teaspoon salt
 1/2 teaspoon baking soda
 1 cup chopped walnuts
 1 1/2 teaspoons ground cinnamon
 1/8 teaspoon ground nutmeg

1. Preheat oven to 350°F. Lightly grease 18 standard (2 1/2-inch) muffin pan cups or line with paper liners.

2. Beat butter and 2 cups sugar in large bowl. Add eggs, one at a time, beating well after each addition. Blend in sour cream and almond extract. Combine flour, salt and baking soda in medium bowl. Add to butter mixture; mix well.

3. Stir together remaining 4 teaspoons sugar, walnuts, cinnamon and nutmeg in small bowl.

4. Fill prepared muffin cups 1/3 full with batter; sprinkle evenly with 2/3 of walnut mixture. Cover with remaining batter. Sprinkle with remaining walnut mixture.

5. Bake 25 to 30 minutes or until toothpick inserted into centers comes out clean. Remove cupcakes from pan; cool on wire rack.   *Makes 1 1/2 dozen cupcakes*

Lemon Poppy Seed Cupcakes

Cupcakes

1 package **DUNCAN HINES**® Moist Deluxe® Lemon Supreme Cake Mix

3 eggs

1 $\frac{1}{3}$ cups water

$\frac{1}{3}$ cup vegetable oil

3 tablespoons poppy seeds

Lemon Frosting

1 container (16 ounces) **DUNCAN HINES**® Vanilla Frosting

1 teaspoon grated lemon peel

$\frac{1}{4}$ teaspoon lemon extract

3 to 4 drops yellow food coloring

Yellow and orange gumdrops for garnish

1. Preheat oven to 350°F. Place paper liners in 30 (2½-inch) muffin cups.

2. For cupcakes, combine cake mix, eggs, water, oil and poppy seeds in large bowl. Beat at medium speed of electric mixer 2 minutes. Fill paper liners about half full. Bake at 350°F for 18 to 21 minutes or until toothpick inserted in center comes out clean. Cool in pans 5 minutes. Remove to cooling racks. Cool completely.

3. For lemon frosting, combine Vanilla frosting, lemon peel and lemon extract in small bowl. Tint with yellow food coloring to desired color. Frost cupcakes with lemon frosting. Decorate with gumdrops.   *Makes 30 cupcakes*

Lemon Poppy Seed Cupcakes

German Chocolate No-Cook Fudge

- **3 packages (4 ounces each) German sweet chocolate, broken into pieces**
- **1 cup (6 ounces) semisweet chocolate chips**
- **1 can (14 ounces) sweetened condensed milk**
- **1 cup chopped pecans**
- **2 teaspoons vanilla**
- **36 pecan halves (optional)**

1. Butter 8-inch square pan; set aside. Melt chocolate and chips in heavy, small saucepan over very low heat, stirring constantly. Remove from heat. Add condensed milk, chopped pecans and vanilla; stir until well blended. Spread in prepared pan. Score fudge into squares with knife. Place pecan half on each square, if desired. Refrigerate until firm.

2. Cut fudge into squares along score marks. Store in refrigerator. Bring to room temperature before serving.

Makes about 2 pounds

Tip

To cut fudge into neat squares, run your knife under hot water and wipe it dry before making each cut.

German Chocolate No-Cook Fudge

The publisher would like to thank the companies and organizations listed below for the use of their recipes and photographs in this publication.

ACH FOOD COMPANIES, INC.

Cherry Marketing Institute

Crisco is a registered trademark of The J.M. Smucker Company

Dole Food Company, Inc.

Duncan Hines® and Moist Deluxe® are registered trademarks of Pinnacle Foods Corp.

Eagle Brand® Sweetened Condensed Milk

Fleischmann's® Yeast

Grandma's® is a registered trademark of Mott's, LLP

Hershey Foods Corporation

Keebler® Company

National Honey Board

Nestlé USA

The Quaker® Oatmeal Kitchens

Smucker's® trademark of The J.M. Smucker Company

Sokol and Company

Southeast United Dairy Industry Association, Inc.

Reprinted with permission of Sunkist Growers, Inc.

Washington Apple Commission

Index

VOLUME MEASUREMENTS (dry)

1/8 teaspoon = 0.5 mL
1/4 teaspoon = 1 mL
1/2 teaspoon = 2 mL
3/4 teaspoon = 4 mL
1 teaspoon = 5 mL
1 tablespoon = 15 mL
2 tablespoons = 30 mL
1/4 cup = 60 mL
1/3 cup = 75 mL
1/2 cup = 125 mL
2/3 cup = 150 mL
3/4 cup = 175 mL
1 cup = 250 mL
2 cups = 1 pint = 500 mL
3 cups = 750 mL
4 cups = 1 quart = 1 L

VOLUME MEASUREMENTS (fluid)

1 fluid ounce (2 tablespoons) = 30 mL
4 fluid ounces (1/2 cup) = 125 mL
8 fluid ounces (1 cup) = 250 mL
12 fluid ounces (1 1/2 cups) = 375 mL
16 fluid ounces (2 cups) = 500 mL

WEIGHTS (mass)

1/2 ounce = 15 g
1 ounce = 30 g
3 ounces = 90 g
4 ounces = 120 g
8 ounces = 225 g
10 ounces = 285 g
12 ounces = 360 g
16 ounces = 1 pound = 450 g

DIMENSIONS

1/16 inch = 2 mm
1/8 inch = 3 mm
1/4 inch = 6 mm
1/2 inch = 1.5 cm
3/4 inch = 2 cm
1 inch = 2.5 cm

OVEN TEMPERATURES

250°F = 120°C
275°F = 140°C
300°F = 150°C
325°F = 160°C
350°F = 180°C
375°F = 190°C
400°F = 200°C
425°F = 220°C
450°F = 230°C

BAKING PAN SIZES

Utensil	Size in Inches/Quarts	Metric Volume	Size in Centimeters
Baking or Cake Pan (square or rectangular)	8 × 8 × 2	2 L	20 × 20 × 5
	9 × 9 × 2	2.5 L	23 × 23 × 5
	12 × 8 × 2	3 L	30 × 20 × 5
	13 × 9 × 2	3.5 L	33 × 23 × 5
Loaf Pan	8 × 4 × 3	1.5 L	20 × 10 × 7
	9 × 5 × 3	2 L	23 × 13 × 7
Round Layer Cake Pan	8 × 1½	1.2 L	20 × 4
	9 × 1½	1.5 L	23 × 4
Pie Plate	8 × 1¼	750 mL	20 × 3
	9 × 1¼	1 L	23 × 3
Baking Dish or Casserole	1 quart	1 L	—
	1½ quart	1.5 L	—
	2 quart	2 L	—

Deployment
Journal
for Kids

Rachel Robertson

Elva Resa ✳ Saint Paul

Deployment Journal for Kids
©2005 Rachel Robertson
Design ©2005 Elva Resa Publishing
All rights reserved.

ISBN-13: 978-0-9657483-0-8
ISBN-10: 0-9657483-0-8

http://www.deploymentkids.com

Elva Resa Publishing http://www.elvaresa.com

T H A N K   Y O U

My editors Tammy Price and Chris Coughenour
Taraschke provided valuable guidance and inspiring
enthusiasm. Karen Pavlicin patiently mentored.

Dawn Payne read my first draft with the sharp eye
of a seasoned military wife.

Adam and Hannah Taraschke, my two awesome advisors,
shared their experience and perspective to ensure
this journal helps all military children.

I especially thank my husband, Travis, for teaching
me about courage, my father for always believing in
me, my brother for being so proud, and my mother
for sharing my joy.   — Rachel

For Hanna Louise and Abigail Jane,
My angels on earth:

Hanna, your hope and laughter during your dad's
deployments gave me the faith and serenity I needed
so much. You are my inspiration for this book.

Abigail, your timing was perfect.

For my grandmother Elvera,
Who always smiled.

Someone you know must be deploying. I know how you feel; my dad had to go to Okinawa for a whole year and Iraq for five months. Sometimes it was really hard because I missed him so much. Then other times it was okay because my mom and I did special things. If someone that is special to you is about to leave on a deployment, I bet you have lots of feelings going on inside of you; I sure did. These are some of the feelings I felt when my dad was gone: angry, scared, hurt, disappointed, lonely and nervous. Maybe you feel this way too. Sometimes it's going to be tough, but you'll be okay. Your special person will be missing you just as much.

My mom wrote this book so kids like you could keep special memories and feelings until you see your special person back home again. You can share this book with that person, or you can keep it private all to yourself. The best part is that there are no rules. This is YOUR book - made to help YOU! You can write your thoughts and feelings down whenever and however you like. You can write in it daily, weekly or once a month. You can write poems, add artwork or just write how you feel.

There's a story about butterflies that my mom told me. Butterflies begin life as fuzzy, crawly caterpillars. Then they go through metamorphosis (met-a-mor-fo-sis, a big word meaning a big change) where they make a cocoon and shelter themselves inside for days while they experience many changes. This is a lot of work for the caterpillars, and while they are in the cocoon, they are very fragile. However, if they go through the struggle, they come out as strong and unique butterflies just as you will after this experience. So keep your chin up and remember that even though you may feel fragile, you are working hard to make yourself extra awesome!

Happy journaling!

Hanna Robertson

My name is:

I am _____ years old.

I live...

My favorite things to do are...

The thing I like the most about myself
is...

The person who is deploying is...

This person is special to me because...

HAPPY, excited, cheerful, proud, surprised, joyous, thrilled, smiley, glad,

ecstatic, elated, brave, hopeful, on cloud nine, loving, awesome. SAD,

scared, tired, lonely, miserable, gloomy, bored, depressed, shy, miserable,

_____

_____

_____

_____

_____

_____

_____

_____

_____

_____

_____

_____

_____

heartbroken, disappointed, confused, embarrassed, exhausted, afraid, icky,

hot, shocked, outraged, offended, guilty, fed up, disgusted, mean, crazy.

bummed out.   MAD, angry, upset, jealous, hurt, furious, livid, fuming,

Find out where your loved one is on the
world map and draw a star.

Go to www.deploymentkids.com for maps,
flags and more information.

About the Deployment

My loved one is deployed to...

I think we are about _____ miles apart.

I think we are about _____ hours apart.

I have learned these things about
the deployment location...

I want to find out more. I wonder...

On the next few pages you'll learn about a few of the places in the world that American military deploy. Find out what people eat, what kind of money they use and what activities they like to do in those places. If your deployed person is in a location not listed, there is a page for you to write in your own information. Go to www.deploymentkids.com for a distance calculator, time zones and more location information. Or go to your library, use an atlas or look up information on other Web sites. There is so much to learn about different places in the world. Have fun!

♀	28 million people	ABC	Speak Dari and Pashto
⊢—⊣ MILE	252,000 square miles	🖐	*Salam* is hello in Dari
⭐	Capital is Kabul	💰	The money is afghanis
☀🌧	Surrounded by land Very hot or very cold	🍢	Specialty is kebabs, meat cooked and served on skewers (sticks)

Other interesting facts:

* A popular sport is kite fighting. Opponents cover their kite strings with powdered glass and flour. When they fly their kites they try to move their kites in a way that will cut the other players' strings. The last kite flying wins.

* Only about 40 of every 100 people in Afghanistan can read.

* Families usually live in a kala. This is a group of buildings where big families live together, including cousins, uncles and aunts. The women work together to raise all of the kids. Grandpas are in charge of everyone's money and grandmas are in charge of all of the housekeeping chores.

Germany

83 million people		ABC Speak German	
137,800 square miles		*Hallo* is hello. *Guten tag* means good day	
Capital is Berlin		The money is euro	
Hot in summer, cool in winter. Cold rainstorms from the mountains.		Get German fast food at an Imbiss. Bratwurst, pretzels, frites (fries).	

Other interesting facts:

* Many fairy tales, such as *Rumplestiltsken* and *Hansel and Gretel* come from German authors.

* Every man is required to serve in the military for 9 months after high school. Women can volunteer to do the same.

* Germany makes Volkswagen cars, such as The Beetle.

* The Berlin Wall separated Germany into two countries, East Germany and West Germany, for almost 40 years because people couldn't agree how to run the country. The wall was torn down in 1989.

* Germans have a big party every October called Oktoberfest. People dance, listen to music, eat lots of food and go on carnival rides.

🧍 1.2 million people	ABC Speak English & Hawaiian
⊢—⊣ MILE 11,000 square miles, 6,500 miles of land	🖐 *Aloha* is hello in Hawaiian
☆ Capital is Honolulu	💵 The money is dollars
🌤 Considered paradise. Between 60 and 90 degrees year round.	🍽 A plate lunch is rice, a scoop of macaroni salad and short ribs or teriyaki.

Other interesting facts:

* People in Hawaii eat 6.9 million cans of SPAM in a year.

* The best surfers in the world compete on Hawaiian shores.

* Hawaii was formed from volcanic eruptions under the sea.

* The volcano Kilauea (kill-a-whey-ah) has been erupting constantly since 1983 and is the world's most active volcano.

* Hawaii is composed of 132 islands, reefs and shoals. The eight main islands, in order of size, are Hawaii, Maui, Oahu, Kauai, Molokai, Lanai, Nihau and Kahoolawe.

* Luaus, similar to backyard barbeques, are a traditional way to celebrate birthdays, graduations, weddings and any other occasions.

* Nutritious poi is made from pounding potato-like taro root after it is cooked in an underground oven called an imu.

(figure)	25 million people	ABC	Speak Arabic
MILE	168,750 square miles	(hand figure)	*Marhaba* is hello
(star)	Capital is Baghdad	(coins)	The money is dinar
(weather)	Mostly desert and more than 100 degrees. Cool in the mountains.	(bread)	Samoons are flat rounds of bread. Tripe, cow's stomach, is popular.

Other interesting facts:

∗ Soccer, called football, is popular.

∗ Some people believe that the Garden of Eden was in Iraq.

∗ They have large shopping areas called *bazaars*. Instead of stores, there are stalls where people sell things they have made or grown. Nothing has a set price; you can bargain.

∗ After the month of Ramadan, a religious fast in which no one eats during the day for a month, everyone celebrates. Girls cover their feet and hands with henna drawings, which look like swirly and decorative brown tattoos.

∗ Showing someone the bottom of your feet is considered rude and disrespectful.

☺	127 million people	ABC	Speak Japanese
⊢MILE⊣	145,880 square miles	✋	*Konichiwa* is hello
☆	Capital is Tokyo	💰	The money is yen
☁☀	Range of weather. Typhoons and monsoons are common.	🍽	Use chopsticks. Eat meat and rice. Specialty is sushi: raw or pickled fish.

Other interesting facts:

✳ Most meals are eaten at a low table, with people seated on the floor on a mat called a tatami.

✳ Tokyo is the largest city in the world and has 27 million people.

✳ Invitations are not sent to weddings because everyone who wants to come is welcome.

✳ It is rude to blow your nose in public.

✳ If you slurp your soup, it means you like it.

✳ Karate was invented in Japan. It means *Japanese hand art.*

✳ Okinawa is a small island 6 miles wide and 70 miles long. It is a prefecture of Japan (like a state). Many U.S. military are assigned to Okinawa. Since it is an island, some people spend time at beach resorts camping, swimming and riding banana boats.

☺	48 million people	ABC	Speak Korean
MILE	38,020 square miles	✋	*Anyong haseyo* is hello
☆	Capital is Seoul	💵	The money is won
☁☀🌧	Very green with lots of mountains. Summers wet from typhoons. Winter can be cold.	🥗	More than 100 kinds of Kimchi, vegetables that are prepared and stored for a long time.

Other interesting facts:

* Taekwondo started in Korea. People break bricks and wood with their bare hands and feet. It is now an Olympic sport.

* When you are at the table for a meal, no one can start eating until the oldest person starts to eat. No one can be excused until that person is finished.

* Most people in Korea eat, sleep and sit on the floor.

* Two important holidays are *Seollal*, the lunar New Year, and *Chuseok,* Korea's thanksgiving feast, also called Harvest Moon Festival.

* North Korea and South Korea are two separate countries because they don't agree how to run as one country.

2 million people		ABC Speak Arabic	
6,880 square miles		*Marhaba* is hello	
Capital is Kuwait City		The money is dinar	
Dry desert. Hot, hot, hot! Sandstorms and tauz (blowing dust everywhere!).		Falafel, deep-fried chick-pea balls, and hummus, cooked chickpea paste with garlic and lemon.	

Other interesting facts:

∗ Sailing is popular. Perfect winds and large marinas.

∗ Kuwait University is free to any Kuwaiti citizen who goes to college. The government will pay for someone to go to school in a different country if Kuwait University does not teach what the person wants to study.

∗ Every year there is a pearl diving festival. Many Kuwaitis used to earn money by diving for pearls. This festival celebrates that old tradition.

∗ If you eat at someone's house in Kuwait the host will keep filling up your plate with food as long as you keep eating every bite. If you stop eating and leave a little food on your plate, the host will stop serving you.

Being deployed on a ship is a different experience from being deployed to another country. Each type of ship can carry a different number of people and equipment. Ask about the ship your loved one is on.

Interesting facts:

*   Each part of the ship has a name. The BOW is the front, the STERN is the rear, PORT is the left and STARBOARD is the right.
*   TOPSIDE is above the main deck. BELOW DECK is beneath the main deck. Stairs are called LADDERS. A door is a HATCH.
*   A GEEDUNK is a snack shop. The GALLEY is the ship's kitchen. The SCULLERY is next to the galley where kitchen cleanup is done. MESS is where the sailors eat.
*   The BRIDGE is the place where the ship's controls are located.
*   SICKBAY is the hospital aboard ship.
*   A RACK is a bed. Ship beds are stacked like bunk beds. There are storage boxes under the mattresses.
*   To be SQUARED AWAY means you are in good position for whatever has to be done next.
*   SCUTTLEBUTT is stories or gossip of the day.
*   SKIVVIES are underwear.
*   USS in the title of a Navy ship stands for United States Ship.
*   LIBERTY is permission to leave ship for off-duty time for a day or a weekend. Longer periods of time off are called LEAVE.

If your loved one's deployment location is
not in this book, use this space to write
information you find out about the location. Also check www.deploymentkids.com.

Name of the location:

How many people live there?

How big is it?

What is the capital?

What language do they speak?

How do you say hello?

What kind of money do they use?

What kind of weather do they have?

What kind of food do they eat?

Other interesting facts:

Now that you know more about the country or ship, find out more about what daily life is like for your loved one. Ask questions such as:

Do you get any time alone?

Is there a place to watch TV?

What do you do during the day?

What do you do in your free time?

What do you miss the most?

Other questions:

Saying Goodbye

How I found out about the deployment...

I got ready for it by...

On the day I said goodbye I felt...

I know at least one friend and one grown-up I can talk to during this deployment.

Name _____

Phone # _____

Name _____

Phone # _____

Things I want to do or learn or accomplish
during the deployment...

1.

2.

3.

When I get lonely there are some things I
can do to cheer myself, for example...

1.

2.

3.

I plan to keep in touch by...

Write in the month and dates to plan or
record special events or days to remember.

Month:

	Sun	Mon	Tues	Wed	Thurs	Fri	Sat

Month:

Sun	Mon	Tues	Wed	Thurs	Fri	Sat

Write in the month and dates to plan or
record special events or days to remember.

	Sat				
	Fri				
	Thurs				
	Wed				
	Tues				
	Mon				
Month:	Sun				

Month:

Sun	Mon	Tues	Wed	Thurs	Fri	Sat

Write in the month and dates to plan or
record special events or days to remember.

Month:	Sun	Mon	Tues	Wed	Thurs	Fri	Sat

Month:

Sun	Mon	Tues	Wed	Thurs	Fri	Sat

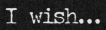
I wish...

_____

_____

_____

_____

_____

_____

_____

_____

_____

_____

_____

_____

We are going to have a homecoming. I
can't wait! This is how I found out...

I feel...

I have lots of plans for the big day. My
plans are...

The first thing I hope we do together...

HAPPY, excited, cheerful, proud, surprised, joyous, thrilled, smiley, glad,

ecstatic, elated, brave, hopeful, on cloud nine, loving, awesome. SAD,

scared, tired, lonely, miserable, gloomy, bored, depressed, shy, miserable,

_____

_____

_____

_____

_____

_____

_____

_____

_____

_____

_____

_____

heartbroken, disappointed, confused, embarrassed, exhausted, afraid, icky,

bummed out. MAD, angry, upset, jealous, hurt, furious, livid, fuming, hot, shocked, outraged, offended, guilty, fed up, disgusted, mean, crazy.

How to Help at Home

Deployment is HARD!!! Everyone in the family feels sad or grumpy at times. That's what happens when you miss someone you love. Sometimes the grownups who are home need help and understanding just like kids do. If everyone works together and understands each other the time will go more quickly. Here are some things to do if you are sad or someone at home is having a bad day.

If you are having a bad day

* Tell a grown up
* Write a letter
* Write a poem
* Watch a happy movie
* Try a new hobby
* Start a collection
* Play a game
* Learn magic

* Draw a picture
* Write a song
* Listen to music
* Exercise
* Beat a record
* Do something silly
* Go bowling
* Plan activities for when your loved one returns home

WRITE IN YOUR JOURNAL!!!

If someone at home is having a bad day

* Ask how you can help
* Write them a poem
* Look at happy pictures together
* Call another grownup like Grandma or Grandpa
* Remember that being sad is okay sometimes

* Give them a hug
* Make something for them
* Be patient
* Do something around the house without being asked

More ideas:

If there is ever a time when you are worried about your mom or dad, tell a grownup. Your teacher, a neighbor or grandparent will be happy to help your whole family.

* Decide how often you want to write letters. Try to write at least every two weeks.

* Write about yourself and what is happening in your life. Remember, your loved one doesn't get to be part of your daily life and will be interested in anything you write, even if you think it's boring.

* Don't be afraid to express your feelings. Your loved one is probably feeling some of the same things.

* Send something you create, such as a picture, a poem, a song or a photograph. Your loved one will see how much you're growing and learning and will be so proud to see your creativity.

* Write a story together. You start by writing one paragraph and then send it back and forth until it is finished.

* Glue a picture on a piece of cardboard to make a postcard.

* Send riddles or mini-mysteries and have your loved one send you guesses.

* Make a timeline out of construction paper. Keep track of all your family events during the deployment.

* Make coupons to send to your loved one, such as one free hug or one day of picking up your room without being asked.

✳ Make an "all about me" picture. Trace yourself, color it in and describe yourself.

✳ Measure yourself with string and send it so your loved one can see how much you're growing.

✳ Write a newspaper article about one of your recent achievements.

✳ Write a letter on a piece of cardboard and cut it into puzzle pieces. Send the pieces to your loved one.

✳ Keep a box in the house and slowly fill it with items to send.

✳ Record a message on a mini tape recorder or CD.

✳ Send a favorite snack you like to share together.

✳ Make a video of yourself.

✳ Start a collection of something small such as cards, agates (shiny rocks), stamps, coins, postcards or something else you are interested in. Keep your eyes out for these items and ask your loved one to bring some home, if possible, to add to the collection.

✳ Save water bottles and send messages in a bottle.

✳ Send your loved one a lightweight frame or mat board and send a new piece of art every month to put in it.

In the military we hear a lot of big, fancy words or letter combinations that are hard to understand. Here are some definitions to help you. Ask your loved one to teach you other military words. On the next page, add words you learn.

Battalion A group of 300-1000 military people who work together.

Bird An airplane or helicopter.

Command The people in charge are called the command. Also, the place where these people work can be called the command.

Company A group of 150-300 military people who work together.

Convoy A group of military people traveling together, moving from one place to another.

Cruise When a military ship goes out to sea.

Deployment A mission that takes military personnel away from home. People are deployed to different places depending on where the world needs help.

Duty Station A place where military personnel are assigned to live and work.

ETD / ETA Estimated time of departure / estimated time of arrival. The best guess for when someone is leaving or coming home.

Float When a ship is at sea.

Installation Another word for base or post, a place where military personnel work. Installations are often called camps or forts, for example, Camp Pendleton or Fort Ripley.

MEU Marine Expeditionary Unit. A group of Marines who prepare for and then deploy on a mission that usually lasts 6 months.

MOS Military Occupational Specialty. A military person's job. Someone may ask a Navy pilot, "What is your MOS?" He would answer, "I am a pilot."

Orders Directions telling military personnel where to go and what to do next. When someone gets orders it usually means being assigned to a new duty station or being deployed.

PCS Permanent Change of Station. Moving to a new base.

Platoon A group of 30-40 military people who work together.

Squadron A group of 100-300 military people who work together.

Stateside In the United States.

Underway When a ship or carrier is leaving its homeport.

Unit A group of military people, such as a battalion or platoon.

WestPac Western Pacific. The part of the world near Japan.

New Words

Word	Meaning

Word	Meaning

You Can Do It!

Remember, each day is one day closer to the day your loved one comes home! Each day between that day and now, you can decide to be mopey (which is okay once in awhile) or happy! Think about one day at a time. Decide to make the best of it, even though it's hard. Work on your goals, help around the house, try something new. Laugh and have fun!

When your loved one comes home you will be so excited to see each other!

Going through a deployment is tough. Remember the butterfly story and be proud of yourself every day. You are a brave, strong and special MILITARY KID!!!

Go online to **www.deploymentkids.com** for fun activities, cool ideas and more information.

FOURTH EDITION

THE
BUSINESS WRITER'S
COMPANION

Gerald J. Alred

Charles T. Brusaw

Walter E. Oliu

BEDFORD / ST. MARTIN'S   Boston   ◆   New York

For Bedford / St. Martin's

Developmental Editor: Caroline Thompson
Editorial Assistant: Amy Hurd
Production Supervisor: Jessie Markland
Senior Marketing Manager: Richard Cadman
Project Management: Books By Design, Inc.
Text Design: Claire Seng-Niemoeller
Cover Design: Donna Lee Dennison
Cover Photo: Office Building at Night by Robin Maddock/Photonica
Composition: Pine Tree Composition, Inc.
Printing and Binding: Haddon Craftsman, an RR Donnelley & Sons Company

President: Joan E. Feinberg
Editorial Director: Denise B. Wydra
Editor in Chief: Karen S. Henry
Director of Marketing: Karen Melton Soeltz
Director of Editing, Design, and Production: Marcia Cohen
Manager, Publishing Services: Emily Berleth

Library of Congress Control Number: 2004101848

Manufactured in the United States of America.

0 9 8 7 6
f e

For information, write: Bedford / St. Martin's, 75 Arlington Street, Boston, MA 02116   (617-399-4000)

ISBN-10: 0-312-41325-4
ISBN-13: 978-0-312-41325-5

Acknowledgments

Acknowledgments and copyrights appear at the back of the book on page 396, which constitutes an extension of the copyright page.

Preface

The Business Writer's Companion, a brief, topically arranged version of the popular *Business Writer's Handbook*, is an easy-to-use guide to the most common types of business writing and communication. By combining effective real-world sample documents, practical advice on specific types of business writing, thorough coverage of the writing process, and in-depth treatment of grammar and usage, we have tried to make the *Companion* a reliable reference in the classroom and on the job.

Our focus in this edition has been on helping students prepare for an increasingly global and technological environment as well as helping them become aware of the ethical concerns of business writing. We have also updated our advice for the job-application process based on a review by Monster.com's Résumé Expert, streamlined the information on research and documentation, and created a thoroughly integrated companion Web site. As always, we have also been guided by the generous reviews of colleagues and users around the country. In response to their suggestions, we have revised and updated entries throughout the book on topics such as writing for the Web, proposals, forms design, graphs, visuals, Web design, presentations, emphasis, and possessive case.

The *Companion*'s Organization and Cross-Referencing System

The *Companion*'s entries are thematically grouped into twelve tabbed sections. At the beginning of each tabbed section, a brief preview lists and introduces the entries, which are alphabetically arranged within that section. Within each entry, underlined cross-references, such as "revision," link readers to related entries both within that section and in other tabbed sections. When referencing an entry in a different tabbed section, the cross-reference includes a tab number in parentheses: "revision (Tab 1)."

For more details on accessing information in the *Companion*, see "How to Use This Book" on the inside back cover.

New to This Edition

New Features for Using Technology in Writing

- **Digital Tips.** New Digital Tips boxes throughout the book suggest ways to use software tools to assist with a variety of writing tasks, such as reviewing collaborative documents, creating indexes and outlines, laying out a page, and revising and proofreading. Corresponding expanded Digital Tips on the companion Web site provide more detailed step-by-step information for completing the tasks described.

- **An Integrated Book Companion Web Site.** The new companion Web site at <bedfordstmartins.com/alred> augments the material in the book with additional sample documents, tutorials, expanded Digital Tips, and links to helpful Web sites related to each entry in the book. Web Link boxes throughout the book now point students to related resources on the companion Web site.

Up-to-Date Topics to Familiarize Students with Today's Business World

- **Greater Attention to Global Communication.** Because of the growing importance of global communication in today's workplace, we have expanded our coverage of this topic and revised our coverage of global graphics, international correspondence, and English as a second language. We have also cross-referenced entries throughout the book to these discussions to make sure students consider the needs of global audiences throughout the writing process.
- **Ethics Notes.** New ⬥ ETHICS NOTE icons throughout the book alert students to ethical concerns in the workplace—such as plagiarism, copyright violations, honesty, and personal and corporate integrity—and highlight advice for handling ethical issues frequently encountered in workplace writing.
- **Updated Coverage of Job Search and Application.** Thoroughly reviewed and updated by Kim Isaacs, Monster.com's Résumé Expert, the résumés entry features new advice and examples for writing effective résumés. Tab 7, "Job Search and Application," guides students through the entire process, from writing application letters, to interviewing, to negotiating a salary and accepting a job offer. Additional sample résumés by Kim Isaacs appear on the companion Web site.

Streamlined Coverage of Research and Documentation

The new Tab 2, "Research and Documentation," gathers all the book's research-related entries into one section to provide students with easier access to advice about the entire research process, from finding and evaluating sources, to taking notes and avoiding plagiarism, to integrating quotations and documenting sources. To better assist students with today's research methods, we have revised our advice for library and Internet research and combined it into one research entry. The research entry now covers search strategies for print and online resources, both in the library and on the Web, and includes a new *Writer's Checklist:*

Evaluating Print and Online Sources. Finally, the documenting sources entry offers the most up-to-date guidelines for using MLA and APA styles and clarifies the reasons and rules for documenting sources.

Improved Reference Features

We have added the Complete List of Model Documents at the front of the book to give students quick access to every sample document in the book. We have also moved the complete table of contents to the front of the book and improved the cross-referencing system to make information in the *Companion* easier to find.

Acknowledgments

We are deeply grateful to the many instructors, students, professional writers, and others who have helped shape *The Business Writer's Companion*, Fourth Edition. For their sound advice on this revision, we wish to express our thanks to the following reviewers who completed questionnaires: Anne Bliss, University of Colorado–Boulder; Diann Dillingham, Texas A&M University; Susan A. Hagedorn, Virginia Tech; Beth L. Hewett, Pennsylvania State University–Fayette; Nancy Hightower, University of Denver; Terry A. Hinch, Johns Hopkins University; Roxanne Kent-Drury, Northern Kentucky University; Nancy D. Kersell, Northern Kentucky University; Judy A. Lange, Chapman University; Lauryn Migenes, University of Central Florida; Norman Pendegraft, University of Idaho; Rolanda P. Farrington Pollard, San José State University; Richard A. Quinn, University of Central Florida; Elizabeth Robinson, Texas A&M University; Christopher Sawyer-Laucanno, Massachusetts Institute of Technology; Terry Zambon, University of Colorado; and Jesseka Zeleike, University of Arizona.

For their helpful reviews of the companion Web site, we thank Anne Bliss, University of Colorado–Boulder; Lesley Baker, Tulane University; Mary Connerty, Pennsylvania State University–Erie; Annette Gooch, Santa Rosa Junior College; Christina Grignon, University of Wisconsin–Milwaukee; Nancy Hightower, University of Denver; Matthias Jonas, University of Wisconsin–Milwaukee; Elizabeth Robinson, Texas A&M University; Charlotte Rosen, Cornell University; and Philip Tietjen, Virginia Tech University.

We are also indebted to many who made important contributions to the first three editions of *The Business Writer's Companion*. In particular, we appreciate the valuable feedback on the first edition provided by Chris Benson, Clemson University; Alma G. Bryant, University of South Florida; Kenneth W. Davis, Indiana University–Purdue University, Indianapolis; and Philip Vassallo. For the second edition, we wish to thank E. Wallace Coyle, Boston College; Zita Ingham, Southwestern Oregon Community College; James S. O'Rourke IV, University of Notre Dame College of Business Administration; and

Robert P. Rimes, University of California, San Diego. For the third edition, we thank Laurence A. Jarvik, Johns Hopkins University; Cynthia Kuhn, University of Denver; N. L. Reinsch, Georgetown University; Jeffrey L. Walls, Indiana Institute of Technology; and Deanna F. Wilson, Collin County Community College.

We are especially grateful to Kim Isaacs of Advanced Career Systems, Inc., for her thorough review of the résumés entry and her work on new sample résumés for this edition. We also thank Renee Tegge and Matthias Jonas, who assisted in the development and improvement of the book in many ways. For contributions to previous editions, we wish to thank Lisa Rivero, Milwaukee School of Engineering; Peter Sands, University of Wisconsin–Milwaukee; and Rachel Spilka, University of Wisconsin–Milwaukee.

We most gratefully acknowledge the leadership of Bedford/St. Martin's, beginning with Joan Feinberg, President; Denise Wydra, Editorial Director; Karen Henry, Editor in Chief; and Charles Christensen, retired president, for their support of this book. We would also like to acknowledge the contributions of others at Bedford/St. Martin's over the years — Nancy Lyman, who conceived the first edition of this book; Carla Samodulski, for her expert editorial guidance; Mimi Melek, for her editorial development of the second edition; and Ellen Thibault, for editing the third edition.

For this edition, we would like to thank Emily Berleth for ensuring the high-quality production of the book, as well as Jessie Markland of Bedford/St. Martin's and Herb Nolan of Books By Design for their energy, care, and professionalism in turning manuscript into bound book. We are also pleased to acknowledge the unfailing support of Amy Hurd, Editorial Assistant at Bedford/St. Martin's. Finally, we would like to thank Caroline Thompson, Associate Editor at Bedford/St. Martin's, for her thoughtful and insightful editorial direction throughout the project.

Special thanks go to Janice Alred for her many hours of substantive assistance and for holding everything together.

Gerald J. Alred
Charles T. Brusaw
Walter E. Oliu

Complete Contents

5. Design and Visuals   133

7. Job Search and Application   203

Five Steps to Successful Writing

Successful writing on the job is not the product of inspiration, nor is it merely the spoken word converted to print; it is the result of knowing how to structure information using both text and design to achieve an intended purpose for a clearly defined audience. The best way to ensure that your writing will succeed—whether it is in the form of a memo, résumé, proposal, or Web page—is to approach writing using the following steps:

1. Preparation
2. Research
3. Organization
4. Writing
5. Revision

You will very likely need to follow those steps consciously—even self-consciously—at first. The same is true the first time you use new software, interview a candidate for a job, or chair a committee meeting. With practice, the steps become nearly automatic. That is not to suggest that writing becomes easy. It does not. However, the easiest and most efficient way to write effectively is to do it systematically.

As you master the five steps, keep in mind that they are interrelated and often overlap. For example, your readers' needs and your purpose, which you determine in step 1, will affect decisions you make in subsequent steps. You may also need to retrace steps. When you conduct research, for example, you may realize that you need to revise your initial impression of the document's purpose and audience. Similarly, when you begin to organize, you may discover the need to return to the research step to gather more information.

The time required for each step varies with different writing tasks. When writing an informal memo, for example, you might follow the first three steps (preparation, research, and organization) by simply listing the points in the order you want to cover them. In such situations, you gather and organize information mentally as you consider your purpose and audience. For a formal report, the first three steps require well-organized research, careful note-taking, and detailed outlining. For a routine e-mail message to a coworker, the first four steps merge as you type the information on the screen. In short, the five steps expand, contract, and at times must be repeated to fit the complexity or context of the writing task.

Dividing the writing process into steps is especially useful for collaborative writing, in which you typically divide work among team members, keep track of a project, and save time by not duplicating effort. When you collaborate, you can use e-mail to share text and other files, suggest improvements to each other's work, and generally keep everyone informed of your progress as you follow the steps in the writing process. See also <u>collaborative writing</u> (Tab 1).*

Preparation

Writing, like most professional tasks, requires solid <u>preparation</u> (Tab 1). In fact, adequate preparation is as important as writing the draft. In preparing to write, your goal is to accomplish the following four major tasks:

- Establish your primary purpose.
- Assess your audience (or readers).
- Determine the scope of your coverage.
- Select the appropriate medium.

Establishing Your Purpose.   To establish your primary <u>purpose</u> (Tab 1), simply ask yourself what you want your readers to know, believe, or be able to do after they have finished reading what you have written. Be precise. Often a writer states a purpose so broadly that it is almost useless. A purpose such as "to report on possible locations for a new research facility" is too general. However, "to compare the relative advantages of Paris, Singapore, and San Francisco as possible locations for a new research facility so top management can choose the best location" is a purpose statement that can guide you throughout the writing process. In addition to your primary purpose, consider possible secondary purposes for your document. For example, a secondary purpose of the research-facilities report might be to make corporate executive readers aware of the staffing needs of the new facility so that they can ensure its smooth operation in whatever location is selected.

Assessing Your Audience.   The next task is to assess your <u>audience</u> (Tab 1). Again, be precise and ask key questions. Who exactly is your reader? Do you have multiple readers? Who needs to see or use the document? What are your readers' needs in relation to your subject? What are their attitudes about the subject? (Skeptical? Supportive? Anxious? Bored?) What do your readers already know about the subject? Should you define basic terminology, or will such definitions merely bore, or even impede, your readers? Are you communicating with international

---

*In this discussion, as elsewhere throughout this book, words and phrases underlined and set in an alternate typeface refer to specific alphabetical entries. The number in parentheses indicates the tabbed topical section in which the alphabetical entry can be found. If no tab number appears, the entry can be found in the same topical section as the entry you are reading.

readers and therefore dealing with issues inherent in <u>global communication</u> (Tab 1)?

For the research-facilities report, the readers are described as "top management." Who is included in that category? Will one of the people evaluating the report be the human resources manager? If so, that person likely would be interested in the availability of qualified professionals as well as in the presence of training, housing, and perhaps even recreational facilities available to potential employees in each city. The purchasing manager would be concerned about available sources for materials needed by the facility. The marketing manager would give priority to the facility's proximity to the primary markets for its products and services and the transportation options that are available. The chief financial officer would want to know about land and building costs and about each country's tax structure. The chief executive officer would be interested in all this information and perhaps more.

In addition to knowing the needs and interests of your readers, learn as much as you can about their background knowledge. Have they visited all three cities? Have they already seen other reports on the three cities? Is this the company's first new facility, or has the company chosen locations for new facilities before? As with this example, many workplace documents have audiences composed of multiple readers. You can accommodate their needs through one of a number of approaches described in the entry <u>readers</u> (Tab 1).

(ESL) TIPS FOR CONSIDERING AUDIENCES

In the United States, <u>conciseness</u> (Tab 9), <u>coherence</u> (Tab 9), and clarity characterize good writing. Make sure readers can follow your writing, and say only what is necessary to communicate your message. Of course, no writing style is inherently better than another, but to be a successful writer in any language, you must understand the cultural values that underlie the language in which you are writing. See also <u>global communication</u> (Tab 1).

Throughout this book we have included ESL Tips boxes like this one with information that may be particularly helpful to nonnative speakers of English. The entry <u>English as a second language</u> (Tab 11) includes a list of entries that may be of particular help to ESL writers.

Determining the Scope.   Determining your purpose and assessing your readers will help you decide what to include and what not to include in your writing. Those decisions establish the <u>scope</u> (Tab 1) of your writing project. If you do not clearly define the scope, you will spend needless hours on research because you will not be sure what kind of information you need or even how much. Given the purpose and audience established for the report on facility locations, the scope would include such information as land and building costs, available labor force, cultural issues, transportation options, and proximity to suppliers. However, it probably would not include the early history of the cities being considered or their climate and geological features, unless those aspects were directly related to your particular business.

Selecting the Medium.   Finally, you need to determine the most appropriate medium for communicating your message. Professionals on the job face a wide array of options—from e-mail, fax, voice mail, videoconferencing, and Web sites to more traditional means like letters, memos, reports, telephone calls, and face-to-face meetings. The most important considerations in selecting the appropriate medium are the audience and the purpose of the communication. For example, if you need to collaborate with someone to solve a problem or if you need to establish rapport with someone, written exchanges, even by e-mail, could be far less efficient than a phone call or a face-to-face meeting. However, if you need precise wording or you need to provide a record of a complex message, communicate in writing. If you need to make information that is frequently revised accessible to employees at a large company, the best choice might be to place the information on the company's Web site. If reviewers or collaborators need to make written comments on a proposal, you may need to provide paper copies that can be faxed or use word-processing software to insert comments electronically. The comparative advantages and primary characteristics of many typical means of business communication are discussed in <u>selecting the medium</u> (Tab 1). See also <u>writing for the Web</u> (Tab 1), <u>Web design</u> (Tab 5), and the entries in Tab 3, "Business Writing Documents and Elements."

Research

The only way to be sure that you can write about a complex subject is to thoroughly understand it. To do that, you must conduct adequate research, whether that means conducting an extensive investigation for a major proposal—through interviewing, library and Internet research, careful note-taking, and documenting sources—or simply checking a company Web site and jotting down points before you send an e-mail to a colleague. The entries in Tab 2, "Research and Documentation," will help you with the research process.

Methods of Research.   Researchers frequently distinguish between primary and secondary <u>research</u> (Tab 2), depending on the types of sources consulted and the method of gathering information. *Primary research* refers to the gathering of raw data compiled from interviews, direct observation, surveys, experiments, questionnaires, and audio and video recordings, for example. In fact, direct observation and hands-on experience are the only ways to obtain certain kinds of information, such as the behavior of people and animals, certain natural phenomena, mechanical processes, and the operation of systems and equipment. *Secondary research* refers to gathering information that has been analyzed, assessed, evaluated, compiled, or otherwise organized into accessible form. Such forms, or sources, include books, articles, reports, Web documents, e-mail discussions, business letters, minutes of meetings, operating manuals, and brochures. Use the methods most appropriate to your needs, recognizing that some projects will require several types of research and that collaborative projects may require those research tasks to be distributed among team members.

Sources of Information.   As you conduct research, numerous sources of information are available to you.

- Your own knowledge and that of your colleagues
- The knowledge of people outside of your workplace, gathered through <u>interviewing for information</u> (Tab 2)
- Internet sources, including Web sites, directories, archives, and discussion groups
- Library resources, including databases and indexes of articles as well as books and reference works
- Printed and electronic sources in the workplace, such as brochures, memos, e-mail, and Web documents

Consider all sources of information when you begin your research, and use those that are appropriate and helpful. The amount of research you will need to do depends on the scope of your project.

Organization

Without organization, the material gathered during your research, will be incoherent to your readers. To organize information effectively, you need to determine the best way to structure your ideas; that is, you must choose a primary method of development. The entry <u>organization</u> (Tab 1) describes typical methods of development used in on-the-job writing.

Methods of Development.   An appropriate method of development is the writer's tool for keeping information under control and the readers' means of following the writer's presentation. As you analyze the information you have gathered, choose the method that best suits your subject, your readers' needs, and your purpose. For example, if you were writing instructions for assembling office equipment, you would naturally present the steps of the process in the order readers should perform them: the sequential method of development. If you were writing about the history of an organization, your account would most naturally go from the beginning to the present: the chronological method of development. If your subject naturally lends itself to a certain method of development, use it—do not attempt to impose another method on it.

Sometimes you may need to use combinations of methods of development. For example, a persuasive brochure for a charitable organization might combine a general and specific method of development with a cause-and-effect method of development. That is, you could begin with persuasive case histories of individual people in need and then move to general information about the positive effects of donations on recipients.

Outlining.   Once you have chosen a method of development, you are ready to prepare an outline. Outlining (Tab 1) breaks large or complex subjects into manageable parts. It also enables you to emphasize key points by placing them in the positions of greatest importance. By structuring your thinking at an early stage, a well-developed outline ensures that your document will be complete and logically organized, allowing you to focus exclusively on writing when you begin the rough draft. An outline can be especially helpful for maintaining a collaborative-writing team's focus throughout a large project. However, even a short letter or memo needs the logic and structure that an outline provides, whether the outline exists in your mind or on-screen or on paper.

At this point, you must begin to consider layout and design elements that will be helpful to your readers and appropriate to your subject and purpose. For example, if visuals, photographs, or tables will be useful, this is a good time to think about where they may be deployed and what kinds of visual elements will be effective, especially if they need to be prepared by someone else while you are writing and revising the draft. The outline can also suggest where headings, lists, and other special design features may be useful. See the entries in Tab 5, "Design and Visuals."

Writing

When you have established your purpose, your readers' needs, and your scope and have completed your research and your outline, you will be well prepared to write a first draft. Expand your outline into paragraphs (Tab 1), without worrying about grammar, refinements of language usage, or punctuation. Writing and revising are different activities; refinements come with revision.

Write the rough draft, concentrating entirely on converting your outline into sentences and paragraphs. You might try writing as though you were explaining your subject to a reader sitting across from you. Do not worry about a good opening. Just start. Do not be concerned in the rough draft about exact word choice unless it comes quickly and easily—concentrate instead on ideas.

Even with good preparation, writing the draft remains a chore for many writers. The most effective way to get started and keep going is to use your outline as a map for your first draft. Do not wait for inspiration—you need to treat writing a draft as you would any on-the-job task. The entry <u>writing a draft</u> (Tab 1) describes tactics used by experienced writers—discover which ones are best suited to you and your task.

Consider writing the introduction last because then you will know more precisely what is in the body of the draft. Your opening should announce the subject and give readers essential background information, such as the document's primary purpose. For longer documents, an introduction should serve as a frame into which readers can fit the detailed information that follows. See <u>introductions</u> (Tab 1).

Finally, you will need to write a conclusion that ties the main ideas together and emphatically makes a final significant point. The final point may be to recommend a course of action, make a prediction or a judgment, or merely summarize your main points—the way you conclude depends on the purpose of your writing and your readers' needs. See <u>conclusions</u> (Tab 1).

Revision

The clearer a finished piece of writing seems to the reader, the more effort the writer has likely put into its <u>revision</u> (Tab 1). If you have followed the steps of the writing process to this point, you will have a rough draft that needs to be revised. Revising, however, requires a different frame of mind than does writing the draft. During revision, be eager to find and correct faults, and be honest. Be hard on yourself for the benefit of your readers. Read and evaluate the draft as if you were a reader seeing it for the first time.

Check your draft for accuracy, completeness, and effectiveness in achieving your purpose and meeting your readers' needs and expectations. Trim extraneous information: your writing should give readers exactly what they need, but it should not burden them with unnecessary information or sidetrack them into loosely related subjects.

Do not try to revise for everything at once. Read your rough draft several times, each time looking for and correcting a different set of problems or errors. Concentrate first on larger issues, such as <u>unity</u> (Tab 9) and <u>coherence</u> (Tab 9); save mechanical corrections, like spelling and punctuation, for later. See also <u>ethics in writing</u> (Tab 1).

Finally, for important documents, consider having others review your writing and make suggestions for improvement. For collaborative writing, of course, it is essential for team members to review each other's work on segments of the document as well as the final master draft. For further advice and useful checklists, see <u>revision</u> (Tab 1) and <u>proofreading</u> (Tab 1).

The Writing Process

Preview

The "Five Steps to Successful Writing" essay (page xxi) describes not only a systematic approach to writing but also a diagnostic tool for assessing problems. That is, when you find that a document is not achieving its primary purpose, the five steps can help you pinpoint where a problem occurred. Was the audience not fully assessed? Is further research needed? Does the document only need further revision? Many of the entries in this section expand on the topics introduced in the "Five Steps," such as **readers**, **collaborative writing**, **selecting the medium**, **writing a draft**, and others. (Entries related to the research process, including such topics as finding, evaluating, and using sources, appear in Tab 2, "Research and Documentation.")

audience

Although the word *audience* can have a slightly different meaning for a writer than a speaker, it is crucial to both. The writer and the speaker must know as much as possible about the people they are trying to reach with their message, regardless of its method of delivery. For the specific requirements of audiences, see <u>global communication</u>, <u>readers</u>, <u>international correspondence</u> (Tab 6), and <u>presentations</u> (Tab 8).

collaborative writing

Collaborative writing occurs when two or more writers work together to produce a single document for which they share responsibility and decision-making authority. Collaborative writing teams are formed when (1) the size of a project or the time constraints imposed on it require collaboration, (2) the project involves multiple areas of expertise, or (3) the project requires the melding of divergent views into a single perspective that is acceptable to the whole team or to another group.

Tasks of the Collaborative Writing Team

The collaborating writers strive to achieve a compatible working relationship by dividing the work in a way that uses each writer's expertise and experience to their collective advantage. The team should also designate a coordinator who will guide the team members' activities and organize the final project. The coordinator's duties can be determined by mutual agreement or, if the team often works together, assigned on a rotating basis.

Planning.   The team collectively identifies the audience, purpose, and scope of the project. The team conceptualizes the document to be produced, creates a broad outline of the document, divides it into segments, and assigns each segment to individual team members, often on the basis of expertise. See also "Five Steps to Successful Writing" (page xxi) and <u>meetings</u> (Tab 8).

In the planning stage, the team projects a schedule and sets any writing style standards that the team is expected to follow. The schedule includes due dates for drafts, reviews of the drafts, revisions, and the final document.

Research and Writing.   Each team member then researches his or her assigned segment of the document, expands and develops the broad outline, and produces a draft from the detailed outline. See also <u>outlining</u>, <u>writing a draft</u>, and <u>research</u> (Tab 2).

Reviewing.   Keeping the readers' needs and the document's purpose in mind, each member critically yet diplomatically reviews the other team members' work, from the overall organization to the clarity of each paragraph, and offers advice to help improve the writer's segment. Team members can easily solicit feedback by sharing files on a network system, by e-mailing documents back and forth, or by exchanging disks. Redlining or highlighting allows the reviewer to show the suggested changes without deleting the original text. The author can then easily accept or reject the proposed changes.

DIGITAL TIP **GIVING ELECTRONIC FEEDBACK**

Adobe Acrobat® and many word-processing packages have options for providing feedback on the drafts of collaborators' documents. You can add text or voice annotations within the text, allowing your reader to read or hear your comments, as well as track changes in your text and allow readers to accept or reject each change. In Acrobat, you can also use a drawing tool to input traditional editing marks. For more on this topic, see <bedfordstmartins.com/alred> and select *Digital Tips*, "Giving Electronic Feedback."

Revising.   In this stage, individual writers evaluate their colleagues' reviews and accept, reject, or build on their suggestions. Then, all drafts can be consolidated into a final master copy maintained by the team coordinator. See also <u>revision</u>.

Conflict

As you collaborate, be ready to tolerate some disharmony, but temper it with mutual respect. Team members may not agree on every subject, and differing perspectives can easily lead to conflict, ranging from mild differences over minor points to major showdowns. However, creative differences resolved respectfully can energize the team and, in fact, strengthen a finished document by compelling writers to reexamine assumptions and issues in unanticipated ways. See also <u>listening</u> (Tab 8).

Writer's Checklist: Writing Collaboratively

- ☑ Designate one person as the team coordinator.
- ☑ Identify the audience, purpose, and scope of the project.
- ☑ Create a working outline of the document.
- ☑ Assign segments or tasks to each team member.
- ☑ Establish a schedule: due dates for drafts, revisions, and final versions.

Writer's Checklist: Writing Collaboratively (continued)

- ☑ Agree on a standard reference guide for style and format.
- ☑ Research and write drafts of document segments.
- ☑ Exchange segments for team member reviews.
- ☑ Revise segments as needed.

conclusions

The conclusion of a document ties the main ideas together and can clinch a final significant point. This final point may, for example, make a prediction or a judgment, summarize the key findings of a study, or recommend a course of action, as shown in Figure 1–1.

CONCLUSION AND RECOMMENDATION

As shown earlier, building and equipping fitness centers at all five company locations would require an initial investment of nearly $2 million. Such facilities would also occupy valuable office space. Therefore, this option would be costly.

Enrolling employees in the corporate program at AeroFitness would allow them to attend on a trial basis. Those interested in continuing could join the club and pay half of the $400 annual membership cost, less a 30-percent discount. The other half of the membership ($140) would be paid for by First Investment. Employees who leave the company would be given the option to purchase First Investment's share of the membership.

I recommend that First Investment, Inc., participate in the corporate membership program at AeroFitness Clubs by subsidizing employee memberships. First Investment benefits from such a program in several ways: We demonstrate our commitment to a fit workforce, we augment our already generous benefits package, and we boost employee morale. Most importantly, implementing this program will help First Investment, Inc., reduce its health-care costs both by building a healthier workforce and by qualifying for insurance premium discounts.

FIGURE 1–1. Sample Conclusion

The way you conclude depends on both the purpose of your writing and your readers' needs. For example, a committee report about possible locations for a new production facility might end with a recommendation. The following examples are typical concluding strategies.

RECOMMENDATION

These results indicate that you need to alter your testing procedure to eliminate the impurities we found in specimens A through E.

SUMMARY

As this report describes, we would attract more recent graduates with the following strategies:
1. Establish a Web site where students can register and submit online résumés.
2. Increase our advertising in local student newspapers and our attendance at college career fairs.
3. Expand our local co-op program.

JUDGMENT

Based on the scope and degree of the tornado's damage, the current construction code for roofing on light industrial facilities is inadequate.

IMPLICATION

Although our estimate calls for a substantially higher budget than in the three previous years, we believe that it is reasonable given our planned expansion.

PREDICTION

Although I have exceeded my original estimate for equipment, I have reduced my original labor estimate; therefore, I will easily stay within the original bid.

The concluding statement may merely present ideas for consideration, call for action, or deliberately provoke thought.

IDEAS FOR CONSIDERATION

The new prices become effective the first of the year. Price adjustments are routine for the company, but some of your customers will not consider them acceptable. Please bear in mind the needs of both your customers and the company as you implement these new prices.

CALL FOR ACTION

Send us a check for $250 now if you wish to keep your account active. If you have not responded to our previous letters because of some special hardship, I will be glad to work out a solution with you personally.

THOUGHT-PROVOKING STATEMENT

Can we continue to accept the losses incurred by inefficiency? Or should we consider steps to control it now?

Be especially careful not to introduce a new topic when you con-clude. A conclusion should always relate to and reinforce the ideas pre-sented earlier in your writing. Moreover, the conclusions must be con-sistent with what the introduction promised the report would examine (its purpose) and how it would do so (its method). Figure 1–1 on page 5 is a conclusion from a proposal to reduce health-care costs by increas-ing employee fitness through health-club subsidies. It makes recom-mendations that pull the various parts of the proposal together.

For guidance about the location of the conclusion section in a re-port, see formal reports (Tab 4). For letter and other short closings, see correspondence (Tab 6) and entries on specific types of documents throughout this book. See also introductions.

defining terms

Good writing ensures that readers understand key terms and concepts. Terms can be defined either formally or informally, depending on your purpose and your readers.

A *formal definition* is a form of classification. You define a term by placing it in a category and then identifying the features that distinguish it from other members of the same category.

TERM	CATEGORY	DISTINGUISHING FEATURES
An *auction* is	a public sale	in which property passes to the highest bidder through successively increased offers.

An *informal definition* explains a term by giving a more familiar word or phrase as a synonym.

- Plants have a *symbiotic,* or *mutually beneficial,* relationship with certain kinds of bacteria.

State definitions positively; focus on what the term *is* rather than on what it is not.

NEGATIVE	In a legal transaction, *real property* is not personal property.
POSITIVE	*Real property* is legal terminology for the right or inter-est a person has in land and the permanent structures on that land.

Avoid circular definitions, which merely restate the term to be defined and therefore fail to clarify it.

CIRCULAR	*Spontaneous combustion* is fire that begins spontaneously.
REVISED	*Spontaneous combustion* is the self-ignition of a flammable material through a chemical reaction.

In addition, avoid "is when" and "is where" definitions. Such definitions fail to include the category and are too indirect.

> *a binding agreement between two or more parties.*
> • A *contract* is ~~when two or more people agree to something.~~

description

The key to effective description is the accurate presentation of details, whether for simple or complex descriptions. In Figure 1–2, notice that the simple description contained in the purchase order includes five specific details in addition to the part number.

PURCHASE ORDER

PART NO.	DESCRIPTION	QUANTITY
IW 8421	Infectious-waste bags, 12″ × 14″, heavy-gauge polyethylene, red double closures with self-sealing adhesive strips	5 boxes containing 200 bags per box

---

FIGURE 1–2. Simple Description

Complex descriptions, of course, involve more details. In describing a mechanical device, for example, describe the whole device and its function before giving a detailed description of how each part works. The description should conclude with an explanation of how each part contributes to the functioning of the whole.

In descriptions intended for readers who are unfamiliar with the topic, details are crucial. For these readers, show or demonstrate (as opposed to "tell") primarily through the use of images and details.

• Their corporate headquarters, which reminded me of a rural college campus, are located north of the city in a 90-acre wooded area. The complex consists of five three-story buildings of colonial design. The buildings are spaced about 50 feet apart and are built in a U shape. . . .

You can also use analogy to explain unfamiliar concepts in terms of familiar ones. See also <u>figures of speech</u> (Tab 9).

Visuals can be powerful aids in descriptive writing. For a discussion of how to incorporate visual material into text, see Tab 5, "Design and Visuals."

ethics in writing

Ethics refers to the choices we make that affect others for good or ill. Ethical issues are inherent in writing and speaking because what we write and say can influence others. Further, how we express ideas affects our readers' perceptions of us and our company's ethical stance.

■ ETHICS NOTE Obviously, no book can describe how to act ethically in every situation, but here are some typical ethical lapses to watch for and address during revision.*

Avoid language that attempts to evade responsibility. Some writers use the passive <u>voice</u> (Tab 11) because they hope to avoid responsibility or obscure an issue.

- It has been decided. [*Who* has decided?]

- Several mistakes were made. [*Who* made them?]

Avoid deceptive language. Do not use words with more than one meaning as a means to circumvent the truth. Consider the company document that stated, "A nominal charge will be assessed for using our facilities." When clients objected that the charge was actually very high, the writer pointed out that the word *nominal* means "the named amount" as well as "very small." In that situation, clients had a strong case in charging that the company was attempting to be deceptive. Various <u>abstract words</u> (Tab 9), technical and legal <u>jargon</u> (Tab 9), and <u>euphemisms</u> (Tab 9) are unethical when they are used to mislead readers or to hide a serious or dangerous situation, even though technical or legal experts could interpret them as accurate. See also <u>word choice</u> (Tab 9).

Do not deemphasize or suppress important information. Not including information that a reader would want to have, such as potential safety hazards or hidden costs for which a customer might be responsible, is unethical. Such omissions may also be illegal. (See also <u>copyright</u>, Tab 2, and <u>plagiarism</u>, Tab 2.) Use <u>layout and design</u> (Tab 5) features like typeface size, bullets, lists, and footnotes to highlight—not hide—information that is important to readers.

*Adapted from Brenda R. Sims, "Linking Ethics and Language in the Technical Communication Classroom," *Technical Communication Quarterly* 2.3 (Summer 1993): 285–99.

Do not emphasize misleading or incorrect information. Similarly, avoid the temptation to highlight a feature or service that readers would find attractive but that is available only with some product models or at extra cost. (See also logic errors, Tab 9, and positive writing, Tab 9.) Readers could justifiably object that you have given them a false impression to sell a product or service, especially if you also deemphasize the extra cost or other special conditions.

In general, treat others — individuals, companies, groups — fairly and with respect. Avoid language that is biased, racist, or sexist, or that perpetuates stereotypes. See also biased language (Tab 9).

Writer's Checklist: Writing Ethically

Ask yourself the following questions:

☑ *Am I willing to take responsibility, publicly and privately, for what the document says?* Will you stand behind what you have written? to your employer? to your family and friends?

☑ *Is the document honest and truthful?* Scrutinize findings and conclusions carefully. Make sure that the data support them.

☑ *Am I acting in my employer's best interest? my client's or the public's best interest? my own best long-term interest?* Have someone outside your company review and comment on what you have written.

☑ *Does the document violate anyone's rights?* Have people from different backgrounds review your writing.

☑ *Am I ethically consistent in my writing?* Apply consistently the principles outlined here and those you have assimilated throughout your life to meet this standard.

☑ *What if everybody acted or communicated in this way?* If you were the intended audience, would the message be acceptable and respectful?

global communication

The prevalence of global communication technology, international trade agreements, and the emergence of Europe as a giant single market means that the ability to communicate with audiences from varied cultural backgrounds is essential. The audiences for such communications include clients, business partners, and colleagues.

Entries such as meetings (Tab 8) and résumés (Tab 7) in this book are based on U.S. cultural patterns. The treatment of such topics might be very different in other cultures where leadership styles, persuasive strategies, and even legal constraints differ. As illustrated in international correspondence (Tab 6), organizational patterns, forms of courtesy, and ideas about efficiency can vary significantly from culture to culture.

What might be seen as direct and efficient in U.S. culture could be seen as blunt and even impolite in other cultures. The reasons behind these differing ways of viewing communication are complex, and those who study cultures have found various ways to measure cultural differences, such as individual versus group orientation, the importance of saving face, and conceptions of time.

Anthropologist Edward T. Hall, a pioneer in cross-cultural research, developed the concept of "context" to assess the predominant communication style of a culture.* By "context" Hall means how much or how little an individual assumes another person understands about a subject under discussion. In a very low-context communication, the participants assume they share little knowledge and must communicate in great detail. In a high-context communication, the participants already understand the context and thus do not feel a need to exchange much background information. Of course, no culture is strictly high or low context; rather, these concepts can be helpful in understanding the complex communication style of a particular culture.†

Obviously, cultural differences and the reasons behind them are often so subtle that only someone who is very familiar with a culture can explain the effect those differences may have on others from that culture. For that reason, it is best to consult with someone from your intended audience's culture.

Writer's Checklist: Communicating Globally

☑ Acknowledge diversity within your organization. Discussing the differing cultures within your company or region will reinforce the idea that people can interpret verbal and nonverbal communications differently.

☑ Invite global and intercultural communication experts to speak to your employees. Companies in your area may have employees who could be resources for cultural discussions.

☑ Understand that the key to effective communication with global audiences is recognizing that cultural differences, despite the challenges they may present, offer growth for both you and your organization.

☑ Consult with someone from your intended audience's culture. Many phrases, gestures, and visual elements are so subtle that only someone who is very familiar with the culture can explain the effect they may have on others from that culture.

For more information on reaching global audiences, see **global graphics** (Tab 5) and **international correspondence** (Tab 6).

---

*Edward Twitchell Hall and Mildred Reed Hall, *Understanding Cultural Differences: Germans, French and Americans* (Yarmouth, ME: Intercultural Press, 1990).
†Gerald J. Alred, "Teaching in Germany and the Rhetoric of Culture," *Journal of Business and Technical Communication* 11.3 (July 1997): 353–78.

WEB LINK INTERCULTURAL RESOURCES

Intercultural Press is a source of publications aimed at specific cultures as well as a wide variety of subjects, from cross-cultural theory to international business. For links to this and other resources for global communication, see <bedfordstmartins.com/alred> and select *Links for Business Writing.*

introductions

This entry discusses opening strategies for short and routine types of correspondence (Tab 6), such as letters and e-mail (Tab 6), as well as full-scale introductions to large writing projects, such as formal reports (Tab 4) and major proposals (Tab 3). See also conclusions.

Routine Openings

Not every document needs a fully developed introduction or opening. If your readers are already familiar with your subject or if what you are writing is short, a brief or routine opening, as shown in the following examples, is adequate.

CORRESPONDENCE

Dear Mr. Ignatowski:

You will be happy to know that we have corrected the error in your bank balance. The new balance shows . . .

PROGRESS REPORT LETTER

Dear Dr. Chang:

To date, 18 of the 20 specimens you submitted for analysis have been examined. Our preliminary analysis indicates . . .

LONGER PROGRESS REPORT

Progress Report on Rewiring the Sports Arena

The rewiring program at the Sports Arena is proceeding ahead of schedule. Although the costs of certain equipment are higher than our original bid, we expect to complete the project without exceeding our budget because the speedy completion will save labor costs.

Work Completed   As of August 15, we have . . .

E-MAIL

Jane, as I promised in my e-mail yesterday, I've attached the human resources budget estimates for fiscal year 2005.

Opening Strategies

Opening strategies are aimed at focusing the readers' attention and motivating them to read the entire document.

Objective.   In reporting on a project, you might open with a statement of the project's objective to give the readers a basis for judging the results.

- The primary goal of this project was to develop new techniques to solve the problem of waste disposal. Our first step was to investigate . . .

Problem Statement.   One way to give readers the perspective of your report is to present a brief account of the problem that led to the study or project being reported.

- Several weeks ago a manager noticed a recurring problem in the software developed by Datacom Systems. Specifically, error messages repeatedly appeared when, in fact, no specific trouble . . . After an extensive investigation, we found that Datacom Systems . . .

Of course, for proposals or formal reports, problem statements may be more elaborate and a part of the full-scale introduction, which is discussed later in this entry.

Scope.   You may want to present the <u>scope</u> of your document in your opening. By providing the parameters of your material, the limitations of the subject, or the amount of detail to be presented, you enable your readers to determine whether they want to or need to read your document.

- This pamphlet provides a review of the requirements for obtaining an FAA pilot's license. It is not intended as a textbook to prepare you for the examination itself; rather, it outlines the steps you need to take and the costs involved.

Background.   The background or history of a subject may be interesting and lend perspective and insight to a subject. Consider the following example from a newsletter describing the process of oil drilling:

- From the bamboo poles the Chinese used when the pyramids were young to today's giant rigs drilling in hundreds of feet of water, there has been considerable progress in the search for oil. But whether in ancient China or a modern city, under water or on a mountaintop, the object of drilling has always been the same — to manufacture a hole in the ground, inch by inch.

Summary.   You can provide a summary opening by describing in ab-breviated form the results, conclusions, or recommendations of your ar-ticle or report. Be concise: Do not begin a summary by writing "This report summarizes . . . "

| CHANGE | This report summarizes the advantages offered by the photon as a means of examining the structural features of the atom. |
| TO | As a means of examining the structure of the atom, the photon offers several advantages. |

Interesting Detail.   Often an interesting detail will gain the readers' attention and arouse their curiosity. Readers of an annual report for a manufacturer of telescopes and scientific instruments, for example, may be persuaded to invest if they believe that the company is developing in-novative, cutting-edge products.

- The rings of Saturn have puzzled astronomers ever since they were discovered by Galileo in 1610 using the first telescope. Recently, even more rings have been discovered. . . .
     Our company's Scientific Instrument Division designs and manufactures research-quality, computer-controlled telescopes that promise to solve the puzzles of Saturn's rings by enabling scientists to use multicolor differential photometry to determine the rings' origins and compositions.

Definition.   Although a definition can be useful as an opening, do not define something with which the reader is familiar or provide a de-finition that is obviously a contrived opening (such as "Webster defines *technology* as . . . "). A definition should be used as an opening only if it offers insight into what follows.

- *Risk* is often a loosely defined term. In this report, risk refers to a qualitative combination of the probability of an event and the severity of the consequences of that event. In fact, . . .

Anecdote.   An anecdote can be used to attract and build interest in a subject that may otherwise be mundane; however, this strategy is best suited to longer documents and presentations.

- In his poem "The Calf Path," Sam Walter Foss tells of a wander-ing, wobbly calf trying to find its way home at night through the lonesome woods. It made a crooked path, which was taken up the next day by a lone dog. Then "a bellwether sheep pursued the trail over vale and steep, drawing behind him the flock, too, as all good bellwethers do." At last the path became a country road; then a lane that bent and turned and turned again. The lane became a village street, and at last the main street of a flourishing city. The poet ends by saying, "A hundred thousand men were led by one calf near calf, three centuries dead."

Many companies today follow a "calf path" because they react to events rather than planning . . .

Quotation.   Occasionally, you can use a quotation to stimulate interest in your subject. To be effective, however, the quotation must be pertinent—not some loosely related remark selected from a book of quotations.

- Richard Smith, founder of PCS Corporation, recently said, "I believe that managers need to be more 'people smart' than ever before. The management style of today involves much more than just managing the operations of a department—it requires understanding the personalities that comprise a corporation." His statement represents a growing feeling among corporate leaders that . . .

Forecast.   Sometimes you can use a forecast of a new development or trend to arouse the reader's interest.

- In the not-too-distant future, we may be able to use a hand-held medical diagnostic device similar to those in science fiction to assess the complete physical condition of accident victims. This project and others are now being developed at The Seldi Group, Inc.

Persuasive Hook.   While all opening strategies contain persuasive elements, the hook is the most overtly persuasive. A <u>brochure</u> (Tab 3) touting the newest innovation in tax-preparation software might address readers as follows:

- Welcome to the newest way to do your taxes! TaxPro EZ ends the headache of last-minute tax preparation with its unique Web-Link feature.

Full-Scale Introductions

The purpose of a full-scale introduction is to give readers enough general information about the subject to enable them to understand the details in the body of the document. An introduction may accomplish any or all of the following:

- *State the subject.* Provide background information, such as definition, history, or theory to supply context for your readers.
- *State the purpose.* Make your readers aware of why the document exists and whether the material provides a new perspective or clarifies an existing perspective.

- *State the scope.* Tell readers the amount of detail you plan to cover.
- *Preview the development of the subject.* Especially in a longer document, outline how you plan to develop the subject. Providing such information allows readers to anticipate how the subject will be presented and helps them evaluate your conclusions or recommendations.

Consider writing an opening or introduction last. Many writers find that only after they have drafted the body of the document do they have enough perspective on the subject to introduce it adequately.

organization

A well-organized document enables your readers to grasp how the pieces of your subject fit together as a coherent whole. An organized document or presentation is based on an effective outline produced from a method of development that suits your subject, fulfills your purpose, and satisfies your readers' need for shape and structure. Following are the most common methods of developing any document—from an e-mail to a formal report to a Web page. See also <u>outlining</u>.

- *Cause-and-effect development* begins with either the cause or the effect of an event. For example, if you were reporting on an airplane accident, you might start your report with the causes and lead up to the accident itself. Conversely, you might start with a description of the accident and trace the events back to the cause. This approach can also be used to develop a report that offers a solution to a problem, beginning with the problem and moving on to the solution, or vice versa.
- *Chronological development* emphasizes the time element of a sequence. For example, a Federal Aviation Administration (FAA) report on an airplane crash might begin with takeoff and proceed sequentially to the crash.
- *Comparison* is useful when writing about a new topic that is in many ways similar to another, more familiar topic. For example, an online tutorial for a new operating system might compare that system to one that is familiar to the readers.
- *Division* separates a whole into component parts and discusses each part separately. Division could be used, for example, to report on a multinational corporation by describing its various operations. *Classification* groups parts into categories that clarify the relationship of the parts. For example, you might discuss local retail businesses by grouping them according to common demographic features of their target customers (such as age, household income, occupation).

- *General-and-specific development* proceeds either from general information to specific details or from specific information to a general conclusion. On the one hand, if you are writing about a new software product, you might begin with a general statement of the function of the total software package, then explain the functions of the major routines in the package, and finally describe the functions of the various subroutines. On the other hand, you might describe a software problem in a minor application, leading to a larger, more global problem with the software.
- *Order-of-importance development* presents a sequence that reflects the relative importance of each detail. The information can be presented in either decreasing or increasing order of importance. For example, you might explain the decision-making responsibilities in a company by discussing the executive staff first and the temporary support staff last, with all other human resources categories arranged in decreasing order of importance within that company.
- *Sequential development* emphasizes the order of elements in a process and is particularly useful when writing step-by-step instructions.
- *Spatial development* describes the physical appearance of an object from top to bottom, inside to outside, front to back, and so on. A crime-scene report might start at the site of the crime and proceed in concentric areas from that point.

Methods of development often overlap; rarely does a writer rely on only one method. Nevertheless, you should select one primary method of development and base your outline on it, and then subordinate any other methods to it. For example, in describing the organization of a company, you could use elements from three methods of development. You could divide the larger topic (the company) into departments, arrange the departments by their order of importance within the company, and present their operations sequentially.

During organization, you must consider a design and layout that will be helpful to your reader and a format appropriate to your subject and purpose. If you intend to include visuals, plan them as you complete your outline, especially if they need to be prepared by someone else while you are writing and revising the draft. See also Tab 3, "Business Writing Documents and Elements," and Tab 5, "Design and Visuals."

outlining

An outline—the skeleton of the document you are going to write—structures your writing by ensuring that it has a beginning (introduction), a middle (main body), and an end (conclusion). An outline provides the foundation for <u>coherence</u> (Tab 9) so that relationships between ideas are clear and one part flows smoothly to the next. An outline also helps with <u>collaborative writing</u> by enabling a team to refine a project's scope, divide responsibilities, and maintain focus.

Types of Outlines

Two types of outlines are most common: short topic outlines and lengthy sentence outlines. A *topic outline* consists of short phrases arranged to reflect your primary method of development. (See also <u>organization</u>.) A topic outline is especially useful for short documents such as letters, e-mail, or memos. See also <u>correspondence</u> (Tab 6).

For a large writing project, create a topic outline first and then use it as a basis for creating a sentence outline. A *sentence outline* summarizes each idea in a complete sentence that may become the topic sentence for a paragraph in the rough draft. If most of your notes can be shaped into topic sentences for paragraphs in your rough draft, you can be relatively sure that your document will be well organized. See also <u>note-taking</u> (Tab 2) and <u>research</u> (Tab 2).

Creating an Outline

When you are outlining large and complex subjects with many pieces of information, the first step is to group related notes into categories. Sort the notes by major and minor division headings. Use an appropriate method of development to arrange items, and label them with Roman numerals. For example, the major divisions for this discussion of outlining could be as follows:

    I. Advantages of outlining
   II. Types of outlines
  III. Creating an outline

The second step is to establish your minor points by deciding on the minor divisions within each major division. Arrange your minor points under their major divisions and label them with capital letters.

   II. Types of outlines
     A. Topic outlines   Division and classification
     B. Sentence outlines
  III. Creating an outline
     A. Establish major and minor divisions.
     B. Sort notes by major and minor divisions.   Sequential
     C. Complete the sentence outline.

You will often need more than two levels of headings. If your subject is complicated, you may need three or four levels of headings to better organize all of your ideas in proper relationship to one another. In that event, use the following numbering scheme:

  I. First-level heading
     A. Second-level heading
        1. Third-level heading
           a. Fourth-level heading

The third step is to mark each of the sorted notes with the appropriate Roman numeral and capital letter. Then arrange the notes logically within each minor heading, and mark each with the appropriate sequential Arabic number. As you do, make sure your organization is logical and your headings have <u>parallel structure</u> (Tab 9). For example, all the second-level headings under "III. Creating an outline" are complete sentences in the active <u>voice</u> (Tab 11).

Treat visuals as an integral part of your outline, and plan approximately where each should appear. Either include a rough sketch of the visual or write "illustration of . . ." at each place. As with other information in an outline, freely move, delete, or add visuals as needed. See also Tab 5, "Design and Visuals."

The outline samples shown earlier use a combination of numbers and letters to differentiate the various levels of information. You could also use a decimal numbering system, such as the following, for your outline.

  1. FIRST-LEVEL HEADING
     1.1 Second-level heading
     1.2 Second-level heading
        1.2.1 Third-level heading
        1.2.2 Third-level heading
             1.2.2.1 Fourth-level heading
             1.2.2.2 Fourth-level heading
     1.3 Second-level heading
  2. FIRST-LEVEL HEADING

This system should not go beyond the fourth level because the numbers get too cumbersome beyond that point. In many documents, the decimal numbering system is carried over from the outline to the final version of the document for ease of cross-referencing sections.

Create your draft by converting your notes into complete sentences and <u>paragraphs</u>. If you have a complete sentence outline, the most

---

DIGITAL TIP CREATING AN OUTLINE

Using the outline feature of your word-processing software permits you to format your outline automatically — fill in, rearrange, and update your outline as well as create alphanumeric or decimal numbering outlining styles. For more on this topic, see <bedfordstmartins.com/alred> and select *Digital Tips*, "Creating an Outline."

difficult part of the writing job is over. However, whether you have a topic or a sentence outline, remember that an outline is not set in stone; it may need to change as you write the draft, but it should always be your point of departure and return.

paragraphs

A paragraph performs three functions: (1) it develops the unit of thought stated in the topic sentence; (2) it provides a logical break in the material; and (3) it creates a visual break on the page, which signals a new topic.

Topic Sentence

A topic sentence states the paragraph's main idea; the rest of the paragraph supports and develops that statement with related details. The topic sentence is often the first sentence because it tells the reader what the paragraph is about.

- *The cost of training new employees is high.* In addition to the cost of classroom facilities and instructors, an organization must pay employees their regular salary while they sit in the classroom. For the companies to break even on the investment, their professional employees must stay in the job for which they have been trained for at least one year.

The topic sentence is usually most effective early in the paragraph, but a paragraph can lead up to the topic sentence, which is sometimes done to achieve <u>emphasis</u> (Tab 9).

- Energy does far more than simply make our daily lives more comfortable and convenient. Suppose you wanted to stop — and reverse — the economic progress of this nation. What would be the surest and quickest way to do it? Find a way to cut off the nation's oil resources! . . . The economy would plummet into the abyss of national economic ruin. *Our economy, in short, is energy-based.*

  — *The Baker World* (Los Angeles: Baker Oil Tools)

On rare occasions, the topic sentence may logically fall in the middle of a paragraph.

- . . . [It] is time to insist that science does not progress by carefully designed steps called "experiments," each of which has a well-defined beginning and end. *Science is a continuous and often a disorderly and accidental process.* We shall not do the young psy-

chologist any favor if we agree to reconstruct our practices to fit the pattern demanded by current scientific methodology.
— B. F. Skinner, "A Case History in Scientific Method"

Paragraph Length

A paragraph should be just long enough to deal adequately with the subject of its topic sentence. A new paragraph should begin whenever the subject changes significantly. A series of short, undeveloped paragraphs can indicate poor <u>organization</u> and sacrifice unity by breaking a single idea into several pieces. A series of long paragraphs, however, can fail to provide the reader with manageable subdivisions of thought.

Occasionally, a one-sentence paragraph is acceptable if it is used as a transition between larger paragraphs or as a one-sentence opening or closing in a letter, e-mail, or memo. See also <u>introductions</u> and <u>conclusions</u>.

Writing Paragraphs

Careful paragraphing reflects the writer's logical organization and helps the reader follow the writer's thoughts. A good working outline makes it easy to group ideas into appropriate paragraphs. (See also <u>outlining</u>.) Notice how the following partial topic outline plots the course of the subsequent paragraphs:

TOPIC OUTLINE (PARTIAL)

I. Advantages of Chicago as location for new facility
  A. Transport infrastructure
    1. Rail
    2. Air
    3. Truck
    4. Sea (except in winter)
  B. Labor supply
    1. Engineering and scientific personnel
      a. Many similar companies in the area
      b. Several major universities
    2. Technical and manufacturing personnel
      a. Existing programs in community colleges
      b. Possible special programs designed for us

RESULTING PARAGRAPHS

Probably the greatest advantage of Chicago as a location for our new facility is its excellent transport facilities. The city is served by three major railroads. Both domestic and international air cargo service is available at O'Hare International Airport; Midway Airport's convenient location adds flexibility for domestic air cargo service. Chicago is a major hub of the trucking industry, and most of the nation's large freight carriers have terminals there. Finally, except in the winter months when the Great Lakes are frozen, Chicago is a seaport, accessible through the St. Lawrence Seaway.

Chicago's second advantage is its abundant labor force. An ample supply of engineering and scientific staff is assured not only by the presence of many companies engaged in activities similar to ours but also by the presence of several major universities in the metropolitan area. Similarly, technicians and manufacturing personnel are in abundant supply. The colleges in the Chicago City College system, as well as half a dozen other two-year colleges in the outlying areas, produce graduates with associate degrees in a wide variety of technical specialties appropriate to our needs. Moreover, three of the outlying colleges have expressed an interest in developing off-campus courses attuned specifically to our requirements.

Paragraph Unity and Coherence

A good paragraph has <u>unity</u> (Tab 9) and <u>coherence</u> (Tab 9), as well as adequate development. Unity is singleness of purpose, based on a topic sentence that states the core idea of the paragraph. When every sentence in the paragraph develops the core idea, the paragraph has unity.

Coherence is holding to one point of view, one attitude, one tense; it is the joining of sentences into a logical pattern. A careful choice of transitional words ties ideas together and thus contributes to coherence in a paragraph, as shown here. Notice how the underlined italicized words tie together the ideas in the following paragraph:

TOPIC SENTENCE *Over the past several months, I have heard complaints about the Merit Award Program. Specifically,* many employees feel that this program should be linked to annual *salary increases*. They believe that *salary increases* would provide a much better incentive than the current $500 to $700 cash awards for exceptional service. *In addition*, these *employees believe* that their supervisors consider the cash awards a satisfactory alternative to salary increases. Although I don't think this practice is widespread, the fact that the *employees believe* that it is justifies a reevaluation of the Merit Award Program.

Simple enumeration (*first, second, then, next*, and so on) also provides effective <u>transition</u> (Tab 9) within paragraphs. Notice how the underlined italicized words and phrases give coherence to the following paragraph.

- Most adjustable office chairs have nylon tubes that hold metal spindle rods. To keep the chair operational, lubricate the spindle rods occasionally. *First*, loosen the set screw in the adjustable bell.

Then lift the chair from the base. _Next,_ apply the lubricant to the spindle rod and the nylon washer. _When you have finished,_ replace the chair and tighten the set screw.

persuasion

Persuasive writing attempts to convince the reader to adopt the writer's point of view or take a particular action. Much workplace writing uses persuasion to reinforce ideas that readers already have, to convince readers to change their current ideas, or to lobby for a particular suggestion or policy (as in Figure 1–3). You may find yourself pleading for

---

Memo

TO: Sales Management and Support Staff
FROM: Bernadine Kovak, MIS Administrator   _BK_
DATE: April 4, 2005
SUBJECT: Plans for Changeover to NRT/R4 System

As you all know, our workload has jumped by 30 percent in the past month. It has increased because our customer base and resulting support services have grown dramatically. This growth is a result, in part, of our recent merger with First Financial.

   This growth has meant that we have all experienced the difficulty of providing our customers with up-to-date technical information when they need it. In the next few months, we anticipate that the workload will increase another 20 percent. Even a staff as experienced as ours cannot handle such a workload without help.

   To cope with this expansion, we will install in the next month the NRT/R4 server and QCS enterprise software with Web-based applications and global sales and service network. This system will speed processing dramatically and give us access to all relevant company-wide databases. It should enable us to access the information both we and our customers need.

   The new system, unfortunately, will cause some disruption at first. We will need to transfer many of our legacy programs and software applications to the new format. And all of us need to learn to navigate in the R4 and QCS environments. However, once we have made these adjustments, I believe we will welcome the changes.

   I would like to put your knowledge and experience to work in getting the new system into operation. Let's meet in my office to discuss the improvements on Friday, April 8, at 1:00 p.m. I will have details of the plan to discuss with you. I'm also eager to get your comments, suggestions, and—most of all—your cooperation.

FIGURE 1–3. Persuasive Memo

safer working conditions, justifying the expense of a new program, or writing a proposal for a large purchase. See also <u>purpose</u>, <u>readers</u>, and <u>proposals</u> (Tab 3).

In persuasive writing, the way you present your ideas is as important as the ideas themselves. You must support your appeal with logic and a sound presentation of facts, statistics, and examples.

⚡ **ETHICS NOTE** Avoid ambiguity: Do not wander from your main point, and above all never make false claims. You should also acknowledge any real or potentially conflicting opinions; doing so allows you to anticipate and overcome objections and builds your credibility. See also <u>ethics in writing</u>.

The memo shown in Figure 1–3 was written to persuade a sales management and support staff to accept and participate in a change to a new computer system. Notice that not everything in this memo is presented in a positive light. Change brings disruption, and the writer acknowledges that fact.

A writer also gains credibility, and thus persuasiveness, through the readers' impressions of the document's appearance. For this reason, consider carefully a document's <u>layout and design</u> (Tab 5). See also <u>promotional writing</u> and <u>résumés</u> (Tab 7).

point of view

Point of view is the writer's relation to the information presented, as reflected in the use of grammatical <u>person</u> (Tab 11). The writer usually expresses point of view in first-, second-, or third-person personal pronouns. Use of first person indicates that the writer is a participant or an observer. Use of second or third person indicates that the writer is giving directions, instructions, or advice or is writing about other people or something impersonal.

FIRST PERSON	*I* scrolled down to find the settings option.
SECOND PERSON	Scroll down to find the settings option and double-click. [*You* is understood.]
THIRD PERSON	*He* scrolled down to the settings option.

Consider the following sentence, revised from an impersonal to a more personal point of view. Although the meaning of the sentence does not change, the revision indicates that people are involved in the communication.

- ~~It is regrettable~~ *I regret* that the equipment shipped on the 12th ~~is~~ *we cannot accept* ~~unacceptable~~.

Many people think they should avoid the pronoun *I* in their business writing. Such practice, however, leads to awkward sentences with people referring to themselves in the third person as *one* or as *the writer* instead of as *I.*

- *I believe*
  ~~The writer believes~~ that this project will be completed by the end
  of June.

However, do not use the personal point of view when an impersonal point of view would be more appropriate or more effective because you need to emphasize the subject matter over the writer or the reader. In the following examples, it does not help to personalize the situation; in fact, the impersonal version may be more tactful.

PERSONAL   I received objections to my proposal from several of your managers.

IMPERSONAL   Several managers have raised objections to the proposal.

Whether you adopt a personal or an impersonal point of view depends on the **purpose** and the **readers** of the document. For example, in an informal e-mail to an associate, you would most likely adopt a personal point of view. However, in a report to a large group, you would probably emphasize the subject by using an impersonal point of view.

⚡ ETHICS NOTE In letters on company stationery, use of the pronoun *we* may be interpreted as reflecting company policy, whereas *I* clearly reflects personal opinion. (See also **correspondence**, Tab 6.) Which pronoun to use should be decided according to whether the matter discussed in the letter is an individual (*I*) or a corporate (*we*) concern.

- *I* understand your frustration with the price increase, but *we* must now add the import tax to the sales price.

> (ESL) **TIPS FOR STATING AN OPINION**
>
> In some cultures, stating an opinion in writing is considered impolite or unnecessary, but in the United States readers expect to see a writer's opinion stated clearly and explicitly. The opinion should be followed by specific examples to help the reader understand the writer's point of view.

preparation

The preparation stage of the writing process is essential. By determining the needs of your **readers**, your primary **purpose**, and your **scope**, you understand the information you will need to gather during **research** (Tab 2). See also "Five Steps to Successful Writing" (page xxi).

Writer's Checklist: Preparing to Write

☑ Determine who your readers are and learn certain key facts about them — their knowledge, attitudes, and needs relative to your subject.

☑ Determine the document's primary purpose. What exactly do you want your readers to know, believe, or be able to do when they have finished reading your document?

☑ Establish the scope of your document — the type and amount of detail you must include — by considering any external constraints, such as word limits for trade journal articles or the space limitations of Web pages, and by understanding your purpose and readers' needs. See also <u>writing for the Web</u>.

☑ Consider the appropriate medium for your message. See <u>selecting the medium</u>.

process explanation

Many kinds of workplace writing explain a process, an operation, or a procedure, such as the steps necessary to start a small business. A process explanation describes the steps that a mechanism or system uses to accomplish a certain result. The opening often presents a brief overview of the process or let readers know why it is important for them to become familiar with the process you are explaining. Be sure to define terms that readers might not understand and provide any <u>visuals</u> (Tab 5) needed to clarify the process. See also <u>defining terms</u>.

In describing a process, transitional words and phrases create unity within paragraphs, and headings often mark the <u>transition</u> (Tab 9) from one step to the next. Notice in the following example how obtaining a company tuition refund is described as a step-by-step process.

Tuition Refund Process
1. PROCEDURES
    1.1 Degree Approval
        1.1.1 An employee who meets academic requirements and is interested in receiving tuition refunds should gain the approval of his or her manager and submit the request to the Human Resources Department. Human Resources may ask the manager to justify, in writing, the benefits of approving the degree request if the reason is not obvious.

        1.1.2 After an agreement has been reached, the employee should complete Section I of Form

F-6970. After Human Resources has obtained two levels of management approval, it authorizes the employee's enrollment in the degree program.

1.1.3 The employee who receives approval then completes Section II of Form F-6970 when registering for each course required for the degree.

promotional writing

Promotional writing is vital to the success of any company or organization; high-quality, state-of-the-art products or services are of little value if customers and clients do not know they exist. The specific types of promotional writing discussed in this book include brochures (Tab 3), newsletters (Tab 3), proposals (Tab 3), sales letters (Tab 6), and Web pages. See also writing for the Web.

Although you may not be a marketing or public relations specialist, you may be asked to prepare promotional (or marketing) materials, especially if you work for a small organization or are self-employed. Even at a large company, you may help prepare a brochure, a Web page, or a department newsletter. See also collaborative writing.

Several elements are central to promotional writing:

- *Understanding your audience.* Analyzing the needs, interests, concerns, and makeup of your audience is crucial. See also readers.
- *Understanding the principles of persuasion.* Good promotional writing must gain attention, build interest, build credibility, reduce resistance, and motivate readers to act.
- *Making information both easy to find and visually appealing.* You need to make the most effective use of organization as well as layout and design. You need to select the most appropriate visuals and integrate them with the text. See also Tab 5, "Design and Visuals."
- *Writing with clarity, coherence, and conciseness.* No matter how attractive the design, if readers don't understand the message, you will not achieve your purpose. To make information accessible, of course, you must thoroughly understand the product or service you are promoting—to do so may require research (Tab 2). See also Tab 9, "Style and Clarity."

ETHICS NOTE Because readers are persuaded only if they believe the source is credible, you need to be careful not to overstate claims and avoid possible logic errors (Tab 9). See also ethics in writing and persuasion.

Keep in mind that many other documents described in this book often include the additional or secondary purpose of promoting an organization. For example, <u>adjustment letters</u> (Tab 6), which are usually concerned with resolving a specific problem, offer opportunities to promote your organization. Likewise, <u>progress and activity reports</u> (Tab 3) provide an opportunity to promote the value of your work in an organization.

proofreading

Computer grammar checkers and spell checkers, while a help to proofreading, can make writers overconfident. If a typographical error results in a legitimate English word (for example, *coarse* instead of *course*), the spell checker will not flag the misspelling. Therefore, you still must proofread your work carefully—both on your monitor and on paper. You may find some of the tactics discussed in <u>revision</u> useful when proofreading; in fact, you may find passages during proofreading that require further revision.

Whether the material you proofread is your own writing or that of someone else, consider proofreading in several stages. Although you need to tailor the stages to the specific document and to your own problem areas, the following Writer's Checklist should provide a useful starting point for proofreading. See also the chart of proofreaders' marks (facing inside back cover).

Writer's Checklist: Proofreading in Stages

FIRST-STAGE REVIEW
- ☑ Appropriate format, as for reports or correspondence
- ☑ Typographical consistency (headings, spacing, fonts)

SECOND-STAGE REVIEW
- ☑ Specific grammar and usage problems
- ☑ Appropriate punctuation
- ☑ Correct abbreviations and capitalization
- ☑ Correct spelling (especially names and places)
- ☑ Complete Web or e-mail addresses and the like
- ☑ Accurate figures in tables and lists
- ☑ Cut-and-paste errors, such as those caused by moved or deleted text and numbers

Writer's Checklist: Proofreading in Stages (continued)

FINAL-STAGE REVIEW

☑ Survey of your overall goals: readers' needs and purpose

☑ Appearance of the document (see <u>layout and design</u>, Tab 5)

☑ Review by a colleague for crucial documents

See also Tab 11, "Grammar," and Tab 12, "Punctuation and Mechanics."

DIGITAL TIP PROOFREADING FOR FORMAT CONSISTENCY

Viewing whole pages on-screen is an effective way to check formatting, spacing, and typographical consistency as well as the general appearance of documents. For comparing layouts, view multiple pages or "tile" separate documents side by side. For more on this topic, see <bedfordstmartins .com/alred> and select *Digital Tips*, "Proofreading for Format Consistency."

---

purpose

What do you want your readers to know, believe, or do after they have read your document? When you answer that question, you have determined the primary purpose, or objective, of your document. Be careful not to state purposes too broadly. A purpose such as "to explain a fax machine" is too general to be helpful to you as you write. In contrast, "to instruct the reader how to use a fax machine to send and retrieve faxes" is a specific purpose that will help you focus on what you need your document to accomplish.

However, the writer's primary purpose is often more complex than simply "to explain" something. To fully understand this complexity, you need to ask yourself not only *why* you are writing the document but *what* you want to influence your reader to believe or do after reading it. Suppose a writer for a newsletter has been assigned to write an article about cardiopulmonary resuscitation (CPR). In answer to the question *what*, the writer could state the purpose as "to emphasize the importance of CPR." To the question *why*, the writer might respond, "to encourage employees to sign up for evening CPR classes." Putting the answers to the two questions together, the writer's purpose might be stated as, "To write a document that will emphasize the importance of CPR and encourage employees to sign up for evening CPR classes." Note that the primary purpose of the document on CPR was to persuade the readers of the importance of CPR, and the secondary goal was to motivate them to register for a class. Secondary goals often involve such abstract notions as to motivate, persuade, reassure, or inspire your reader. See also <u>persuasion</u>.

If you answer the questions *what* and *why* and put the answers into writing as a stated purpose that includes both primary and secondary goals, you will simplify your writing task and more likely achieve your purpose. For a <u>collaborative writing</u> project, it is especially important to collectively write a statement of your purpose to ensure that the document achieves its goals. Be careful not to lose sight of that purpose as you become engrossed in the other steps of the writing process. See also "Five Steps to Successful Writing" (page xxi).

readers

The first rule of effective writing is to *help your readers.* If you overlook this commitment, your writing will not achieve its <u>purpose</u>, either for you or for your business or organization.

Determining Your Readers' Needs

To help your readers, first determine their needs relative to your purpose and goals by asking key questions during <u>preparation</u>.

- Who specifically is your reader? Do you have multiple readers? Who needs to see or use the document?
- What do your readers already know about your subject? What are your readers' attitudes about the subject? (Skeptical? Supportive? Anxious? Bored?)
- Do you need to adapt your message for international readers? If so, see <u>global communication</u>, <u>global graphics</u> (Tab 5), and <u>international correspondence</u> (Tab 6).

In the workplace, your readers are usually less familiar with the subject than you are. You have to be careful, therefore, when writing on a topic that is unique to your area of specialization. Be sensitive to the needs of those whose training or experience lies in other areas; provide definitions of nonstandard terms and explanations of principles that you, as a specialist, take for granted.

Writing to Individual Readers

When you write to an individual reader, empathize with that reader by considering the <u>"you" viewpoint</u> (Tab 9) and writing in an appropriate <u>tone</u> (Tab 9). You may find it useful to visualize that person sitting across from you as you write. Likewise, when you write to a group of readers who are relatively homogeneous, you might create an image of a composite reader and write for *that* reader. You could also list that reader's characteristics (experience, training, attitudes, and work habits, for example) to help you write at the appropriate level with good <u>business writing style</u> (Tab 9).

Writing for Diverse Audiences

For documents aimed at multiple readers with different needs, consider segmenting the document for different groups of readers: an executive summary for top managers, an appendix with detailed data for technical specialists, and the body for those readers who need to make decisions based on the details. See also <u>proposals</u> (Tab 3) and <u>formal reports</u> (Tab 4).

When you have multiple readers with various needs but cannot segment your document, first determine your primary or most important readers—such as those who will make decisions based on the document—and be sure to meet their needs. Then, meet the needs of secondary readers, such as those who need only some of the document's contents, as long as you do not sacrifice the needs of your primary readers. See also "Five Steps to Successful Writing" (page xxi), <u>persuasion</u>, <u>correspondence</u> (Tab 6), and <u>e-mail</u> (Tab 6).

revision

When you revise your draft, read and evaluate it primarily from the point of view of your readers. In fact, revising requires a different frame of mind than <u>writing a draft</u>. To achieve that frame of mind, experienced writers have developed the following tactics:

- Allow a "cooling period" between writing the draft and revision in order to evaluate the draft objectively.
- Print out your draft and mark up the paper copy; it is often difficult to revise on-screen.
- Read your draft aloud—often, hearing the text will enable you to spot problem areas that need improvement.
- Revise in passes by reading through your draft several times, each time searching for and correcting a different set of problems.

When you can no longer spot improvements, you may wish to give the draft to a colleague for review—especially for projects that are crucial for you or your organization as well as for collaborative projects as described in <u>collaborative writing</u>.

Writer's Checklist: Revising Your Draft

☑ *Completeness.* Does the document achieve its primary purpose? Will it fulfill the readers' needs? Your writing should give readers exactly what they need but not overwhelm them.

☑ *Appropriate introduction and conclusion.* Check to see that your introduction frames the rest of the document and your conclusion ties the main ideas together. Both should account for revisions to the content of the document.

☑ *Accuracy.* Look for any inaccuracies that may have crept into your draft.

☑ *Unity and coherence.* Check to see that sentences and ideas are closely tied together (coherence, Tab 9) and contribute directly to the main idea expressed in the topic sentence of each paragraph (unity, Tab 9). Provide transitions (Tab 9) where they are missing and strengthen those that are weak.

☑ *Consistency.* Make sure that layout and design (Tab 5), visuals (Tab 5), and use of language are consistent. Do not call the same item by one term on one page and a different term on another page.

☑ *Conciseness.* Tighten your writing so that it says exactly what you mean. Prune unnecessary words, phrases, sentences, and even paragraphs. See conciseness (Tab 9).

☑ *Awkwardness.* Look for awkwardness (Tab 9) in sentence construction —especially any garbled sentences (Tab 9).

☑ *Ethical writing.* Check for ethics in writing and eliminate biased language (Tab 9).

☑ *Active voice.* Use the active voice (Tab 11) unless the passive voice is more appropriate.

☑ *Word choice.* Delete or replace vague words (Tab 9) and unnecessary intensifiers (Tab 9). Check for affectation (Tab 9) and unclear pronoun references (Tab 11). See also word choice (Tab 9).

☑ *Jargon.* If you have any doubt that all your readers will understand any jargon (Tab 9) or special terms you have used, eliminate or define them.

☑ *Clichés.* Replace clichés (Tab 9) with fresh figures of speech (Tab 9) or direct statements.

☑ *Grammar.* Check your draft for grammatical errors. Use computer grammar checkers with caution. Because they are not always accurate, treat their recommendations only as *suggestions.* See also Tab 11, "Grammar."

☑ *Typographical errors.* Check your final draft for typographical errors both with your spell checker and through proofreading.

1

> **DIGITAL TIP INCORPORATING TRACKED CHANGES**
>
> When colleagues review your document, they can track changes and insert comments within the document itself. Tracking and commenting vary with types and versions of word-processing programs, but in most programs you can view the tracked changes on a single draft or review the multiple drafts of your reviewers' versions. For more on this topic, see <bedford stmartins.com/alred> and select *Digital Tips*, "Incorporating Tracked Changes."

scope

Scope is the depth and breadth of detail needed to cover a subject. Determine the scope of your document during the <u>preparation</u> stage of the writing process, even though you may refine it later. The needs of your <u>readers</u> and your primary <u>purpose</u> determine the kind of information and the amount of detail you will need to include. Defining your scope will expedite your <u>research</u> (Tab 2) and help determine team members' responsibilities in <u>collaborative writing</u>.

Your scope will also be affected by the type of document you are writing as well as the medium you select for your message. For example, government agencies often prescribe the general content and length for proposals and some organizations set limits for the length of memos and e-mail. See <u>selecting the medium</u> and "Five Steps to Successful Writing" (page xxi).

selecting the medium

You must select the most appropriate medium for communicating your message early in your <u>preparation</u>. You can choose from such technologies as e-mail, fax, voice mail, and videoconferencing to more traditional means such as letters and memos, telephone calls, and face-to-face meetings.

The most important considerations in selecting the medium are the expectations of your <u>readers</u> and the <u>purpose</u> of the communication. For example, if you need to collaborate with someone to solve a problem or if you need to establish rapport, written exchanges (even by e-mail) may be far less efficient than a phone call or a face-to-face meeting. However, if you need precise wording or a record of a complex message, communicate in writing. Understanding the typical means of communicating on the job will help you select the most appropriate medium.

Letters on Organizational Stationery

Letters are often the most appropriate choice for initial contacts with new business associates or customers and for other formal communications. Letters written on your organization's letterhead communicate formality, respect, and authority. See also <u>correspondence</u> (Tab 6).

Memos

<u>Memos</u> (Tab 6) on printed company stationery or attached to an e-mail are appropriate for internal communication among members of the same organization, even when offices are geographically separated. They have many of the same characteristics as letters, such as formality and authority, but they are used for a wider variety of functions — from reminders to short reports.

E-mail

<u>E-mail</u> (Tab 6) can replace letters and memos or transmit documents as attachments. E-mail can also be a less-formal medium to send information, elicit discussions, collect opinions, and transmit many other kinds of messages quickly. Because e-mail recipients can print copies of messages and attachments they receive and easily forward them to others, always write your e-mail with care, and reread the message carefully before you send it.

Faxes

A <u>fax</u> (Tab 6) is useful when speed is essential and when the information — a drawing or contract, for example — must be viewed in its original form. Faxes are especially useful when the recipient does not have e-mail or when the material is not available in electronic form.

Telephone Calls

Information exchanged through telephone calls can range from a brief exchange to answer a question to a lengthy conversation to negotiate or clarify the conditions of a contract. Because phone calls enable participants to interpret tone of voice, they can make it easier to resolve misunderstandings, although they do not provide the visual cues possible during face-to-face meetings.

In addition, when there are three or more participants, a conference call is a less-expensive alternative to face-to-face meetings requiring travel. To ensure maximum efficiency, the person coordinating the call works from an agenda shared by all the participants and directs the discussion as though he or she were leading a meeting. Telephone calls in which a decision has been reached should be followed up with written confirmation.

Voice Mail

Voice mail allows callers to leave a brief message ("Call me about the deadline for the new project" or "I got the package, so you don't need to call the distributor"). If the message is complicated or contains numerous details, use another medium, such as an e-mail message or a letter. If you want to discuss a subject at length, let the recipient know the subject so that he or she can prepare a response before returning your call. When you leave a message, give your name, phone number, the date, and the time of the call.

Face-to-Face Meetings

Face-to-face meetings are most appropriate for initial or early contacts with associates and clients with whom you intend to develop an important, long-term relationship. Meetings may also be best for brainstorming, negotiating, solving a technical problem, or handling a controversial issue. For advice on how to record discussions and decisions, see both <u>meetings</u> (Tab 8) and <u>minutes of meetings</u> (Tab 8).

Videoconferencing

Videoconferencing is particularly useful for meetings when travel is impractical. Unlike telephone conference calls, videoconferences have the advantage of allowing participants to see as well as to hear one another. Videoconferences work best with participants who are at ease in front of the camera.

word processing and writing

Word-processing software can help your writing in many ways; you must determine which features will be useful to you. Be aware that working on-screen may focus your attention too narrowly on sentence-level problems and cause you to lose sight of the larger problems of <u>scope</u> or <u>organization</u>. The rapid movement of the text on the screen, together with last-minute editing changes, may allow errors to creep into the text.

Writer's Checklist: Getting the Most from Word Processing

☑ Avoid the temptation of writing first drafts on the computer without any planning. See "Five Steps to Successful Writing" (page xxi).

☑ Use the outline feature to brainstorm and organize an initial outline for your topic. Cut and paste to try alternative ways of organizing the information. See <u>outlining</u>.

Writer's Checklist: Getting the Most from Word Processing (continued)

☑ Use the search command to find and revise wordy phrases such as *that is, there are, the fact that,* and *to be* and unnecessary helping verbs such as *will.* See also **conciseness** (Tab 9).

☑ When writing for readers who are unfamiliar with your topic, use the search command to find technical terms, abbreviations, and other information that may need further explanation.

☑ Use a spell checker and other specialized programs to identify and correct typographical, spelling, grammar, and word-choice errors. Because grammar checkers do not consider context, however, treat their recommendations only as *suggestions*.

☑ Do not make all of your revisions on-screen. Print a double-spaced copy of your drafts periodically for major revisions and reorganizations. See also **revision**.

☑ Print copies of your final version for yourself or others to proofread because catching errors on the screen is difficult. See also **proofreading**.

☑ Use the software for effective document design, for example, by highlighting major headings and subheadings with bold or italic type and by increasing their size relative to the regular text. Use the copy command to duplicate parallel headings throughout your document, and insert blank lines (hard returns) above and below examples and visuals to set them off from the surrounding text. See also **layout and design** (Tab 5).

☑ Routinely save to your hard drive and create a backup copy of your documents on separate disks or on the company network.

writing a draft

You are well prepared to write a rough draft when you have established your purpose and readers' needs, defined your scope, completed adequate research, and prepared an outline (whether rough or developed). Writing a draft is simply transcribing and expanding the notes from your outline into paragraphs, without worrying about grammar, refinements of language, or spelling. Refinement will come with revision and proofreading. See also "Five Steps to Successful Writing" (page xxi) and **word processing and writing**.

Writing and revising are different activities. Do not let worrying about a good opening slow you down. Instead, concentrate on getting your ideas on paper—now is not the time to polish or revise. Do not wait for inspiration—treat writing a draft as you would any other on-the-job task.

Writer's Checklist: Writing a Rough Draft

☑ Set up your writing area with whatever supplies you need (notepads, pens and pencils, reference material, etc.) to keep going once you get started. Then hang out the "Do Not Disturb" sign.

☑ Use a good outline as a springboard to start and keep going. See also **outlining**.

☑ Keep in mind your readers' needs, expectations, and knowledge of the subject. Doing so will help you write directly to your readers and suggest which ideas need further development. See **readers**.

☑ When you are trying to write quickly and you come to something difficult to explain, try to relate the new concept to something with which the readers are already familiar, as discussed in **figures of speech** (Tab 9).

☑ Start with the section that seems easiest. Your readers will neither know nor care that the middle section of the document was the first section you wrote.

☑ Give yourself a set time (ten or fifteen minutes, for example) in which you write continuously, regardless of how good or bad your writing seems to be. Don't stop when you are rolling along easily — if you stop and come back, you may lose momentum.

☑ Give yourself a small reward — a short walk, a soft drink, a brief chat with a friend, an easy task — after you have finished a section.

☑ Reread what you have written when you return to your writing. Seeing what you have already written can return you to a productive frame of mind.

writing for the Web

In the workplace, those who write content for Web sites are not always the same people who design the sites. This entry provides guidelines only for writing for an online audience; for more information on site design, see **Web design** (Tab 5).

Crafting Content for the Web

Because most readers scan Web sites for specific information, the way you write and organize your information will greatly affect your readers' understanding. State your important points first, before any detailed supporting information. (This method is called *inverted pyramid organization*.) Keep your writing style simple and straightforward, and eliminate any **biased language** (Tab 9). Use the following techniques to make your content more accessible to readers.

Headings.   Divide your text into short passages, each focusing on one facet of your topic. Use informative <u>headings</u> (Tab 5) to help the reader decide at a glance whether to read a passage. Headings also simplify text by highlighting structure and organization, and they signal transitions from one topic to the next.

Lists.   Use bullets and numbered <u>lists</u> (Tab 5) to break up dense paragraphs, reduce text length, and highlight important content.

Directional Cues.   Avoid directional cues, such as "as shown in the example below," that make sense on the printed page but not on a Web screen.

Keywords.   To help search engines and your audience find your site, use keywords in the first 50 or so words of your text.

WITHOUT KEYWORDS	We are proud to introduce a new commemorative coin honoring our company's founder and president. The item will be available on this Web site after December 1, 2005, which is the 100th anniversary of our first sale.
WITH KEYWORDS	The new *Reynolds Corporation's* commemorative coin features a portrait of *George G. Reynolds*, the founder and president of *Reynolds Corporation*. The coin can be purchased after December 1, 2005, in honor of the 100th anniversary of the sale of the first *Reynolds* product.

Graphics.   Graphics provide visual relief from text and make your site attractive and appealing. Use only images that illustrate essential information, and use graphics that load as quickly as possible. See also <u>visuals</u> (Tab 5).

Hyperlinks.   Use hyperlinks to help readers navigate the information in your site. If a passage of text is longer than two or three screens, create a table of contents of hyperlinks for it at the top of the Web page and link each item to the relevant content further down the page. Avoid hyperlinks within text paragraphs because they can distract readers, make scanning the text difficult, and tempt readers to leave before reaching the end of your content.

Fonts.   Font sizes and styles affect screen legibility. Because computer screens display fonts at lower resolutions than printed text, sans serif fonts work better for online text passages. Consult with your Web master about your site's font preferences. Do not use capital letters or boldface type for blocks of text because they slow the reader. For content that contains special characters (such as mathematical or chemical content), consult your Web master about the best way to submit the files for HTML (hypertext markup language) coding.

Line Length.   Line length also affects readability because short line lengths reduce the amount of eye movement necessary to scan text. Optimal length is approximately half the width of the screen. To achieve this length, draft text that is between 50 and 70 characters (or between 10 and 12 words) to a line.

Writing for a Global Audience

Eliminate expressions and references that make sense only to someone very familiar with American English. Express <u>dates</u> (Tab 12), clock times, and measurements consistent with international practices. For visuals, choose symbols and icons, colors, representations of human beings, and captions that can be easily understood. For additional information, see <u>global communication</u>, <u>global graphics</u> (Tab 5), and <u>English as a second language</u> (Tab 11).

Linking to External Sites

Links to outside sites can expand your content. However, review such sites carefully before linking to them. Is the site's author or sponsoring organization reputable? Is its content accurate, current, and unbiased? Does the site date-stamp its content with notices such as "This page was last updated on January 1, 2005"? (For more advice on evaluating Web sites, see <u>research</u>, Tab 2.) Link directly to the page or specific area of an outside site that is relevant to your users, and be sure that you provide a clear context for why you are sending your readers there.

Posting an Existing Document

If you post files for existing paper documents to a Web site, try to retain the document's original sequence and page layout. If you shorten or revise the original document for posting to the Web, add a notice informing readers that it differs from the printed original.

Regardless of format or version used, be sure to

- Obtain permission from the copyright holder for the use of copyrighted text, tables, or images.
- Ask the Web master or site administrator about the preferred file format to submit for coding and posting. On campus, consult your instructor or campus computer support staff.
- Request that the Web master optimize any slow-loading graphics files for quick access.

- Review the document internally before it is posted to the public site: Is it the correct version? Is any information missing? Do all links work and go to the right places?
- Ask the Web master to create a single-file version of the document (a version formatted as a single, long Web page) for readers who will print it to read offline.

DIGITAL TIP USING PDF FILES

Converting documents such as reports, articles, and brochures to PDF (portable document format) allows you to retain the identical look of the printed documents. The PDF pages will display on-screen in black and white exactly as they appear on the printed page. Readers can read the document online, download and save it, or print it in whole or in part. For more on this topic, see <bedfordstmartins.com/alred> and select *Digital Tips*, "Using PDF Files."

Documenting Sources of Information

ETHICS NOTE Document sources of information or of help received — text, images, streaming video, and other multimedia material. Seek prior approval before using any copyrighted information. Documenting your sources is not only required, but it also bolsters the credibility of your site. See copyright (Tab 2) and documenting sources (Tab 2).

Protecting the Privacy of Users

ETHICS NOTE Put a link on your page to the site's privacy statement, particularly if you solicit comments about your content or have an e-mail link for unsolicited comments for site users. A privacy statement informs site visitors about how the site sponsor handles solicited and unsolicited information from individuals, its policy on the use of cookies,* and legal action it takes against hackers. Inform users if you intend to use their information for marketing or intend to share their information with third parties, and give visitors the option of refusing you permission to use or share their information.

---

*"Cookies" are small files that are downloaded to your computer when you browse certain Web pages. Cookies hold information, such as your user name and password, so you do not need to reenter it each time you visit the site.

Research and Documentation

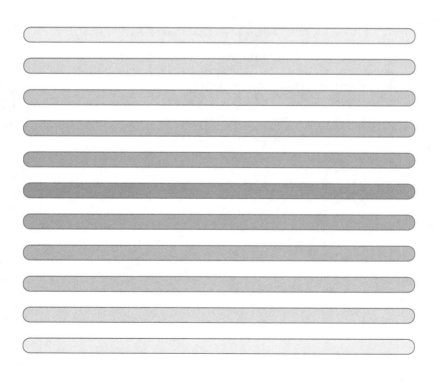

Preview

This section contains entries related to the process of __research__ using both library and Internet sources, __interviewing for information__, and __note-taking__. Entries in this section provide help for incorporating what you gather from research into a document, including using __quotations__ and avoiding __plagiarism__. The entry __documenting sources__ provides not only examples of bibliographic citations in two major systems, both American Psychological Association (APA) and the Modern Language Association (MLA) styles, but also sample pages using those styles.

WEB LINK RESEARCH AND DOCUMENTATION RESOURCES

For links to research-related resources—including library catalogs, databases, and guidelines for documenting sources—see <bedfordstmartins .com/alred> and select *Diana Hacker's Research and Documentation Online* as well as *Links for Business Writing*.

bibliographies

A bibliography is an alphabetical list of books, articles, Web sources, and other materials that records the works consulted in preparing a document. It provides a convenient listing of sources in a standardized form for readers interested in getting further information on the topic or in assessing the scope of the research.

While a list of references (APA style) and a works-cited list (MLA style) refer to works actually cited in the text, a bibliography includes works consulted for general background information. For information on using APA and MLA styles, see <u>documenting sources</u>. See <u>formal reports</u> (Tab 4) for guidance on the placement of a bibliography in a report.

Entries in a bibliography are listed alphabetically by the author's last name. If an author is unknown, the entry is alphabetized by the first word in the title (other than *A*, *An*, or *The*). Entries also can be arranged by subject and then ordered alphabetically within those categories.

An annotated bibliography includes complete bibliographic information about a work (author, title, publisher) followed by a brief description or evaluation of what the work contains.

copyright

◆ ETHICS NOTE The Copyright Act protects all original works from the moment of their creation, regardless of whether they are published or even contain a notice of copyright (©). However, all works created by U.S. government agencies are in the public domain—that is, they are not copyrighted—and can be used without permission. For information on the Copyright Act, visit the Library of Congress copyright Web site at <www.copyright.gov>.

Writer's Checklist: Using Copyrighted Materials (Printed and Online)

☑ In general, give credit to any source from which material is taken, unless it is boilerplate or common knowledge, as described in <u>plagiarism</u>. See also <u>documenting sources</u>.

☑ With the exception of works created by U.S. government agencies, any work first published after March 1, 1989, receives copyright protection regardless of whether it bears a notice of copyright. Works published before March 1, 1989, without a notice of copyright are in the public domain.

*Writer's Checklist: Using Copyrighted Materials
(Printed and Online) (continued)*

☑   A small amount of material from a copyrighted source may be used, especially for educational purposes, without permission or payment as long as the use satisfies the fair-use criteria, as described at the Library of Congress Web site (<www.copyright.gov>).

☑   Copyright law applies to electronic works just as it does to their print counterparts. Web pages that are copyrighted include the symbol © and provide information on terms of use.

☑   If you plan to reproduce or further distribute copyrighted works posted on the Internet, you must obtain permission from the copyright holder, unless the fair-use provision of the copyright law applies to your intended use. To obtain permission, read the site's terms-of-use information and e-mail your request to the appropriate party. As with printed works, document the source of all materials (text, graphics, tables) obtained.

documenting sources

Documenting sources achieves three important purposes:

*   It allows readers to locate and consult the sources used and to find further information on the subject.
*   It enables writers to support their assertions and arguments in such documents as proposals, reports, and trade journal articles.
*   It helps writers to give proper credit to others and thus avoid plagiarism by identifying the sources of facts, ideas, quotations, and paraphrases. See also paraphrasing.

This entry shows citation models and sample pages for two principal documentation systems.

- The American Psychological Association (APA) system of citation is often used in the social sciences. It is referred to as an author/date method of documentation because parenthetical in-text citations and a references list (at the end of the paper) in APA style emphasize the author(s) and date of publication so that the currency of the research is clear.
- The Modern Language Association (MLA) system is used in the humanities. MLA style uses parenthetical in-text citations and a list of works cited and places greater importance on the pages on which cited information can be found than on the publication date.

The following examples compare APA and MLA styles for citing a book by one author: *Management Challenges for the 21st Century* by Peter F. Drucker, which was published in 2001 by HarperBusiness in New York.

In-Text Citations

APA STYLE   (Author's Last Name, year)

                              (Drucker, 2001)

MLA STYLE   (Author's Last Name page number)

                              (Drucker 162)

Documentation Models

APA REFERENCES ENTRY

Author's Last Name, Initials. (year). *Title in italics*. City: Publisher

Drucker, P. F. (2001). *Management challenges for the 21st century.* New York: HarperBusiness.

MLA WORKS-CITED ENTRY

Author's Last Name, First Name Middle Initial. Title Underlined. City: Publisher, year.

Drucker, Peter F. Management Challenges for the 21st Century. New York: HarperBusiness, 2001.

These systems are described in full detail in the following publications:

American Psychological Association. *Publication Manual of the American Psychological Association.* 5th ed. Washington, D.C.: American Psychological Association, 2001. See also <www .apastyle.org>.

2

Research and Documentation

> *MLA Handbook for Writers of Research Papers.* 6th ed. New York: Modern Language Association of America, 2003. See also <www.mla.org>.

For additional bibliographic advice and documentation models, consult these style manuals or those listed at the end of this entry. See also bibliographies, copyright, research, and abbreviations (Tab 12).

APA Documentation

APA In-Text Citations.   APA parenthetical documentation within the text of a paper gives a brief citation—in parentheses—of the author, year of publication, and relevant page number if it helps locate a passage in a lengthy document.

When APA parenthetical citations are needed midsentence, place them after the closing quotation marks and continue with the rest of the sentence. If the APA parenthetical citation follows a block quotation, place it after the final punctuation mark.

- World War II was the occasion of radar's first application in warfare, and Great Britain led the way in radar research (Butrica, 2000).

- According to Butrica (2000), the use of radar as an offensive and defensive warfare agent made World War II "the first electronic war" (p. 2).

- The "first electronic war" (Butrica, 2000, p. 2) was fought as much in the research laboratory as on the battlefield.

When a work has two authors, always cite both names joined by an ampersand: (Hey & Walters, 1997). For the first citation of a work with three, four, or five authors, include all names. For subsequent citations and for works with six or more authors, include only the name of the first author followed by *et al.* (not italicized). When two or more works by different authors are cited in the same parentheses, list the citations alphabetically and use semicolons to separate them: (Hey & Walters, 1997; Ostro, 1993).

APA Documentation Models

BOOKS

Single Author

> Hassab, J. C. (1997). *Systems management: People, computers, machines, materials.* New York: CRC Press.

Multiple Authors

Testerman, J. O., Kuegler, T. J., Jr., & Dowling, P. J., Jr. (1998). *Web advertising and marketing* (2nd ed.). Rocklin, CA: Prima.

Corporate Author

Ernst and Young. (1999). *Ernst and Young's retirement planning guide.* New York: Wiley.

Edition Other Than First

Estes, J. C., & Kelley, D. R. (1998). *McGraw-Hill's interest amortization tables* (3rd ed.). New York: McGraw-Hill.

Multivolume Work

Standard and Poor. (1998). *Standard and Poor's register of corporations, directors and executives* (Vols. 1–3). New York: McGraw-Hill.

Work in an Edited Collection

Thorne, K. S. (1997). Do the laws of physics permit wormholes for interstellar travel and machines for time travel? In Y. Terzian & E. Bilson (Eds.), *Carl Sagan's universe* (pp. 121–134). Cambridge, England: Cambridge University Press.

Encyclopedia or Dictionary Entry

Gibbard, B. G. (1997). Particle detector. In *World Book encyclopedia* (Vol. 15, pp. 186–187). Chicago: World Book.

ARTICLES IN PERIODICALS (See also Electronic Sources)

Magazine Article

Coley, D. (1997, June). Compliance for the right reasons. *Business Geographics, 12,* 30–32.

Journal Article

Rossouw, G. J. (1997). Business ethics in South Africa. *Journal of Business Ethics, 16,* 1539–1547.

Newspaper Article

Mathews, A. W. (1997, October 1). The Internet generation taps into Morse code. *Wall Street Journal,* pp. B1, B7.

Article with Unknown Author

American City adds Nashville, Memphis. (1997, September 26). *The Business Journal,* p. 16.

2

Research and
Documentation

APA

ELECTRONIC SOURCES

An Entire Web Site

The APA recommends that at minimum, a reference to a Web source should provide a document title or description, a date (of the publication or retrieval of the document), an address (URL) that links directly to the document or section, and an author, whenever possible. On the rare occasion that you need to cite multiple pages of a Web site (or the entire site), provide a URL that links to the site's homepage.

> Association for Business Communication. (2002). Retrieved April 20, 2002, from http://www.theabc.org [no period with URLs]

A Document on a Web Site, with an Author

> Locker, K. O. (1995). *The history of the association for business communication.* Retrieved April 20, 2001, from the Association for Business Communication Web site: http://www.theabc.org/history.html

A Document on a Web Site, with a Corporate Author

> General Motors. (2001). *Company profile.* Retrieved April 20, 2001, from http://www.gm.com/company/corp_info/profiles/

A Document on a Web Site, with an Unknown Author

> *Forgotten inventors.* (2001). PBS Online. Retrieved April 19, 2001, from http://www.pbs.org/wgbh/amex/telephone/sfeature/index.html

Article or Other Work from a Database

> Goldbort, R. C. (2001, March). Scientific writing as an art and as a science. *Journal of Environmental Health, 63*(7). Retrieved April 19, 2001, from Expanded Academic ASAP database.

Article in an Online Periodical

> Tiernen, R. (2001, April 18). Waiting for wireless. *SmartMoney.com.* Retrieved April 19, 2001, from http://www.smartmoney.com/techmarket/index.cfm?story=20010418

Publication on CD-ROM

> *Money 99.* (1997). [CD-ROM]. Redmond, WA: Microsoft.

MULTIMEDIA SOURCES (PRINT AND ELECTRONIC)

Map or Chart

> Asia. (2001). [Map]. Maps.com. Retrieved April 20, 2001, from http://www.maps.com/explore/atlas/political/asia.html

> Wisconsin. (2000). [Map]. Chicago: Rand.

Film or Video

> Lawrence, D. (Director), & Christopher, J. (Editor). (2001). *Emergency film group video* [Video]. Retrieved April 20, 2001, from http://www .efilmgroup.com/video1.rm

> Massingham, G. (Director), & Christopher, J. (Editor). (1998). *Introduction to hazardous chemicals* [Motion picture]. Edgartown, MA: Emergency Film Group.

Radio or Television Program

> Norris, R. (Host). (2001, April 3). Energy supplies. *All things considered* [Radio broadcast]. Boston: WGBH. Retrieved April 20, 2001, from http://www.npr.org/programs/atc

> Novak, R. (Host). (2001, April 16). Do Americans really want a tax cut? *CNN: Crossfire* [Television broadcast]. Washington, DC: CNN.

OTHER SOURCES

Published Interview

> Gates, B. (2000, April 17). The view from the very top [Interview]. *Newsweek, 135,* 36–39.

Personal Communications

Personal communications such as letters, interviews, e-mail, and messages from discussion groups and electronic bulletin boards are not cited in a reference list. They can be cited in the text as follows: "According to J. D. Kahl (personal communication, October 2, 2001), Web pages need to reflect . . ."

Brochure or Pamphlet

> Library of Congress. U.S. Copyright Office. (1999). *Copyright registration for online works* [Brochure]. Washington, DC: U.S. Government Printing Office.

Government Document

> U.S. Department of Energy. (1998). *The energy situation in the next decade* (Technical Publication No. 11346–53). Washington, DC: U.S. Government Printing Office.

Report

> Bertot, J. C., McClure, C. R., & Zweizig, D. L. (1996). *The 1996 national survey of public libraries and the Internet: Progress and issues. Final report.* Washington, DC: U.S. Government Printing Office.

Unpublished Data

> Wisniewski, K., & Hussar, D. (2002). [Oregon small business statistics by county]. Unpublished raw data.

Shortened title and page number.

One-inch margins. Text double-spaced.

This report examines the nature and disposition of the 3,458 ethics cases handled companywide by CGF's ethics officers and managers during 2002. The purpose of such reports is to provide the Ethics and Business Conduct Committee with the information necessary for assessing the effectiveness of the first year of CGF's Ethics Program (Davis, Roland, & Tegge, 2001). According to Matthias Jonas (1999), recommendations are given for consideration "in planning for the second year of the Ethics Program" (p. 152).

The Office of Ethics and Business Conduct was created to administer the Ethics Program. The director of the Office of Ethics and Business Conduct, along with seven ethics officers throughout CGF, was given the responsibility for the following objectives, as described by Rossouw (1997):

Long quote indented five to seven spaces, double-spaced, without quotation marks.

> Communicate the values, standards, and goals of CGF's Program to employees. Provide companywide channels for employee education and guidance in resolving ethics concerns. Implement companywide programs in ethics awareness and recognition. Employee accessibility to ethics information and guidance is the immediate goal of the Office of Business Conduct in its first year. (p. 1543)

The purpose of the Ethics Program, established by the Committee, is to "promote ethical business conduct through open communication and compliance with company ethics standards" (Jonas, 2001, p. 89). This report examines the nature and disposition of the 3,458 ethics cases handled companywide by CGF's ethics officers and

In-text citation gives name, date, and page number.

FIGURE 2–1. APA Sample Page

2

Research and Documentation

APA

Ethics Cases   21

Heading
centered.

References

Davis, W. C., Roland, M., & Tegge, D. (2001). *Working in the system:*
Five new management principles. New York: St. Martin's Press.

List alpha-
betized by
authors'
last names
and double-
spaced.

Hassab, J. C. (1997). *Systems management: People, computers,*
machines, materials. New York: CRC Press.

Jonas, M. (1999). The Internet and ethical communication: Toward a
new paradigm. *Journal of Ethics and Communication, 27,*
147–177.

Jonas, M. (2001). Ethics in organizational communication: A review of
the literature. *Journal of Ethics and Communication, 29,* 79–99.

Library of Congress. U.S. Copyright Office. (1999). *Copyright*
registration for online works [Brochure]. Washington, DC: U.S.
Government Printing Office.

Hanging-
indent style
used for
entries.

The one-minute manager. (1998). [CD-ROM]. Boston: Bedford/St.
Martin's.

Rossouw, G. J. (1997). Business ethics in South Africa. *Journal of*
Business Ethics, 16, 1539–1547.

FIGURE 2–2. APA Sample List of References

MLA Documentation

MLA In-Text Citations.   MLA parenthetical citation within the text of a paper gives a brief citation — in parentheses — of the author and relevant page numbers, separated only by a space.

- As Peterson writes, preparing a videotape of measurement methods is cost effective and can expedite training (151).

- The results of these studies have led even the most conservative managers to adopt technologies that will "catapult the industry forward" (Peterson 183–84).

If the parenthetical citation refers to a long indented quotation, place it outside the punctuation of the last sentence.

- . . . a close collaboration with the physics and technology staff is essential. (Minsky 42)

If no author is named or if you are using more than one work by the same author, give a shortened version of the title in the parenthetical citation, unless you mention it in a signal phrase in the text. A proper citation for Thomas J. Peterson's book *The Pursuit of Wow: Every Person's Guide to Topsy-Turvy Times* would appear as (Peterson, <u>Pursuit</u> 93).

MLA Documentation Models

BOOKS

Single Author

> Hassab, Joseph C. <u>Systems Management: People, Computers, Machines, Materials</u>. New York: CRC, 1997.

Multiple Authors

> Testerman, Joshua O., Thomas J. Kuegler, Jr., and Paul J. Dowling, Jr. <u>Web Advertising and Marketing</u>. 2nd ed. Roseville, CA: Prima, 1998.

Corporate Author

> Ernst and Young. <u>Ernst and Young's Retirement Planning Guide</u>. New York: Wiley, 1999.

Edition Other Than First

> Estes, Jack C., and Dennis R. Kelley. <u>McGraw-Hill's Interest Amortization Tables</u>. 3rd ed. New York: McGraw, 1998.

Multivolume Work

> Standard and Poor. <u>Standard and Poor's Register of Corporations, Directors and Executives</u>. 3 vols. New York: McGraw, 1998.

Work in an Edited Collection

Gueron, Judith M. "Welfare and Poverty: Strategies to Increase Work." Reducing Poverty in America: Views and Approaches. Ed. Michael R. Darby. Thousand Oaks, CA: Sage, 1996. 237–55.

Encyclopedia or Dictionary Entry

Gibbard, Bruce G. "Particle Detector." World Book Encyclopedia. 1999 ed.

ARTICLES IN PERIODICALS (See also Electronic Sources)

Magazine Article

Coley, Don. "Compliance for the Right Reasons." Business Geographics June 1997: 30–32.

Journal Article

Rossouw, G. J. "Business Ethics in South Africa." Journal of Business Ethics 16 (1997): 1539–47.

Newspaper Article

Mathews, Anna Wilde. "The Internet Generation Taps into Morse Code." Wall Street Journal 1 Oct. 1997, natl. ed.: B1+.

Article with Unknown Author

"American City Adds Nashville, Memphis." Business Journal 26 Sept. 1997: 16.

ELECTRONIC SOURCES

An Entire Web Site

Association for Business Communication. Aug. 1999. Assn. for Business Communication. 20 Apr. 2001 <http://www.theabc.org/>.

A Short Work from a Web Site, with an Author

Locker, Kitty O. "The History of the Association for Business Communication." Association for Business Communication. 25 Oct. 1995. Assn. for Business Communication. 20 Apr. 2001 <http://www.theabc.org/history.htm>.

A Short Work from a Web Site, with a Corporate Author

General Motors. "Company Profile." General Motors. 2001. 19 Apr. 2001 <http://www.gm.com/company/corp_info/profiles/>.

A Short Work from a Web Site, with an Unknown Author

"Forgotten Inventors." Forgotten Inventors. PBS Online. 2001. 19 Apr. 2001 <http://www.pbs.org/wgbh/amex/telephone/sfeature/index.htm>.

2

Research and Documentation

MLA

Article from a Database

Goldbort, Robert C. "Scientific Writing as an Art and as a Science." Journal of Environmental Health 63.7 (2001): 22. Expanded Academic ASAP. InfoTrac. Salem State Coll. Lib., Salem, MA. 19 Apr. 2001.

Article in an Online Periodical

Ray, Tiernan. "Waiting for Wireless." SmartMoney.com 18 Apr. 2001. 19 Apr. 2001 <http://www.smartmoney.com/techmarket/index.cfm?story=20010418>.

Publication on CD-ROM

Money 99. CD-ROM. Redmond, WA: Microsoft, 1998.

E-mail Message

Kahl, Jonathan D. "Re: Web page." E-mail to the author. 2 Oct. 2001.

MULTIMEDIA SOURCES (PRINT AND ELECTRONIC)

Map or Chart

Wisconsin. Map. Chicago: Rand, 2000.

"Asia." Map. Maps.com. 2000. 20 Apr. 2001 <http://www.maps.com/explore/atlas/political/asia.html>.

Film or Video

Massingham, Gordon, dir., and Jane Christopher, ed. Introduction to Hazardous Chemicals. Videocassette. Edgartown, MA: Emergency Film Group, 1998.

Lawrence, Detrick, dir. Emergency Film Group: Homepage Web Video. 2001. 20 Apr. 2001 <http://www.efilmgroup.com/video1.rm>.

Radio or Television Program

"Do Americans Really Want a Tax Cut?" CNN: Crossfire. Host Robert Novak. CNN. 16 Apr. 2001.

"Energy Supplies." Host Emily Harris. All Things Considered. Natl. Public Radio. WGBH, Boston. 3 Apr. 2001. 20 Apr. 2001 <http://www.npr.org/programs/atc/>.

OTHER SOURCES

Published Interview

Gates, Bill. "The View from the Very Top." Interview. Newsweek 17 Apr. 2000: 36–39.

Personal Interview

Sariolgholam, Mahmood. Personal interview. 29 Nov. 2004.

Personal Letter

Viets, Hermann. Letter to all students, fac., and staff. University of
Wisconsin–Milwaukee. 1 Sept. 2003.

Brochure or Pamphlet

Library of Congress. US Copyright Office. Copyright Registration for
Online Works. Washington: GPO, 1999.

Government Document

United States. Dept. of Energy. The Energy Situation in the Next Decade.
Technical Pub. 11346-53. Washington: GPO, 1998.

Report

Bertot, John Carlo, Charles R. McClure, and Douglas L. Zweizig. The 1996
National Survey of Public Libraries and the Internet: Progress and
Issues: Final Report. Washington: GPO, 1996.

Lecture or Speech

McKinney, Scott. Lecture. Demarest Hall, Hobart and William Smith
Colls., Geneva, NY. 3 May 2002.

Krug, Steve. "Don't Make Me Think: The Art of Designing User-Friendly
Websites." New England School of Art & Design at Suffolk U. Boston
Public Lib. 3 Apr. 2001.

2

Research and
Documentation

MLA

Author's last name and page number.

Marks 14

One-inch margins. Text double-spaced.

This report examines the nature and disposition of the 3,458 ethics cases handled companywide by CGF's ethics officers and managers during 2002. The purpose of such reports is to provide the Ethics and Business Conduct Committee with the information necessary for assessing the effectiveness of the first year of CGF's Ethics Program (Davis 142). According to Matthias Jonas, recommendations are given for consideration "in planning for the second year of the Ethics Program" ("Internet" 152).

The Office of Ethics and Business Conduct was created to administer the Ethics Program. The director of the Office of Ethics and Business Conduct, along with seven ethics officers throughout CGF, was given the responsibility for the following objectives, as described by Rossouw:

Long quote indented one inch (or 10 spaces), double-spaced, without quotation marks.

> Communicate the values, standards, and goals of CGF's Program to employees. Provide companywide channels for employee education and guidance in resolving ethics concerns. Implement companywide programs in ethics awareness and recognition. Employee accessibility to ethics information and guidance is the immediate goal of the Office of Business Conduct in its first year. (1543)

In-text citations give author and page number. Title used when multiple works by same author(s) cited.

According to Jonas, the purpose of the Ethics Program, established by the Committee, is to "promote ethical business conduct through open communication and compliance with company ethics standards" ("Ethics" 89). This report examines the nature and the

FIGURE 2–3. MLA Sample Page

Marks 21

Heading centered.

Works Cited

Association for Business Communication. Aug. 1999. Assn. for Business
Communication. 20 Apr. 2001 <http://www.theabc.org/>.

List alphabetized by authors' last names or title and doublespaced.

Davis, W. C., Roland Marks, and Diane Tegge. Working in the System:
Five New Management Principles. New York: St. Martin's, 2001.

Hassab, Joseph C. Systems Management: People, Computers, Machines,
Materials. New York: CRC, 1997.

Jonas, Matthias. "Ethics in Organizational Communication: A Review of
the Literature." Journal of Ethics and Communication 29 (2001):
79–99.

---. "The Internet and Ethical Communication: Toward a New
Paradigm." Journal of Ethics and Communication 27 (1999):
147–77.

Hanging-indent style used for entries.

Library of Congress. US Copyright Office. Copyright Registration for
Online Works. Washington: GPO, 1999.

The One-Minute Manager. CD-ROM. Boston: Bedford, 1998.

Rossouw, George J. "Business Ethics in South Africa." Journal of
Business Ethics 16 (1997): 1539–47.

Sariolgholam, Mahmood. Personal interview. 29 Nov. 2000.

FIGURE 2–4. MLA Sample List of Works Cited

Other Style Manuals

Many professional societies, publishing companies, and other organizations publish manuals that prescribe bibliographic reference formats for their publications or for publications in their fields. In addition, several general style manuals are well known and widely used.

General

> The Chicago Manual of Style. 15th ed. Chicago: University of Chicago Press, 2003. See also <www.press.uchicago.edu/Misc/Chicago/cmosfaq/cmosfaq.html>.

Government Documents

> United States Government Printing Office. *Style Manual.* Washington, DC: Government Printing Office, 2000. See also <www.gpo.gov>.

Journalism

> Goldstein, Norm, ed. *Associated Press Stylebook and Briefing on Media Law.* 35th ed. New York: Associated Press, 2000. See also <www.ap.org>.

Law

> Harvard Law Review et al. *The Bluebook: A Uniform System of Citation.* 17th ed. Cambridge: Harvard Law Review Association, 2000. See also <www.legalbluebook.com>.

Political Science

> American Political Science Association. *Style Manual for Political Science.* Rev. ed. Washington, DC: APSA, 2001. See also <www.apsanet.org>.

Social Work

> National Association of Social Workers. *An Author's Guide to Social Work Journals.* 4th ed. Washington, DC: National Association of Social Workers Press, 1997. See also <www.naswpress.org>.

interviewing for information

The process of interviewing for information can be divided into three parts: (1) determining the proper person to interview, (2) preparing for the interview, and (3) conducting the interview.

Determining the Proper Person to Interview

Many times, your subject or __purpose__ (Tab 1) logically points to the proper person to interview for information. If you were writing about using the Web to market a software-development business, you would want to interview someone with extensive experience in Web marketing as well as someone who has built a successful business developing software. The following sources can help you determine the appropriate person to interview: (1) workplace colleagues or faculty in appropriate academic departments, (2) information from the Internet, (3) local chapters of professional societies, and (4) yellow or business pages of the local telephone directory. For advice on finding sources, see research.

Preparing for the Interview

Before the interview, learn as much as possible about the person you are going to interview and the organization for which he or she works. When you contact the prospective interviewee, explain who you are, why you would like to interview him or her, the subject and purpose of the interview, and how much time it will take. You should also let your interviewee know that you will allow him or her to review your draft.

After you have made the appointment, prepare a list of questions to ask your interviewee. Avoid vague, general questions. A question such as "What do you think of the Internet?" is too general to elicit useful information. It is more helpful to ask specific but open-ended questions; for example, "Some local professionals in your field are making extensive use of the Internet for helping clients. How has the Internet helped your organization?"

Conducting the Interview

Arrive promptly for the interview and be prepared to guide the discussion. The following *Writer's Checklist: Interviewing Successfully* should help you to do so. During the interview, take only memory-jogging notes that will help you recall the conversation later. Do not ask your interviewee to slow down so you can take detailed notes. As the interview is reaching a close, take a few minutes to skim your notes and ask the interviewee to clarify anything that is ambiguous. Immediately after leaving the interview, use your memory-jogging notes to help you mentally review the interview and record your detailed notes. Do not postpone this step. No matter how good your memory is, you will forget some important points if you do not do this at once. See also note-taking.

Writer's Checklist: Interviewing Successfully

☑ Be pleasant but purposeful. You are there to get information, so don't be timid about asking leading questions on the subject.

☑ Use the list of questions you have prepared, starting with the less-controversial aspects of the topic to get the conversation started and then going on to the more-controversial aspects.

Writer's Checklist: Interviewing Successfully (continued)

- ☑ Let your interviewee do most of the talking. Remember that the interviewee is the expert. See also <u>listening</u> (Tab 8).
- ☑ Be objective. Don't offer your opinions on the subject. You are there to get information, not to debate.
- ☑ Some answers prompt additional questions; ask them as they arise.
- ☑ Don't get sidetracked. If the interviewee strays too far from the subject, ask a specific question to direct the conversation back on track.
- ☑ If you use a tape recorder, do not let it lure you into relaxing so that you neglect to ask crucial questions.

note-taking

The purpose of note-taking is to summarize and record information you extract during <u>research</u>. The challenge in taking notes is to condense someone else's thoughts into your own words without distorting the original thinking. As you extract information, let your knowledge of the audience and the purpose of your writing guide you.

⚡ ETHICS NOTE Resist copying your source word for word as you take notes; instead, paraphrase the author's idea or concept. You must do more than just change a few words in the original passage; otherwise, you will be guilty of <u>plagiarism</u>. See also <u>paraphrasing</u> and <u>minutes of meetings</u> (Tab 8).

On occasion, when your source concisely sums up a great deal of information or points to a trend important to your subject, you are justified in directly quoting the source and incorporating it into your document. If you use a direct quote, enclose the material in <u>quotation marks</u> (Tab 12) in your notes. In your finished writing, provide the source of your quotation. As a general rule, you will rarely need to quote anything longer than a paragraph. See also <u>documenting sources</u> and <u>quotations</u>.

Writer's Checklist: Taking Notes

- ☑ Ask yourself the following questions: What information do you need to fulfill your <u>purpose</u> (Tab 1)? What are the needs of your <u>readers</u> (Tab 1)?
- ☑ Record only the most important ideas and concepts. Be sure to record all vital names, dates, and definitions.
- ☑ When in doubt about whether to take a note, consider the difficulty of finding the source again should you want it later.

Writer's Checklist: Taking Notes (continued)

☑ Use <u>quotations</u> when sources summarize a great deal of information or point to important trends.

☑ Ensure proper credit: Record the author, title, publisher, place and date of publication, and page number. (On subsequent notes from the same source, include only the author and page number.)

☑ Use your own shorthand and record notes in a way that you find efficient, whether in an electronic document or on note cards.

☑ Photocopy and highlight passages that you intend to quote.

☑ Print out key sections from online documents or download the information to a notes file: Be sure to copy the full URL and your retrieval date for Web sites.

☑ Check your notes for accuracy against the original material before moving on to another source.

2

Research and
Documentation

paraphrasing

Paraphrasing is restating or rewriting in your own words the essential ideas of another writer. The following example is an original passage explaining the concept of object blur. The paraphrased version restates the essential information of the passage in a form appropriate for a report.

ORIGINAL	One of the major visual cues used by pilots in maintaining precision ground reference during low-level flight is that of object blur. We are acquainted with the object-blur phenomenon experienced when driving an automobile. Objects in the foreground appear to be rushing toward us, while objects in the background appear to recede slightly.
	—Wesley E. Woodson and Donald W. Conover, *Human Engineering Guide for Equipment Designers*
PARAPHRASED	Object blur refers to the phenomenon by which observers in a moving vehicle report that foreground objects appear to rush at them, while background objects appear to recede slightly (Woodson & Conover, 1964).

⬛ ETHICS NOTE Because the paraphrase does not quote the source word for word, quotation marks are not necessary. However, paraphrased material should be credited because the *ideas* are taken from someone else. See also <u>ethics in writing</u> (Tab 1), <u>note-taking</u>, <u>plagiarism</u>, and <u>quotations</u>.

plagiarism

✦ ETHICS NOTE Plagiarism is the use of someone else's unique ideas without acknowledgment or the use of someone else's exact words without quotation marks and appropriate credit. Plagiarism is considered to be the theft of someone else's creative and intellectual property and is not accepted in business, science, journalism, academia, and other fields.

You may, however, quote or paraphrase the words and ideas of another if you document your source. (See also <u>paraphrasing</u> and <u>documenting sources</u>.) Although you do not enclose paraphrased ideas or materials in quotation marks, you must document their sources. Paraphrasing a passage without citing the source is permissible only when the information paraphrased is common knowledge in a field. *Common knowledge* refers to information on a topic that is widely known and readily available in handbooks, manuals, atlases, and other references.

Quoting a passage—including cutting and pasting a passage from the Internet into your work—is permissible only if you enclose the passage in quotation marks and properly cite the source. For detailed guidance on quoting correctly, see <u>quotations</u>. If you intend to publish, reproduce, or distribute material that includes quotations from published works, including Web sites, you may need to obtain written permission from the copyright holder to do so.

In the workplace, employees often borrow from in-house manuals, reports, and other company documents. Using such boilerplate material is neither plagiarism nor a violation of copyright. See also <u>ethics in writing</u> (Tab 1) and <u>copyright</u>.

> ✷ WEB LINK AVOIDING PLAGIARISM
>
> For a tutorial on using sources correctly, see <bedfordstmartins.com/alred> and select *Tutorials*, "The St. Martin's Tutorial on Avoiding Plagiarism." For links to helpful related resources, select *Links for Business Writing*.

quotations

Using direct and indirect quotations is an effective way to make or support a point. However, avoid the temptation to overquote during the note-taking phase of your research; concentrate on summarizing what you read.

⚡ ETHICS NOTE When you do use a quotation (or an idea of another writer), cite your source properly. If you do not, you will be guilty of <u>plagiarism</u>. For specific details on APA and MLA systems, see <u>documenting sources</u>. See also <u>note-taking</u> and <u>research</u>.

Direct Quotations

A direct quotation is a word-for-word copy of the text of an original source. Choose direct quotations (which can be of a word, a phrase, a sentence, or, occasionally, a paragraph) carefully and use them sparingly. Enclose direct quotations in <u>quotation marks</u> (Tab 12) and separate them from the rest of the sentence by a <u>comma</u> (Tab 12) or <u>colon</u> (Tab 12). Use the initial capital letter of a quotation if the quoted material originally began with a capital letter.

- The economist stated, "Regulation cannot supply the dynamic stimulus that in other industries is supplied by competition."

When dividing a quotation, set off the material that interrupts the quotation with commas, and use quotation marks around each part of the quotation.

- "Regulation," he said in a recent interview, "cannot supply the dynamic stimulus that in other industries is supplied by competition."

Indirect Quotations

An indirect quotation is a paraphrased version of an original text. It is usually introduced by the word *that* and is not set off from the rest of the sentence by punctuation marks. (See also <u>paraphrasing</u>.)

- In a recent interview he said that regulation does not stimulate the industry as well as competition does.

Deletions or Omissions

Deletions or omissions from quoted material are indicated by three ellipsis dots (. . .) within a sentence and a period plus three ellipsis dots (. . . .) at the end of a sentence.

- "If monopolies could be made to respond . . . we would be able to enjoy the benefits of . . . large-scale efficiency. . . ."

When a quoted passage begins in the middle of a sentence rather than at the beginning, ellipsis dots are not necessary; the fact that the first letter of the quoted material is not capitalized tells the reader that the quotation begins in midsentence.

- Rivero goes on to conclude that "coordination may lessen competition within a region."

Inserting Material into Quotations

When it is necessary to insert a clarifying comment within quoted material, use brackets.

- "The industry is an integrated system that serves an extensive [geographic] area, with divisions existing as islands within the larger system's sphere of influence."

When quoted material contains an obvious error or might be questioned in some other way, insert the expression *sic* (Latin for "thus"), in italic type and enclosed in brackets, following the questionable material to indicate that the writer has quoted the material exactly as it appeared in the original.

- The company considers the Baker Foundation to be a "guilt-edged [*sic*] investment."

Incorporating Quotations into Text

Quote word for word only when your source concisely sums up a great deal of information or reinforces a point you are making. Quotations must also relate logically, grammatically, and syntactically to the rest of the sentence and surrounding text.

Depending on the length, MLA and APA use different mechanical methods of handling quotations in your text. For MLA style, a quotation of three or fewer lines is incorporated into the text and enclosed in quotation marks. For APA style, a quotation of fewer than 40 words is incorporated into the text and enclosed in quotation marks.

Material that runs longer than four lines (MLA style) or at least 40 words (APA style) is usually inset; that is, set off from the body of the text by being indented from the left margin one inch (MLA style) or five to seven spaces (APA style). The quoted passage is spaced the same as the surrounding text (APA and MLA styles), and is not enclosed in quotation marks, as shown in Figure 2–5, which uses MLA style. If you are not following a specific style manual, you may block indent one inch from both the left and right margins for reports and other documents.

Notice in Figure 2–5 that the quotation blends with the content of the surrounding text, which uses transitions to introduce and comment on the quotation. (See transition, Tab 9.) At the end of the document, the following entry appears in the MLA-style list of works cited as the source of the quotation in Figure 2–5.

- Alred, Gerald J. The St. Martin's Bibliography of Business and Technical Communication. New York: St. Martin's, 1997.

Do not rely too heavily on the use of quotations in the final version of your document. Generally, avoid quoting anything that is more than one paragraph.

After reviewing a large number of works in business and technical communication, Alred sees an inevitable connection between theory, practice, and pedagogy:

> Therefore, theory is necessary to prevent us from being overwhelmed by what is local, particular, and temporal. In turn, pedagogy both mediates practice and transforms our theory. Indeed, one reason I find this work rewarding is that I sense it puts me at the intersection of theory, practice, and pedagogy as they are involved with writing in the workplace. (ix–x)

The use of the Web today has reinforced this connection because it calls on the Web page designer to engage in a teaching function as well as reflect on the practice of Web design. For example, the widespread use of . . .

FIGURE 2–5. Long Quotation (MLA Style)

research

Research is the process of investigation—the discovery of facts. To be focused, research must be preceded by preparation, especially consideration of your readers (Tab 1), purpose (Tab 1), and scope (Tab 1). See also "Five Steps to Successful Writing" (page xxi).

In an academic setting, your preparatory resources include conversations with your peers, instructors, and especially a research librarian. On the job, your main resources are your own knowledge and experience and that of your colleagues. In this setting, begin by brainstorming with colleagues about what sources will be most useful to your topic and how you can track them down.

Primary Research

Primary research is the gathering of raw data from interviews, direct observation, surveys and questionnaires, experiments, recordings, and the like. In fact, direct observation and interaction are the only ways to obtain certain kinds of information, such as behavior, certain natural phenomena, and the operation of systems and equipment. You can also conduct primary research on the Internet by participating in discussion groups and newsgroups, and by using e-mail to request information from specific audiences. See also <u>interviewing for information</u>.

⚡ ETHICS NOTE If you are planning research that involves observation, choose your sites and times carefully, and be sure to obtain permission in advance. During your observations, remain as unobtrusive as possible, and keep accurate, complete records that indicate date, time of day, duration of the observation, and so on. Save interpretations of your observations for future analysis. Be aware that observation can be valuable research, but it may also be time-consuming, complicated, and expensive, and you may inadvertently influence the subjects you are observing.

Secondary Research

Secondary research is the gathering of information that has been analyzed, assessed, evaluated, compiled, or otherwise organized into accessible form. Sources include books, articles, reports, Web documents, e-mail discussions, business letters, minutes of meetings, operating manuals, brochures, and so forth. The following sections, Library Research Strategies (below) and Internet Research Strategies (page 70), provide methods for finding secondary sources.

As you seek information, keep in mind that in most cases the more recent the information, the better. Recently published periodicals and newspapers as well as academic (.edu), organizational (.org), and government (.gov) Web sites can be good sources of current information and can include interviews, articles, papers, and conference proceedings. See especially the *Writer's Checklist: Evaluating Print and Online Sources* (page 74). See also <u>documenting sources</u>, <u>paraphrasing</u>, and <u>plagiarism</u>.

When a resource seems useful, read it carefully and take notes that include any additional questions about your topic. Some of your questions may eventually be answered in other sources; those that remain unanswered can guide you to further primary research. For example, you may discover that you need to talk with an expert. Not only can someone skilled in a field answer many of your questions, but he or she can also suggest further sources of information. See <u>interviewing for information</u>, <u>note-taking</u>, and <u>listening</u> (Tab 8).

Library Research Strategies

The library is a gateway to all types of sources—including Internet sources—that can help you find the best, most reliable information. The first step in using library resources, either in an academic institution or in a workplace, is to develop a search strategy appropriate to the information needed for your topic. You may want to begin by meeting with a research librarian who can help you quickly find the best print or online resources for your topic — a brief conversation can focus your research and save you time. In addition, use your library's homepage for access to its catalogs, databases of articles, subject directories to the Web, and more. A sample of a library's homepage is shown in Figure 2–6.

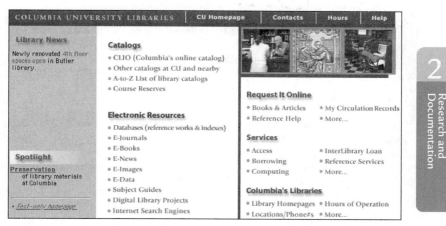

FIGURE 2–6. Library Homepage

Your search strategy depends on the kind of information you are seeking. For example, if you need the latest data offered by government research, check the Web, as described later in this entry. Likewise, if you need a current article on a topic, search an online database — such as InfoTrac — subscribed to by your library. For an overview of a subject, you might turn to an encyclopedia; for historical background, your best resources are books, journals, and primary documents.

Online Catalogs (Locating Books).   An online catalog — accessed through a library terminal and through the Internet — allows you to search a library's holdings, indicates an item's location and availability, and may allow you to arrange an interlibrary loan.

You can search a library's online catalog by author, title, keyword, or subject. The most typical ways of searching for a specific topic are by subject or by keyword. If your search turns up too many results, you can usually narrow it by using the "limit search" or "advanced search" option.

Online Databases and Indexes (Locating Articles).   Most libraries subscribe to online databases — such as collections of online articles — many of which are available through a library's Web site.

- *InfoTrac:* a collection of databases of articles, with many available in full text, which can also provide specialized databases in business, health, and other fields.
- *ProQuest:* a database of articles, with many available in full text, which can also provide specialized databases for nursing, biology, and psychology.
- *EBSCOhost:* a database of articles, with many available in full text, which can also provide specialized databases in a range of subjects.
- *FirstSearch:* a collection of specialized databases such as WorldCat (library collections) and ArticleFirst (articles, some in full text).
- *Lexis/Nexis Universe:* a collection of databases containing news, business, legal, and congressional information (most in full text).

These databases, sometimes called *periodical indexes,* are excellent resources for articles published within the last ten to twenty years. Some include descriptive abstracts and full texts of articles. To find older articles, you may need to consult a print index, such as the *Readers' Guide to Periodical Literature* and the *New York Times Index,* or a reference librarian. (For more information on print indexes, see "General Guides" in the Reference Works section, page 69.)

To locate articles in a database, conduct a keyword search, as shown in Figure 2–7. If your search turns up too many results, refine your search by connecting two search terms with AND — "business management AND employment" — or use other options offered by the database, such as a limited, modified, or advanced search.

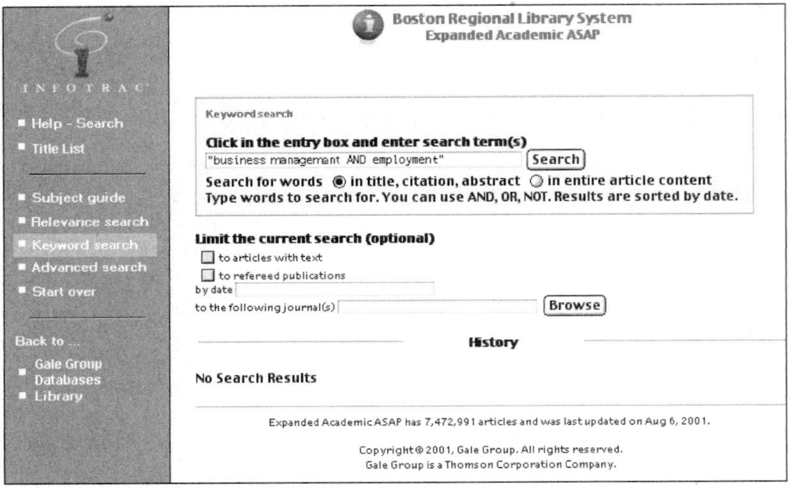

FIGURE 2–7. InfoTrac Search Page

Reference Works.   In addition to articles, books, and Web sources, you may want to consult reference works such as encyclopedias, dictionaries, and atlases for a brief overview of your subject. Bibliographies, which are lists of works written about a topic, can direct you to more specialized sources. Ask your reference librarian to recommend reference works and bibliographies that are most relevant to your topic. Many are available in print, on CD-ROM, and online.

ENCYCLOPEDIAS.   Encyclopedias are comprehensive, multivolume collections of articles arranged alphabetically. Some, such as the *Encarta Encyclopedia,* cover a wide range of subjects, while others, such as *The Encyclopedia of Careers and Vocational Guidance,* 12th ed., edited by Andrew Morkes (Chicago: Ferguson, 2002), focus on specific areas.

DICTIONARIES.   General dictionaries can be compact or comprehensive, unabridged publications. Specialized dictionaries define terms used in a particular field, such as business, computers, architecture, or consumer affairs, and offer detailed definitions of field-specific terms, usually written in straightforward language.

HANDBOOKS AND MANUALS.   Handbooks and manuals are typically one-volume compilations of frequently used information in a particular field. They offer brief definitions of terms or concepts, standards for presenting information, procedures for documenting sources, and visuals such as graphs and tables.

BIBLIOGRAPHIES.   Bibliographies list books, periodicals, and other research materials published in areas such as business, engineering, medicine, the humanities, and the social sciences. One example is *The St. Martin's Bibliography of Business and Technical Communication* by Gerald J. Alred (New York: St. Martin's, 1997).

GENERAL GUIDES.   The annotated *Guide to Reference Books,* 11th ed., by Robert Balay (Chicago: American Library Association, 1996) can help you locate reference books, indexes, and other research materials. The following are specialized indexes. Check your library's homepage or with your reference librarian to find out if your library subscribes to a particular index, and whether it is available online.

Business Periodicals Index, 1958–. Alphabetical subject listing; issued monthly.

Government Reports Announcements and Index, 1965–. Semimonthly index of reports, arranged by subject, author, and report number.

Index to the Times (London), 1790–. Monthly.

Monthly Catalog of U.S. Government Publications, 1895–. Unclassified publications of all federal agencies, listed by subject, author, and report number; issued monthly.

New York Times Index, 1851–. Alphabetical list of subjects covered in *New York Times* articles; issued bimonthly.

Readers' Guide to Periodical Literature, 1900–. Monthly index of about 200 general U.S. periodicals, arranged alphabetically by subject.

Wall Street Journal Index, 1958–. Monthly index of business and financial news covered in the *Journal*.

ATLASES.   Atlases provide representations of the physical and political boundaries of countries, climate, population, or natural resources. One example on CD-ROM is the *Microsoft® Encarta® World Atlas 2000* (Redmond, WA: Microsoft Corporation, 2000).

STATISTICAL SOURCES.   Statistical sources are collections of numerical data. They are the best source for such information as the U.S. gross domestic product, the consumer price index, or the demographic breakdown of the general population.

American Statistics Index. Washington, D.C.: Congressional Information Service, 1978–. Monthly, quarterly, and annual supplements.

United States Bureau of the Census. *Statistical Abstract of the United States.* Washington, DC: Government Printing Office, 1879–. Annual. (<www.census.gov>)

Internet Research Strategies

The Internet provides access to a staggering amount of information. However, the information on the Web varies widely in its completeness and accuracy, and it can seriously affect the quality and accuracy of your completed project. You need to spend extra time and effort to critically evaluate Internet sources by following the advice in the *Writer's Checklist: Evaluating Print and Online Sources* (page 74).

As comprehensive as search engines and directories may seem, keep in mind that none is complete or objective. Most search sites are incomplete, carrying only a preselected range of content. Many, for example, do not index Adobe PDF files or Usenet newsgroups, and many cannot index databases and other non-HTML-based content. Further, search sites' ranking of the sites they believe will be relevant to you is based on a number of different strategies. Some sites base relevance on how high on the given page your search term appears, on the number of appearances of your term, or on the number of other sites that link to the page. Almost all major search sites now sell high rankings to the highest bidders, so your results may not highlight the pages most relevant to your search. Your best strategy is to research how your favorite search engines work; nearly all provide detailed methodologies on their help pages.

Search Engines.   Search engines—like Google or AltaVista—are machine-generated databases created by "spiders" or "bots" that travel the Web looking for new or updated pages; search engines typically have databases of billions of pages. The following search engines are used widely on the Web:

> AltaVista <www.altavista.com>
> Excite <www.excite.com>
> Google <www.google.com>
> Hotbot <www.hotbot.lycos.com>
> Lycos <www.lycos.com>
> WebCrawler <www.webcrawler.com>
> Yahoo! <www.yahoo.com>

Search sites may use a hybrid approach. For example, some search engines, such as Northern Light (<www.northernlight.com>), search not only the Web but also their own database of articles—content that is edited and compiled by staff librarians and not available elsewhere on the Web.

Many search engines allow advanced searches with options that provide more selective results. Figure 2–8 shows an advanced search conducted on Google for business writing programs—a search limited

FIGURE 2–8. Advanced Google Search

to results in English and to sites within the ".edu" domain. This particular advanced search resulted in ten selective hits. Although search engines vary in what and how they search, you can use some basic strategies, as in the *Writer's Checklist: Using Search Engines* that follows.

Writer's Checklist: Using Search Engines

☑ Enter words and phrases that are as specific to your topic as possible. For example, if you are looking for information about *nuclear power* and enter only the term *nuclear*, the search will also yield listings for *nuclear* family, *nuclear* medicine, and *nuclear* winter.

Writer's Checklist: Using Search Engines (continued)

☑ Use Boolean operators (AND, OR, NOT) to narrow your search. For example, if you're searching for information on breast cancer and are finding references to nothing but prostate cancer, try breast AND cancer NOT prostate.

☑ Consider conducting an advanced search (see Figure 2–8).

☑ Check any search tips available at the engine you use. For example, some engines allow you to narrow your search by combining phrases with double quotation marks: "usability testing" will return only pages that have the full compound phrase.

☑ Use a variety of search engines.

☑ Consider using a metasearch engine, such as Dogpile (<www.dogpile .com>) and Metacrawler (<www.metacrawler.com>), if you are interested in obtaining as many hits as possible. Be prepared to refine and narrow your results.

Web Directories.   Directories are human generated, so they index fewer pages but offer subject directory trees to help organize their content, as shown in Figure 2–9. In addition to the subject directories

FIGURE 2–9. Google's Main Subject Directory

offered by many search engines, the following directories will help you to conduct selective, scholarly research on the Web:

Infomine <http://infomine.ucr.edu>
The Internet Public Library <www.ipl.org>
World Wide Web Virtual Library <www.vlib.org>

The Web includes numerous directories and sites devoted to specific subject areas. Following are some suggested resources for researching a business topic.

Business Internet Resources <www.pace.edu/library/links/links.html>

CIO's Research Centers <www.cio.com/research>

Inc.com Articles by Topic <www.inc.com/articles>

Yahoo's Business Resources <http://dir.yahoo.com/business_and_economy>

Federal Government Agencies Directory <www.lib.lsu.edu/gov/fedgov.html>

FedStats <www.fedstats.gov>

Some combine search engines with directories; for example, Google operates both a standard search engine and directory as well as a special contributor-generated directory referred to as an "Open Directory" (<http://dmoz.org>).

Evaluating Sources

The easiest way to ensure that information is valid is to obtain it from a reputable source. For Internet sources, be especially concerned about the validity of the information provided. Because anyone can publish on the Web, it is sometimes difficult to determine authorship of a document, and frequently a person's qualifications for speaking on a topic are absent or questionable. The Internet versions of established, reputable journals in medicine, management, engineering, computer software and the like merit the same level of trust as the printed versions. However, as you move away from established, reputable sites, exercise more caution. Be especially wary of unmoderated discussion groups on Usenet and other public Web forums. Use the following domain abbreviations to determine an Internet site sponsor:

.aero	aerospace industry	.int	international
.biz	business	.mil	U.S. military
.com	company or individual	.museum	museum
.coop	business cooperative	.name	individual
.edu	college or university	.net	network provider
.gov	federal government	.org	nonprofit organization
.info	general use	.pro	professionals

In addition, keep in mind the following four criteria when evaluating Internet sources: authority, accuracy, bias, and currency.

Writer's Checklist: Evaluating Print and Online Sources

FOR ALL SOURCES

☑ Is the source recent enough and relevant to your topic? Is it readily available?

☑ Who is the intended audience? The mainstream public? A small group of professionals?

☑ Who is the author(s)? Is the author(s) an authority on the subject of the resource?

☑ Does the author(s) provide enough supporting evidence and document sources so that you can verify the information's accuracy?

☑ Is the information presented in an objective, unbiased way? Are any biases made clear?

☑ Are opinions clearly labeled? Are viewpoints balanced, or are opposing opinions acknowledged?

☑ Are the language, tone, and style inviting?

FOR A BOOK

☑ Does the preface or introduction indicate the author's or book's purpose?

☑ Does the table of contents relate to your topic? Does the index contain terms related to your topic?

☑ Are the chapters useful? Skim through one that seems related to your topic — notice especially the introduction, headings, and closing.

FOR AN ARTICLE

☑ Is the publisher of the magazine or other periodical well known?

☑ What is the article's purpose? For a journal article, read the abstract; for a newspaper article, read the headline and lead sentences.

☑ Does the article contain informative diagrams or other visuals that indicate its scope?

FOR AN INTERNET SITE

☑ Does a reputable group or organization sponsor or maintain the site?

☑ Are the purpose and scope of the site clearly stated? Check the "Mission Statement" or "About Us" pages. Are there any disclaimers?

☑ Is the site updated, thus current? Are the links functional and up to date?

Writer's Checklist: Evaluating Print and Online Sources (continued)

☑ Is the documentation authoritative and credible? Check the links, which often replace traditional documentation on Web sites, and cross-check facts at other reputable Web sites, such as academic ones.

☑ What do you think of the presentation of the site? Is it well designed? Is it easily navigated? Is the material well written and error-free?

 WEB LINK EVALUATING ONLINE SOURCES

For a tutorial on evaluating information online, see <bedfordstmartins .com/alred> and select *Tutorials*, "Evaluating Online Sources." For links to additional related resources, select *Links for Business Writing*.

2

Research and
Documentation

Business Writing Documents and Elements

Preview

This section contains entries on various forms of business documents, including **proposals** and such typical **reports** as **progress and activity reports**, **trip reports**, and **trouble reports**. Also included in this section are **brochures** and **newsletters**—types of promotional writing that you may encounter on the job. (See also **promotional writing**, Tab 1.) Because of their size and complexity, formal reports and their parts are covered separately in Tab 4, "Formal Reports," which includes a sample formal report (page 116).

WEB LINK   ANNOTATED SAMPLE DOCUMENTS

For additional samples of some of the types of writing covered in this section, see <bedfordstmartins.com/alred> and select *Model Documents Gallery*. For links to additional resources and advice, select *Links for Business Writing*.

3

Business Writing
Documents
and Elements

brochures

Brochures are printed publications that promote the products and services offered by a business or that promote the image of a business or an organization by providing information important to a target audience. The goal of a brochure is to inform, to persuade, or to do both. See persuasion (Tab 1) and promotional writing (Tab 1).

There are two major types of brochures: sales brochures and informational brochures. *Sales brochures* are created specifically to sell a company's products and services. For example, a brochure for a cellphone company might describe the various phones and calling plans available; a brochure for a consulting company would detail its seminars or specific services. *Informational brochures* are created to inform and educate the reader as well as to promote goodwill and raise the profile of an organization. For example, a health-food company might create an informational brochure that shows the reader how to clean fruits and vegetables before they are eaten and offers healthful recipes; a psychiatric hospital might create a brochure describing how to recognize depression in teenagers.

Before you begin to write, you must decide on the specific purpose (Tab 1) of the brochure—to sell a product? to provide information about a service? You must also identify your target audience—general reader? expert? potential client? (See readers, Tab 1.) Understanding your purpose and audience is crucial to creating content and design that will be both rhetorically appropriate and persuasive to your target audience. Once you make these decisions, gather samples of brochures for similar products or services to stimulate your thinking.

The main goal of the cover panel of a sales or promotional brochure is to gain the audience's attention. The cover panel, which should clearly identify the company being promoted, usually features a carefully selected visual image or headline geared toward the interest of your audience. Accompanying the image, there may be a minimal amount of text—for example, a statement about the company's mission and success or a brief promotional quotation from a satisfied customer.

The first inside panel of a sales or promotional brochure should again identify the company and attract the reader with headlines and brief, readable content, such as that used in advertising. In subsequent panels of your brochure, describe the product or service with your readers' needs in mind, clearly stating the benefits and solutions that the product offers. Include relevant and accurate supporting facts and visuals, and you might further establish credibility with a company history, a product history, and a list of current clients or testimonials. Use subheadings and bulleted lists to break up the text and make the brochure easy to read. In the final panel, be clear about the action you want the

reader to take, such as calling for an appointment, e-mailing for technical support, or mailing an enclosed reply card.

Writer's Checklist: Designing Brochures

- ☑ Collect other brochures to stimulate your thinking as you consider the goals and content for your brochure and each panel.
- ☑ Create a rough sketch that maps out the content of each panel to help you select visuals, color schemes, and the number of panels. See also **layout and design** (Tab 5) and **visuals** (Tab 5).
- ☑ Experiment with margins, spacing, and the arrangement and amount of text on each panel; make appropriate changes to content or length and allow adequate white space for readability.
- ☑ Experiment with fonts and formatting, such as enlarging the first letter of the first word in a paragraph, but do not overuse unusual fonts or alternative styles, such as running type vertically.
- ☑ Consider color choices: black and white, which is inexpensive, can be effective; in some circumstances (such as brochures for travel) color, although more expensive, is a must.
- ☑ Evaluate the impact of the design with your content. Does the design complement the content and make the brochure more persuasive? Have you adequately considered the needs of your readers? When your brochure is distributed, will it fulfill its purposes?
- ☑ Depending on your budget and the scale of your project, consider using a professional printer.

feasibility reports

When organizations consider a new project—developing a new product or service, expanding a customer base, purchasing equipment, or
moving operations—they first try to determine the project's chances
for success. A feasibility report presents evidence about the practicality
of a proposed project based on specific criteria. It answers such questions as the following: Is new construction or development *necessary*? Is
sufficient *staff* available? What are the *costs* involved? What are the *legal
ramifications*? Based on the findings of this analysis, the writer offers
logical conclusions and recommends whether the project should be
carried out. In the sample feasibility report in Figure 3–1, a financial
consulting firm conducts a feasibility study to determine how to upgrade its computer system and Internet capability.

Introduction

The purpose of this report is to determine which of two proposed options would best enable ACM Technology Consulting to upgrade its file servers and its Internet capacity to meet its increasing data and communication requirements.

Background.   In October 2003, the Information Development and Technical Support Group at ACM put the MISSION System into operation. Since then, the volume of processing transactions has increased fivefold (from 1,000 to 5,000 updates per day). This increase has severely impaired system response time; in fact, average response time has increased from less than 10 seconds to 120 seconds. Further, our new Web-based client services system has increased exponentially the demand for processing speed and access capacity.

Scope.   Two alternative solutions to provide increased processing capacity have been investigated: (1) purchase of a new ARC 98 processor to supplement the first, and (2) purchase of an HRS 60/EP with PRS enterprise software and expandable peripherals to replace the current ARC 98. The two alternatives are evaluated here according to cost and, to a lesser extent, according to expanded capacity for future operations.

Purchasing a Second ARC 98 Processor

This alternative would require additional annual maintenance costs, salary for an additional computer specialist, increased energy costs, and a one-time construction cost for necessary remodeling as well as installing Internet and other connections.

Annual maintenance costs	$35,000
Annual costs for computer specialist	75,000
Annual increased energy costs	7,500
Annual operating costs	$117,500
Construction cost (one-time)	50,000
Total first-year cost	$167,500

The costs for the installation and operation of another ARC 98 processor are expected to produce savings in system reliability and readiness.

FIGURE 3–1. Feasibility Report

Before beginning to write a feasibility report, analyze your readers' needs and the purpose of your study. Then write a purpose statement: "The purpose of this study is to determine the feasibility of expanding our Pacific Rim operations." See also <u>readers</u> (Tab 1) and <u>purpose</u> (Tab 1).

System Reliability.   A second ARC 98 would reduce current downtime periods from four to two per week. Downtime recovery averages 30 minutes and affects 40 users. Assuming that 50 percent of users require the system at a given time, we determined that the following reliability savings would result:

$$\text{2 downtimes} \times \text{0.5 hours} \times \text{40 users} \times 50\%$$
$$\times\ \$12.00/\text{hour overtime} \times \text{52 weeks} = \$12{,}480 \text{ (annual savings)}$$

Conclusion

A comparison of costs for both systems indicates that the HRS 60/EP would cost $2,200 more in first-year costs.

ARC 98 Costs

Net additional operating	$56,300
One-time (construction)	50,000
First-year total	$106,300

HRS 60/EP Costs

Net additional operating	$84,000
One-time (facility)	24,500
First-year total	$108,500

Installation of a second ARC 98 processor would permit the present information-processing systems to operate relatively smoothly and efficiently. It would not, however, provide the expanded processing capacity that the HRS 60/EP processor would for implementing new subsystems required to increase processing speed and Internet access.

Recommendation

The HRS 60/EP processor should be purchased because of the long-term savings and because its additional capacity and flexibility will allow for greater expansion in the future.

3

FIGURE 3–1. Feasibility Report (*continued*)

Report Sections

Every feasibility report should contain an introduction, a body, a conclusion, and a recommendation. See also proposals and formal reports (Tab 4).

Introduction.   The introduction states the purpose of the report, describes the circumstances that led to the report, and includes any pertinent background information. It may also discuss the scope of the report, any procedures or methods used in the analysis of alternatives, and any limitations of the study. See introductions (Tab 1).

Body.   The body of the report presents a detailed evaluation of all the alternatives under consideration. Evaluate each alternative according to specific criteria, such as cost, availability of staff and financing, and other relevant requirements, identifying the subsections with headings (Tab 5) to guide readers.

Conclusion.   The conclusion summarizes the available options and evaluates each alternative, pointing to one as the best or most feasible. See conclusions (Tab 1).

Recommendation.   This section clearly presents the writer's opinion on which alternative best meets the criteria as summarized in the conclusion.

investigative reports

Investigative reports may be written for a variety of reasons—most often in response to a request for information. You might be asked, for instance, to determine how your Web site compares to those of competing companies in your industry or to learn the level of satisfaction among your customers. An example of an investigative report is shown in Figure 3–2.

An investigative report gives a precise analysis of a topic and offers conclusions and recommendations. Open the report with a statement of its primary and (if any) secondary purposes, then define the scope of your investigation. (See also purpose, Tab 1, and scope, Tab 1.) If the report includes a survey of opinions, indicate the number of people surveyed, income categories, occupations, and other related information. Include any information that is pertinent in defining the extent of the investigation. Then report your findings and, if necessary, discuss their significance. End the report with your conclusions and any recommendations.

Memo

To: Noreen Rinaldo, Training Manager
From: Charles Lapinski, Senior Instructor   *CL*
Date: February 7, 2005
Subject: Adler's Basic English Program

As requested, I have investigated Adler Medical Instruments' (AMI's) Basic English Program to determine whether we might adopt a similar program.

The purpose of AMI's program is to teach medical technologists outside the United States who do not speak or read English to understand procedures written in a special 800-word vocabulary called *Basic English*. This program eliminates the need for AMI to translate its documentation into a number of different languages. The Basic English Program does not attempt to teach the medical technologists to be fluent in English but, rather, to recognize the 800 basic words that appear in Adler's documentation.

Course Requirements
The course does not train technologists. Students must know, in their own language, what a word like *hemostat* means; the course simply teaches them the English term for it. As prerequisites, students must have basic knowledge of their specialty, must be able to identify a part in an illustrated parts book, must have used AMI products for at least one year, and must be able to read and write in their own language.

Students are given an instruction manual, an illustrated book of equipment with parts and their English names, and pocket references containing the 800 words of the Basic English vocabulary plus the English names of parts. Students can write the corresponding word in their language beside the English word and then use the pocket reference as a bilingual dictionary. The course consists of 30 two-hour lessons, each lesson introducing approximately 27 words. No effort is made to teach pronunciation; the course teaches only recognition of the 800 words, which include 450 nouns, 70 verbs, 180 adjectives and adverbs, and 100 articles, prepositions, conjunctions, and pronouns.

Course Outcomes
The 800-word vocabulary enables the writers of documentation to provide medical technologists with any information that might be required because the subject areas are strictly limited to usage, troubleshooting, safety, and operation of AMI medical equipment. All nonessential words (such as *apple, father, mountain*, and so on) have been eliminated, as have most synonyms (for example, *under* appears, but *beneath* does not).

Conclusions and Recommendations
AMI's program appears to be quite successful, and a similar approach could also be appropriate for us. I see two possible ways in which we could use some or all of the elements of AMI's Program: (1) in the preparation of our student manuals or (2) as AMI uses the program.

I think it would be unnecessary to use the Basic English methods in the preparation of manuals for *all* of our students. Most of our students are English speakers to whom an unrestricted vocabulary presents no problem.

As for our initiating a program similar to AMI's, we could create our own version of the Basic English vocabulary and write our instructional materials in it. Because our product lines are much broader than AMI's, however, we would need to create illustrated parts books for each of the different product lines.

FIGURE 3–2. Investigative Report

newsletters

Newsletters are publications that are designed to inform and to create and sustain interest and membership in an organization. They can also be used to sell products and services. There are two main types of newsletters: organizational newsletters and subscription newsletters.

Organizational newsletters like the one shown in Figure 3–3 are sent to employees or members of an association to keep them informed

FIGURE 3–3. Company Newsletter (Front Page)

about issues regarding their company or group, such as the development of new products or policies, or the accomplishments of individuals or teams. Stories in organizational newsletters can also urge members to take a specific action. For example, a health club's newsletter could describe new equipment being installed, its purpose, and how to use it.

Subscription newsletters are designed to attract and build a readership interested in buying specific products or services or in learning more about investing or financial matters. Subscribers are buying information, and they expect a certain level of value for their money. For example, a person with experience in the stock market could create a financial newsletter and charge subscribers a monthly fee for the investing advice in that newsletter; a person who collects movie memorabilia could create an online newsletter that includes stories about ways to find and sell rare movie posters.

Before you begin to develop a newsletter, decide on its specific <u>purpose</u> (Tab 1) and the specific <u>readers</u> (Tab 1) you will be targeting; then make sure the newsletter's appearance and editorial choices create a sense of identification among the readership. Because newsletters often involve different individuals who work on design, content, and project management, see <u>collaborative writing</u> (Tab 1). See also <u>persuasion</u> (Tab 1) and <u>promotional writing</u> (Tab 1).

You will need to acquire a mailing list (names and addresses of your readers), and you will need to decide on the most strategic way to get the newsletter to the readers, whether through interoffice mail, the post office, or online. Because it can be time-consuming and technically problematic to send out hundreds or thousands of online newsletters by yourself, you may also need to subscribe to a list-hosting service.

As you develop and edit articles, you need to research the topics and interview relevant sources. As you research trade journals, business and technology magazines, newspapers, or the Internet, find specific angles for the articles that will appeal to your select audience. Attempt to provide content that they won't read elsewhere. Other strategies include interviewing and profiling customers or your employees. Be aware that your fact-checking needs to be meticulous. Unlike the general readership of a newspaper, newsletter readers are often specialists in their fields. Because newsletters are often distributed to branches and clients abroad, see <u>global communication</u> (Tab 1) and <u>global graphics</u> (Tab 5). See also <u>interviewing for information</u> (Tab 2) and <u>research</u> (Tab 2).

As shown in Figure 3–3, a newsletter's format should be simple and consistent, yet visually appealing to your readership. Use the active voice and a conversational tone. Boldface names of customers or association members included in your articles to identify them and bring attention to their contributions. Use subheadings and bullets to break up the text and make the newsletter easy to read. Keep your sentences simple and paragraphs short. See <u>layout and design</u> (Tab 5), <u>conciseness</u> (Tab 9), <u>tone</u> (Tab 9), and <u>voice</u> (Tab 11).

Using word-processing or desktop-publishing software, create newspaper columns and one or two visuals per page that complement the text. On the front page, identify the organization, and include the date, volume and issue numbers (if any), and a contents box. Depending on the length and quantity of the text and photographs or other visuals to be included, newsletters are usually 8½" × 11" or 17" × 22" pages folded in half. If your budget is generous and the scale of your project is substantial, you may want to work with a professional printer to produce your newsletter. See also photographs (Tab 5) and visuals (Tab 5).

policies and procedures

A policy states an organization's position on a subject; a procedure provides instructions for carrying out the policy. They are often written at the same time, usually by top or middle managers. Policies and procedures are subjected to a careful review process, often by legal staff. Writing these documents requires careful thought and planning as well as precise language and word choice (Tab 9) so that the policies and procedures are clear and understandable.

Policies

A statement of policy is often preceded by an explanation of the policy's purpose or rationale. Specific details then follow in numbered sections as in the following company policy regarding tuition refunds.

2. POLICY
   2.1 The Tuition Refund Plan is intended for all full-time staff.
   2.2 To receive a refund, an individual must be employed by the company at the time of enrollment and at the completion of the course. Should an individual's employment be terminated because of a reduction of staff, fees will be refunded for approved courses upon their satisfactory completion.
   2.3 Satisfactory completion means that the employee has completed the course work and has achieved a grade at least one level above passing. If a course is not satisfactorily completed, reimbursement may be deferred if the employee, upon completion of the degree, attains a cumulative grade average of at least C (B for most graduate-degree programs).

Policies may be kept in loose-leaf binders or posted on an organization's intranet Web site so that they can be easily referred to and updated.

Procedures

Procedures provide a step-by-step explanation of how to carry out a policy. They provide instructions not only for employees but also for managers who must ensure that the company's policy is properly implemented.

To prepare for writing procedures, keep track of who must do what. An easy and effective way is to create a chart, as shown in Figure 3–4. Draw a vertical line down a page. Label the left column "Actor" and the right "Directions." Under "Actor," list who must perform the action in each step; under "Directions," describe each step of the procedure. Describe each step fully and in the correct sequence. In effect, the list serves as an outline for the procedure you will write.

ACTOR	DIRECTIONS
Employee	Determines his or her eligibility for degree program, gains approval of manager, and submits request to Human Resources
Human Resources Department	Reviews request and, if reason is not obvious, asks manager to justify, in writing, the benefits of approving the degree program
Employee	Completes Sections I and II of Form F-6970
Human Resources Department	Sends form to the employee's supervisor and the head of the department for approval

FIGURE 3–4. Procedures Chart

3

progress and activity reports

Progress reports are often used to report on major workplace projects, whereas activity reports (also called *status reports*) focus on the work of individual employees.

Progress Reports

A progress report provides information about a project—its status, whether it is on schedule and within budget, and so on. Progress reports are often submitted by a contracting company to a client company, as shown in Figure 3–5. They are used mainly for projects that involve many steps over a period of time and are issued at regular intervals to state what has been done and what remains to be done. Progress reports help keep projects running smoothly by helping managers assign work, adjust schedules, allocate budgets, and order supplies and equipment. All progress reports for a particular project should have the same format.

Hobard Construction Company
9032 Salem Avenue
Lubbock, TX 79409

www.hobardcc.com
(808) 769-0832
Fax: (808) 769-5327

August 15, 2005

Walter M. Wazuski
County Administrator
109 Grand Avenue
Manchester, NH 03103

Subject: Progress Report 8 for July 1–July 29, 2005

Dear Mr. Wazuski:

The renovation of the County Courthouse is progressing on schedule and within budget. Although the cost of certain materials is higher than our original bid indicated, we expect to complete the project without exceeding the estimated costs because the speed with which the project is being completed will reduce overall labor expenses.

Costs
Materials used to date have cost $78,600, and labor costs have been $193,000 (including some subcontracted plumbing). Our estimate for the remainder of the materials is $59,000; remaining labor costs should not exceed $64,000.

Work Completed
As of August 12, we had finished the installation of the circuit-breaker panels and meters, of level-one service outlets, and of all subfloor wiring. The upgrading of the courtroom, the upgrading of the records-storage room, and the replacement of the air-conditioning units are in the preliminary stages.

Work Schedule
We have scheduled the upgrading of the courtroom to take place from August 29 to October 7, the upgrading of the records-storage room from October 11 to November 18, and the replacement of the air-conditioning units from November 21 to December 16. We see no difficulty in having the job finished by the scheduled date of December 23.

Sincerely yours,

Tran Nuguélen

Tran Nuguélen
ntran@hobardcc.com

FIGURE 3–5. Progress Report

INTEROFFICE MEMO

Date: June 6, 2005
To: Kathryn Hunter, Director of IT
From: Wayne Tribinski, Manager, Applications Programs   *WT*
Subject: Activity Report for May 2005

We are dealing with the following projects and problems, as of May 31.

Projects

1. For the *Software Training Mailing Campaign*, we anticipate producing a set of labels for mailing software training information to customers by June 10.
2. The *Search Project* is on hold until the PL/I training has been completed, probably by the end of June.
3. The project to provide a database for the *Information Management System* has been expanded in scope to provide a database for all training activities. We are rescheduling the project to take the new scope into account.

Problems

The *Information Management System* has been delayed. The original schedule was based on the assumption that a systems analyst who was familiar with the system would work on this project. Instead, the project was assigned to a newly hired systems analyst who was inexperienced and required much more learning time than expected.

Bill Michaels, whose activity report is attached, is correcting a problem in the *CNG Software*. This correction may take a week.

Plans for Next Month

- Complete the *Software Training Mailing Campaign.*
- Resume the *Search Project.*
- Restart the project to provide a database on information management with a schedule that reflects its new scope.
- Write a report to justify the addition of two software developers to my department.
- Congratulate publicly the recipients of Meritorious Achievement Awards: Bill Thomasson and Nancy O'Rourke.

Current Staffing Level

Current staff: 11
Open requisitions: 0

Attachment

FIGURE 3–6. Activity Report

The introduction to the first progress report should identify the project, any materials needed, and the project's completion date. Subsequent reports summarize the progress to date; include the status of schedules and costs; list the steps that remain to be taken; and conclude with recommendations about changes in the schedule, materials, and so on.

Activity Reports

Within an organization, employees often submit activity reports on the progress of ongoing projects. Managers may combine the activity reports of several individuals or teams into larger activity reports and, in turn, submit those larger reports to their own managers. The activity report shown in Figure 3–6 was submitted by a manager (Wayne Tribinski) who supervises eleven employees; the reader of the report (Kathryn Hunter) is Tribinski's manager.

Because the activity report is issued periodically (usually monthly) and contains material familiar to its readers, it normally needs no introduction or conclusion, although it may need a brief opening to provide context. (See also introductions, Tab 1.) Although format varies from company to company, the following sections are typical: Current Projects, Current Problems, Plans for the Next Period, and Current Staffing Level (for managers).

proposals

3

Business Writing
Documents
and Elements

DIRECTORY

A proposal is a document written to persuade readers (Tab 1) to follow a plan or course of action that you are proposing. (See also persuasion, Tab 1.) You may need to send a proposal to a colleague within your organization (an internal proposal) or to a potential customer or client outside the organization (an external or sales proposal). Often, you will collaborate with others in preparing a proposal.

Strategies

Regardless of the type of proposal you write, begin by considering its audience and purpose, the project management, and the proposal structure.

Audience and Purpose.   A proposal offers a plan to fill a need, and readers will evaluate your plan based on how well you answer their questions about what you are proposing to do, how you plan to do it, when you plan to do it, and how much it will cost. Because proposals often require more than one level of approval, take all your readers into account as you answer their questions. Consider especially their levels of technical knowledge of the subject. For example, if your primary reader is an expert on your subject but a supervisor who must also approve the proposal is not, provide an executive summary written in nontechnical language. You might also include a glossary of terms used in the body of the proposal or an appendix that explains highly detailed information in nontechnical language. If your primary reader is not an expert but a supervisor is, write the proposal with the nonexpert in mind and include an <u>appendix</u> (Tab 4) that contains the technical details.

Often the complicated task of writing a persuasive proposal can be simplified by composing a concise statement of exactly the problem or opportunity that your proposal is designed to address. Determining the problem that your proposal addresses helps you and your reader understand the value, scope, and limitations of your proposed solution. Doing so will also enable you to construct a clear statement of the proposal's <u>purpose</u> (Tab 1). Some readers even set requirements so proposals meet their needs.

Project Management.   Proposal writers are often faced with writing high-quality, persuasive proposals under tight organizational deadlines. Breaking the task down into manageable parts is the key to accomplishing your goal. For details about working with others on such writing projects, see <u>collaborative writing</u> (Tab 1).

Proposal Structure.   Proposals vary widely in length, formality, and structure. A short or medium-length proposal typically consists of an introduction, a body, and a conclusion.

INTRODUCTION.   The <u>introduction</u> (Tab 1) should state the purpose and scope of your proposal, as well as the problem you propose to solve and your solution to it. It should also indicate the dates on which you propose to begin and complete work, any special benefits of your proposed approach, and the cost of the project. For a sales (external) proposal, refer to any previous positive associations your organization has had with the potential client or customer.

BODY.   The body should offer the details of your solution to the problem and explain (1) the product or service you are offering, (2) how the job will be done, (3) how you will perform the work and any special materials you may use, (4) a schedule of when each phase of the project will be completed and (5) a breakdown of project costs.

CONCLUSION. The <u>conclusion</u> (Tab 1) should persuasively resell your proposal by emphasizing the benefits of your solution, product, or service over any competing ideas. Also include details about the time period during which the proposal is valid. Effective conclusions show confidence in your solution, your appreciation for the opportunity to submit the proposal, and your willingness to provide further information as well as encouraging your reader to act on your proposal.

TYPICAL SECTIONS. The list that follows describes the possible sections found in longer, more formal proposals. The number of sections in any particular proposal depends on the audience, the purpose, and the scope of the proposal, as well as on the standard practice within an organization. For more information on many of the following components, see <u>formal reports</u> (Tab 4).

FRONT MATTER
- *Copy of the Request for Proposals (RFP) or Invitation for Bids (IFB).* Include a copy of the RFP or IFB with a formal proposal.
- *Cover Letter or Letter of Transmittal.* In the <u>cover letter</u> (Tab 6), express appreciation for the opportunity to submit your proposal, any assistance from the customer, and any previous positive associations. Then summarize the proposal's recommendations and express confidence that they will satisfy the customer's needs.
- *Title Page.* Include the <u>title</u> of the proposal, the date, the organization to which it is being submitted, and your company name.
- *Table of Contents.* Include a <u>table of contents</u> (Tab 4) in longer proposals to guide readers to important headings, which should be listed according to beginning page numbers.
- *List of Figures.* If your proposal has six or more figures, include a list of figures with captions as well as figure and page numbers.

BODY
- *Executive Summary.* Briefly summarize the proposal's highlights in persuasive, nontechnical language for decision makers. See <u>executive summaries</u> (Tab 4).
- *Introduction.* Explain the reasons for the proposal; emphasize reader benefits; and, when appropriate, discuss your understanding of the problem. See <u>introductions</u> (Tab 1).
- *Background or Problem.* Describe the problem or opportunity your proposal addresses. To make your proposal more persuasive, your problem statement should illustrate how your proposal will benefit your client's organization.
- *Product Description.* If your proposal offers products as well as services, include a general description of the products and any technical specifications.

3

Business Writing Documents and Elements

- *Detailed Solutions (Rationale)*. Explain in a detailed section that will be read by technical specialists exactly how you plan to do what you are proposing.
- *Cost Analysis*. Itemize the estimated costs of all the products and services you are offering.
- *Delivery Schedule*. Outline how you will accomplish the work, and show a timetable for each phase of the project.
- *Staffing*. Summarize the expertise (education, experience, and certifications) of key personnel who will work on the project. Include their full <u>résumés</u> (Tab 7) in the appendix.
- *Site Preparation*. If your recommendations include modifying the customer's physical facilities, include a site-preparation description that details the required modifications.
- *Training Requirements*. If the products and services you are proposing require training the customer's employees, specify the required training and its cost.
- *Statement of Responsibilities*. To prevent misunderstandings about what you and your customer's responsibilities will be, state those responsibilities.
- *Organizational Sales Pitch*. Describe your company, its history, and its present position in the industry. An organizational sales pitch is designed to sell your company and its general capability in the field. It promotes the company and concludes the proposal on an upbeat persuasive note.
- *Authorization Request and Deadline*. Close with a request for approval and a deadline that explains how long the proposed prices are valid.
- *Conclusion*. Include a persuasive <u>conclusion</u> (Tab 1) that summarizes the proposal's key points and stresses your company's strong points.

BACK MATTER
- *Appendixes*. Provide résumés of key personnel or material of interest to some readers, such as statistical analysis and maps, in an <u>appendix</u> (Tab 4).
- *Bibliography*. List all sources consulted to prepare the proposal. See <u>bibliographies</u> (Tab 2) and <u>documenting sources</u> (Tab 2).
- *Glossary*. If your proposal contains terms that will be unfamiliar to your intended audience, list and define them in the <u>glossary</u> (Tab 4).

Internal Proposals

Two common types of internal proposals are often distinguished from each other by the frequency with which they are written and by the degree of change proposed.

Routine Internal Proposals. Routine internal proposals are common in most organizations. Usually in memo format, they typically include small spending requests, permission to hire new employees or increase salaries, and requests to attend conferences or purchase new equipment. (See also <u>memos</u>, Tab 6.) In writing these routine proposals, use the introduction-body-conclusion format, and highlight any benefits to be realized.

Formal Internal Proposals.   Formal internal proposals are often written to commit relatively large sums of money. These proposals have various names, but the most common designation is a *capital appropriations request* or a *capital appropriations proposal.* Figure 3–7 shows a typical formal internal proposal.

The introduction to a formal internal proposal should persuasively

---

ABO, Inc.
InterOffice Memo

To: Joan Marlow, Director, Human Resources Division
From: Leslie Galusha, Chief, Employee   *LG*
           Benefits Department
Date: June 13, 2005
Subject: Employee Fitness and Health-Care Costs

Health-care and worker-compensation insurance costs at ABO, Inc., have risen 100 percent over the last five years. In 2000, costs were $5,675 per employee per year; in 2005, they have reached $11,560 per employee per year. This doubling of costs mirrors a national trend, with health-care costs anticipated to continue to rise at the same rate for the next 10 years. Controlling these escalating expenses will be essential. They are eating into ABO's profit margin because the company currently pays 70 percent of the costs for employee coverage.

Healthy employees bring direct financial benefits to companies in the form of lower employee insurance costs, lower absenteeism rates, and reduced turnover. Regular physical exercise promotes fit, healthy people by reducing the risk of coronary heart disease, diabetes, osteoporosis, hypertension, and stress-related problems. I propose that to promote regular, vigorous physical exercise for our employees, ABO implement a health-care program that focuses on employee fitness. . . .

FIGURE 3–7. Introduction to a Formal Internal Proposal

Joan Marlow   2   June 13, 2005

Background

The U.S. Department of Health and Human Services recently estimated that health-care costs in the United States will triple by the year 2015. Corporate expenses for health care are rising at such a fast rate that, if unchecked, in eight years they will significantly erode corporate profits.

Researchers have found that people who do not participate in a regular and vigorous exercise program incur double the health-care costs and are hospitalized 30 percent more days than people who exercise regularly. Nonexercisers are also 41 percent more likely to submit medical claims over $10,000 at some point during their careers than are those who exercise regularly.

U.S. companies are recognizing this trend. Tenneco, Inc., for example, found that the average health-care claim for unfit men was $2,006 per illness compared with an average claim of $862 for those who exercised regularly. For women, the average claim for those who were unfit was $2,535, more than double the average claim of $1,039 for women who exercised. Additionally, Control Data Corporation found that nonexercisers cost the company an extra $515 a year in health-care expenses.

These figures are further supported by data from independent studies. A model created by the National Institutes of Health (NIH) estimates that the average white-collar company could save $596,000 annually in medical costs (per 1,000 employees) just by promoting wellness. NIH researchers estimated that for every $1 a firm invests in a health-care program, it saves up to $3.75 in health-care costs. Another NIH study of 667 insurance-company employees showed savings of $2.65 million over a five-year period. The same study also showed a 400-percent drop in absentee rates after the company implemented a company-wide fitness program.

Solution

The benefits of regular, vigorous physical activity for employees and companies are compelling. To achieve these benefits at ABO, I propose that we choose from one of two possible options: Build in-house fitness centers at our warehouse facilities, or offer employees several options for membership at a national fitness club.

FIGURE 3–7. Body of a Formal Internal Proposal (*continued*)

Joan Marlow   3   June 13, 2005

Conclusion and Recommendation
I recommend that ABO, Inc., participate in the corporate membership program at AeroFitness Clubs, Inc., by subsidizing employee memberships. By subsidizing memberships, ABO shows its commitment to the importance of a fit workforce. Club membership allows employees at all five ABO warehouses to participate in the program. The more employees who participate, the greater the long-term savings in ABO's health-care costs. Building and equipping fitness centers at all five warehouse sites would require an initial investment of nearly $2.5 million. These facilities would also occupy valuable floor space—on average, 4,000 square feet at each warehouse. Therefore, this option would be very costly.

Enrolling employees in the corporate program at AeroFitness would allow them to receive a one-month free trial membership. Those interested in continuing could then join the club and pay half of the one-time membership fee of $900 and receive a 30-percent discount on the $600 yearly fee. The other half of the membership fee ($450) would be paid for by ABO. If employees leave the company, they would have the option of purchasing ABO's share of the membership to continue at AeroFitness or selling their half of the membership to another ABO employee wishing to join AeroFitness.

Implementing this program will help ABO, Inc., reduce its health-care costs while building stronger employee relations by offering employees a desirable benefit. If this proposal is adopted, I have some additional thoughts about publicizing the program to encourage employee participation. I look forward to discussing the details of this proposal with you and answering any questions you may have.

FIGURE 3–7. Conclusion of a Formal Internal Proposal (*continued*)

3

Business Writing
Documents
and Elements

establish that a problem exists that needs a solution and provide any background information your reader needs to help him or her make the decision in question. The introduction should also briefly describe any supporting evidence you are including, such as a feasibility study you may have conducted. See also <u>feasibility reports</u>.

The body of a formal internal proposal should offer a practical solution to the problem; compare possible alternatives; respond to possible objections; and describe all the equipment, property, or services you are proposing to purchase and their key benefits to the organization. You should include any justifications for each expenditure: the calculated return on investment or the internal rate of return; the volume of use over, for example, the next two years; the product life expectancy, technical support, or warranties; and the most economical purchasing option.

The conclusion should emphasize the benefits of what you are proposing and express your willingness to provide any further information that may be required.

External Proposals

External proposals to be submitted to other companies or organizations could be either solicited or unsolicited.

Unsolicited and Solicited Proposals.   Unsolicited proposals are submitted to a company without a prior request for a proposal. Companies often operate for years with a problem they have never recognized (unnecessarily high maintenance costs, for example, or poor inventory-control methods). You might prepare an unsolicited proposal if you were convinced that the potential customer could realize substantial benefits by adopting your solution to a problem. Of course, you would need to convince the customer of the need for what you are proposing and that your solution would be the best one. Many unsolicited proposals are preceded by an inquiry to determine potential interest. If you receive a positive response, you would conduct a detailed study of the prospective customer's needs to determine whether you can be of help, and, if so, exactly how. You would then prepare your proposal on the basis of your study.

Solicited proposals are prepared in response to a request for goods or services. Procuring organizations that would like competing companies to bid for a job commonly issue a request for proposals (RFP) or an invitation for bids (IFB).

An IFB is commonly issued by government agencies to solicit bids on clearly defined products or services. An IFB is restrictive, binding the bidder to produce an item that meets the exact requirements of the agency. The goods or services to be procured are defined in the IFB by references to performance standards stated in specifications. Bidders must be prepared to prove that their product will meet all requirements of the specifications.

In contrast to an IFB, an RFP is flexible. It is negotiable, and it does not necessarily specify exactly what goods or services are required. Often an RFP will define a problem and allow those who respond to suggest possible solutions. Sometimes, RFPs are presented in several stages: (1) development of a concept, (2) construction of a prototype or mock-up, and (3) production of the device or plan selected.

The procuring organization generally publishes its IFB or RFP in trade journals, on its Web site, or in a specialized venue such as Federal Business Opportunities at <www.fedbizopps.gov/>.

Sales Proposals.   A persuasive sales proposal must demonstrate above all that the prospective customer's purchase of the seller's products or services will solve a problem, improve operations, or offer other benefits. Sales proposals vary greatly in size and sophistication—from several pages written by one person, to dozens of pages written collaboratively by several people, to hundreds of pages written by a team of professional proposal writers. A short sales proposal might bid for the construction of a single home, a moderate-length proposal might bid for the installation of a computer network, and a large proposal might bid for the construction of a multimillion-dollar water purification system.

✪ ETHICS NOTE Always keep in mind that, once submitted, a sales proposal is a legally binding document that promises to offer goods or services within a specified time and for a specified price.

Your first task in writing a sales proposal is to find out exactly what your prospective customer needs. To do that, survey your potential customer's business, and determine whether your organization can satisfy the customer's needs. Before preparing a sales proposal, try to find out who your principal competitors are. Then compare your company's strengths with those of the competing firms, determine your advantages over your competitors, and emphasize those advantages in your proposal.

🔆 **WEB LINK ANNOTATED SAMPLE SALES PROPOSAL**

For an annotated example of a full sales proposal, see <bedfordstmartins .com/alred> and select *Model Documents Gallery.*

3

Business Writing
Documents
and Elements

Grant and Research Proposals.   Grant and research proposals are written to request the approval of, and usually funding for, particular projects. For example, a professor of education might submit a research or grant proposal to the Department of Education to request funding for research on the relationship of class size to educational performance. Many government and private agencies solicit research and grant proposals. The granting agencies usually have their own requirements for format and content of the proposals submitted to them, but the proposals must always be persuasive. Tailor your grant or research proposal to your audience carefully by explaining the project's goals, your plan for achieving those goals, and your qualifications to perform the project.

Writer's Checklist: Writing Persuasive Proposals

☑ Analyze your audience carefully to determine how to best meet your readers' needs or requirements.

☑ Write a concise purpose statement to clarify your proposal's goals.

☑ Emphasize the proposal's benefits to readers and anticipate their questions or objections.

☑ Incorporate evidence to support the claims of your proposal.

☑ Break the writing task into manageable segments and develop a work schedule.

☑ Review the purpose of the proposal sections and their uses.

☑ Select an appropriate, visually appealing format. (See <u>layout and design</u>, Tab 5.)

☑ Use a confident, upbeat <u>tone</u> (Tab 9) throughout the proposal.

reports

A report is an organized presentation of factual information, often aimed at multiple audiences, that may present the results of an investigation, a trip, or a research project. For any report—whether formal or informal—assessing the readers' needs is essential. (See <u>readers</u>, Tab 1.) Following is a list of report entries in this book:

<u>feasibility reports</u>   <u>progress and activity reports</u>
<u>formal reports</u> (Tab 4)   <u>trip reports</u>
<u>investigative reports</u>   <u>trouble reports</u>

Formal reports often present the results of long-term projects or those that involve multiple participants. (See also <u>collaborative writing</u>, Tab 1.) Such projects may be done either for your own organization or as a contractual requirement for another organization. Formal reports generally follow a precise format and include such elements as <u>abstracts</u> (Tab 4) and <u>executive summaries</u> (Tab 4). See also <u>proposals</u>.

Informal and short reports normally run from a few paragraphs to a few pages and ordinarily include only an introduction, a body, conclusions, and (if necessary) recommendations. Because of their brevity, informal reports are customarily written as letters (if sent outside your organization) and memos or e-mails (if internal). See also <u>correspondence</u> (Tab 6), <u>e-mail</u> (Tab 6), and <u>memos</u> (Tab 6).

The <u>introduction</u> (Tab 1) announces the subject of the report, states its purpose, and gives any essential background information. It may also summarize the conclusions, findings, or recommendations made in the report. The body presents a clearly organized account of the report's subject—the results of a test carried out, the status of a project, and so on. The amount of detail to include depends on the complexity of the subject and on your readers' familiarity with it.

The conclusion (Tab 1) summarizes your findings and tells readers what you think their significance may be. In some reports, a final, separate section gives recommendations; in others, the conclusions and the recommendations sections are combined into one section. This final section makes suggestions for a course of action based on the conclusions you have reached. See also persuasion (Tab 1).

titles

Titles are important because many readers decide to read a document, such as a trade journal article, based solely on the title. The title of a report or other document should both state its topic and indicate its purpose (Tab 1) and scope (Tab 1), such as "Using Chaos Theory to Explain Small Business Growth Management." A title should be concise but not so short that it is not specific. For example, the title "Chaos Theory and Small Businesses" announces the topic of a report, but it does not answer important questions, such as "What is the relationship between chaos theory and small businesses?" and "What aspect of small business is explained by chaos theory?"

For guidelines on how to capitalize titles and when to use italics (Tab 12) and quotation marks (Tab 12), see those entries and capitalization (Tab 12).

trip reports

A trip report provides a permanent record of a business trip and its accomplishments. It provides managers essential information about the results of the trip and can enable many employees to benefit from the information.

A trip report is normally written as a memo (Tab 6) or an e-mail (Tab 6) and addressed to an immediate superior, as shown in Figure 3–8. The subject line identifies the destination and dates of the trip. The body of the report explains why you made the trip, whom you visited, and what you accomplished. The report should devote a brief section to each major event and may include a heading (Tab 5) for each section. You need not give equal space to each event — instead, elaborate on the more important events. Follow the body of the report with the appropriate conclusions and recommendations. Finally, a record of expenses is often attached to a trip report.

Subject: **Trip to Smith Electric Co., Huntington, West Virginia,**
                 January 2005
To: Roberto Camacho <rcamacho@psys.com>
From: James D. Kerson <jdkerson@psys.com>
Date: Fri, 14 Jan 2005 12:16:30 EST
Attachments: 📎 Expense Report.xls (25 KB)

I visited the Smith Electric Company in Huntington, West Virginia, to determine the cause of a recurring failure in a Model 247 printer and to fix it.

Problem
The printer stopped printing periodically for no apparent reason. Repeated efforts to bring it back online eventually succeeded, but the problem recurred at irregular intervals. Neither customer personnel operating the printer nor the local maintenance specialist was able to solve the problem.

Action
On January 3, I met with Ms. Ruth Bernardi, the Office Manager, who explained the problem. My troubleshooting did not reveal the cause of the problem then or on January 4.

Only when I tested the logic cable did I find that it contained a broken wire. I replaced the logic cable and then ran all the normal printer test patterns to make sure no other problems existed. All patterns were positive, so I turned the printer over to the customer.

Conclusion
There are over 12,000 of these printers in the field and to my knowledge this is the first occurrence of a bad cable. Therefore, I do not believe the logic cable problem found at Smith Electric Company warrants further investigation.

==================================
James D. Kerson, Maintenance Specialist
Printer Systems, Inc.
1366 Federal St., Allentown, PA 18101
(610) 747-9955 Fax: (610) 747-9956
jdkerson@psys.com
www.psys.com
==================================

FIGURE 3–8. Trip Report Sent as E-mail (with Attachment)

trouble reports

The trouble report is used to analyze such events as accidents, equipment failures, or health emergencies. For example, the report shown in Figure 3–9 describes an accident involving personal injury. The report assesses the causes of the problem and suggests changes necessary to prevent its recurrence. Because it is usually an internal document, the trouble report normally follows a simple memo format. See memos (Tab 6).

In the subject line of the memo, state the precise problem you are reporting. Then, in the body of the report, provide a detailed, precise description of the problem. What happened? Where and when did it occur? Was anybody hurt? Was there any property damage? Was there a work stoppage?

⚡ ETHICS NOTE Because insurance claims, worker's compensation awards, and even lawsuits may hinge on the information contained in a trouble report, be sure to include precise times, dates, locations, treatment of injuries, names of any witnesses, and any other crucial information. (Notice the careful use of language and factual detail in Figure 3–9.) Be thorough and accurate in your analysis of the problem and support any judgments or conclusions with facts. Be objective: always use a neutral tone (Tab 9) and avoid assigning blame. If you speculate about the cause of the problem, make it clear to your reader that you are speculating. See also ethics in writing (Tab 1).

In your conclusion, state what has been or will be done to correct the conditions that led to the problem. That may include training in safety practices, improved equipment, protective clothing, and so on.

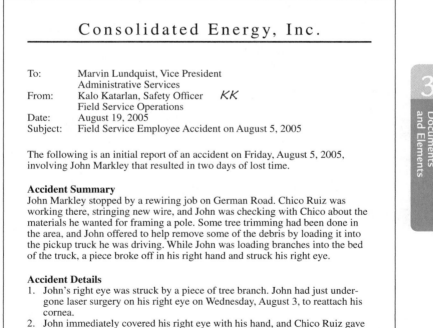

Consolidated Energy, Inc.

To: Marvin Lundquist, Vice President
           Administrative Services
From: Kalo Katarlan, Safety Officer   KK
           Field Service Operations
Date: August 19, 2005
Subject: Field Service Employee Accident on August 5, 2005

The following is an initial report of an accident on Friday, August 5, 2005, involving John Markley that resulted in two days of lost time.

Accident Summary
John Markley stopped by a rewiring job on German Road. Chico Ruiz was working there, stringing new wire, and John was checking with Chico about the materials he wanted for framing a pole. Some tree trimming had been done in the area, and John offered to help remove some of the debris by loading it into the pickup truck he was driving. While John was loading branches into the bed of the truck, a piece broke off in his right hand and struck his right eye.

Accident Details
1. John's right eye was struck by a piece of tree branch. John had just undergone laser surgery on his right eye on Wednesday, August 3, to reattach his cornea.
2. John immediately covered his right eye with his hand, and Chico Ruiz gave him a paper towel with ice to cover his eye and help ease the pain.

FIGURE 3–9. Trouble Report

7. On Thursday, August 11, John returned to his eye surgeon. Although bruised, his eye was not damaged, and the surgically implanted lens was still in place.

Recommendations
To prevent a recurrence of such an accident, the Safety Department will require the following actions in the future:

*   When working around and moving debris, such as tree limbs or branches, all service crew employees must wear safety eyewear with side shields.
*   All service crew employees must always consider the possibility of shock for an injured employee. If crew members cannot leave the job site to care for the injured employee, someone on the crew must call for assistance from the Service Center. The Service Center phone number is printed in each service crew member's Handbook.

FIGURE 3–9. Trouble Report (*continued*)

Formal
Reports

Preview

This section includes entries about the formal report and its components. Although the number and arrangement of elements in formal reports vary, often depending on an organization's preferred style, the guidelines given in the **formal reports** entry follow the most common pattern. This section also includes entries that provide more detailed guidance for preparing key sections often included in formal reports. A sample formal report (Figure 4–2) appears on pages 115–31. For specific types of reports and other documents that may be presented in formal-report form, see Tab 3, "Business Writing Documents and Elements."

abstracts

An abstract summarizes and highlights the major points of a <u>formal report</u>, trade journal article, dissertation, or other work. Its primary purpose is to enable readers to decide whether to read the work in full. For a discussion of how summaries differ from abstracts, see <u>executive summaries</u>.

Although abstracts, typically 200 to 250 words long, are published with the longer works they condense, they can also be published separately in periodical indexes and abstracting services (see <u>research</u>, Tab 2). For this reason, an abstract must be readable apart from the original document.

Depending on the kind of information they contain, abstracts are often classified as descriptive or informative. A *descriptive abstract* summarizes the purpose, scope, and methods used to arrive at the reported findings. It is a slightly expanded table of contents in sentence and paragraph form. A descriptive abstract need not be longer than several sentences. An *informative abstract* is an expanded version of the descriptive abstract. In addition to information about the <u>purpose</u> (Tab 1), <u>scope</u> (Tab 1), and research methods used, the informative abstract summarizes the results, conclusions, and any recommendations. The informative abstract retains the <u>tone</u> (Tab 9) and essential scope of the report, omitting its details. The first two paragraphs of the abstract shown in Figure 4–1 alone would be descriptive; with the addition of the paragraphs that detail the conclusions of the report, the abstract becomes informative.

The type of abstract you should write depends on your <u>readers</u> (Tab 1) and the organization or publication for which you are writing. Informative abstracts work best for wide audiences that need to know conclusions and recommendations; descriptive abstracts work best for compilations, such as proceedings and progress reports, that do not contain conclusions or recommendations.

Writing Style

Write the abstract *after* finishing the report or document. Otherwise, the abstract may not accurately reflect the longer work. Begin with a topic sentence that announces the subject and scope of your report or document. Then, using the major and minor headings of your <u>outline</u> (Tab 1) or <u>table of contents</u> to distinguish primary ideas from secondary ones, decide what material is relevant to your abstract. Write with clarity and <u>conciseness</u> (Tab 9), eliminating unnecessary words and ideas. (See Tab 9, "Style and Clarity.") Do not, however, become so terse that you omit articles (*a, an, the*) and important transitional words and

ABSTRACT

Purpose

This report investigates the long-term effects of long-distance running on the bones, joints, and general health of runners aged 50 to 72. The Sports Medicine Institute of Columbia Hospital sponsored this investigation, first to decide whether to add a geriatric unit to the Institute, and second to determine whether physicians should recommend long-distance running for their older patients.

Methods and scope

The investigation is based on recent studies conducted at Stanford University and the University of Florida. The Stanford study tested and compared male and female long-distance runners between 50 and 72 years of age with a control group of runners and nonrunners. The groups were also matched by sex, race, education, and occupation. The Florida study used only male runners who had run at least 20 miles a week for five years and compared them with a group of runners and nonrunners. Both studies based findings on medical histories and on physical and X-ray examinations.

Findings and conclusions

Both studies conclude that long-distance running is not associated with increased degenerative joint disease. Control groups were more prone to spur formation, sclerosis, and joint-space narrowing and showed more joint degeneration than runners. Female long-distance runners exhibited somewhat more sclerosis in knee joints and the lumbar spine area than matched control subjects. Both studies support the role of exercise in retarding bone loss with aging. The investigation concludes that the health risk factors are fewer for long-distance runners than for those less active between the ages of 50 and 72.

Recommendations

The investigation recommends that the Sports Medicine Institute of Columbia Hospital consider the development of a geriatric unit a priority and that it inform physicians that an exercise program that includes long-distance running can be beneficial to their patients' health.

iii

FIGURE 4–1. Informative Abstract

phrases (*however, therefore, but, in summary*). Write complete sentences, but avoid stringing a group of short sentences end to end; instead, combine ideas by using <u>subordination</u> (Tab 9) and <u>parallel structure</u> (Tab 9). Spell out all but the most common <u>abbreviations</u> (Tab 12). Typically, in a formal report, an abstract follows the title page and is numbered page iii.

appendixes

An appendix, located at the end of a <u>formal report</u>, a <u>proposal</u> (Tab 3), or other major document, supplements or clarifies the information in the body of the document. Appendixes (or *appendices*) can provide information that is too detailed or lengthy for the primary audience of the document. For example, an appendix could contain material of interest to secondary <u>readers</u> (Tab 1), such as maps, statistical analysis, or résumés of key personnel involved in a proposed project.

A document may have more than one appendix, with each offering only one type of information. When the document contains more than one appendix, arrange them in the order they are mentioned in the text. Begin each appendix on a new page, and identify each with a letter, starting with the letter A ("Appendix A: Sample Questionnaire"). If you have only one appendix, title it simply "Appendix." List the titles and beginning page numbers of the appendixes in the <u>table of contents</u>.

executive summaries

An executive summary consolidates the principal points of a report or proposal. Executive summaries differ from <u>abstracts</u> in that readers scan abstracts to decide whether to read the work in full. However, they often read an executive summary instead of reading the longer work, so it must accurately and concisely reflect the original document. Executive summaries tend to be about 10 percent the length of the documents they summarize and generally follow the same sequence.

Write the executive summary so that it can be read independently of the report or proposal. Do not refer by number to figures, tables, or references contained elsewhere in the document. Executive summaries may occasionally include a figure, table, or footnote if that information is essential to the summary. For an example, see the executive summary in Figure 4–2 on page 119.

Writer's Checklist: Writing Executive Summaries

☑ Write the executive summary after you have completed the original document.

☑ Avoid using terminology that may not be familiar to your readers.

☑ Spell out all uncommon symbols and abbreviations because executive summaries frequently are read in place of the full document.

4

Formal Reports

Writer's Checklist: Writing Executive Summaries (continued)

☑ Make the summary concise, but do not omit transitional words and phrases (*however, moreover, therefore, for example, in summary*).

☑ Include only information discussed in the original document.

☑ Place the executive summary at the very beginning of the body of the report, as described in **formal reports**.

formal reports

Formal reports are usually written accounts of major projects that require substantial <u>research</u> (Tab 2), and they often involve more than one writer. See also <u>collaborative writing</u> (Tab 1).

Most formal reports are divided into three primary parts—front matter, body, and back matter—each of which contains a number of elements. The number and arrangement of the elements may vary, depending on the subject, the length of the report, and the kinds of material covered. Further, many organizations have a preferred style for formal reports and furnish guidelines for report writers to follow. If you are not required to follow a specific style, use the format recommended in this entry. The following list includes most of the elements a formal report might contain, in the order they typically appear. (The items shown with page numbers appear in Figure 4–2 on pages 115–31.) Often, a <u>cover letter</u> (Tab 6) precedes the front matter and identifies the report by title, the person or persons to whom it is being sent, and the reason it was written.

FRONT MATTER
Title page   (116)
Abstract   (117)
Table of contents   (118)
List of figures
List of tables
Foreword
Preface
List of abbreviations and symbols

BODY
Executive summary   (119)
Introduction   (121)
Text (including headings)   (124)
Conclusions   (129)
Recommendations   (129)
Explanatory notes
References (or Works Cited)   (131)

BACK MATTER
Appendixes
Bibliography
Glossary
Index

Front Matter

The front matter serves several functions: it gives the readers a general idea of the writer's purpose, it gives an overview of the type of information in the report, and it lists where specific information is covered in the report. Not all formal reports include every element of front matter described here. A title page and table of contents are usually mandatory, but the scope of the report and its intended audience determine whether the other elements are included.

Title Page.   Although the formats of title pages may vary, they may include the following items:

- *The full title of the report.* The title describes the topic, <u>scope</u> (Tab 1), and <u>purpose</u> (Tab 1) of the report, as described in <u>titles</u> (Tab 3).
- *The name of the writer(s), principal investigator(s), or compiler(s).* Sometimes contributors identify themselves by their job title in the organization or by their tasks in contributing to the report (Gina Hobbs, Principal Investigator).
- *The date or dates of the report.* For one-time reports, the date shown is the date the report is distributed. For periodic reports (monthly, quarterly, or yearly), the subtitle shows the period that the report covers. Elsewhere on the title page, the date shown is the date the report is distributed.
- *The name of the organization for which the writer(s) works.*
- *The name of the organization to which the report is being submitted.* This information is included if the report is written for a customer or client.

The title page, although unnumbered, is considered page i. The back of the title page, which is blank and unnumbered, is considered page ii, and the abstract falls on page iii. The body of the report begins with Arabic number 1, and a new chapter or large section typically begins on a new right-hand (odd-numbered) page. Reports with printing on only one side of each sheet can be numbered consecutively regardless of where new sections begin. Center page numbers at the bottom of the page throughout the report.

Abstract.   An <u>abstract</u>, which normally follows the title page, highlights the major points of the report, enabling readers to decide whether to read the report.

4

Formal Reports

Table of Contents.   A <u>table of contents</u> lists all the major sections or <u>headings</u> (Tab 5) of the report in their order of appearance, along with their page numbers.

List of Figures.   When a report contains more than five figures, list them, along with their page numbers, in a separate section beginning on a new page immediately following the table of contents. Number figures consecutively with Arabic numbers. Figures include all visuals — drawings, photographs, maps, charts, and graphs — contained in the report. See Tab 5, "Design and Visuals."

List of Tables.   When a report contains more than five <u>tables</u> (Tab 5), list them, along with their titles and page numbers, in a separate section immediately following the list of figures (if there is one). Number tables consecutively with Arabic numbers.

Foreword.   A foreword is an optional introductory statement about a formal report or book that is written by someone other than the author(s). The foreword author is usually an authority in the field or an executive of the organization sponsoring the report. The foreword author's name and affiliation appear at the end of the foreword, along with the date it was written. The foreword generally provides background information about the publication's significance and places it in the context of other works in the field. The foreword precedes the preface when a work has both.

Preface.   The preface, another type of optional introductory statement, is written by the author(s) of the book or formal report. The preface may announce the work's purpose, scope, and background (including any special circumstances leading to the work). A preface may also specify the audience for a work, it may contain acknowledgments of those who helped in its preparation, and it may cite permission obtained for the use of copyrighted works. See also <u>copyright</u> (Tab 2).

List of Abbreviations and Symbols.   When the report uses numerous <u>abbreviations</u> (Tab 12) and symbols and there is a chance that readers will not be able to interpret them, the front matter may include a section that lists symbols and abbreviations with their meanings.

Body

The body is the section of the report that describes in detail the methods and procedures used to generate the report, demonstrates how results were obtained, describes the results, draws conclusions, and, if appropriate, makes recommendations.

4

Formal Reports

Executive Summary.   The body of the report begins with the <u>ex-ecutive summary</u>, which provides a more complete overview of the re-port than an abstract does.

Introduction.   The <u>introduction</u> (Tab 1) gives readers any general in-formation, such as the report's purpose and scope, necessary to under-stand the detailed information in the rest of the report.

Text.   The text of the body presents, as appropriate, the details of how the topic was investigated, how a problem was solved, what alternatives were explored, and how the best choice among them was selected. This information is enhanced by the use of illustrations, tables, and refer-ences that both clarify and persuade the reader.

Conclusions.   The conclusions section pulls together the results of the research and offers conclusions based on the analysis. See <u>conclu-sions</u> (Tab 1).

Recommendations.   Recommendations, which are sometimes combined with the conclusions, state what course of action should be taken based on the earlier arguments and conclusions of the study. The recommendations section may state, for example, "We should pursue new markets in . . ." or "I recommend we expand our marketing efforts on the Internet by . . ."

Explanatory Notes.   Occasionally, reports contain notes that am-plify terms or points for some readers that would be a distraction for others. If such notes are not included as footnotes on the page where the term or point appears, they may appear in a final "Notes" section.

References (or Works Cited).   A list of references or works cited appears in a separate section if the report refers to material in, or quotes directly from, published works or other research sources, including on-line sources. If your employer has a preferred reference style, follow it;

DIGITAL TIP AUTOMATING REPORT FORMATTING

Use your word-processing software to create style sheets to automate for-matting for your reports. Once you've specified the format guidelines, save them as a file and use them each time you create a formal report. You can automate and make consistent elements such as fonts and font sizes, para-graphs, lists, columns, and tables of contents. For more on this topic, see <bedfordstmartins.com/alred> and select *Digital Tips*, "Automating Report Formatting."

4

Formal Reports

otherwise, use the guidelines provided in the entry <u>documenting sources</u> (Tab 2). For a relatively short report, place the references at the end of the body of the report. For a report with a number of sections or chapters, place the reference section at the end of each major section or chapter. In either case, title the reference or works-cited section as such and begin it on a new page. If a particular reference appears in more than one section or chapter, repeat it in full in each appropriate reference section. See also <u>plagiarism</u> (Tab 2) and <u>quotations</u> (Tab 2).

Back Matter

The back matter of a formal report contains supplementary material, such as where to find additional information about the topic (bibliography), and expands on certain subjects (appendixes). Other back-matter elements clarify the terms used (glossary) and provide information on how to easily locate information in the report (index). For very large formal reports, back-matter sections may be individually numbered.

Appendixes.   An <u>appendix</u> clarifies or supplements the body with information that is too detailed or lengthy for the primary audience but that is relevant to secondary audiences.

Bibliography.   A <u>bibliography</u> (Tab 2) is an alphabetical list of all sources that were consulted (not just those cited) in researching the report. A bibliography is not necessary if the reference listing contains a complete list of sources.

Glossary.   A <u>glossary</u> is an alphabetical list of specialized terms used in the report and their definitions.

Index.   An index is an alphabetical list of all the major topics and subtopics discussed in the report. It cites the page numbers where discussion of each topic can be found and allows readers to find information on topics quickly and easily. The index is always the final section of a report.

Sample Formal Report

The following sample shows the typical sections of a <u>formal report</u>. Keep in mind that the number and arrangement of the elements vary, depending on the specific subject and requirements of an organization or a client.

 WEB LINK **ANNOTATED SAMPLE FORMAL REPORT**

For an annotated version of this formal report, see <bedfordst martins.com/alred> and select *Model Documents Gallery.*

CGF Aircraft Corporation
Memo

To: Members of the Ethics and Business Conduct Committee   *SL*
From: Susan Litzinger, Director of Ethics and Business Conduct
Date: March 4, 2005
Subject: Reported Ethics Cases, 2004

Enclosed is the annual Ethics and Business Conduct Report, as required by
CGF Policy CGF-EP-01, for your evaluation, covering the first year of our
Ethics Program. This report contains a review of the ethics cases handled
by CGF ethics officers and managers during 2004.

The ethics cases reported are analyzed according to two categories:
(1) major ethics cases, or those potentially involving serious violations
of company policy or illegal conduct, and (2) minor ethics cases, or those
that do not involve serious policy violations or illegal conduct. The report
also examines the mode of contact in all of the reported cases and the
disposition of the substantiated major ethics cases.

It is my hope that this report will provide the Committee with the information needed to assess the effectiveness of the first year of CGF's Ethics
Program and to plan for the coming year. Please let me know if you have
any questions about this report or if you need any further information. I
may be reached at (555) 211-2121 and by e-mail at <sl@cgf.com>.

Enc.

FIGURE 4–2. Cover Letter for a Formal Report. Reprinted and adapted by permission of Susan Litzinger, a student at Pennsylvania State University, Altoona.

REPORTED ETHICS CASES
Annual Report, 2004

Prepared by Susan Litzinger
Director of Ethics and Business Conduct

Report Distributed March 4, 2005

Prepared for
The Ethics and Business Conduct Committee
CGF Aircraft Corporation

FIGURE 4–2. Title Page for a Formal Report (*continued*)

Reported Ethics Cases — 2004

ABSTRACT

This report examines the nature and disposition of 3,458 ethics cases handled companywide by CGF Aircraft Corporation's ethics officers and managers during 2004. The purpose of this annual report is to provide the Ethics and Business Conduct Committee with the information necessary for assessing the effectiveness of the Ethics Program's first year of operation. Records maintained by ethics officers and managers of all contacts were compiled and categorized into two main types: (1) major ethics cases, or cases involving serious violations of company policies or illegal conduct, and (2) minor ethics cases, or cases not involving serious policy violations or illegal conduct. This report provides examples of the types of cases handled in each category and analyzes the disposition of 30 substantiated major ethics cases. Recommendations for planning for the second year of the Ethics Program are (1) continuing the channels of communication now available in the Ethics Program, (2) increasing financial and technical support for the Ethics Hotline, (3) disseminating the annual ethics report in some form to employees to ensure employee awareness of the company's commitment to uphold its Ethics Policies and Procedures, and (4) implementing some measure of recognition for ethical behavior to promote and reward ethical conduct.

iii

FIGURE 4–2. Abstract for a Formal Report (*continued*)

250 words

Descriptive/
Inform.
1. Purpose
2. methods/scope
3. findings/conclusions
4. Recommendations

Reported Ethics Cases — 2004

TABLE OF CONTENTS

iv

FIGURE 4–2. Table of Contents for a Formal Report (*continued*)

Reported Ethics Cases — 2004

EXECUTIVE SUMMARY

This report examines the nature and disposition of the 3,458 ethics cases handled by the CGF Aircraft Corporation's ethics officers and managers during 2004. The purpose of this report is to provide CGF's Ethics and Business Conduct Committee with the information necessary for assessing the effectiveness of the first year of the company's Ethics Program.

Effective January 1, 2004, the Ethics and Business Conduct Committee (the Committee) implemented a policy and procedures for the administration of CGF's new Ethics Program. The purpose of the Ethics Program, established by the Committee, is to "promote ethical business conduct through open communication and compliance with company ethics standards." The Office of Ethics and Business Conduct was created to administer the Ethics Program. The director of the Office of Ethics and Business Conduct, along with seven ethics officers throughout the corporation, was given the responsibility for the following objectives:

- Communicate the values and standards for CGF's Ethics Program to employees.

- Inform employees about company policies regarding ethical business conduct.

- Establish companywide channels for employees to obtain information and guidance in resolving ethics concerns.

- Implement companywide ethics-awareness and education programs.

Employee accessibility to ethics information and guidance was available through managers, ethics officers, and an ethics hotline.

Major ethics cases were defined as those situations potentially involving serious violations of company policies or illegal conduct. Examples of major ethics cases included cover-up of defective workmanship or use of defective parts in products; discrimination in hiring and promotion; involvement in monetary or other kickbacks; sexual harassment; disclosure of proprietary or company information; theft; and use of corporate Internet resources for inappropriate purposes, such as conducting personal business, gambling, or access to pornography.

1

FIGURE 4–2. Executive Summary for a Formal Report (*continued*)

4

Formal Reports

Reported Ethics Cases — 2004

Minor ethics cases were defined as including all reported concerns not classified as major ethics cases. Minor ethics cases were classified as informational queries from employees, situations involving coworkers, and situations involving management.

The effectiveness of CGF's Ethics Program during the first year of implementation is most evidenced by (1) the active participation of employees in the program and the 3,458 contacts employees made regarding ethics concerns through the various channels available to them, and (2) the action taken in the cases reported by employees, particularly the disposition of the 30 substantiated major ethics cases. Disseminating information about the disposition of ethics cases, particularly information about the severe disciplinary actions taken in major ethics violations, sends a message to employees that unethical or illegal conduct will not be tolerated.

Based on these conclusions, recommendations for planning the second year of the Ethics Program are (1) continuing the channels of communication now available in the Ethics Program, (2) increasing financial and technical support for the Ethics Hotline, the most highly utilized mode of contact in the ethics cases reported in 2004, (3) disseminating this report in some form to employees to ensure their awareness of CGF's commitment to uphold its Ethics Policy and Procedures, and (4) implementing some measure of recognition for ethical behavior, such as an "Ethics Employee of the Month" award to promote and reward ethical conduct.

2

FIGURE 4–2. Executive Summary for a Formal Report (*continued*)

Reported Ethics Cases — 2004

INTRODUCTION

This report examines the nature and disposition of the 3,458 ethics cases handled companywide by CGF's ethics officers and managers during 2004. The purpose of this report is to provide the Ethics and Business Conduct Committee with the information necessary for assessing the effectiveness of the first year of CGF's Ethics Program. Recommendations are given for the Committee's consideration in planning for the second year of the Ethics Program.

Ethics and Business Conduct Policy and Procedures

Effective January 1, 2004, the Ethics and Business Conduct Committee (the Committee) implemented Policy CGF-EP-01 and Procedure CGF-EP-02 for the administration of CGF's new Ethics Program. The purpose of the Ethics Program, established by the Committee, is to "promote ethical business conduct through open communication and compliance with company ethics standards" (CGF, "Ethics and Conduct").

The Office of Ethics and Business Conduct was created to administer the Ethics Program. The director of the Office of Ethics and Business Conduct, along with seven ethics officers throughout CGF, was given the responsibility for the following objectives:

- Communicate the values, standards, and goals of CGF's Ethics Program to employees.

- Inform employees about company ethics policies.

- Provide companywide channels for employee education and guidance in resolving ethics concerns.

- Implement companywide programs in ethics awareness, education, and recognition.

- Ensure confidentiality in all ethics matters.

Employee accessibility to ethics information and guidance became the immediate and key goal of the Office of Ethics and Business Conduct in its first year of operation. The following channels for contact were set in motion during 2004:

3

FIGURE 4–2. Introduction to a Formal Report (*continued*)

Reported Ethics Cases — 2004

- Managers throughout CGF received intensive ethics training; in all ethics situations, employees were encouraged to go to their managers as the first point of contact.
- Ethics officers were available directly to employees through face-to-face or telephone contact, to managers, to callers using the ethics hotline, and by e-mail.
- The Ethics Hotline was available to all employees, 24 hours a day, 7 days a week, to anonymously report ethics concerns.

Confidentiality Issues

CGF's Ethics Policy ensures confidentiality and anonymity for employees who raise genuine ethics concerns. Procedure CGF-EP-02 guarantees appropriate discipline, up to and including dismissal, for retaliation or retribution against any employee who properly reports any genuine ethics concern.

Documentation of Ethics Cases

The following requirements were established by the director of the Office of Ethics and Business Conduct as uniform guidelines for the documentation by managers and ethics officers of all reported ethics cases:

- Name, position, and department of individual initiating contact, if available
- Date and time of contact
- Name, position, and department of contact person
- Category of ethics case
- Mode of contact
- Resolution

Managers and ethics officers entered the required information in each reported ethics case into an ACCESS database file, enabling efficient retrieval and analysis of the data.

4

FIGURE 4–2. Introduction to a Formal Report (*continued*)

4

Formal Reports

Reported Ethics Cases—2004

Major/Minor Category Definition and Examples

Major ethics cases were defined as those situations potentially involving serious violations of company policies or illegal conduct. Procedure CGF-EP-02 requires notification of the Internal Audit and the Law Departments in serious ethics cases. The staffs of the Internal Audit and the Law Departments assume primary responsibility for managing major ethics cases and for working with the employees, ethics officers, and managers involved in each case.

Examples of situations categorized as major ethics cases:

- Cover-up of defective workmanship or use of defective parts in products
- Discrimination in hiring and promotion
- Involvement in monetary or other kickbacks from customers for preferred orders
- Sexual harassment
- Disclosure of proprietary customer or company information
- Theft
- Use of corporate Internet resources for inappropriate purposes, such as conducting private business, gambling, or gaining access to pornography

Minor ethics cases were defined as including all reported concerns not classified as major ethics cases. Minor ethics cases were classified as follows:

- Informational queries from employees
- Situations involving coworkers
- Situations involving management

5

FIGURE 4–2. Introduction to a Formal Report (*continued*)

4

Formal Reports

Reported Ethics Cases—2004

ANALYSIS OF REPORTED ETHICS CASES

Reported Ethics Cases by Major/Minor Category

CGF ethics officers and managers companywide handled a total of 3,458 ethics situations during 2004. Of these cases, only 172, or 5 percent, involved reported concerns of a serious enough nature to be classified as major ethics cases (see Figure 1). Major ethics cases were defined as those situations potentially involving serious violations of company policy or illegal conduct.

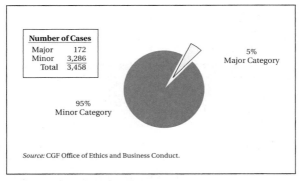

Number of Cases	
Major	172
Minor	3,286
Total	3,458

5%
Major Category

95%
Minor Category

Source: CGF Office of Ethics and Business Conduct.

Figure 1.   Reported ethics cases by major/minor category in 2004.

Major Ethics Cases

Of the 172 major ethics cases reported during 2004, 57 percent, upon investigation, were found to involve unsubstantiated concerns. Incomplete information or misinformation most frequently was discovered to be the cause of the unfounded concerns of misconduct in 98 cases. Forty-four cases, or 26 percent of the total cases reported, involved incidents partly substantiated by ethics officers as serious misconduct; however, these cases were discovered to also involve inaccurate information or unfounded issues of misconduct.

6

FIGURE 4–2. Body of a Formal Report (*continued*)

Reported Ethics Cases — 2004

Only 17 percent of the total number of major ethics cases, or 30 cases, were substantiated as major ethics situations involving serious ethical misconduct or illegal conduct (CGF, "2004 Ethics Hotline Results") (see Figure 2).

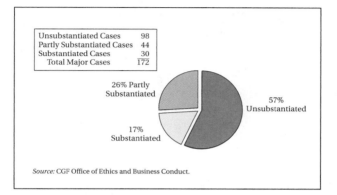

Unsubstantiated Cases	98
Partly Substantiated Cases	44
Substantiated Cases	30
Total Major Cases	172

26% Partly Substantiated

57% Unsubstantiated

17% Substantiated

Source: CGF Office of Ethics and Business Conduct.

Figure 2.   Major ethics cases in 2004.

Of the 30 substantiated major ethics cases, seven remain under investigation at this time, and two cases are currently in litigation. Disposition of the remainder of the 30 substantiated reported ethics cases included severe disciplinary action in five cases: the dismissal of two employees and the demotion of three employees. Seven employees were given written warnings, and nine employees received verbal warnings (see Figure 3).

FIGURE 4–2. Body of a Formal Report (*continued*)

Reported Ethics Cases — 2004

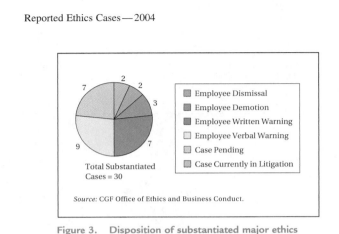

Figure 3.   Disposition of substantiated major ethics cases in 2004.

Minor Ethics Cases

Minor ethics cases included those that did not involve serious violations of company policy or illegal conduct. During 2004, ethics officers and company managers handled 3,286 such cases. Minor ethics cases were further classified as follows:

• Informational queries from employees

• Situations involving coworkers

• Situations involving management

As might be expected during the initial year of the Ethics Program implementation, the majority of contacts made by employees were informational, involving questions about the new policies and procedures. These informational contacts comprised 65 percent of all contacts of a minor nature and numbered 2,148. Employees made 989 contacts regarding ethics concerns involving coworkers and 149 contacts regarding ethics concerns involving management (see Figure 4).

8

FIGURE 4–2. Body of a Formal Report (*continued*)

Reported Ethics Cases — 2004

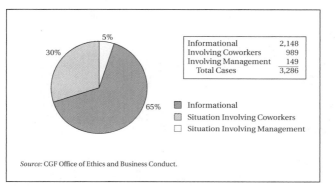

Informational	2,148
Involving Coworkers	989
Involving Management	149
Total Cases	3,286

■ Informational
▦ Situation Involving Coworkers
☐ Situation Involving Management

Source: CGF Office of Ethics and Business Conduct.

Figure 4.   Minor ethics cases in 2004.

Mode of Contact

The effectiveness of the Ethics Program rested on the dissemination of information to employees and the provision of accessible channels through which employees could gain information, report concerns, and obtain guidance. Employees were encouraged to first go to their managers with any ethical concerns, because those managers would have the most direct knowledge of the immediate circumstances and individuals involved.

Other channels were put into operation, however, for any instance in which an employee did not feel able to go to his or her manager. The ethics officers companywide were available to employees through telephone conversations, face-to-face meetings, and e-mail contact. Ethics officers also served as contact points for managers in need of support and assistance in handling the ethics concerns reported to them by their subordinates.

The Ethics Hotline became operational in mid-January 2004 and offered employees assurance of anonymity and confidentiality. The Ethics Hotline was accessible to all employees on a 24-hour, 7-day basis. Ethics officers companywide took responsibility on a rotational basis for handling calls reported through the hotline.

9

FIGURE 4–2. Body of a Formal Report (*continued*)

Reported Ethics Cases—2004

In summary, ethics information and guidance was available to all employees during 2004 through the following channels:

- Employee to manager
- Employee telephone, face-to-face, and e-mail contact with ethics officer
- Manager to ethics officer
- Employee Hotline

The mode of contact in the 3,458 reported ethics cases was as follows (see
Figure 5):

- In 19 percent of the reported cases, or 657, employees went to managers with concerns.
- In 9 percent of the reported cases, or 311, employees contacted an
  ethics officer.
- In 5 percent of the reported cases, or 173, managers sought assistance
  from ethics officers.
- In 67 percent of the reported cases, or 2,317, contacts were made
  through the Ethics Hotline.

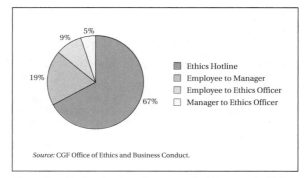

Source: CGF Office of Ethics and Business Conduct.

Figure 5.   Mode of contact in reported ethics cases in 2004.

10

FIGURE 4–2. Body of a Formal Report (*continued*)

Reported Ethics Cases — 2004

CONCLUSIONS AND RECOMMENDATIONS

The effectiveness of CGF's Ethics Program during the first year of implementation is most evidenced by (1) the active participation of employees in the program and the 3,458 contacts employees made regarding ethics concerns through the various channels available to them, and (2) the action taken in the cases reported by employees, particularly the disposition of the 30 substantiated major ethics cases.

One of the 12 steps to building a successful Ethics Program identified by Frank Navran in *Workforce* magazine is an ethics communication strategy. Navran explains that such a strategy is crucial in ensuring

> that employees have the information they need in a timely and usable fashion and that the organization is encouraging employee communication regarding the values, standards and the conduct of the organization and its members. (Navran 119)

The 3,458 contacts by employees during 2004 attest to the accessibility and effectiveness of the communication channels that exist in CGF's Ethics Program.

An equally important step in building a successful ethics program is listed by Navran as "Measurements and Rewards," which he explains as follows:

> In most organizations, employees know what's important by virtue of what the organization measures and rewards. If ethical conduct is assessed and rewarded, and if unethical conduct is identified and dissuaded, employees will believe that the organization's principals mean it when they say the values and code of ethics are important. (Navran 121)

Disseminating information about the disposition of ethics cases, particularly information about the severe disciplinary actions taken in major ethics violations, sends a message to employees that unethical or illegal conduct will not be tolerated. Making public the tough-minded actions taken in cases of ethical misconduct provides "a golden opportunity to make other employees aware that the behavior is unacceptable and why" (Ferrell and Gardiner 129).

11

FIGURE 4–2. Conclusions and Recommendations for a Formal Report (*continued*)

Reported Ethics Cases — 2004

With these two points in mind, I offer the following recommendations for consideration for plans for the Ethics Program's second year:

- Continuation of the channels of communication now available in the Ethics Program

- Increased financial and technical support for the Ethics Hotline, the most highly utilized mode of contact in the reported ethics cases in 2004

- Dissemination of this report in some form to employees to ensure employees' awareness of CGF's commitment to uphold its Ethics Policy and Procedures

- Implementation of some measure of recognition for ethical behavior, such as an "Ethics Employee of the Month," to promote and reward ethical conduct

To ensure that employees see the value of their continued participation in the Ethics Program, feedback is essential. The information in this annual review, in some form, should be provided to employees. Knowing that the concerns they reported were taken seriously and resulted in appropriate action by Ethics Program administrators would reinforce employee involvement in the program. While the negative consequences of ethical misconduct contained in this report send a powerful message, a means of communicating the *positive* rewards of ethical conduct at CGF should be implemented. Various options for recognition of employees exemplifying ethical conduct should be considered and approved.

Continuation of the Ethics Program's successful 2004 operations, with the implementation of the above recommendations, should ensure the continued pursuit of the Ethics Program's purpose: "to promote a positive work environment that encourages open communication regarding ethics and compliance issues and concerns."

12

FIGURE 4–2. Conclusions and Recommendations for a Formal Report (*continued*)

Reported Ethics Cases — 2004

WORKS CITED

CGF. "Ethics and Conduct at CGF Aircraft Corporation." 1 Jan. 2004.

11 Feb. 2005. <www.cgfac.com/aboutus/ethics.html>.

---. "2004 Ethics Hotline Investigation Results." 15 Jan. 2005. 11 Feb.

2005. <www.cgfac.com/html/ethics.html>.

Ferrell, O. C., and Gareth Gardiner. In Pursuit of Ethics: Tough Choices in

the World of Work. Springfield, IL: Smith Collins, 1991.

Kelley, Tina. "Corporate Prophets, Charting a Course to Ethical Profits."

New York Times 8 Feb. 1998: BU12.

Navran, Frank. "12 Steps to Building a Best-Practices Ethics Program."

Workforce Sept. 1997: 117-22.

13

FIGURE 4–2. Works Cited for a Formal Report (*continued*)

glossaries

A glossary is an alphabetical list of definitions of specialized terms used in a <u>formal report</u>, a manual, or another long document.

If you are writing a document that will go to readers who are not familiar with specialized or technical terms you use, you may want to include a glossary. If you do, keep the entries concise and be sure they are written in plain language that all readers can understand. Arrange the terms alphabetically, with each entry beginning on a new line. The definitions then follow the terms, dictionary style. In a formal report, the glossary appears after the appendix(es) and bibliography, and it begins on a new page.

Including a glossary does not relieve you of the responsibility of defining in the text any terms your reader will not know when those terms are first mentioned. See also <u>defining terms</u> (Tab 1).

tables of contents

A table of contents is typically included in a document longer than ten pages. It previews what the work contains and how it is organized, and it allows readers looking for specific information to locate sections quickly and easily.

When creating a table of contents, use the major headings and subheadings of your document exactly as they appear in the text, as shown in Figure 4-2 (page 118). Note that the table of contents is typically placed in the front matter so that it follows the title page and abstract and precedes the list of tables or figures, the foreword, and the preface. See <u>formal reports</u>.

5

Design
and Visuals

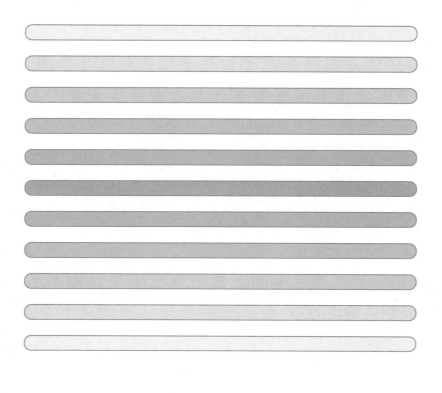

Preview

This section includes entries related to the general physical appearance of a document, as discussed in <u>layout and design</u>, and entries concerning specific types of visuals, such as <u>drawings</u>, <u>graphs</u>, and <u>tables</u>. For an overview of creating and integrating specific types of illustrations into documents, read the entry <u>visuals</u>. Because many visuals are seen by international audiences, we have included the entry <u>global graphics</u>. See also <u>Web design</u> and <u>writing for the Web</u> (Tab 1).

drawings

The types of drawings discussed in this entry are conventional line drawings and cutaway drawings. Each type of drawing has unique advantages—the type of drawing you use should be determined by its purpose (Tab 1).

A conventional drawing, like that in Figure 5–1, is appropriate if your readers need a representation of an object's general appearance or an overview of a series of steps. A cutaway drawing, like the one in Figure 5–2, is used to show the internal parts of a piece of equipment and illustrate their relationship to the whole.

FIGURE 5–1. Conventional Drawing Illustrating Instructions

Drawings that require a high degree of accuracy and precision generally are prepared by graphics specialists. If you need only general-interest images to illustrate newsletters and brochures or to create presentation overheads, use noncopyrighted photographs or images from clip-art libraries. Such libraries contain thousands of noncopyrighted symbols, shapes, and images.

■ ETHICS NOTE Be careful not to use drawings from copyrighted sources without proper documentation, especially from the Web—the same copyright laws that apply to printed material also apply to Web-based graphics. See also copyright (Tab 2), documenting sources (Tab 2), and plagiarism (Tab 2).

Think about your need for drawings during the preparation (Tab 1) and research (Tab 2) stages of writing. Include them in your outline, indicating approximately where each should appear throughout the outline with "drawing of . . ." enclosed in brackets. For integrating drawings into your text, see visuals.

5

Design and Visuals

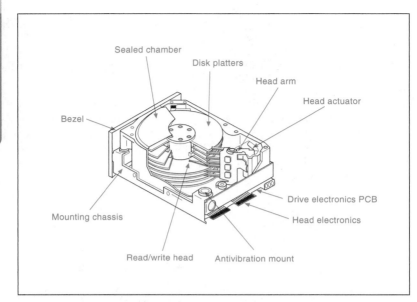

FIGURE 5–2. Cutaway Drawing (Hard Disk Drive)

flowcharts

A flowchart is a diagram of a process that involves stages, shown in sequence from beginning to end. A flowchart provides an overview of a process and allows the reader to identify its essential steps quickly and easily. Flowcharts can take several forms: the steps might be represented by labeled blocks, as shown in Figure 5–3; pictorial symbols, as shown in Figure 5–4; or ISO (International Organization for Standardization) symbols for information processing, as shown in Figure 5–5.

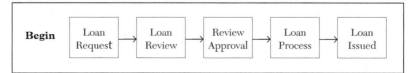

FIGURE 5–3. Flowchart Using Labeled Blocks

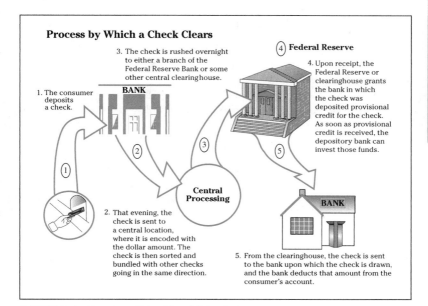

FIGURE 5–4. Flowchart Using Pictorial Symbols

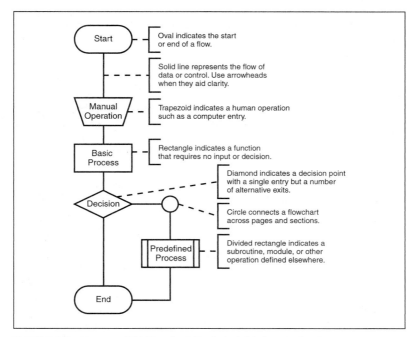

FIGURE 5–5. Common ISO Flowchart Symbols (with Annotations)

5

Design and Visuals

Writer's Checklist: Creating Flowcharts

☑ Label each step in the process or identify each step with labeled blocks, pictorial representations, or standardized symbols.

☑ Follow the standard flow directions: left to right and top to bottom. When the flow is otherwise, indicate that with arrows.

☑ Include a key if the flowchart contains symbols your readers may not understand.

☑ Use standardized symbols for flowcharts that document computer programs and other information-processing procedures, as set forth in *Information Processing — Documentation Symbols and Conventions for Data, Program and System Flowcharts, Program Network Charts, and System Resources Charts*, ISO publication 5807-1985 (E).

For advice on integrating flowcharts into your text, see **visuals**. See also **global graphics**.

forms design

Forms provide an economical and uniform way to gather, record, and evaluate data. They help respondents provide necessary information in the form of standardized answers that are easy for you to evaluate and tabulate. Figures 5–6 and 5–7 are two examples of forms.

Preparing a Form

An effective form makes it easy for one person to supply information and for another person to retrieve, record, and interpret that information. Ideally, a form should be self-explanatory to someone seeing it for the first time. When preparing a form, determine the kind of information you are seeking and arrange the questions in a logical order.

Choosing Online or Paper.   Many organizations are moving their forms online. Forms especially well suited for online use include job applications, conference or seminar registrations, medical records, and order forms. Web-based and other online forms both standardize respondents' interfaces and link easily to databases, thus automating the tabulation and interpretation of data. Online forms ensure that the form will be completed correctly because their programs do not accept a form until all the necessary fields are completed. In addition, using online forms can eliminate the problems associated with distributing and collecting forms. However, using online forms can be difficult for people with limited computer literacy or access, so consider your **readers**

Annual Reappointment Form   Effective July 1, 20___ to June 30, 20___

CHILDREN'S MEDICAL CENTER
1735 Chapel Street
Toledo, Ohio 43692

NAME:

List appointments or offices held, teaching positions, independent studies
in medical or dental societies or other medical organizations, and any
other professional recognitions you would like to have included in your file:

_____   Open-ended
_____   questions
_____
_____
_____
_____

Do you wish a change in your privileges? If so, specify: _____
_____

Have there been any changes in your board specialties? Yes ☐ No ☐   Labeled
          If yes: Date _____   box
                Specialty Board _____

Signature_____   Signature
Date_____   and date

WHITE: Committee Chair   BLUE: Human Resources   Routing
PINK: Employee   instructions

FIGURE 5–6. Form (for Staff Reappointment)

(Tab 1) carefully before opting to collect your responses online. See also
Web design.

Writing Instructions.   Place instructions at the beginning of the
form or at the beginning of each section of the form and use headings
or other design elements, such as the boldface type and shading in
Figure 5–7, to attract the reader's attention. When necessary, place instructions for distributing the various copies of multiple-copy forms at

104-M S A
Section 125 Flexible Spending Account (FSA) Claim Form

Form title

Employee Name: _____

Social Security Number: _____-____-_____   *Writing lines*

Name of Employer: _____

Employee Signature: _____

Instructions

Complete section below for medical, dental, or vision reimbursement

CLAIM TYPE I: MEDICAL CARE ACCOUNT

Amount of Expense Incurred: $_____

Dates of Services: From: _____   To: _____

Instructions

Complete section below for reimbursement of care for your dependent provided by a child-care facility, adult dependent-care center, or caretaker

CLAIM TYPE II: DEPENDENT CARE ACCOUNT

Amount of Expense Incurred: $_____

Name of Dependent Care Provider: _____

Provider Social Security or Federal ID Number: _____-____-_____

Mail or fax form with documentation to:
   Specialized Benefit Services, Inc.
   P. O. Box 498
   Framingham, MA 01702
   Fax: (508) 877-1182
For additional claim forms: www.sbsclaims.com

Mailing and contact information

FIGURE 5-7. Form (for a Medical Claim)

the bottom of the form and repeat them on every copy of the form, as in Figure 5–6. Instructions for mailing or faxing the form should be clearly indicated, as in Figure 5–7.

Choosing Response Types.   Forms should ask questions in ways that are best suited to the types of data you hope to collect. In general, there are two types of questions:

- *Open-ended questions* allow respondents the freedom to choose their own words. Such questions are most appropriate if you wish to elicit answers you may not have anticipated (as in a complaint form) or if there are too many possible answers to use a multiple-choice format. However, the responses to open-ended questions are difficult to tabulate and analyze.
- *Closed-ended questions* provide a list of answers from which the respondent can select, limiting the range of possible responses. When you want to make sure you receive a standardized, easy-to-tabulate response, use any of the types of closed-ended questions that follow:
  - *Multiple choice:* Choose one (or sometimes more) from a preset list of options.
  - *Ranked choice:* Rank items according to preference, such as selecting vacation days or choosing job assignments.
  - *Forced choice:* Choose yes/no or male/female.

Wording Captions.   Questions are normally presented as captions. Keep them brief, specific, and to the point; avoid unnecessary repetition by combining related information under an explanatory heading.

WORDY   What make of car do you drive? _____

What year was it manufactured? _____

What model is it? _____

What is the body style? _____

CONCISE   Vehicle Information

Make _____ Year _____

Model _____ Body Style _____

If a requested date is other than the date on which the form is being filled out, the caption should read, for example, "Effective date" or "Date issued," rather than simply "Date." As in all business writing, put yourself in your reader's place and imagine what sorts of requests would be clear. See Figure 5–6.

Sequencing Data.   At the top of the form, clearly indicate preliminary information, such as the name of your organization, the title of your form, and any reference number. In the main portion of the form,

5

Design and Visuals

include the entries you need to obtain the necessary data. At the end of the form, include space for a signature and a date.

Arrange requests for information in an order that will be the most logical to the person filling out the form.

- Sequence entries to fit the subject matter. For instance, a form requesting reimbursement for travel expenses would logically begin with the first day of the week (or month) and end with the last day of the appropriate period.
- If the response to one item is based on the response to another item, be sure the items appear in the correct order.
- Group requests for related information together whenever possible.
- For ease of reading, arrange entries from left to right and from top to bottom.

Ensuring Confidentiality

ETHICS NOTE Information gathered on forms can be of a sensitive or personal nature. All effort should be made to present questions in a way that is not invasive or illegal. Unless otherwise indicated on the form, the person filling out the form has the right to expect confidentiality. If you are concerned about issues of confidentiality or legality, check with your organization's policy or check with your instructor.

Designing a Form

You can design computer-generated forms specific to your needs with form design and management software or with word-processing software. However you prepare the final version of a form, pay particular attention to design details, especially to the placement of entry lines and the amount of space allowed for responses.

Entry Lines.   A form can be designed so that the person filling it out provides information on a writing line, in a writing block, or in square boxes. A *writing line* is simply a rule with a caption, as shown in Figure 5–7.

A *writing block* is essentially the same as a writing line, except that each entry is enclosed in a ruled block, making it impossible for the respondent to associate a caption with the wrong line, as shown in Figure 5–8.

When it is possible to anticipate all likely responses, you can make the form easy to fill out by writing the question on the form, supplying a labeled box for each possible answer, and asking the respondent to check the appropriate boxes. Such a design also makes it easy to tabulate the data. Be sure your questions are both simple and specific.

- Would your department order another MAX-PC? Yes ☐ No ☐

NAME		TELEPHONE
STREET ADDRESS		
CITY	STATE	ZIP CODE

FIGURE 5–8. Writing Block for a Form

Spacing.   Provide enough space to enable the person filling out the form to enter the data. Insufficient writing space makes it difficult for people to respond, resulting in responses that are hard to read. Reading responses that are too tightly spaced or that snake around the side of the form can cause eyestrain and errors. To ensure the usability of the form, have a coworker complete it before printing the final version.

global graphics

In the global business and technological environment, <u>graphs</u> and <u>visuals</u> require the same careful attention given to other aspects of <u>global communication</u> (Tab 1). The complex cultural connotations of visuals challenge writers to think beyond their own experience.

Symbols, images, and even colors are not free from cultural associations—they depend on context, and context is culturally determined. For instance, in North America, a red cross is commonly used as a symbol for first aid or hospital. In Muslim countries, however, a cross (red or otherwise) represents Christianity, whereas a crescent (usually green) signifies first aid or hospital. A manual for export to Honduras could indicate "caution" by using a picture of a person touching a finger below the eye. In France, however, that gesture means "You can't fool me."

Careful attention to the connotations that visual elements may have for a diverse audience makes translations easier, prevents embarrassment, and earns respect for the company and its products and services. See also <u>presentations</u> (Tab 8).

Writer's Checklist: Communicating with Global Graphics

☑ Consult with someone from your intended audience's country who can recognize and explain the effect that your graphic elements will have on readers.

Writer's Checklist: Communicating with Global Graphics (continued)

☑ Organize visual information for the intended audience. For example, North Americans tend to read visuals from left to right in clockwise rotation. Middle Eastern cultures read visuals from right to left in counterclockwise rotation.

☑ Be sure that the graphics you use have no unintended religious implications.

☑ Carefully consider how you depict people in visuals. Nudity in advertising, for example, is generally acceptable in Europe but much less so in North America and Asia. In some cultures, showing even isolated bare body parts can alienate audiences.

☑ Use outlines or neutral abstractions to represent human beings. For example, use stick figures and, when possible, avoid representing men and women.

☑ Examine how you display body positions in signs and visuals. Body positioning can carry unintended cultural meanings very different from your own. For example, some Middle Eastern cultures regard the display of the soles of one's shoes to be disrespectful and offensive.

☑ Try to use neutral colors in your graphics. Generally, black-and-white and gray-and-white illustrations work well. Colors can be problematic. For example, in North America, Europe, and Japan, red indicates danger. In China, however, red symbolizes joy. In Europe and North America, blue generally has a positive connotation; in Japan, blue represents villainy.

☑ Check your use of punctuation marks, which are as language specific as symbols. For example, in North America, the question mark generally represents the need for information or the help function in a computer manual or program. In many countries, that symbol has no meaning at all.

☑ Create simple visuals and use consistent labels for all visual items. In most cultures, simple shapes with fewer elements are easier to read.

☑ Explain the meaning of icons or symbols. Include a **glossary** (Tab 4) to explain technical symbols that cannot be changed, such as company logos.

graphs

A graph presents numerical data in visual form and offers several advantages over presenting data within the text or in tables. Trends, movements, distributions, comparisons, and cycles are more readily apparent in graphs than they are in tables. However, although graphs present data in a more comprehensible form than tables do, they are less precise. For that reason, graphs are often accompanied by tables that give exact data. The most common types of graphs are line graphs, bar graphs, pie graphs, and picture graphs. For additional advice, see <u>visuals</u>; for information about using presentation graphics, see <u>presentations</u> (Tab 8).

Line Graphs

A line graph shows the relationship between two variables or sets of numbers by plotting points in relation to two axes drawn at right angles. The vertical axis usually represents amounts, and the horizontal axis usually represents increments of time. Line graphs that portray more than one set of variables (double-line graphs) allow for comparisons between two sets of statistics for the same period of time. You can emphasize the difference between the two lines by shading the space between them, as shown in Figure 5–9.

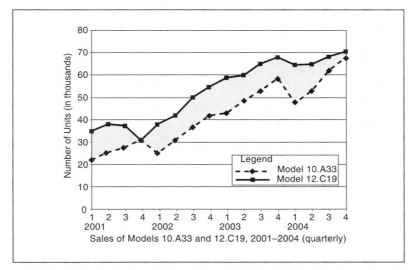

FIGURE 5–9. Double-Line Graph (with Shading)

⬗ ETHICS NOTE Be especially careful to proportion the vertical and horizontal scales so they give a precise presentation of the data that is free of visual distortion. To do otherwise is not only inaccurate but potentially unethical. (See <u>ethics in writing</u>, Tab 1.) In Figure 5–10, the graph on the left gives the appearance of a dramatic decrease in accidents because the scale is unevenly compressed with some of the years selectively omitted. The graph on the right represents the trend more accurately because the years are evenly distributed without omissions.

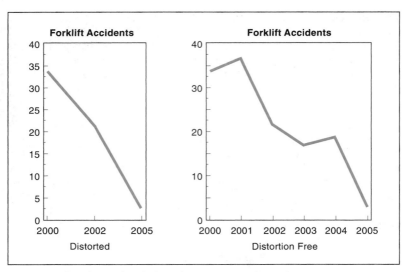

FIGURE 5–10. Distorted and Distortion-Free Expressions of Data

Bar Graphs

Bar graphs consist of horizontal or vertical bars of equal width, scaled in length to represent some quantity. They are commonly used to show (1) quantities of the same item at different times, (2) quantities of different items at the same time, and (3) quantities of the different parts of an item that make up a whole—in this case, the segments of the bar graph must total 100 percent. The horizontal graph in Figure 5–11 shows the quantities of different items for the same period of time.

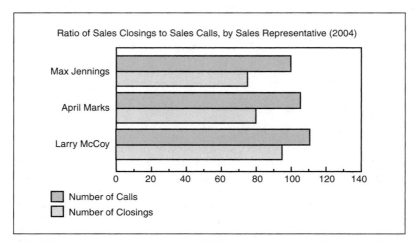

FIGURE 5–11. Bar Graph (Quantities of Different Items During a Fixed Period)

5

Pie Graphs

A pie graph presents data as wedge-shaped sections of a circle. Like the bar graph that shows quantities of different parts that comprise a whole, the total value of the graph (the circle) must equal 100 percent. Pie graphs, such as that shown in Figure 5–12, also provide a way of presenting information that is more immediate than a table; in fact, a table with a more detailed breakdown of the same information often accompanies a pie graph.

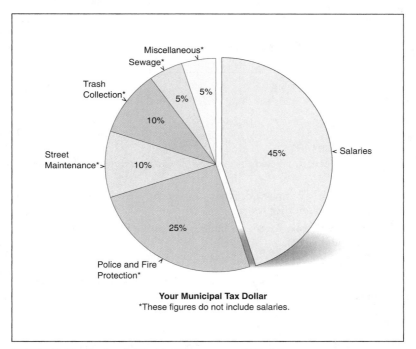

FIGURE 5–12. Pie Graph (Showing Percentages of Whole)

Picture Graphs

Picture graphs are modified bar graphs that use pictorial symbols of the item portrayed. Each symbol corresponds to a specified quantity of the item, as shown in Figure 5–13. Note that for precision and clarity, the picture graph includes the total quantity following the symbols.

Design and Visuals

5

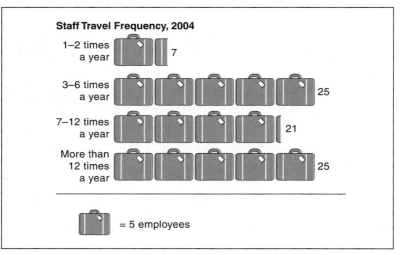

FIGURE 5–13. Picture Graph

Writer's Checklist: Creating Graphs

FOR ALL GRAPHS

☑ Use, as needed, a key or legend that lists and defines symbols (see Figure 5-9).

☑ Include a source line under the graph at the lower left when the data comes from another source.

☑ Place explanatory footnotes directly below the figure caption or label (see Figure 5-12).

FOR LINE GRAPHS

☑ Indicate the zero point of the graph (the point where the two axes intersect).

☑ Insert a break in the scale if the range of data shown makes it inconvenient to begin at zero.

☑ Divide the vertical axis into equal portions, from the least amount at the bottom (or zero) to the greatest amount at the top.

☑ Divide the horizontal axis in equal units from left to right. If a label is necessary, center it directly beneath the scale.

☑ Make all lettering read horizontally if possible, although the caption or label for the vertical axis is usually positioned vertically (see Figure 5-9).

FOR PIE GRAPHS

☑ Make sure that the complete circle is equivalent to 100 percent.

☑ Sequence the wedges clockwise from largest to smallest, beginning at the 12 o'clock position, whenever possible.

Writer's Checklist: Creating Graphs (continued)

☑ Limit the number of items in the pie graph to avoid clutter and to ensure that the slices are thick enough to be clear.

☑ Give each wedge a distinctive color, pattern, shade, or texture.

☑ Label each wedge with its percentage value and keep all call-outs (labels that identify the wedges) horizontal.

☑ Detach a slice, as shown in Figure 5–12, if you wish to draw attention to a particular segment of the pie graph.

FOR PICTURE GRAPHS

☑ Use picture graphs to add interest to **presentations** (Tab 8) and documents, such as **newsletters** (Tab 3), that are aimed at wide audiences.

☑ Choose symbols that are easily recognizable. (See also **global graphics**.)

☑ Let each symbol represent a specific number of units.

☑ Indicate larger quantities by using more symbols, instead of larger symbols, because relative sizes are difficult to judge accurately.

headings

Headings (also called *heads*) are titles or subtitles within the body of a document that help readers find information, divide the material into comprehensible segments, highlight the main topics, and signal topic changes. A formal report or proposal may need several levels of headings to indicate major divisions, subdivisions, and even smaller units. However, it is better to avoid using more than three levels of headings. See also **proposals** (Tab 3), **formal reports** (Tab 4), and **layout and design**.

Headings typically represent the major topics of a document. In a short document, you can use the major divisions of your outline as headings; in a longer document, you may need to use both major and minor divisions.

General Heading Style

No one format for headings is correct. Often a company settles on a standard format, which everyone in the company follows. Sometimes a customer for whom a report or proposal is being prepared requires a particular format. In the absence of specific guidelines, follow the system illustrated in Figure 5–14. For an example of a different system (the decimal system of headings), see **outlining** (Tab 1).

First-level head
DISTRIBUTION CENTER LOCATION REPORT

The committee initially considered 30 possible locations for the proposed new distribution center. Of these, 20 were eliminated almost immediately for one reason or another (unfavorable zoning regulations, inadequate transportation infrastructure, etc.). Of the remaining ten locations, the committee selected for intensive study the three that seemed most promising: Chicago, Minneapolis, and Salt Lake City. We have now visited these three cities and our observations and recommendations follow.

Second-level head
CHICAGO

Of the three cities, Chicago presently seems to the committee to offer the greatest advantages, although we wish to examine these more carefully before making a final recommendation.

Third-level head
Selected Location

Though not at the geographic center of the United States, Chicago is the demographic center to more than three-quarters of the U.S. population. It is within easy reach of our corporate headquarters in New York. And it is close to several of our most important suppliers of components and raw materials—those, for example, in Columbus, Detroit, and St. Louis. Several considerations were considered essential to the location, although some may not have had as great an impact on the selection. . . .

Fourth-level heads
Air Transportation. Chicago has two major airports (O'Hare and Midway) and is contemplating building a third. Both domestic and international air-cargo service are available. . . .

Sea Transportation. Except during the winter months when the Great Lakes are frozen, Chicago is an international seaport. . . .

Rail Transportation. Chicago is served by the following major railroads. . . .

FIGURE 5–14. Headings Used in a Document

Writer's Checklist: Using Headings

☑ Use headings to signal a new topic. Use a lower-level heading to indicate a new subtopic within the larger topic.

☑ Make headings concise but specific enough to be informative, as in Figure 5–14.

☑ Avoid too many or too few headings or levels of headings; too many clutter a document and too few fail to provide recognizable structure.

☑ Ensure that headings at the same level are of relatively equal importance and have **parallel structure** (Tab 9).

☑ Subdivide sections only as needed; when you do, however, subdivide them into at least two lower-level headings.

Writer's Checklist: Using Headings (continued)

- ☑ Do not leave a heading as the final line of a page. If two lines of text cannot fit below a heading, start the section at the top of the next page.
- ☑ Do not allow a heading to substitute for discussion; the text should read as if the heading were not there.

layout and design

The layout and design of a document can make even the most complex information look accessible and give readers a favorable impression of the writer and the organization. To accomplish those goals, a design should help readers find information easily; offer a simple and uncluttered presentation; and highlight structure, hierarchy, and order. The design should also reinforce an organization's image. For example, if clients are paying a high price for consulting services, they may expect a sophisticated, polished design; if employees inside an organization expect management to be frugal, they may accept—even expect—economical and standard company design.

Effective design is based on visual simplicity and harmony and can be achieved through the selection of fonts, the choice of devices to highlight information, and the arrangement of text and visual components on a page.

Typography

Typography refers to the style and arrangement of type on a printed page. A complete set of all the letters, numbers, and symbols available in one typeface (or style) is called a *font*. The letters in a typeface have a number of distinctive characteristics, as shown in Figure 5–15.

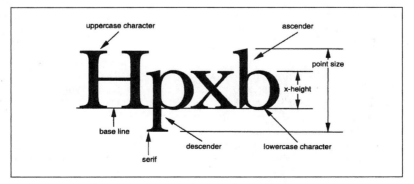

FIGURE 5–15. Primary Components of Letter Characters

Typeface and Type Size.   For most on-the-job writing, select a typeface primarily for its legibility. Avoid typefaces that may distract readers. Instead, choose popular typefaces with which readers are familiar, such as Times Roman, Garamond, or Gill Sans. Do not use more than two typefaces in the text of a document. For certain documents, such as brochures (Tab 3) and newsletters (Tab 3), you may wish to create a contrast between headings and text. To do so, use typefaces that are distinctively different. Always experiment before making final decisions.

One way typefaces are characterized is by the presence or absence of serifs. *Serif* typefaces have projections, as shown in Figure 5–15; *sans serif* styles do not. (*Sans* is French for "without.") The text of this book is set in Plantin, a serif typeface. Although sans serif type has a modern look, serif type is easier to read, especially in the smaller sizes. Sans serif, however, works well for headings (like the entry titles in this book) and for Web sites and other documents read on-screen.

Ideal font sizes for the main text of paper documents range from 8 to 13 points; 11- and 12-point type are the most common sizes, as shown in Figure 5–16. Your readers and the distance from which a document will be read should help determine type size. For example, instructions that will rest on a table at which the reader stands require a larger typeface than a document that will be read up close. For presentations (Tab 8) and writing for the Web (Tab 1), preview your document to see the effectiveness of your choice of point sizes and typefaces. See also Web design.

6 pt. This size might be used for dating a source.
8 pt. This size might be used for footnotes.
10 pt. This size might be used for figure captions.
12 pt. This size might be used for main text.
14 pt. This size might be used for headings.

FIGURE 5–16. Type Sizes (6- to 14-Point)

Left- or Full-Justified Margins.   Left-justified (ragged-right) margins are generally easier to read, especially for texts using standard margins on 8½ × 11″ pages. Left-justified is also better if full justification causes your word-processing software to insert irregular spaces between words, producing unwanted white space or unevenness in blocks of text. Full-justified text is more appropriate for publications aimed at a broad readership that expects a more formal, polished appearance. Full justification is also useful with multiple-column formats because the spaces between the columns (called *alleys*) need the definition that full justification provides.

Highlighting Devices

Thoughtfully used highlighting devices — typography; headings and captions; headers and footers; rules, icons, and color — give a document visual logic and organization. For example, rules and boxes can set off steps and illustrations from surrounding explanations. Consistency and moderation are important: use the same technique to highlight a particular feature throughout your document and be careful not to overuse any single device.

Typographical Devices.   One method of achieving emphasis through typography is to use capital letters. HOWEVER, LONG STRETCHES OF ALL UPPERCASE LETTERS ARE DIFFICULT TO READ. (See also <u>e-mail</u>, Tab 6.) Use all uppercase letters only in short spans, such as in headings. Likewise, use italics sparingly because *continuous italic type reduces legibility and thus slows readers.* Of course, italics are useful if your aim is to slow readers, as in cautions and warnings. **Boldface**, used in moderation, may be the best cuing device because it is visually different yet retains the customary shapes of letters and numbers. See also <u>emphasis</u> (Tab 9).

Headings and Captions.   <u>Headings</u> (or *heads*) reveal the organization of a document and help readers decide which sections they need to read. Headings appear in many typeface variations (boldface being the most common) and often use sans serif typefaces.

Captions are titles that highlight or describe illustrations or blocks of text. Captions often appear below or above figures and tables and in the left or right margins next to blocks of text. See also <u>tables</u>.

Headers and Footers.   A header in a report, letter, or other document appears at the top of each page and a footer appears at the bottom of each page. Document pages may have headers or footers or both that include such elements as the topic or subtopic of a section, identifying numbers, the date the document was written, page numbers, and the document name. Keep your headers and footers concise — too much information in them can create visual clutter. For headers used in letters and memos, see <u>correspondence</u> (Tab 6).

Rules, Icons, and Color.   Rules are vertical or horizontal lines used to divide one area of the page from another or to create boxes. They highlight elements and make information more accessible.

An icon is a pictorial representation of an idea. Commonly used icons include the small envelopes used in Web design to symbolize e-mail links and national flags to symbolize different language versions of a document. To be effective, icons must be simple and easily recognized or defined. See also global graphics.

Color and screening (shaded areas on a page) can distinguish one part of a document from another or unify a series of documents. They can set off sections within a document, highlight examples, or emphasize warnings. In tables, screening can highlight column titles or sets of data to which you want to draw the reader's attention.

Page Design

Page design is the process of combining the various design elements on a page to make a coherent whole. The flexibility of your design is based on the capabilities of your software, how the document will be reproduced, and the budget.

Thumbnail Sketches.   Before you spend time positioning actual text and visuals on a page, you may want to create a thumbnail sketch, in which blocks indicate the placement of elements. You can go further by roughly assembling all the thumbnail pages to show the size, shape, form, and general style of a large document. Such a mock-up, called a *dummy*, allows you to see how a finished document will look.

Columns.   As you design pages, consider how columns may improve the readability of your document. A single-column format works well with larger typefaces, double spacing, and left-justified margins. For smaller typefaces and single-spaced lines, the two-column structure keeps text columns narrow enough so readers need not scan back and forth across the width of the entire page for every line.

A word on a line by itself at the end of a column or page is called an *orphan*. A single word carried over to the top of a column or page is called a *widow*. Avoid both.

White Space.   White space visually frames information and breaks it into manageable chunks. For example, white space between paragraphs helps readers see the information in each paragraph as a unit. White space between sections can also serve as a visual cue to signal that one section is ending and another is beginning.

Lists.   Lists are an effective way to highlight words, phrases, and short sentences. Lists are particularly useful for certain types of information, such as steps in sequence, materials or parts needed, concluding points, and recommendations.

Illustrations.   Readers notice illustrations before they notice text, and they notice larger illustrations before they notice smaller ones.

Thus, the size of an illustration suggests its relative importance. For newsletter articles and publications aimed at wide audiences, consider especially the proportion of the illustration to the text. Magazine designers often use the three-fifths rule: Page layout is more dramatic and appealing when the major element (photograph, drawing, or other visual) occupies three-fifths rather than half the available space. The same principle can be used to enhance the visual appeal of a report.

Remember that clarity and usefulness take precedence over aesthetics in many business and technical documents. Illustrations can be gathered in one place (for example, at the end of a report), but placing them in the text closer to their accompanying explanations makes them more effective. Using illustrations in the text also provides visual relief. For advice on the placement of illustrations, see <u>visuals</u>.

WEB LINK DESIGNING DOCUMENTS

Word-processing programs offer features you can use to improve the layout and other design elements of your document. For a tutorial on using these features, see <bedfordstmartins.com/alred> and select *Tutorials*, "Designing Documents with a Word Processor." For additional advice, select *Digital Tips*, "Laying Out a Page."

---

lists

Lists can save readers time by allowing them to see at a glance specific items, questions, or directions. Lists also help readers by breaking up complex statements and by allowing key ideas to stand out, as in the following example:

- Before we agree to hold the district meeting at the Brent Hotel, we should make sure the hotel facilities provide the following:
  - Service center with phones, faxes, Internet hookup, PCs, and copying services for the conference committee
  - Ground-floor exhibit area large enough for thirty 8-by-15-foot booths
  - Eight meeting rooms to accommodate 25 people each
  - Internet hookups, projection screens for presentations, and overhead projectors in each room
  - Ballroom and dining facilities for 250 people

  To confirm that the Brent Hotel is our best choice, we should tour the facilities during our stay in Kansas City.

5

Design and Visuals

Writer's Checklist: Using Lists

☑ List only comparable items and use __parallel structure__ (Tab 9).

☑ Use only words, phrases, or short sentences of the same general length.

☑ Provide context by introducing each list, typically with a complete sentence followed by a __colon__ (Tab 12).

☑ Ensure __coherence__ (Tab 9) by providing for adequate __transition__ (Tab 9) before and after a list.

☑ Use bullets, as opposed to numbers, when rank or sequence is not important.

☑ Do not overuse lists or include too many items, as in entire pages of lists.

organizational charts

An organizational chart shows how the various components of an organization are related to one another. This type of visual, illustrated in Figure 5–17, is useful when you want to give your readers an overview of an organization or to display the lines of authority within it. As with all illustrations, place the organizational chart as close as possible to the text that refers to it. See __visuals__.

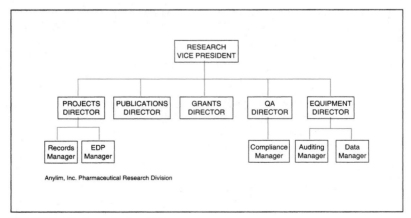

FIGURE 5–17. Organizational Chart

photographs

Photographs are the best way to show the surface of an object, record an event, or demonstrate the development of a phenomenon over a period of time. Photographs, however, cannot depict the internal workings of a mechanism or below-the-surface details of objects or structures. Such details are better represented in <u>drawings</u>.

An effective photograph shows important details and indicates relative size of the subject by including a familiar object—such as a ruler or a person—near the subject being photographed. For example, the photograph in Figure 5–18 shows the drop-down door of an aircraft with part of the nose and landing gear to illustrate relative size.

Treat photographs as you do other <u>visuals</u>. Give the photograph a figure number, call-outs (labels) to identify key features, and a caption, if needed.

FIGURE 5–18. Photo (of Aircraft Door). Photo courtesy of Ken Cook Company.

tables

A table can present data, such as statistics, more concisely than text and more accurately than <u>graphs</u>. A table facilitates comparisons among data by organizing it into rows and columns. However, overall trends are more easily conveyed in charts, graphs, and other <u>visuals</u>.

Table Elements

Tables typically include the elements shown in Figure 5–19.

Table 1. Estimated Emissions from Electric Power Generation (tons per gigawatthour)

Fuel	Sulphur Dioxide	Nitrogen Oxides	Particulate Matter	Carbon Dioxide	Volatile Organic Compounds
Eastern coal	1.74	2.90	0.10	1,000	0.06
Western coal	0.81	2.20	0.06	1,039	0.09
Gas	0.003	0.57	0.02	640	0.05
Biomass	0.06	1.25	0.11	0*	0.61
Oil	0.51	0.63	0.02	840	0.03
Wind	0	0	0	0	0
Geothermal	0	0	0	0	0
Hydro	0	0	0	0	0
Solar	0	0	0	0	0
Nuclear	0	0	0	0	0

*Net emissions.

SOURCE: Department of Energy

Labels: Table number, Table title, Box head, Column headings, Stub, Rule, Footnote, Source line, Body

FIGURE 5–19. Elements of a Table

Table Number.   Table numbers are usually Arabic and should be assigned sequentially to the tables throughout the document.

Table Title.   The title, which is normally placed just above the table, should describe concisely what the table represents.

Box Head.   The box head contains the column headings, which should be brief but descriptive. Units of measurement, where necessary, should be either specified as part of the heading or enclosed in parentheses beneath the heading. Standard abbreviations and symbols are acceptable. Avoid vertical lettering whenever possible.

Stub.   The stub, the left vertical column of a table, lists the items about which information is given in the body of the table.

Body. The body comprises the data below the column headings and to the right of the stub. Within the body, arrange columns so that the items to be compared appear in adjacent rows and columns. Where no information exists for a specific item, substitute a row of dots or a dash to acknowledge the gap.

Rules. Rules are the lines that separate the table into its various parts. Horizontal rules are placed below the title, below the body of the table, and between the column headings and the body of the table. Tables should be open at the sides. The columns within the table may be separated by vertical rules only if such lines aid clarity.

Footnotes. Footnotes are used for explanations of individual items in the table. Symbols (such as * and †) or lowercase letters (sometimes in parentheses) rather than numbers are ordinarily used to key table footnotes because numbers might be mistaken for numerical data or could be confused with the numbering system for text footnotes.

Source Line. The source line identifies where the data originated. When a source line is appropriate, it appears below the table. Many organizations place the source line below the footnotes. See also <u>copyright</u> (Tab 2) and <u>plagiarism</u> (Tab 2).

Continued Tables. When a table must be divided so that it can be continued on another page, repeat the column headings and give the table number at the head of each new page a "continued" label (for example, "Table 3, *continued*").

Informal Tables

To list relatively few items that would be easier for the reader to grasp in tabular form, you can use an informal table, as long as you introduce it properly.

- Dear Customer:
  To order replacement parts, use the following part numbers and prices:

PART	PART NUMBER	PRICE ($)
Diverter valve	2-912	12.50
Gasket kit	2-776	0.95
Adapter	3-212	0.90

Although informal tables do not need titles or table numbers to identify them, they do require column headings that accurately describe the information listed.

visuals

Visuals can express ideas or convey information in ways that words alone cannot. They communicate by showing how things look (drawings, photographs, maps), by representing numbers and quantities (graphs, tables), by depicting relationships (flowcharts, schematic diagrams), and by making abstract concepts and relationships concrete (organizational charts). They also highlight the most important information and emphasize key concepts succinctly and clearly, especially in documents such as brochures (Tab 3) and newsletters (Tab 3).

Selecting Visuals

Consider your purpose and your audience carefully in selecting visuals. You would need different illustrations for an automobile owner's manual or an auto dealer's Web site, for example, than you would for a mechanic's diagnostic guide.

Many of the qualities of good writing — simplicity, clarity, conciseness, directness — are equally important in the creation and use of visuals. Presented with clarity and consistency, visuals can help the audience focus on key portions of your document, presentation, or Web site. Be aware, though, that even the best visual only enhances or supports the text. Your writing must provide context for the visual and point out its significance.

The following entries are related to specific visuals and their use in printed and online documents as well as in presentations.

drawings	organizational charts
flowcharts	photographs
formal reports (Tab 4)	presentations (Tab 8)
global graphics	tables
graphs	Web design
layout and design	writing for the Web (Tab 1)

Integrating Visuals with Text

To integrate visuals smoothly with your text, consider your graphics requirements before you begin writing a draft. Jot down visual options when you are considering your scope (Tab 1) and organization (Tab 1). Make visuals an integral part of your outline. (See outlining, Tab 1.) At appropriate points in your outline, either make a rough sketch of the visual, if you can, or write "illustration of . . . ," noting the source of the visual and enclosing each suggestion in a text box. Planning your graphics requirements from the beginning stages of your outline ensures their integration throughout all versions of the draft to the finished product.

⚡ ETHICS NOTE Obtain written permission for copyrighted visuals, and acknowledge borrowed material in a source line below the caption for a figure and in a footnote at the bottom of a table. Acknowledge your use of any public (uncopyrighted) information, such as demographic or economic data from government publications, with a source line. See also <u>copyright</u> (Tab 2), <u>documenting sources</u> (Tab 2), and <u>plagiarism</u> (Tab 2).

Writer's Checklist: Using and Integrating Visuals

☑ Clarify for <u>readers</u> (Tab 1) why each visual is included in the text. The amount of description needed will vary, depending on the readers' backgrounds—nonexperts may require lengthier explanations than do experts.

☑ Use consistent terminology; for example, do not refer to a "proportion" in the text and a "percentage" in the visual.

☑ Define <u>abbreviations</u> (Tab 12) the first time they appear in the text and in figures and tables. If any symbols are not self-explanatory, include a key.

☑ Place a visual as close as possible to the text where it is discussed—no visual should precede its first text mention.

☑ Consider placing lengthy, detailed visuals in an <u>appendix</u> (Tab 4) and refer to it in the text.

☑ Give each visual a concise title that clearly describes its content.

☑ Assign figure and table numbers, particularly if your document contains more than one illustration or table. (Graphical illustrations—drawings, maps, and photographs—are generically labeled "figures," while tables are labeled "tables.")

☑ Refer to visuals in the text of your document by their figure or table numbers.

☑ In documents with more than five illustrations or tables, include a section following the table of contents titled "List of Figures" or "List of Tables" that identifies each by number, title, and page number.

☑ Keep visuals simple: include only information needed for discussion in the text and eliminate unneeded labels, arrows, boxes, and lines.

☑ Specify the units of measurement used, make sure relative sizes are clear, and indicate distance with a scale, when appropriate.

☑ Position the lettering of any explanatory text or labels horizontally.

☑ Allow adequate white space around and within the visual.

☑ Check the editorial guidelines or recommended style manual when preparing visuals for a trade journal article.

5

Design and Visuals

Web design

Designing Web sites and pages requires that you stay current with changes in technology, so the best sources for guidance are on the Web itself. To find many useful tutorials, use a search engine to search for *tutorial* along with other keywords such as *HTML* or *Web design*. For advice on developing your site's content for online readers, see <u>writing for the Web</u> (Tab 1).

🌐 **WEB LINK** **WEB-DESIGN RESOURCES**

For Mike Markel's helpful overview of the process and principles of designing Web sites, see <bedfordstmartins.com/alred> and select *Tutorials*, "Designing for the Web." For links to more tutorials as well as sites that provide advice for improving accessibility for people with disabilities, select *Links for Business Writing*.

Audience and Purpose

Your main goal when designing a Web site is to establish a predictable environment in which users can comfortably navigate and easily find the information they need. To do so, you can apply many of the business writing principles covered in this book. For example, you should consider carefully your <u>purpose</u> (Tab 1) and the needs of your <u>readers</u> (Tab 1) when choosing the visual style of your Web site. Most organizational sites have well-defined goals, such as reference, training, education, publicity, advocacy, or marketing. Before you begin building your site, create a clear statement of purpose that identifies your target audience, using one of the two general kinds of sites: external or internal.

EXTERNAL SITE   The purpose of this site is to enable our customers to locate product information, place online orders, and contact our customer-service department.

INTERNAL SITE   The purpose of this site is to provide SNR Security Corporation employees with a single, consistent, and up-to-date resource for materials about SNR Security's Employee Benefits Package.

External sites target an Internet audience; *internal sites* are designed for audiences on an intranet (a computer network within an educational institution or a company that is not accessible to audiences outside that institution or company).

Access for People with Disabilities

The many advantages of Web sites include colorful graphics, animation, and streaming video and audio. However, these design elements can be barriers to people with impaired vision or hearing or those who are color-blind. Use the following strategies to meet the needs of such audiences.

- Avoid frames, complex tables, animation, JavaScript, and other design elements incompatible with text-only browsers and adaptive technologies, such as voice or large-print software.
- Provide HTML versions of pages and documents whenever possible because this format is most compatible with the current generation of screen readers.
- Attach text equivalents for graphic or audio elements.
- Design for the color-blind reader by making meaning independent of color. For example, rather than asking users to "click on the green button for more information," label the button ("Click Here") or embed a link in a sentence: "See our catalog for more information."

Writer's Checklist: Designing Web Sites

Many of the guidelines in **layout and design** are applicable to designing Web sites; however, not all apply, so keep the following in mind.

☑ Work with the Web master or site administrator to optimize your site for speed of access and to maintain technical and design standards. On campus, consult your instructor or campus computer support staff about standards for posting content.

☑ Draft a navigation chart or map of your site early in the design process to make information logically accessible in the fewest possible steps (or clicks).

☑ Anchor links on relevant words in the sentence ("For more information about employment opportunities, visit Human Resources").

☑ Avoid overusing complex graphics and animation that can clutter or slow access to your site. For high-resolution graphics, consider using thumbnails (images reduced to 10–15 percent of the original file size) that link to the original size image.

☑ Avoid bold and multiple colors; instead, use lighter colors, especially for backgrounds. Limit the number of typeface colors as well as styles. Use typeface colors that contrast (but do not clash) with background colors.

☑ Use uppercase letters or boldface type sparingly. Use underlined text only for links. Use sans serif fonts for text passages; they are more legible at a computer screen's low resolution.

Writer's Checklist: Designing Web Sites (continued)

☑ Format your text to achieve the most readable line length — typically fifty to seventy characters, or ten to twelve words, per line.

☑ Separate text from graphics with generous blank space (the equivalent of white space).

☑ Limit the types of heading and subheading styles, and be consistent.

☑ Block indent text sections that you expect viewers to read in detail.

☑ Incorporate the name of your organization and its logo in a banner at the top of each page.

☑ Include a link to your site's Privacy Statement.

☑ Check that all your links work, particularly after site changes.

DIGITAL TIP TESTING YOUR WEB SITE

It's important to test your design by viewing it on different browsers and platforms. You might take advantage of Web sites that will test a limited sample of your site's features for free. The services can test your site's browser and hardware platform compatibility, page-load speed, and links. For more on this topic, see <bedfordstmartins.com/alred> and select *Digital Tips*, "Testing Your Web Site."

6

Correspondence

Preview

The entries <u>correspondence</u> and <u>memos</u> cover the general principles that will help you get the most out of the more-specific entries in this section. You may also wish to review the entry <u>e-mail</u>, especially the discussion of netiquette, for correspondence sent in e-mail form or attached to an e-mail. The other entries in this section cover specific situations, such as complaints, adjustments, and <u>international correspondence</u>. Finally, remember that the process of writing letters and memos involves many of the same steps that go into most other on-the-job writing tasks, as described in "Five Steps to Successful Writing" (page xxi).

> **WEB LINK ANNOTATED SAMPLE CORRESPONDENCE**
>
> For annotated examples of letters, e-mail, and memos, including poorly written correspondence with appropriate, revised versions, see <bedfordst martins.com/alred> and select *Model Documents Gallery*. For links to additional resources, including advice on addressing memos, select *Links for Business Writing*.

acknowledgment letters

One way to build goodwill with colleagues and clients is to send an acknowledgment letter, letting them know that something they sent arrived and expressing thanks. It is usually a short, polite note. If you have established a working relationship with someone, an e-mail message is appropriate. The example shown in Figure 6–1 is typical and could be sent as a letter or an e-mail. See also correspondence.

Dear Mr. Evans:

I received your comprehensive report today. When I finish studying it in detail, I'll send you our cost estimate for the installation of the Mark II Energy Saving System.

Again, thanks for your effort in preparing such a thorough analysis.

Regards,

Roger Vonblatz

FIGURE 6–1. Acknowledgment Letter or E-mail

adjustment letters

An adjustment letter is written in response to a complaint letter and tells the customer what your company intends to do about the complaint. Although sent in response to a problem, an adjustment letter actually provides an excellent opportunity to build goodwill for your company. Effective adjustment letters, such as those shown in Figures 6–2 and 6–3, can both repair any damage done and restore the customer's confidence in your company.

No matter how unreasonable the complaint, your response and tone should be positive and respectful. Avoid emphasizing the problem, but do take responsibility for it and focus on what you are doing to correct it. You should settle such matters quickly and courteously, and always try to satisfy the customer at a reasonable cost to your company. See also refusal letters.

Full Adjustments

Before granting an adjustment to a claim for which your company is at fault, first determine what happened and what you can do to satisfy the

International Hotels

EXECUTIVE OFFICE

September 26, 2005

Ms. Elizabeth Shapiro
2374 N. Kenwood Ave.
Fresno, CA 93650

Dear Ms. Shapiro:

We are sorry that your and your husband's stay with us did not go smoothly. Providing dependable service is what's expected of us — and when our staff doesn't provide high-quality service, it's easy to understand our guests' disappointment. I truly wish we had performed better and that your vacation plans had not been disrupted.

We are eager to restore your confidence in our ability to provide dependable, high-quality service. Please accept the enclosed certificate for one weekend's stay at any of our 500 hotels worldwide. I hope we will have the pleasure of welcoming you and your husband again soon.

Ms. Shapiro, in addition, we appreciate your taking the time to write. It helps to receive comments such as yours, and we conscientiously follow through to be sure proper procedures are met. I assure you your letter is being put to good use.

Yours truly,

Ms. M. J. Matthews

Ms. M. J. Matthews
Executive Office

Enclosure: Certificate

10113 Executive Drive/Chicago, Illinois 60601
800-964-9400   http://www.interhotel.com

FIGURE 6–2. Adjustment Letter (When Company Is at Fault)

customer. Be certain that you are familiar with your company's adjustment policy. In addition, be careful about your wording; for example, "We have just received your letter of May 7 about our *defective product*" could be ruled in a court of law as an admission that the product is in fact defective. Treat every claim individually, and lean toward giving the customer the benefit of the doubt.

Grant adjustments graciously; a settlement made grudgingly will do more harm than good. Not only must you be gracious, but you must also acknowledge the error in such a way that the customer will not lose confidence in your company. (See also <u>tone</u>, Tab 9, and <u>correspondence</u>). Emphasize early what the reader will consider good news.

- Yes, you were incorrectly billed for the delivery.

- Please accept our apologies for the error in your account.

- Enclosed is a replacement for the damaged part.

If an explanation will help restore your reader's confidence, explain what caused the problem. You might point out any steps you may be taking to prevent a recurrence of the problem. Explain that customer feedback helps your firm keep the quality of its product or service high.

6

Correspondence

Dear Mr. Ortiz:

Enclosed is your SWELCO Coffeemaker, which you sent to us on August 17.

In various parts of the country, tap water may have a high mineral content. If you fill your SWELCO Coffeemaker with water for breakfast coffee before going to bed, a mineral scale will build up on the inner wall of the water tube—as explained on page 2 of your SWELCO Instruction Booklet.

We have removed the mineral scale from the water tube of your coffeemaker and thoroughly cleaned the entire unit. To ensure the best service from your coffeemaker in the future, clean it once a month by operating it with four ounces of white vinegar and eight cups of water. To rinse out the vinegar taste, operate the unit twice with clear water.

With proper care, your SWELCO Coffeemaker will serve you well for many years to come.

Sincerely,

FIGURE 6–3. **Partial Adjustment Letter (Accompanying a Product)**

Close pleasantly, looking forward, not back. Avoid recalling the problem in your closing ("Again, we apologize . . .").

The adjustment letter in Figure 6–2, for example, begins by accepting responsibility and offers an apology for the customer's inconvenience (note the use of the pronouns *we* and *us*). The second paragraph expresses a desire to restore goodwill and describes specifically how the writer intends to make the adjustment. The third paragraph expresses appreciation to the customer for calling attention to the problem and assures her that her complaint has been taken seriously.

Partial Adjustments

You may sometimes need to grant a partial adjustment—even if a claim is not really justified—to regain the lost goodwill of a customer or client. If, for example, a customer incorrectly uses a product or service, you may need to help the reader better understand the correct use of that product or service. In such a circumstance, remember that your customer or client believes that his or her claim is justified. Therefore, you should give the explanation before granting the claim—otherwise, your reader may never get to the explanation. If your explanation establishes customer responsibility, do so tactfully. Figure 6–3 is an example of a partial adjustment letter.

collection letters

Collection letters serve two purposes: (1) collecting the overdue bill and (2) preserving the customer relationship. In some states, collection letters may be prepared by attorneys because certain language and requirements must be followed to demand payment.

Most companies use a series of collection letters like the series shown in Figures 6–4, 6–5, and 6–6, in which the letters become increasingly demanding and urgent. All letters should be courteous and show a genuine interest in the customer as well as concern for whatever problems may be preventing prompt payment. See also tone (Tab 9) and "you" viewpoint (Tab 9).

The first stage consists of reminders stamped on the invoice ("overdue"), form letters, or brief personal notes. These early reminders should maintain a friendly tone that emphasizes the customer's good credit record until now. As in the example of a first-stage collection letter in Figure 6–4, you might suggest that nonpayment may be a result of a simple oversight.

In the second stage, your tone should be firmer and more direct than in the first stage, but it should never be rude, sarcastic, or threatening. Ask directly for payment, and inquire whether some circum-

Dear Mr. Holland:

With the new school year about to begin, your shoe store must be busier than ever as students purchase their back-to-school footwear. Perhaps in the rush of business you've overlooked paying your account of $1,200, which is now 60 days overdue.

Enclosed is our fall sales list. When you send in your check for your outstanding account, why not send in your next order and take advantage of these special prices.

Sincerely,

FIGURE 6–4. First-Stage Collection Letter

stances are preventing payment. Perhaps suggest an installment payment plan if you are able to offer one. Mention the importance of good credit and remind the customer that he or she has always received good value from you. Make it easy to respond by enclosing a return envelope or by offering a toll-free telephone or fax number or a Web address

Dear Mr. Holland:

We are concerned that we have not heard from you about your overdue account of $1,200 even though we have written three times in the past 90 days. Because you have always been one of our best customers, we have to wonder if some special circumstances have caused the delay. If so, please feel free to discuss the matter with us.

By sending us a check today, you can preserve your excellent credit record. Because you have always paid your account promptly in the past, we are sure that you will want to settle this balance now. If your balance is more than you can pay at present, we will be happy to work out mutually satisfactory payment arrangements.

Please use the enclosed envelope to send in your check, or call (800) 526-1945, toll-free, to discuss your account.

Sincerely,

FIGURE 6–5. Second-Stage Collection Letter

Dear Mr. Holland:

Your account in the amount of $1,200 is now 180 days overdue. You have already received a generous extension of time and, in fairness to our other customers, we cannot permit a further delay in payment.

Because you have not responded to any of our letters, we will be forced to turn your account over to our attorney for collection if we do not receive payment immediately. Such action, of course, will damage your previously fine credit rating.

Why not avoid this unpleasant situation by sending your check in the enclosed return envelope within 10 days or by calling (800) 526-1945 to discuss payment.

Sincerely,

FIGURE 6–6. Third-Stage Collection Letter

where the customer can pay with a credit card. Notice how the second-stage letter in Figure 6–5 is more direct than the first letter, but it is no less polite.

Third-stage collection letters reflect a sense of urgency because the customer has not responded to your previous letters. Although your tone should remain courteous, make your demand for payment explicit, as shown in Figure 6–6. Point out how reasonable you have been and urge the customer to pay at once to avoid a collection-service or legal action.

complaint letters

The tone of a complaint letter is important; the most effective ones do not sound complaining. If your letter reflects only your annoyance and anger, you may not be taken seriously. Assume that the recipient will be conscientious in correcting the problem. However, anticipate reader reactions or rebuttals.

- I reviewed carefully the "safe operating guidelines" in the user manual before I installed the device.

Without such explanations, readers may be tempted to dismiss your complaint. Figure 6–7 shows a typical complaint letter.

Subject: HV3 Monitors

On July 9, I ordered nine HV3 monitors for your model MX-15 diagnostic scanner. The monitors were ordered from your Web site.

On August 2, I received from your Newark, New Jersey, parts warehouse seven HL monitors. I immediately returned these monitors with a note indicating the mistake that had been made. However, not only have I failed to receive the HV3 monitors I ordered, but I have also been billed repeatedly.

I have enclosed a copy of my confirmation e-mail, the shipping form, and the most recent bill. If you cannot send me the monitors I ordered by November 1, please cancel my order.

Sincerely,

FIGURE 6–7. Complaint Letter

Although the circumstances and severity of the problem may vary, effective complaint letters generally follow this pattern:

1. Identify the problem or faulty item(s) and include relevant invoice numbers, part names, and dates. Include a copy of the receipt, bill, or contract, and keep the original for your records.
2. Explain logically, clearly, and specifically what went wrong, especially for a problem with a service. (Avoid guessing why you *think* some problem occurred.)
3. State what you expect the reader to do to solve the problem.

Begin by checking to see if the company's Web site provides instructions for submitting a complaint. Otherwise, for large organizations, you may address your complaint to Customer Service. In smaller organizations, you might write to a vice president in charge of sales or service, or directly to the owner. As a last resort, you may find that sending copies of a complaint letter to more than one person in the company will get faster results. See also adjustment letters and refusal letters.

correspondence

The process of writing letters or <u>memos</u> (or <u>e-mail</u> that functions as either) involves many of the same steps that go into writing most other documents, as described in "Five Steps to Successful Writing" (page xxi). One important consideration in correspondence is the impression you convey to <u>readers</u> (Tab 1). To convey a professional image—of yourself and your company or organization—take particular care with the <u>tone</u> (Tab 9) and style of your writing. See also <u>business writing style</u> (Tab 9).

Writing Style and Accuracy

Letter-writing style varies from informal (or casual), as in a letter to a close business associate, to formal (or restrained), as in a letter to someone you do not know.

INFORMAL	It worked! The new process is better than we had dreamed.
RESTRAINED	You will be pleased to know that the new process is more effective than we had expected.

You will probably find yourself using the restrained style more frequently than the casual one. Remember that an overdone attempt to sound casual or friendly can sound insincere. However, do not adopt so formal a style that your letters read like legal contracts. See also <u>affectation</u> (Tab 9).

AFFECTED	Per our dialogue yesterday, we no longer possess an original copy of the brochure requested. Please be advised that a PDF copy is attached to this e-mail.
IMPROVED	We are out of original copies of the brochure we discussed yesterday, so I am attaching a PDF copy to this e-mail.

The improved version is both less stuffy and more concise. Do not be so concise, however, that you become blunt. Responding to a written request that is vague with "Your request was unclear" or "I don't understand" could offend your reader. Instead, ask for more information and establish goodwill to encourage your reader to provide the information.

- I will need more information before I can answer your request. Specifically, can you give me the title and the date of the report you are looking for?

Although this version is a bit longer, it is more tactful and will elicit a faster response. See also <u>telegraphic style</u> (Tab 9).

6

Correspondence

Check your letters for accuracy. Facts, figures, and dates that are incorrect or misleading may cost time, money, and goodwill. Incorrect punctuation or grammar and unconventional usage can undermine your credibility. Remember that when you sign a letter, you are accepting responsibility for it. Therefore, allow yourself time to review correspondence carefully before sending it.

Audience: Tone and Goodwill

Correspondence is always more personal than reports or other forms of business writing because it is written directly to another person. To achieve a conversational style, imagine your reader sitting across the desk from you and write to the reader as if you were talking face to face.

Take into account your reader's needs and feelings. Ask yourself, "How might I feel if I received this letter?" and then tailor your message accordingly. Remember, an impersonal and unfriendly letter to a customer or client can tarnish the image of you and your business, but a thoughtful and sincere letter can enhance it. Suppose, for example, you received a refund request from a customer who forgot to enclose the receipt with the request. In a response to that customer, you might write the following:

- We must receive the sales receipt with your letter before we can process a refund. [writer's needs (*we*) emphasized]

If you consider how you might keep the customer's goodwill, you might word the request this way:

- Please mail or fax the sales receipt with your letter so that we can process your refund. [polite, but writer's needs (*we*) emphasized]

You can put the reader's needs and interests foremost in the letter by writing from the reader's perspective. Often, doing so means using the words *you* and *your* rather than *we, our, I,* and *mine* — a technique called the "you" viewpoint (Tab 9). Consider the following revision:

- So you can receive your refund promptly, please mail or fax the sales receipt with your letter. [reader's needs emphasized with *you* and *your*]

This revision stresses the reader's benefit and interest. By emphasizing the reader's needs, the writer will be more likely to accomplish the objective: to get the reader to act. See also purpose (Tab 1) and positive writing (Tab 9).

Keep in mind that, if overdone, goodwill and the "you" viewpoint can produce writing that is fawning and insincere. Messages that are full of excessive praise and inflated language may be ignored — or even resented — by the reader.

EXCESSIVE	You are just the kind of client that deserves the finest service that anyone can offer—and you deserve our best deal. Knowing how careful you are at making decisions, I know you'll think about the advantages of using our consulting service.
REASONABLE	From our earlier correspondence, I can understand your need for reliable service—we strive to give all our priority clients our full attention. After you have reviewed our proposal, I am confident you will appreciate our "five-star" consulting option.

Writer's Checklist: Using Tone to Build Goodwill

Use the following guidelines to achieve a tone that builds goodwill with your recipients.

☑ Be respectful, not demanding.

DEMANDING	Submit your answer within one week.
RESPECTFUL	I would appreciate your answer within one week.

☑ Be modest, not arrogant.

ARROGANT	My attached report is thorough, and I'm sure that you won't be able to continue without it.
MODEST	The attached report contains details of the refinancing options, and I hope you find it useful.

☑ Be polite, not sarcastic.

SARCASTIC	I just now received the shipment we ordered six months ago. I'm sending it back—we can't use it now. Thanks a lot!
POLITE	I am returning the shipment we ordered on March 12. Unfortunately, it arrived too late for us to be able to use it.

☑ Be positive and tactful, not negative and condescending.

NEGATIVE	Your complaint about our prices is way off target. Our prices are definitely not any higher than those of our competitors.
TACTFUL	Thank you for your suggestion concerning our prices. We believe, however, that our prices are competitive with, and in some cases are below, those of our competitors.

Good-News and Bad-News Patterns

Although the relative directness of correspondence may vary, it is generally more effective to present good news directly and bad news indirectly, especially if the stakes are high.* This principle is based on the fact that readers form their impressions and attitudes very early in letters and that you as a writer may want to subordinate the bad news to reasons that make the bad news understandable. Further, if you are writing international correspondence, be aware that far more cultures are generally indirect in business messages than are direct.

Consider the thoughtlessness and direct rejection in Figure 6–8. Although the letter is concise and uses the pronouns *you* and *your*, the writer does not consider how the recipient is likely to feel as she reads the letter. Its pattern is (1) the bad news, (2) an explanation, (3) the closing.

Ms. Barbara L. Mauer
157 Beach Drive
San Diego, CA 92113

Dear Ms. Mauer:

Your application for the position of records administrator at Southtown Dental Center has been rejected. We have found someone more qualified than you.

Sincerely,

FIGURE 6–8. A Poor Bad-News Letter

A better general pattern for bad-news letters is (1) an opening that provides context (often called a "buffer"), (2) an explanation, (3) the bad news, and (4) a goodwill closing. (See also refusal letters.) The opening introduces the subject and establishes a professional tone. The body provides an explanation by reviewing the facts that make the bad news understandable. Although bad news is never pleasant, information that either puts the bad news in perspective or makes it seem reasonable maintains goodwill between the writer and the reader. The closing should reinforce a positive relationship through goodwill or helpful information. Consider, for example, the rejection letter shown in Figure 6–9. It carries the same disappointing news as does the letter in Figure 6–8, but the writer is careful to thank the reader for her time and effort, explain why she was not accepted for the job, and offer her encouragement.

*Gerald J. Alred, "'We Regret to Inform You': Toward a New Theory of Negative Messages," in *Studies in Technical Communication*, ed. Brenda R. Sims, 17–36 (Denton: University of North Texas and NCTE, 1993).

Dear Ms. Mauer:

Context
(or "buffer")   Thank you for your time and effort in applying for the position of records administrator at Southtown Dental Center.

Explanation
leading to
bad news   Because we need someone who can assume the duties here with a minimum of training, we have selected an applicant with over ten years of experience.

Goodwill   I am sure that with your excellent college record you will find a position in another office.

Sincerely,

FIGURE 6–9. A Courteous Bad-News Letter

Presenting good news is, of course, easier. Present good news at the beginning of the letter. By presenting the good news first, you increase the likelihood that the reader will pay careful attention to details, and you achieve goodwill from the start. The pattern for good-news letters should be (1) a good-news opening, (2) an explanation of facts, and (3) a goodwill closing. Figure 6–10 is an example of an effective good-news letter.

Dear Ms. Mauer:

Good news   Please accept our offer of the position of records administrator at Southtown Dental Center.

Explanation   If the terms we discussed in the interview are acceptable to you, please come in at 9:30 a.m. on November 15. At that time, we will ask you to complete our benefits form, in addition to . . .

Goodwill   I, as well as the others in the office, look forward to working with you. Everyone was favorably impressed with you during your interview.

Sincerely,

FIGURE 6–10. A Good-News Letter

Openings and Closings

To focus the relevance of any correspondence for the reader, identify your subject in the opening.

- Yesterday, I received your letter and the pager, number AJ 50172. I sent the pager to our quality-control department for tests.

Your closing should let the reader know what he or she should do next and should reinforce goodwill.

- Thanks again for the report, and let me know if you want me to send you a copy of the tests.

Because a closing is in a position of emphasis, consider it carefully. Before you simply use a routine closing ("If you have further questions, please let me know"), consider how you might make your closing work for you. It may be helpful to provide prompts to which the reader can respond.

- If you would like further information, such as a copy of the questionnaire we used, please e-mail me at delgado@prn.com.

See also <u>conclusions</u> (Tab 1) and <u>introductions</u> (Tab 1).

Format and Design

Although word-processing software provides templates for correspondence, it may not provide specific dimensions and spacing. To achieve a professional appearance, center the letter on the page vertically and horizontally. Although one-inch margins are the default standard in many word-processing programs, it is more important to establish a picture frame of blank space surrounding the page of text. When you use organizational letterhead stationery, consider the bottom of the letterhead as the top edge of the paper. The right margin should be approximately as wide as the left margin. To give a fuller appearance to very short letters, increase both margins to about an inch and a half. Use your computer's full-page or print-preview feature to check for proportion.

The two most common formats for business letters are the full-block style shown in Figure 6–11 and the modified-block style shown in Figure 6–12. In the *full-block style*, which should be used only with letterhead, the entire letter is aligned at the left margin. In the *modified-block style*, the return address, date, and complimentary closing begin at the center of the page and the other elements are aligned at the left margin. All other letter styles are variations of the full-block and modified-block styles.

If your employer requires a particular format, use it. Otherwise, follow the guidelines provided here, and review the examples shown in Figures 6–11 and 6–12.

6

Correspondence

520 Niagara Street
Braintree, MA 02184

Phone: (781) 787-1175
Fax: (781) 787-1213
E-mail: mail@evans.com

Letterhead

Date   May 16, 2005

Inside   Mr. George W. Nagel
address   Director of Operations
                Boston Transit Authority
                57 West City Avenue
                Boston, MA 02210

Salutation   Dear Mr. Nagel:

                Enclosed is our final report evaluating the safety measures for
                the Boston Intercity Transit System.

Body   We believe that the report covers the issues you raised and that it
                is self-explanatory. However, if you have any further questions,
                we would be happy to meet with you at your convenience.

                We would also like to express our appreciation to Mr. L. K.
                Sullivan of your committee for his generous help during our
                trips to Boston.

Compli-
mentary   Sincerely,
close

Signature   *Carolyn Brown*

Typed name   Carolyn Brown, Ph.D.
Title   Director of Research

                CB/ls
End   Enclosure: Final Safety Report
notations   cc: ITS Safety Committee Members

FIGURE 6–11. Full-Block-Style Letter (with Letterhead)

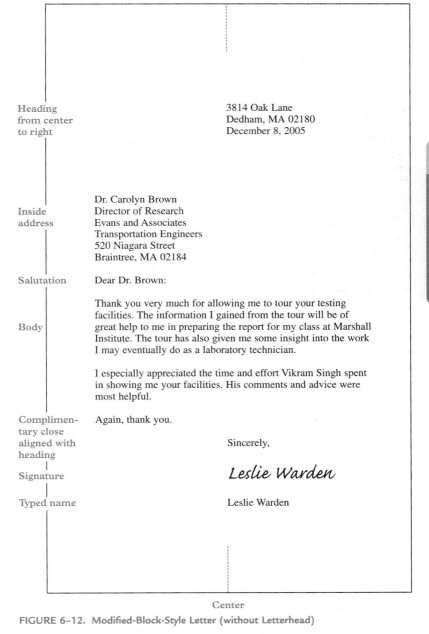

Center

| Heading from center to right | 3814 Oak Lane
Dedham, MA 02180
December 8, 2005 |

Inside address

Dr. Carolyn Brown
Director of Research
Evans and Associates
Transportation Engineers
520 Niagara Street
Braintree, MA 02184

Salutation

Dear Dr. Brown:

Body

Thank you very much for allowing me to tour your testing facilities. The information I gained from the tour will be of great help to me in preparing the report for my class at Marshall Institute. The tour has also given me some insight into the work I may eventually do as a laboratory technician.

I especially appreciated the time and effort Vikram Singh spent in showing me your facilities. His comments and advice were most helpful.

Complimentary close aligned with heading

Again, thank you.

Sincerely,

Signature

Leslie Warden

Typed name

Leslie Warden

Center

FIGURE 6–12. Modified-Block-Style Letter (without Letterhead)

Heading.   Place your full return address and the date in the heading. Because your name appears at the end of the letter, it need not be included in the heading. Spell out words like *street, avenue, first,* and *west* rather than abbreviating them. You may either spell out the name of the state in full or use the standard Postal Service abbreviation. The date usually goes directly beneath the last line of the return address. Do not abbreviate the name of the month. Begin the heading about two inches from the top of the page. If you are using company letterhead that gives the address, enter only the date, three lines below the last line of printed copy.

Inside Address.   Include the recipient's full name, title, and address in the inside address, two to six lines below the date, depending on the length of the letter. The inside address should be aligned with the left margin, and the left margin should be at least one inch wide.

Salutation.   Place the salutation, or greeting, two lines below the inside address and align it with the left margin. In most business letters, the salutation contains the recipient's personal title (such as *Mr., Ms., Dr.*) and last name, followed by a colon. If you are on a first-name basis with the recipient, use only the first name in the salutation.

Address women as *Ms.*, unless they have expressed a preference for *Miss* or *Mrs.* However, professional titles (such as *Professor, Senator, Major*) take precedence over *Ms.* If you do not know whether the recipient is a man or a woman, use a title appropriate to the context of the letter (*Dear Customer, Dear Colleague, Dear IT Professional*).

If you are writing to a large company and do not know the name or title of the recipient, you may address the letter to an appropriate department or identify the subject in a subject line and use no salutation.

- National Business Systems
  501 West National Avenue
  Minneapolis, MN 55407

  Attention: Customer Relations Department

  I am returning three pagers that failed to operate. . . .

- National Business Systems
  501 West National Avenue
  Minneapolis, MN 55407

  Subject: Defective Parts for SL-100 Pagers

  I am returning three pagers that failed to operate. . . .

When a person's first name could be either feminine or masculine, one solution is to use both the first and last names in the salutation (*Dear Pat Smith:*). Avoid "To Whom It May Concern" because it is impersonal and dated.

For multiple recipients, the following salutations are appropriate:

- Dear Professor Allen and Dr. Rivera: [two recipients]
- Dear Ms. Becham, Ms. Moore, and Mr. Stein: [three recipients]
- Dear Colleagues: [Members, or other suitable collective term]

Body. The body of the letter should begin two lines below the salutation (or any element that precedes the body, such as a subject or an attention line). Single-space within paragraphs, and double-space between paragraphs. To provide a fuller appearance to a very short letter, you can increase the side margins or increase the font size. You can also insert extra space above the inside address, the typed (signature) name, and the initials of the person keying the letter—but do not exceed twice the recommended space for each of these elements.

Complimentary Closing. Type the complimentary closing two spaces below the body. Use a standard expression like *Sincerely, Sincerely yours,* or *Yours truly.* (If the recipient is a friend as well as a business associate, you can use a less-formal closing, such as *Best wishes* or *Best regards* or, simply, *Best.*) Capitalize only the initial letter of the first word, and follow the expression with a comma. Place your full name four lines below, aligned on the left with the closing. On the next line include your business title, if it is appropriate to do so. Sign the letter in the space between the complimentary closing and your name.

Second Page. If a letter requires a second page, always carry at least two lines of the body text over to that page. Use plain (nonletterhead) paper of quality equivalent to that of the letterhead stationery for the second page. It should have a header with the recipient's name, the page number, and the date. The heading can go in the upper left-hand corner or across the page, as shown in Figure 6–13.

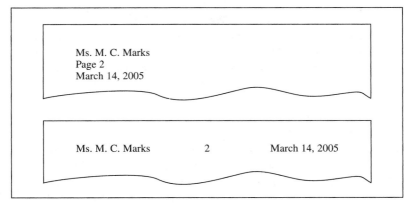

FIGURE 6–13. Headers for the Second Page of a Letter

End Notations.   Business letters sometimes require additional information that is placed at the left margin, two spaces below the typed name and title of the writer in a long letter, four spaces below in a short letter.

Reference initials identify the person keying the letter if that person is not the writer. Show the letter writer's initials in capital letters, followed by a slash mark, and then the initials of the person keying the letter in lowercase letters, as shown in Figure 6–11. When the writer is also the person keying the letter, no initials are needed.

Enclosure notations indicate that the writer is sending material along with the letter (an invoice, an article, and so on). Note that you must mention the enclosure in the body of the letter. Enclosure notations may take several forms:

- Enclosure: Final Safety Report
- Enclosures (2)
- Enc. or Encs.

Copy notation (cc:) tells the reader that a copy of the letter is being sent to the named recipients (see Figure 6–11). Use a blind-copy notation (bcc:) when you do not want the addressee to know that a copy is being sent to someone else. A blind-copy notation appears only on the copy, not on the original (bcc: Dr. Brenda Shelton).

For additional details on letter format and design, you may wish to consult a guide such as *The Gregg Reference Manual* by William A. Sabin.

Writer's Checklist: Writing Correspondence

☑ Establish your purpose, analyze your readers' needs, and determine your **scope** (Tab 1).

☑ Prepare an outline, even if it is only a list of points to be covered in the order you want to cover them (see **outlining**, Tab 1).

☑ Write the first draft (see **writing a draft**, Tab 1).

☑ Allow for a cooling period prior to **revision** (Tab 1) or seek a colleague's advice, especially for correspondence that addresses a problem.

☑ Revise the draft, checking for key problems in clarity and **coherence** (Tab 9).

☑ Use the appropriate or prescribed format.

☑ Check for accuracy: make sure that all facts, figures, and dates are correct.

☑ Check for appropriate punctuation (see Tab 12, "Punctuation and Mechanics") and use effective **proofreading** (Tab 1) techniques.

☑ Remember that when you sign a letter, initial a memo, or send an e-mail, you are accepting responsibility for it. See also **point of view** (Tab 1).

cover letters

A cover letter identifies an item that is being sent, the person to whom it is being sent, and the reason that it is being sent; it provides a permanent record for both the writer and the reader. See also <u>application letters</u> (Tab 7).

Keep your remarks brief in a cover letter. Your opening should explain what is being sent and why. Then, you might highlight or briefly summarize the information you are sending. The example in Figure 6–14 is concise, but it also includes details such as how the report's information was gathered.

Dear Mr. Hammersmith:

Enclosed is the report estimating our energy needs for the year as requested by John Brenan, Vice President, on September 4.

The report is a result of several meetings with the Manager of Plant Operations and her staff and an extensive survey of all our employees. The survey was delayed by the transfer of key staff in Building A. We believe, however, that the report will provide the information you need in order to furnish us with a cost estimate for the installation of your Mark II Energy Saving System.

We would like to thank Diana Biel of ESI for her assistance in preparing the survey. If you need any more information, please let me know.

Sincerely,

FIGURE 6–14. Cover Letter (for a Report)

e-mail

E-mail (or email) functions in the workplace as a medium to send information, elicit discussions, collect opinions, and transmit documents and files of all types electronically. Although e-mail may take the form of informal notes, you should generally follow the same guidelines for writing style and strategy described in the entries <u>correspondence</u> and <u>memos</u>. See also <u>collaborative writing</u> (Tab 1) and <u>selecting the medium</u> (Tab 1).

Review and Confidentiality

E-mail is a quick and easy way to communicate, but avoid the temptation to dash off a first draft and send it as is. Be careful to observe the rules of netiquette (Inter*net* + *etiquette*) in the *Writer's Checklist* that follows. As with other workplace correspondence, your message should be free of grammatical or factual errors, ambiguities, or unintended implications. It should include crucial details. Be especially careful when sending messages to superiors in your organization or to people outside the organization. Time you spend reviewing your e-mail before you send it can save a great deal of time and embarrassment sorting out misunderstandings caused by a careless message.

Keep in mind, also, the issue of confidentiality when sending e-mail. Remember, e-mail can be intercepted by someone other than the intended recipient, and e-mail messages are never truly deleted. Most companies back up and save all company e-mail and are legally entitled to monitor e-mail. Companies can also be compelled legally to provide e-mail in a court of law. Consider the content of all your messages in the light of these possibilities, and carefully review your text before you click "Send."

Writer's Checklist: Observing Workplace Netiquette

To maintain a high level of professionalism in workplace e-mail, observe the rules of netiquette.

☑ Use company e-mail only for appropriate business.
  • Do not send or forward jokes or humorous stories, use **biased language** (Tab 9), or discuss office gossip.
  • Do not send *flames* (e-mail that contains abusive, obscene, or derogatory language) to attack someone.
  • Do not send *spam* (mass-distributed e-mail that often promotes personal projects and interests).

☑ Respond to incoming e-mail promptly. If you receive an assignment by e-mail that will take a few days or longer to complete, send a courtesy response saying so.

☑ Be scrupulous about typing e-mail addresses and otherwise ensuring that the intended recipient gets the message.

☑ Send an attachment only after verifying that your recipient wants or needs the file and that your recipient's software will accept it. Be aware that attachments can consume download time and disk space.

☑ Consider posting a large file at an Internet server and supplying the file's address so that your recipient may download the file at his or her convenience.

☑ Do not write in ALL-UPPERCASE LETTERS; such a message is difficult to read and is considered the equivalent of shouting. Likewise, do not write in all-lowercase letters; it is considered lazy and too informal for professional work.

Writer's Checklist: Observing Workplace Netiquette (continued)

☑ Avoid e-mail abbreviations used in personal e-mail and chat rooms (BTW for *by the way*, for example).

☑ Do not use emoticons (keyboard characters used to create sideways faces conveying emotions) for business and professional e-mail. For advice on providing typographic emphasis, review the next section on design considerations.

DIGITAL TIP SENDING AN E-MAIL ATTACHMENT

Large files, like graphics, slow transmission speed, and the recipient's software or Internet provider may not be able to accept large files. Consider using a compression software utility like WinZip at <www.winzip.com/>, which can reduce the file size by 80 percent or more. A note of caution: viruses can be embedded in e-mail attachments, so regularly update your virus-scanning software. For more on this topic, see <bedfordstmartins .com/alred> and select *Digital Tips*, "Sending an E-mail Attachment."

Design Considerations

Some e-mail systems allow you to use sophisticated typographical features, such as various fonts and bullets. Because these options increase your e-mail file size and may display unpredictably in your recipient's software, set your e-mail software to send messages in "plain text" and use alternative highlighting devices. For example, capital letters or asterisks, used sparingly, can substitute for boldface, italics, and underlines as emphasis.

- Dr. Wilhoit's suggestions benefit doctors AND patients.

- Although the proposal is sound in *theory*, it will never work in *practice*.

Intermittent underlining can replace solid underlining or italics when referring to published works in an e-mail message.

- My report follows the format given in _The Business Writer's Companion_.

Keep in mind the following additional design considerations when sending e-mail.

- Break the text into short paragraphs to avoid dense blocks of text.
- Consider providing an overview at the top in a brief paragraph for messages that run longer than a screen of text.

- Attach documents containing formatted elements, such as tables and bulleted lists, that do not transmit well in e-mails.
- Place your response to someone else's message at the beginning (or top) of the e-mail window so that recipients can see your response immediately.
- When replying to a message, quote only relevant parts. If your system does not distinguish the quoted text, note it with a greater-than symbol (>).
- Use the "cc:" (carbon copy) and "bcc:" (blind carbon copy) address lines with great care because some recipients use their placement in the address lists to filter their mail.
- Provide a concise phrase in the subject line (as in memos) that describes the topic of your message; recipients use subject lines to prioritize and file their incoming messages.

Salutations, Closings, and Signature Blocks

Because e-mail can function as a letter, memo, or personal note, finding a suitable greeting and a complimentary closing can be difficult. If your employer follows a certain form, adopt that practice. Otherwise, use the following guidelines:

- When e-mail functions as a personal note to a friend, you can vary informal salutations (*Hi Mike,* or *Hello Jenny,*) and closings (*Take care,* or *Cheers,*).
- When e-mail goes outside an organization to someone with whom you have not yet corresponded, you can use the standard letter salutation (*Dear Professor Tucker:* or *Dear Docuform Customer:*) and a slightly informal closing (*Best wishes,* or *Sincerely,*).
- When e-mail functions as a memo, you may omit the salutation and closing because both your name and the name(s) of the recipient(s) appear in the "To" and "From" sections of the message. However, some e-mail users adopt a slightly more personal greeting, especially if the distribution list is relatively small or a single individual (*Project Colleagues,* or *Andreas,* [recipient's first name]).

Note that in some cultures, business correspondents do not use first names as quickly as they do in American correspondence. See <u>international correspondence</u>.

Because e-mail does not provide letterhead with standard addresses and contact information, many companies and individual writers include signature blocks (also called *signatures*) at the bottom of their messages. Signature blocks, which writers can usually preprogram to appear on every e-mail they send, supply information that company letterhead usually provides as well as links to Web sites. If your organization requires a certain format, adhere to that standard. Otherwise, use the pattern shown in Figure 6–15.

```
===============================
Daniel J. Vasquez, Publications Manager    ←    Name and Title
Medical Information Systems                ←    Department or Division
TechCom Corporation                        ←    Company Name
P.O. Box 5413   Salinas, CA 93962          ←    Mailing Address
Office Phone 888-229-4511 (x 341)          ←    Phone Number
General Office Fax 888-229-1132            ←    Fax Number
www.tcc.com                                ←    Web Address (URL)
===============================
```

FIGURE 6–15. E-mail Signature Block

For signature blocks, consider the following guidelines:

- Include as few lines as possible. Most netiquette guides advocate using five lines or fewer, but more are acceptable in business correspondence because it typically requires more contact information.
- Keep line length to 60 characters or fewer to avoid unpredictable line wraps.
- Test your signature block in plain text e-mail readers to verify your format; centered text and vertical lines may look fine in one system but chaotic in another.
- Use highlighting cues, such as hyphens, equal signs, and white space, to separate the signature from the message.
- Avoid using quotations, aphorisms, and other messages ("May the Force be with you") in professional signatures.

DIGITAL TIP LEAVING AN AWAY-FROM-DESK MESSAGE

Many e-mail systems allow you to create an away-from-desk, automatic response message. Your message should inform senders when you are expected back and, if necessary, whom they can contact in your absence. For more on this topic, see <bedfordstmartins.com/alred> and select *Digital Tips*, "Leaving an Away-from-Desk Message."

Writer's Checklist: Managing Your E-mail

☑ Check your in-box several times each day; try to clear your in-box by the end of the day.

☑ Set priorities for reading e-mail by skimming sender names and subject lines.

Writer's Checklist: Managing Your E-mail (continued)

☑ Use the search command to find topics and individual names.

☑ Review all messages on a subject before you respond, so you don't waste time responding to an issue that is no longer relevant.

☑ Learn the advanced features of your system so that you can use filters that organize messages as they arrive.

☑ Create electronic folders for e-mail, using personal names and key topics.

☑ Copy or save sent copies of important e-mails in your electronic folders.

☑ Print and file hard copies of crucial e-mail messages that are complex or that you will need for meetings.

☑ Keep an up-to-date address book.

fax

Fax (facsimile transmission) is used to send documents with elements that must be viewed as originally created, such as handwritten corrections and notes. When you have to send a drawing or diagram or a document such as a contract that contains one or more signatures, a fax ensures authenticity. Keep in mind, however, that faxes almost never transmit as clearly as the original document and may be reduced in size. Therefore, use generous margins and avoid small font sizes and styles that will not transmit well.

When you fax, be aware that the document can be read by persons other than the intended recipient. If you have to fax confidential or sensitive messages, call the intended recipient first so that he or she can be waiting at the machine as you transmit your fax. Some recipients are resistant, or even hostile, to faxes they view as unnecessary or overly long. A scanned electronic document attached to an e-mail may be a better option.

inquiries and responses

Your purpose in writing an inquiry letter or e-mail is often to obtain answers to specific questions, as shown in Figure 6–16. You will be more likely to receive a prompt, helpful reply if you follow these guidelines:

• Keep your questions specific and clear but concise.
• Phrase your questions so that the reader will immediately know the type of information you are seeking, why you need it, and how you will use it.

- If possible, present your questions in a numbered list to make it easy for your reader to respond to them.
- Keep the number of questions to a minimum to improve your chances of receiving a prompt response.
- Offer some inducement for the reader to respond, such as promising to share the results of what you are doing. See also <u>persuasion</u> (Tab 1).
- Promise to keep responses confidential, if appropriate.

In the closing, thank the reader for taking the time to respond. In addition, make it convenient for the recipient to respond by providing contact information, such as a phone number or an e-mail address, as shown in Figure 6–16. See also <u>correspondence</u> and <u>"you" viewpoint</u> (Tab 9).

Dear Ms. Metcalf:

Could you please send me some information on heating systems for a computerized, energy-efficient house that a team of engineering students at the University of Dayton is designing?

The house, which contains 2,000 square feet of living space (17,600 cubic feet), meets all the requirements in your brochure "Insulating for Efficiency." We need the following information, based on the southern Ohio climate:

1. The proper-size heat pump for such a home.
2. The wattage of the supplemental electrical heating units required.
3. The estimated power consumption and rates for those units for one year.

We will be happy to send you our preliminary design report. If you have questions or suggestions, please contact me at kjp@fly.ud.edu or call 513-229-4598.

Thank you for your help.

FIGURE 6–16. Inquiry

Responding to Inquiries

When you receive an inquiry, determine whether you have both the information and authority to respond. If you are the right person in your organization to respond, answer as promptly as you can, and be sure to answer every question asked, as shown in Figure 6–17. How long and how detailed your response should be depends on the nature of the question and the information provided in the letter by the writer. If you have received a letter that you feel you cannot answer, find out who can and forward the letter to that person. Notify the letter writer that you have forwarded the letter. When an inquiry is forwarded, the person who

Dear Ms. Parsons:

Jane Metcalf forwarded to me your inquiry of March 11 about the house that your engineering team is designing. I can estimate the heating requirements of a typical home of 17,600 cubic feet as follows:

1. For such a home, we would generally recommend a heat pump capable of delivering 40,000 BTUs, such as our model AL-42 (17 kilowatts).
2. With the AL-42's efficiency, you don't need supplemental heating units.
3. Depending on usage, the AL-42 unit averages between 1,000 and 1,500 kilowatt-hours from December through March. To determine the current rate for such usage, check with Dayton Power and Light Company.

I can give you an answer that would apply specifically to your house based on its particular design (such as number of stories, windows, and entrances). If you send me more details, I will be happy to provide more precise figures for your interesting project.

Sincerely,

Michael Wang

Michael Wang
Engineering Assistant
mwang@mvpc.org

FIGURE 6–17. Response to an Inquiry

replies should state in the first paragraph of the response why someone else is answering the original inquiry.

international correspondence

Business practice varies among cultures, as described in <u>global communication</u> (Tab 1). Organizational patterns, persuasive strategies, forms of courtesy, and ideas about efficiency vary from country to country. For example, in the United States, direct, concise correspondence may demonstrate courtesy by not wasting another person's time; in other cultures, such directness and brevity may seem rude, suggesting that the writer wishes to end the communication as soon as possible. Further, where an American writer might consider one brief letter sufficient to communicate a request, a writer in another culture may expect an exchange of three or four longer letters to pave the way for action.

When you read correspondence from businesspeople in other cultures or countries, be alert to differences in such features as customary expressions, openings, and closings. Japanese business writers, for example, have traditionally used indirect openings that reflect on the season, compliment the reader's success, and offer hopes for the reader's continued prosperity. They have also traditionally expressed negative messages and <u>refusal letters</u> indirectly to avoid embarrassing the recipient.

When you are writing for international readers, rethink the ingrained habits that define how you express yourself, learn as much as you can about the cultural expectations of others, and focus on politeness strategies that demonstrate your respect for readers. Doing so will help you achieve clarity and mutual understanding with international readers.

> **WEB LINK SAMPLE INTERNATIONAL CORRESPONDENCE**
>
> For an example of an inappropriate letter and an appropriate revised version for an international reader, see <bedfordstmartins.com/alred> and select *Model Documents Gallery*.

6

Correspondence

Writer's Checklist: Writing International Correspondence

- ☑ Write clear and complete sentences: unusual word order or rambling sentences will frustrate and confuse readers. See <u>garbled sentences</u> (Tab 9).
- ☑ Avoid an overly simplified style that may offend the reader. See also <u>English as a second language</u> (Tab 11).
- ☑ Avoid humor, irony, and sarcasm; they are easily misunderstood outside their cultural context.
- ☑ Avoid idioms ("give a heads up"), unusual figures of speech, and allusions to events or attitudes particular to American life. See <u>idioms</u> (Tab 9).
- ☑ Consider whether <u>jargon</u> (Tab 9) or technical terminology can be found in abbreviated English-language dictionaries. See also <u>affectation</u> (Tab 9).
- ☑ Avoid using first names too quickly.
- ☑ Write out <u>dates</u> (Tab 12), whether in the month-day-year style (June 11, 2005, not 6/11/05) used in the U.S. or the day-month-year style (11 June 2005, not 11/6/05) used in many other parts of the world.
- ☑ Specify time zones or refer to international standards, such as Greenwich mean time (GMT) or Coordinated Universal Time (UTC).
- ☑ Where possible, use international measurement standards, such as the metric system (18°C, 14 cm, 45 kg, and so on). See also <u>global graphics</u> (Tab 5).

☑ Ask someone from your intended audience's culture to review your draft before you complete your final **proofreading** (Tab 1).

memos

Memos — paper or electronic — are used within organizations for many types of writing that are described in entries throughout this book. Memos, for example, report results, instruct employees, announce policies, disseminate information, and delegate responsibilities. The memo in Figure 6–18 assigns a project and provides instructions for completing it. Memos provide a record of decisions made and actions taken. They also can play a key role in the management of many organizations because managers use memos to inform and motivate employees.

Writing Memos

Many of the principles discussed in **correspondence** apply to memos, whether they are sent on paper, attached to e-mail, or in **e-mail** form. See also "Five Steps to Successful Writing" (page xxi).

Development and Protocol.   To produce an effective memo, outline it first, even if you simply jot down points to be covered and then order them logically. With careful preparation, your memos will be both concise and adequately developed. Adequate development of your thoughts is crucial to the memo's clarity, as the following example indicates.

ABRUPT	Be more careful on the loading dock.
DEVELOPED	To prevent accidents on the loading dock, follow these procedures: 1. Check . . . 2. Load only . . . 3. Replace . . .

Although the abrupt version is concise, it is not as clear and specific as the developed revision. Do not assume your **readers** (Tab 1) will know what you mean. Readers who are pressed for time may misinterpret a vague memo. See also **conciseness** (Tab 9).

Although such practices vary, be alert to the protocol of addressing and sending memos in your organization. Consider who should receive a memo and in what order — senior managers, for example, take precedence over junior managers. If rank does not apply, alphabetizing recipients by last name is safe. Who should be copied on a memo or an

PROFESSIONAL PUBLISHING SERVICES
MEMORANDUM

TO: Barbara Smith, Publications Manager
FROM: Hannah Kaufman, Vice President   *HK*
DATE: April 14, 2005
SUBJECT: Schedule for ACM Electronics Brochure

ACM Electronics has asked us to prepare a comprehensive brochure for its Milwaukee office by August 8, 2005. We have worked with electronics firms in the past, so this job should be relatively easy to prepare. My guess is that the job will take nearly two months. Ted Harris has requested time and cost estimates for the project. Fred Moore in production will prepare the cost estimates, and I would like you to prepare a tentative schedule for the project.

Additional Personnel

In preparing the schedule, check the status of the following:
1. Production schedule for all staff writers
2. Available freelance writers
3. Dependable graphic designers

Ordinarily, we would not need to depend on outside personnel; however, because our bid for the *Wall Street Journal* special project is still under consideration, we could be short of staff in June and July. Further, we have to consider vacations that have already been approved.

Time Estimates

Please give me time estimates by April 18. A successful job done on time will give us a good chance to obtain the contract to do ACM Electronics' annual report for its stockholders' meeting this fall.

I know your staff can do the job.

cc: Ted Harris, President
     Fred Moore, Production Editor

FIGURE 6–18. Typical Memo Format

6

Correspondence

e-mail is often a sensitive matter, and you need to learn both the formal and informal practices in an organization. The best general advice, however, is to copy only those who need to see the information.

Openings.   Although methods of development vary, a memo normally begins with a statement of its main point. Consider the following example:

- Because of the recent hacker attack on our Web site, I recommend that we no longer post the e-mail addresses of our loan officers. This practice . . .

When your reader is not familiar with the subject or with the background of a problem, provide an introductory paragraph before stating the main point of the memo. Doing so is especially important in memos that will serve as records of crucial information. Generally, longer or complex subjects benefit most from more-thorough <u>introductions</u> (Tab 1). However, even when you are writing a short memo about a familiar subject, remind readers of the context. In the following example, words that provide context are shown in *italics.*

- *As Maria Lopez recommended*, I reviewed the office reorganization plan. I like most of the features; however, . . .

Do not state the main point first when (1) the reader is likely to be highly skeptical or (2) you are disagreeing with your superiors. In such cases, a more persuasive tactic is to state the problem first, then present the specific points supporting your final recommendation. See also <u>persuasion</u> (Tab 1) and <u>refusal letters</u>.

Writing Style and Tone.   Whether your memo is formal or informal depends entirely on your readers and your <u>purpose</u> (Tab 1). A message to a coworker who is also a friend is likely to be informal, while an internal proposal to several readers or to someone two or three levels higher in your organization is likely to be more formal. Consider the following versions of a statement:

| TO AN EQUAL | I can't go along with the plan because I think it poses serious logistical problems. First, . . . |
| TO A SUPERIOR | The logistics of moving the department may pose serious problems. First, . . . |

A memo that gives instructions to a subordinate should also be relatively formal, impersonal, and direct, unless you are trying to reassure or praise. When writing to subordinates, remember that *managing* does not mean *dictating.* If you are too formal, sprinkling your writing with fancy words, you may seem stuffy and pompous. In fact, <u>affectation</u> (Tab 9) may both irritate and baffle readers, cause a loss of time, and produce costly errors. Consider the unintended secondary messages the following notice conveys:

- It has been decided that the office will be open the day after Thanksgiving.

"It has been decided" not only sounds impersonal but also communicates an authoritarian, management-versus-employee tone. The passive voice also suggests that the decision-maker does not want to say "I have decided" and thus be identified. (See voice, Tab 11.) One solution is to remove the first part of the sentence.

- The office will be open the day after Thanksgiving.

The best solution would be to suggest both that there is a good reason for the decision and that employees are privy to (if not a part of) the decision-making process.

- Because we must meet the December 15 deadline for submitting the Bradley Foundation proposal, the office will be open the day after Thanksgiving.

By subordinating the bad news (the need to work on that day), the writer focuses on the reasoning behind the decision to work. Employees may not necessarily like the message, but they will at least understand that the decision is not arbitrary and is tied to an important deadline.

Lists and Headings.   Lists (Tab 5) can give impact to important points by making it easier for your reader to quickly grasp information. Be careful, however, not to overuse lists. A memo that consists almost entirely of lists is difficult to understand because it forces the reader to connect the separate and disjointed items on the page. Further, lists lose their effectiveness when they are overused.

Headings (Tab 5) are another attention-getting device, particularly in long memos. They divide material into manageable segments, call attention to main topics, and signal a shift in topic. Readers can scan the headings and read only the section or sections appropriate to their needs.

Closings.   A memo closing can accomplish many important tasks, such as building positive relationships with readers, encouraging colleagues and employees, and letting recipients know what you will do or what you expect of them.

- I will discuss the problem with the marketing consultant and let you know by Monday what we are able to change.

Although routine statements are sometimes unavoidable ("Thanks again for your help"), make your closing work for you by providing specific prompts to which the reader can respond. See also <u>conclusions</u> (Tab 1).

- If you would like further information, such as a copy of the questionnaire we used, please e-mail me at delgado@prn.com.

Format and Design

Memo formats and conventions vary greatly. Although there is no single standard, Figure 6–18 shows a typical $8^{1}/_{2}'' \times 11''$ format with a printed company name.

Subject Lines.   Subject lines announce the topic; because they also aid filing and later retrieval, they must be specific and accurate.

VAGUE	Subject: Tuition Reimbursement
VAGUE	Subject: Time-Management Seminar
SPECIFIC	Subject: Tuition Reimbursement for Time-Management Seminar

Capitalize all major words in a subject line except articles, prepositions, and conjunctions with fewer than five letters unless they are the first or last words. Remember that the subject line should not substitute for an opening that provides context for the message.

Signature.   If you are sending a printed memo, the final step is signing or initialing it, a practice that lets readers know that you approve of its contents. Where you sign or initial the memo depends on the practice of your organization. Figure 6–18 shows a typical placement of initials.

refusal letters

When you must deliver a negative (or bad news) message, you may need to write a refusal letter, a <u>memo</u>, or an <u>e-mail</u> message.

The ideal refusal letter says "no" in such a way that you not only avoid antagonizing your reader but also maintain goodwill. As discussed in <u>correspondence</u>, if the stakes are high, you must convince your reader *before* you present the bad news that your reasons for refusing are logical or understandable. Stating a negative message in your opening may cause your reader to react too quickly and dismiss your logic. The following pattern, used in the letter shown in Figure 6–19, is an effective way to deal with this problem.

1. In the opening, provide a context (often called a "buffer").
2. Review the facts leading to the refusal or bad news.

Dear Mr. Coleman:

Thank you for your cooperation and your patience with us as we struggled to reach a decision. We believe our long involvement with your company indicates our confidence in your products.

Based on our research, we found that the Winton Check Sorter has all the features that your sorter offers and, in fact, has two additional features that your sorter does not. The more important one is a backup feature that retains totals in its memory, even if the power fails. The second additional feature is stacked pockets, which are less space-consuming than the linear pockets on your sorter. After much deliberation, therefore, we have decided to purchase the Winton Check Sorter.

Although we did not select your sorter, we were very favorably impressed with your system and your people. Perhaps we will be able to use other Abbott products in the future.

Sincerely,

6

Correspondence

FIGURE 6–19. Letter Rejecting a Proposal

3. Give the negative message based on the facts.
4. In the closing, establish or reestablish a positive relationship.

Your opening can establish a positive and professional tone, for example, by expressing appreciation for your reader's time, effort, or interest.

- The Screening Procedures Committee appreciates the time and effort you spent on your proposal for a new security-clearance procedure.

Next, review the circumstances of the situation sympathetically by placing yourself in the reader's position. Clearly establish the reasons you cannot do what the reader wants—even though you have not yet said you cannot do it. A good explanation, as shown in the following example, should detail the reasons for your refusal so thoroughly that the reader will accept the negative message as a logical conclusion.

- We reviewed the potential effects of implementing your proposed security-clearance procedure company-wide. We asked the Security Systems Department to review the data, surveyed industry practices, sought the views of senior management, and submitted the idea to our legal staff. As a result of this process, we have reached the following conclusions:

- The cost savings you project are correct only if the procedure could be required universally.
- The components of your procedure are legal, but most are not widely accepted by our industry.
- Based on our survey, some components could alienate employees who would perceive them as violating an individual's rights.
- Enforcing company-wide use would prove costly and impractical.

Do not belabor the negative message—state your refusal quickly, clearly, and as positively as possible.

- For those reasons, the committee recommends that divisions continue their current security-screening procedures.

Close your message in a way that reestablishes goodwill—do not repeat the bad news (avoid writing "Again, we're sorry we can't use your idea"). You might provide an option, offer a friendly remark, assure the reader of your high opinion of his or her product or service, or merely wish the reader success.

- Because some components of your procedure may apply in certain circumstances, we would like to feature your ideas in the next issue of *The Guardian.* I have asked the editor to contact you next week. On behalf of the committee, thank you for the thoughtful proposal.

For responding to a complaint letter, see <u>adjustment letters</u>. For refusing a job offer, see <u>acceptance/refusal letters</u> (Tab 7).

sales letters

A sales letter—a printed or an electronic message that promotes a product, service, or business—requires both a thorough knowledge of the product or service and an understanding of the potential customer's needs.

An effective sales letter (1) catches readers' attention, (2) arouses their interest, (3) convinces them that your product or service will fulfill a need or desire, and (4) confidently asks them to take the course of action you suggest. See also <u>persuasion</u> (Tab 1) and <u>promotional writing</u> (Tab 1).

Your first task is to determine to whom your message should be sent. One good source of names is a list of your customers; people who have at some time purchased a product or service from you may do so again. Other sources are lists of people who may be interested in similar products or services. Companies that specialize in marketing techniques compile such lists from the membership rolls of professional associations, lists of trade-show attendees, and the like. Because outside lists tend to be expensive, select them with care.

Once you determine who is to receive your sales letter, learn as much as you can about your readers so that you can effectively tell them how your product or service will satisfy their needs. Knowledge of their gender, age, vocation, geographical location, educational level, financial status, and interests will help determine your approach.

Analyze your product or service carefully to determine your strongest psychological sales points. Psychological selling involves stressing a product's benefits, which may be intangible, rather than its physical features. Select the most important psychological selling point about your product or service and build your sales message around it. Show how your product or service will make your readers' jobs easier, increase their status, make their personal lives more pleasant, and so on. Show how your product or service can satisfy your readers' needs or desires, which you identified in your opening. Then describe the physical features of your product in terms of their benefit to your readers. Help your readers imagine themselves using your product or service—and enjoying the benefits of doing so. See also "you" viewpoint (Tab 9).

⟨▸⟩ ETHICS NOTE Be certain that any claim you make in a sales message is valid. To claim that a product is safe guarantees its absolute safety; therefore, say that the product is safe "provided that normal safety precautions are taken." Further, do not exaggerate or speak negatively about a competitor. For further ethical and legal guidelines, visit the Direct Marketing Association at <www.the-dma.org>. See also ethics in writing (Tab 1).

Writer's Checklist: Writing Sales Letters

☑ Attract your readers' attention and arouse their interest in the opening, for example by describing a product's feature that would appeal strongly to their needs.

☑ Convince readers that your product or service is everything you say it is through testimonials, case histories, free-trial use, or a money-back guarantee.

☑ Suggest ways readers can make immediate use of the product or service.

☑ Minimize the negative effect price can have on readers.
  • Mention the price along with a reminder of the benefits of the product.
  • State the price in terms of units rather than sets ($20 per item instead of $600 per set).

Writer's Checklist: Writing Sales Letters (continued)

- Identify the daily, monthly, or even yearly cost based on the esti-mated life of the product.
- Suggest a series of payments rather than one total payment.
- Compare the cost of your product with that of something readers ac-cept readily ("This entire package costs no more than a DVD.")

☑ Make it easy and worthwhile for customers to respond: include a **brochure** (Tab 3), a discount coupon, instructions for phone-in or-ders, information about free delivery, or a Web address where cus-tomers can view special discounts and order online.

Job Search and Application

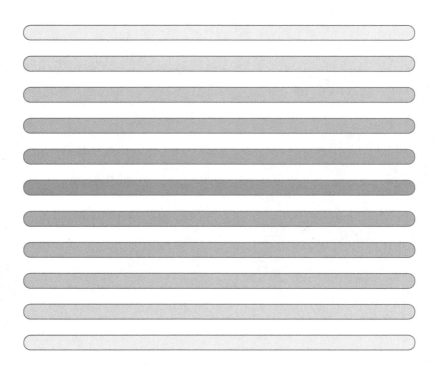

Preview

This section includes entries related to a successful <u>job search</u> — from the crucial <u>application letters</u> and <u>résumés</u> to <u>acceptance/refusal letters</u>. This section also offers strategies for <u>interviewing for a job</u> and advice on the often-sensitive process of <u>salary negotiations</u>.

7

Job Search and Application

acceptance / refusal letters

When you decide to accept a job offer, you can notify your new employer by telephone or in a meeting—but to make your decision official, you need to send an acceptance letter to your new employer. For general advice on letter writing, see <u>correspondence</u> (Tab 6).

Figure 7–1 shows an example of an acceptance letter written by a college student. Of course, the details you include in your own letter will vary depending on your previous conversations with your new employer. Note that in the first paragraph of Figure 7–1, the student identifies the job he is accepting and the salary he has been offered—doing so can avoid any misunderstandings about the job or the salary. In the second paragraph, the student details his plans for moving and reporting for work. Even if the student discussed these arrangements during earlier conversations, he needs to confirm them, officially, in this letter.

2647 Sitwell Road
Charlotte, NC 28210
March 26, 2005

Mr. F. E. Vallone
Manager of Human Resources
Calcutex Industries, Inc.
3275 Commercial Park Drive
Raleigh, NC 27609

Dear Mr. Vallone:

I am pleased to accept your offer of $34,500 per year as an ACR designer in the Calcutex Group.

After graduation, I plan to leave Charlotte on Tuesday, June 21. I should be able to find suitable living accommodations within a few days and be ready to report for work on the following Monday, June 27. Please let me know if this date is satisfactory to you.

I look forward to working with the design team at Calcutex.

Sincerely,

Philip Ming

Philip Ming

FIGURE 7–1. Acceptance Letter

7

Job Search and Application

The student then concludes with a brief but enthusiastic statement that he looks forward to working for his new employer.

When you decide to reject a job offer, send a job-refusal letter to make that decision official, even if you have already notified the employer during a meeting or on the phone. Writing a letter is a gesture that the employer will appreciate. Be especially tactful and courteous — the employer you are refusing has spent time and effort interviewing you and may have counted on your accepting the job. Remember, you may apply for another job at that company in the future. In Figure 7–2, an example of a job-refusal letter, the applicant mentions something positive about his contact with the employer and refers to the specific job offered. He indicates his serious consideration of the offer, provides a logical reason for the refusal, and concludes on a pleasant note. For further strategy on handling refusals and negative messages generally, see refusal letters (Tab 6).

Dear Mr. Vallone:

I enjoyed talking with you about your opening for a technical writer, and I was gratified to receive your offer. Although I have given the offer serious thought, I have decided to accept a position as a copywriter with an advertising agency. I feel that the job I have chosen is better suited to my skills and long-term goals.

I appreciate your consideration and the time you spent with me. I wish you the best of luck in filling the position.

                                    Sincerely,

FIGURE 7–2. Refusal Letter

application letters

When applying for a job, you usually need to submit both a résumé and an application letter (also referred to as a *cover letter*). Unless the prospective employer requests a résumé only, be sure to submit an application letter as well. See also job search.

The application letter is essentially a sales letter in which you market your skills, abilities, and knowledge. Therefore, your application letter must be persuasive. The successful application letter accomplishes four tasks: (1) it catches the reader's attention favorably, (2) it explains which particular job interests you and why, (3) it convinces the reader that you are qualified for the job by drawing your reader's attention to particular elements in your résumé, and (4) it requests an interview. See also <u>persuasion</u> (Tab 1), <u>readers</u> (Tab 1), <u>correspondence</u> (Tab 6), <u>sales letters</u> (Tab 6), <u>interviewing for a job</u>, and <u>salary negotiations</u>.

The three sample application letters shown in Figures 7–3 through 7–5 follow the application-letter structure described in this entry. Each is adapted according to the emphasis, tone, and style to fit the applicant's experience and the particular audience.

Opening

In the opening paragraph, provide context and show your enthusiasm:

1. Indicate how you heard about the opening. If you have been referred to a company by an employee, a career counselor, a professor, or someone else, be sure to mention this even before you state your job objective ("Karen Jarrett informed me of a possible opening in your hospital").
2. State your job objective and mention the specific job title ("Your position of Cath Lab Manager is ideal because my goal is to use my management skills together with my background in nursing"). Those who make hiring decisions review many application letters. To save them time while also calling attention to your strengths as a candidate, state your job objective directly in your first paragraph.
3. Explain why you are interested in the job ("Your position interests me because I can use my skills and talents for a nonprofit organization" or "Your firm's buyer training program is considered one of the most effective").

Body

In the middle paragraphs, show through examples that you are qualified for the job. Limit each of these paragraphs to one basic point that is clearly stated in the topic sentence. (See also <u>paragraphs</u>, Tab 1.) For example, your second paragraph might focus on work experience and your third paragraph on educational achievements. Don't just *tell* readers that you're qualified — *show* them by including examples and details. Come across as proud of your achievements and refer to your enclosed résumé. Indicate how you with your talents can make valuable contributions to their company, such as "I am confident that my ability to take the initiative would be a valuable asset to your company."

Closing

In the final paragraph, request an interview. Let the reader know how to reach you by including your phone number or e-mail address. End with a statement of goodwill, even if only a "thank you."

Proofread your letter very carefully. Research indicates that if employers notice even one spelling, grammatical, or mechanical error,

7188 Virginia Avenue
Pittsburgh, PA 15232
February 28, 2005

Patrice C. Crandal
Executive Recruiter
Abel's Department Stores, Inc.
599 Seventh Avenue
Pittsburgh, PA 15219

Dear Ms. Crandal:

Recently, I learned that you may be hiring undergraduates for summer internships. Through personal research and sources in the retailing industry, I have discovered that your firm's buyer training program is considered one of the most effective. For this reason, I am interested in your company and I would like to be considered as a possible summer intern.

As indicated in my résumé, I have the professional and analytical qualities necessary to excel at an innovative company such as Abel's. My experiences with the Alumni Relations Program and the University Center Committee have enhanced my communication and persuasive abilities as well as my understanding of compromise and negotiation. For example, in the alumni program, my priority focused on convincing both uninvolved and active alumni to become more engaged with the direction of the university. On the University Center Committee, my goal was to balance the students' demands with financial and structural constraints of the administration. In both cases, I succeeded in achieving these important goals through persuasion.

I'd also like to point out that throughout my work experiences and education I have been determined and innovative. My efforts to excel at Abel's will reflect my commitment to these qualities.

I would appreciate the opportunity to meet with you to discuss your summer internship further. If you have questions or would like to speak with me personally, please contact me at (412) 863-2289 any weekday after 3 p.m. Thank you for your time and consideration.

Sincerely,

Marsha S. Parker

Marsha S. Parker

Enclosure: Résumé

FIGURE 7–3. Application Letter (Student Applying for Retailing Internship)

449 Samson Street, Apt. 19
Providence, RI 02906
September 19, 2005

Alice Tobowski
Employee Relations Department
Advertising Media, Inc.
1007 Market Street
Providence, RI 02912

Dear Ms. Tobowski:

I recently learned from Jodi Hammel, a graphic designer at Advertising Media, Inc., and a former colleague, that you are looking for outstanding advertising assistants. Your position interests me greatly, not only because your firm is number one in the region but also because I feel that Advertising Media is, as Jodi and I have discussed, the kind of place where I can further develop my skills and talents.

I understand that you especially need bilingual assistants because of your zone's ethnic diversity. As noted in my enclosed résumé, I speak and write Spanish fluently. I would welcome the chance to apply my language skills at Advertising Media. Ms. Tobowski, I am aware that hundreds of applicants are applying for this position, but I have a combination of qualities probably few can match: in addition to my bilingual skills, I have a degree and experience in advertising, outstanding verbal and written communication skills, an innate ability to work well with colleagues, and the common sense to solve both simple and challenging problems. I have developed my skills by contributing to advertising for Quilted Bear in Providence, where we develop campaigns for diverse audiences. I have also been promoted to leadership positions in my jobs, schools, and community organizations, and I have worked well both individually and in team efforts in each environment.

I would enjoy meeting with you at your convenience to discuss this career opportunity further. Also, I have many references that I encourage you to contact. Feel free to call me any weekday morning or e-mail me at <singh@pcexec.com> if you have any questions, need further information, or would like to set up an interview. Thank you for your consideration.

Sincerely,

Sarah Singh

Sarah Singh

Enclosure: Résumé

FIGURE 7–4. Application Letter (Recent Graduate Applying to Advertising Firm)

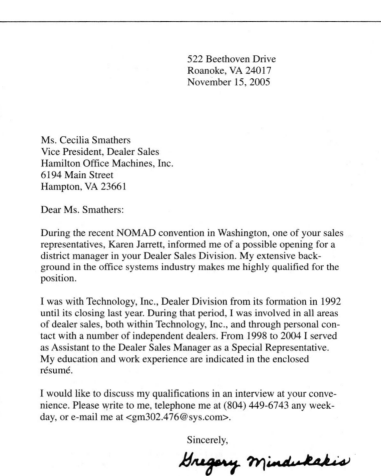

522 Beethoven Drive
Roanoke, VA 24017
November 15, 2005

Ms. Cecilia Smathers
Vice President, Dealer Sales
Hamilton Office Machines, Inc.
6194 Main Street
Hampton, VA 23661

Dear Ms. Smathers:

During the recent NOMAD convention in Washington, one of your sales representatives, Karen Jarrett, informed me of a possible opening for a district manager in your Dealer Sales Division. My extensive background in the office systems industry makes me highly qualified for the position.

I was with Technology, Inc., Dealer Division from its formation in 1992 until its closing last year. During that period, I was involved in all areas of dealer sales, both within Technology, Inc., and through personal contact with a number of independent dealers. From 1998 to 2004 I served as Assistant to the Dealer Sales Manager as a Special Representative. My education and work experience are indicated in the enclosed résumé.

I would like to discuss my qualifications in an interview at your convenience. Please write to me, telephone me at (804) 449-6743 any weekday, or e-mail me at <gm302.476@sys.com>.

Sincerely,

Gregory Mindukakis

Gregory Mindukakis

Enclosure: Résumé

FIGURE 7–5. Application Letter (Applicant with Years of Experience)

Job Search and Application

7

they often immediately eliminate candidates from consideration. Such errors will give employers the impression that you lack writing skills or that you are careless in the way you present yourself professionally. See also <u>proofreading</u> (Tab 1).

interviewing for a job

A job interview may last 30 minutes, an hour, several hours, or more. Sometimes, an initial job interview is followed by a series of job interviews that can last a half or full day. Often, just one or two people conduct a job interview, but at times a group of four or more might do so. Job interviews can take place in person, by phone, or by teleconference. Because it is impossible to know exactly what to expect, it is important that you be well prepared.

Before the Interview

The interview is not a one-way communication. It presents you with an opportunity to ask questions of your potential employer. In preparation, learn everything you can about the company before the interview. Use the following questions as a guide.

- What kind of organization is it? (e.g., nonprofit, government)
- How diversified is the organization?
- Is it locally owned?
- Does it provide a product or service? If so, what kind?
- How large is the business? How large are its assets?
- Is the owner self-employed? Is the company a subsidiary of a larger operation? Is it expanding?
- How long has it been in business?
- Where will you fit in?

You can obtain information from current employees, the Internet, company publications, and the business section of back issues of local newspapers (available in the library or online). You may be able to learn the company's size, sales volume, product line, credit rating, branch locations, subsidiary companies, new products and services, building programs, and other such information from its annual reports and from publications such as *Moody's Industrials, Dun and Bradstreet, Standard and Poor's,* and *Thomas' Register,* as well as other business reference sources a librarian might suggest. Ask your interviewer about what you cannot find through your own <u>research</u> (Tab 2). Now is your chance to demonstrate your interest and make certain you are considering a healthy and growing company.

Try to anticipate the questions your interviewer might ask, and prepare your answers in advance. Be sure you understand a question

7

Job Search and
Application

before answering it, and avoid responding too quickly with a rehearsed answer—be prepared to answer in a natural and relaxed manner. Interviewers typically ask the following questions:

- What are your short-term and long-term occupational goals?
- Where do you see yourself five years from now?
- What are your major strengths and weaknesses?
- Do you work better with others or alone?
- How do you spend your free time?
- What are your personal goals?
- Describe an accomplishment you are particularly proud of.
- Why are you leaving your current job?
- Why do you want to work for this company?
- Why should I hire you?
- What salary and benefits do you expect?

Many employers use behavioral interviews. Rather than traditional, straightforward questions, the behavioral interview focuses on asking the candidate to provide examples or respond to hypothetical situations. Interviewers who use behavior-based questions are looking for specific examples from your experience. Prepare for the behavioral interview by recollecting challenging situations or problems that were successfully resolved. Examples of behavior-based questions include the following:

- Tell me about a time when you experienced conflict on a team.
- If I were your boss and you disagreed with a decision I made, what would you do?
- How have you used your leadership skills to bring about change?
- Tell me about a time when you failed.

Arrive for your interview on time, or even ten or fifteen minutes early—you may be asked to fill out an application or other paperwork before you meet your interviewer. Always bring extra copies of your résumé and samples of your work (if applicable). If you are asked to complete an application form, read it carefully before you write and proofread it when you are finished. The form provides a written record for company files and indicates to the company how well you follow directions and complete a task.

During the Interview

The interview actually begins before you are seated: What you wear and how you act make a first impression. In general, dress simply and conservatively and avoid extremes in fragrance and cosmetics. Be well-groomed.

Behavior.   First, thank the interviewer for his or her time, express your pleasure at meeting him or her, and remain standing until you are offered a seat. Then sit up straight (good posture suggests self-assurance), look directly at the interviewer, and try to appear relaxed and confident. During the interview, you may find yourself feeling a little nervous. Use that nervous energy to your advantage by channeling it into the alertness that you will need to listen and respond effectively. Do not attempt to take extensive notes during the interview, although it is acceptable to jot down a few facts and figures. See also listening (Tab 8).

Responses.   When you answer questions, do not ramble or stray from the subject. Say only what you must to answer each question properly and then stop, but avoid giving just yes or no answers — they usually don't allow the interviewer to learn enough about you. Some interviewers allow a silence to fall just to see how you will react. The burden of conducting the interview is the interviewer's, not yours — and he or she may interpret your rush to fill a void in the conversation as a sign of insecurity. If such a silence makes you uncomfortable, be ready to ask an intelligent question about the company.

If the interviewer overlooks important points, bring them up. However, let the interviewer mention salary first, if possible. Doing so yourself may indicate that you are more interested in the money than the work. However, make sure you are aware of prevailing salaries and benefits in your field, and review salary negotiations.

Interviewers look for a degree of self-confidence and an applicant's understanding of the field, as well as genuine interest in the field, the company, and the job. Ask questions to communicate your interest in the job and company. Interviewers respond favorably to applicants who can communicate and present themselves well.

Conclusion.   At the conclusion of the interview, thank the interviewer for his or her time. Indicate that you are interested in the job (if true) and try to get an idea of the company's hiring time frame. Reaffirm friendly contact with a firm handshake.

After the Interview

After you leave the interview, jot down the pertinent information you obtained, as it may be helpful in comparing job offers. A day or two following a job interview, send the interviewer a note of thanks in a brief letter or e-mail. Such notes often include the following:

- Your thanks for the interview and to individuals or groups that gave you special help or attention during the interview
- The name of the specific job for which you interviewed
- Your impression that the job is attractive
- Your confidence that you can perform the job well
- An offer to provide further information or answer further questions

Figure 7–6 shows a typical follow-up letter.

Dear Mr. Vallone:

Thank you for the informative and pleasant interview we had last Wednesday. Please extend my thanks to Mr. Wilson of the Media Group as well.

I came away from our meeting most favorably impressed with Calcutex Industries. I find the position of ACR designer to be an attractive one and feel confident that my qualifications would enable me to perform the duties to everyone's advantage.

If I can answer any further questions, please let me know.

Sincerely yours,

FIGURE 7–6. Follow-up Letter

If you are offered a job you want, accept the offer verbally and write a brief letter of acceptance as soon as possible—certainly within a week—or if you do not want the job, write a refusal letter, as described in acceptance/refusal letters.

job search

Whether you are applying for your first job or you want to change careers entirely, begin by assessing your skills, interests, and abilities, perhaps through brainstorming.* Next, consider your career goals and values. For instance, do you prefer working independently or collaboratively? Do you enjoy public settings? meeting people? How important are career stability and location? Finally, ask yourself what you would most like to be doing in the immediate future, in two years, and in five years.

Once you have reflected and brainstormed about the job that is right for you, a number of sources can help you locate the job you want. Of course, you should not rely on any one of these sources exclusively.

- Networking
- Campus career services
- Internet resources

*A good source for stimulating your thinking is the most recent edition of *What Color Is Your Parachute? A Practical Manual for Job-Hunters and Career-Changers* by Richard Nelson Bolles, published by Ten Speed Press.

- Advertisements
- Trade and professional journal listings
- Private (or temporary) employment agencies
- Letters of inquiry

Keep a file during your job search of dated job ads, copies of <u>application letters</u> and <u>résumés</u>, notes requesting interviews, and the names of important contacts. This collection can serve as a future resource and reminder. See also <u>interviewing for a job</u> and <u>salary negotiations</u>.

Networking

Networking involves communicating with people who may provide useful advice or may know of potential jobs in your interest areas. They may include people already working in your chosen field, contacts in professional organizations, professors, family members, or friends. Use your contacts to develop a network of even more contacts. Consider that of all open positions, an estimated 80 percent are filled through networking.*

Campus Career Services

A visit to a college career-development center is another good way to begin your job search. Government, business, and industry recruiters often visit campus career offices to interview prospective employees; recruiters also keep career counselors aware of their companies' current employment needs and submit job descriptions. Not only can career counselors help you select a career, they can also put you in touch with the best, most current resources—identifying where to begin your search and saving you time. Career development centers often hold workshops on résumé preparation and offer other job-finding resources on their Web sites.

Internet Resources

Using the Web can enhance your job search in a number of ways. First, you can consult sites that give advice to college graduates about careers, job seeking, and résumé preparation. Second, you can learn about businesses and organizations that may hire employees in your area by visiting their Web sites. Such sites often list job openings and provide instructions for applicants and offer other information, such as employee benefits. Third, you can learn about jobs in your field and post your résumé for prospective employers at employment databases, such as Monster.com at <www.monster.com/> or America's Job Bank at <www.ajb.dni.us/>. Fourth, you can post your résumé at your

*From JobStar Central, an online job-search guide hosted by the *Wall Street Journal* at <http://jobstar.org>.

7

Job Search and
Application

personal Web site. Although posting your résumé at an employment database will undoubtedly attract more potential employers, including your résumé at your own site has benefits. For example, you might provide a link to your site in e-mail correspondence or provide your Web site's URL in an inquiry letter to a prospective employer.

Employment specialists suggest that you spend time on the Web in the evening or early morning so that you can focus on in-person contacts during working hours.

Advertisements

Many employers advertise in the classified sections of newspapers and on their own Web sites. For the widest selection of help-wanted listings, look in the Sunday editions or the help-wanted Web pages of local and big-city newspapers. An item-by-item check is necessary because many times a position can be listed under various classifications. A human relations specialist interested in training, for example, might find the specialty listed under "Human Resources" or "Consulting Services." Depending on a company's or government agency's needs, the listing could be even more specific, such as "Software Education Specialist" or "Learning and Development Coordinator." As you read the ads, take notes on salary ranges, job locations, job duties and responsibilities, and even the terminology used in the ads to describe the work. A knowledge of keywords and expressions that are generally used to describe a particular type of work can be helpful when you prepare your résumé and letters of application.

Trade and Professional Journal Listings

In many industries, associations publish periodicals of interest to people working in the industry. Such periodicals (print and online) often contain job listings. To learn about the trade or professional associations for your occupation, consult resources on the Web, such as Google's Directory of Professional Organizations at <http://directory.google.com/Top/Society/Organizations/Professional> or online resources offered by your library or campus career office. You may also consult the following print references at a library: *Encyclopedia of Associations, Encyclopedia of Business Information Sources,* and *National Directory of Employment Services.* See also <u>research</u> (Tab 2).

Private (or Temporary) Employment Agencies

Private employment agencies are profit-making organizations that are in business to help people find jobs—for a fee. Reputable agencies provide you with job leads, help you organize your job search, and supply information on companies doing the hiring. A staffing agency, or temporary-placement agency, could match you with an appropriate temporary or permanent job in your field. Temporary work for an organization for which you might want to work permanently is an excellent way to build your network while continuing your job search.

Choose an employment or a temporary-placement agency carefully. Some are well established and reputable; others are not. Check with your local Better Business Bureau at <www.bbb.org> and your college career office before you sign an agreement with a private employment agency. Further, be sure you understand who is paying the agency's fee. Often the employer pays the agency's fee; however, if you have to pay, make sure you know exactly how much. As with any written agreement, read the fine print carefully.

Letters of Inquiry

If you would like to work for a particular firm, write and ask whether it has any openings for people with your qualifications. Normally, you can send the letter to the department head, the director of human resources, or both; for a small firm, however, write to the head of the firm. See application letters.

Other Sources

Local, state, and federal government agencies offer many employment services. Local government agencies are listed in telephone and Web directories under the name of your city, county, or state.

> 🌐 WEB LINK FINDING A JOB
>
> For job-hunting tips, sample documents, and more, see <bedford stmartins.com/alred> and select *Finding an Internship or Job* and *Links for Business Writing*.

résumés

A résumé, the key tool of the job search, itemizes the qualifications that you summarize in your application letter. A résumé* should be limited to one page—or two pages if you have substantial experience. On the basis of the information in the résumé and application letter, prospective employers decide whether to ask you to come in for an interview. If you are invited to an interview, the interviewer can base specific questions on the contents of your résumé. See also interviewing for a job.

*A detailed résumé for someone in an academic or scientific area is often called a *curriculum vitae* (also *vita* or *c.v.*). It may include education, publications, projects, grants, and awards as well as a full work history. Outside the United States, the term *curriculum vitae* is often a synonym for the term *résumé*.

Because résumés affect a potential employer's first impression, make sure that yours is well organized, carefully designed, consistently formatted, easy to read, and free of errors. Consider first an organization that highlights your strengths and fits your goals, as suggested by the examples later in this entry. Experiment to determine a <u>layout and design</u> (Tab 5) that is attractive and uncluttered. Consistency is especially important on a résumé. Be sure to use, for example, the same date formats (5/2005 or May 2005), punctuation, and spacing throughout. Proofreading is essential. Verify the accuracy of the information, and have someone else review it. Use a quality printer and high-grade paper. See also <u>organization</u> (Tab 1) and <u>proofreading</u> (Tab 1).

The sample résumés in this entry are here to stimulate your thinking; your own résumé, tailored to your own job search, will look quite different. Before you design and write your résumé, look at as many samples as possible, and then organize and format your own to best suit your previous experience and your professional goals and to make the most persuasive case to your target employers.

- Figure 7–7 presents a conventional student résumé in which the student is seeking an entry-level business position.
- Figure 7–8 shows a résumé with a variation of the conventional headings to highlight professional credentials.
- Figure 7–9 presents a student résumé with a format that is appropriately a bit nonconventional because this student needs to demonstrate skills in graphic design for his potential audience.
- Figure 7–10 shows a résumé that focuses on the applicant's management experience.
- Figure 7–11 focuses on how the applicant advanced and was promoted within a single company.
- Figure 7–12 illustrates how an applicant can organize a résumé by combining functional and chronological elements.
- Figure 7–13 presents an electronic résumé in ASCII (American Standard Code for Information Interchange) format. Notice how this résumé emphasizes keywords so that potential employers searching online for applicants will be able to find it easily.

Analyzing Your Background

In preparing to write your résumé, determine what kind of job you are seeking. Then ask yourself what information about you and your background would be most important to a prospective employer. List the following:

- Schools you attended, degrees you hold, your major field of study, academic honors you were awarded, your grade point average, particular academic projects that reflect your best work

CAROL ANN WALKER

SCHOOL
148 University Drive
Bloomington, Indiana 47405
(812) 652-4781
caw2@iu.edu

HOME (after June 2005)
1436 W. Schantz Avenue
Laurel, Pennsylvania 17322
(717) 399-2712
caw@yahoo.com

OBJECTIVE

Position in financial research, leading to management in corporate finance.

EDUCATION

Bachelor of Science in Business Administration, expected June 2005
Indiana University

Emphasis: Finance   Minor: Professional Writing
Grade Point Average: 3.88 out of possible 4.0
Senior Honor Society

FINANCIAL EXPERIENCE

FIRST BANK, INC., Bloomington, Indiana, 2004
Research Assistant, Summer and Fall Quarters
    Developed long-range planning models for the manager of corporate
    planning.

MARTIN FINANCIAL RESEARCH SERVICES, Bloomington, Indiana, 2003
Financial Audit Intern
    Created a design concept for in-house financial audits and provided re-
    search assistance to staff.
Associate Editor, *Martin Client Newsletter*, 2002–2003
    Wrote articles on financial planning with computer models; developed
    article ideas from survey of business periodicals; edited submissions.

COMPUTER SKILLS

Software: Microsoft Word, Excel, PowerPoint, Pagemaker, QuarkXPress
Hardware: Macintosh, IBM-PC, scanners
Languages: FORTRAN, PASCAL

REFERENCES

Available upon request.

7

Job Search and
Application

FIGURE 7–7. Student Résumé (for an Entry-Level Position)

CHRIS RENAULT, RN

3785 Raleigh Court, #46 • Phoenix, AZ 67903 • (555) 467-1115 • chris@resumepower.com

Qualifications

➢ Recent Honors Graduate of Approved Nursing Program
➢ Current Arizona Nursing Licensure and BLS Certification
➢ Presently Completing Clinical Nurse Internship Program

Education & Licensure

ARIZONA STATE UNIVERSITY • Tempe, AZ
Bachelor of Science in Nursing (BSN), 2004
Graduated summa cum laude (GPA: 4.0)

MOHAVE COMMUNITY COLLEGE • Kingman, AZ
Associate Degree in Nursing (AN), 2002
Graduated cum laude (GPA: 3.5)

Coursework Highlights: Family and Community Nursing, Health Care Delivery Models, Health Assessment, Pathology, Microbiology, Nursing Research, Nursing of Older Adults, Health Care Ethics

Arizona RN License, 2004
BLS Certification, 2004

Clinical Internship

CAMELBACK MEDICAL CENTER – Phoenix, AZ
Nurse Intern, 2004 to Present

• Accepted into new graduate RN training program and completing in-depth, eight-month rotation working under a trained preceptor.
• Gaining valuable clinical experience to assume the role of a professional nurse within an acute care setting. Rotating through all medical center areas, including Post Surgical, Orthopedics, Pediatrics, Oncology, Emergency Department, Psychiatric Nursing, Cardiac Telemetry, and Critical Care.
• Developing speed and skill in the day-to-day functions of a staff nurse. Participating in patient assessment, treatment, medication disbursement, and surgical preparation as a member of the healthcare team.
• Earning written commendations from preceptor for *"...excellent ability to interact with patients and their families, showing a high degree of empathy, medical knowledge, and concern for quality and continuity of patient care."*

Community Involvement

Active Volunteer and Fundraising Coordinator, The American Cancer Society – Scottsdale, AZ Chapter (2003 to Present)
Participant, Annual AIDS Walkathon (2001 to 2004) and "Find the Cure" Breast Cancer Awareness Marathon (2002, 2003)

FIGURE 7–8. Résumé (Combining Functional and Chronological Elements). Prepared by Kim Isaacs, Advanced Career Systems, Inc.

**Joshua S. Goodman
222 Morewood Avenue
Pittsburgh, PA 15212
Jgoodman@aol.com**

OBJECTIVE

A position as a graphic designer with responsibilities in information design, packaging, and media presentations.

EDUCATION

**Carnegie Mellon University, Pittsburgh, Pennsylvania
BFA in Graphic Design — May 2005.**

*Graphic Design
Corporate Identity
Industrial Design
Graphic Imaging Processes
Color Theory
Computer Graphics
Typography
Serigraphy
Photography
Video Production*

GRAPHIC DESIGN EXPERIENCE

**Assistant Designer • Dyer/Khan, Los Angeles, California
Summer 2003, Summer 2004**
Assistant Designer in a versatile design studio. Responsible for design, layout, comps, mechanicals, and project management.
Clients: Paramount Pictures, Mattel Electronics, and Motown Records.

**Photo Editor • Paramount Pictures Corporation, Los Angeles, California
Summer 2002**
Photo Editor for merchandising department. Established art files for movie and television properties. Edited images used in merchandising. Maintained archive and database.

Production Assistant • Grafis, Los Angeles, California, Summer 2001
Production assistant at fast-paced design firm. Assisted with comps, mechanicals, and miscellaneous studio work.
Clients: ABC Television, A&M Records, and Ortho Products Division.

COMPUTER SKILLS

XML, HTML, JavaScript, Forms, Macromedia Dreamweaver 3, Macromedia Flash 4, Photoshop 5.5, Image Ready (Animated GIFs), Corel-DRAW, DeepPaint, iGrafx Designer, MapEdit (Image Mapping), Scanning, Microsoft Access/Excel, QuarkXPress.

ACTIVITIES

Member, Pittsburgh Graphic Design Society; Member, The Design Group.

7

Job Search and Application

FIGURE 7–9. Student Résumé (for a Graphic Design Job)

ROBERT MANDILLO
7761 Shalamar Drive
Dayton, Ohio 45424
(513) 255-4137
mand@juno.com

OBJECTIVE

A management position in aerospace industry with responsibility for developing new designs and products.

MANAGEMENT EXPERIENCE

MANAGER, ENGINEERING DRAFTING DEPARTMENT — May 1996–Present
Wright-Patterson Air Force Base, Dayton, Ohio

Supervise 17 drafting mechanics in support of the engineering design staff. Develop, evaluate, and improve materials and equipment for the design and construction of exhibits. Write specifications, negotiate with vendors, and initiate procurement activities for exhibit design support.

SUPERVISOR, GRAPHICS ILLUSTRATORS — June 1983–April 1996
Henderson Advertising Agency, Cincinnati, Ohio

Supervised five illustrators and four drafting mechanics after promotion from Graphics Technician. Analyzed and approved work-order requirements. Selected appropriate media and techniques for orders. Rendered illustrations in pencil and ink. Converted department to CAD system.

EDUCATION

BACHELOR OF SCIENCE IN MECHANICAL ENGINEERING TECHNOLOGY, 1983
Edison State College, Wooster, Ohio

ASSOCIATE'S DEGREE IN MECHANICAL DRAFTING, 1981
Wooster Community College, Wooster, Ohio

PROFESSIONAL AFFILIATION

National Association of Mechanical Engineers and Drafting Mechanics

REFERENCES

References, letters of recommendation, and a portfolio of original designs and drawings available online at <www.juno.com/mand>.

FIGURE 7–10. Résumé (Applicant with Management Experience)

CAROL ANN WALKER
1436 W. Schantz Avenue
Laurel, Pennsylvania 17322
(717) 399-2712
caw@yahoo.com

FINANCIAL EXPERIENCE

KERFHEIMER CORPORATION, Philadelphia, Pennsylvania

Senior Financial Analyst, June 2001–Present
Report to Senior Vice President for Corporate Financial Planning.
Develop manufacturing cost estimates totaling $30 million annually for
mining and construction equipment with Department of Defense.

Financial Analyst, November 1998–June 2001
Developed $50-million funding estimates for major Department of
Defense contracts for troop carriers and digging and earth-moving
machines. Researched funding options, resulting in savings of
$1.2 million.

FIRST BANK, INC., Bloomington, Indiana

Planning Analyst, September 1993–November 1998
Developed successful computer models for short- and long-range planning.

EDUCATION

Ph.D. in Finance: expected, June 2005
The Wharton School of the University of Pennsylvania

M.S. in Business Administration, 1997
University of Wisconsin–Milwaukee
"Executive Curriculum" for employees identified as promising by their
employers.

B.S. in Business Administration (*magna cum laude*), 1993
Indiana University
Emphasis: Finance   Minor: Professional Writing

PUBLISHING AND MEMBERSHIP

Published "Developing Computer Models for Financial Planning," Midwest
Finance Journal 34.2 (2003): 126–36.

Association for Corporate Financial Planning, Senior Member.

REFERENCES

References and a portfolio of financial plans are available upon request.

FIGURE 7–11. Advanced Résumé (Showing Promotion within Single Company)

--- **CAROL ANN WALKER** ---

1436 W. Schantz Avenue • Laurel, PA 17322
(717) 399-2712 • caw@yahoo.com

Award-Winning Senior Financial Analyst

Astute senior analyst and corporate financial planner with 11 years of experience and proven success enhancing P&L scenarios by millions of dollars. Demonstrated ability to apply critical thinking and sound strategic/economic analysis to multidimensional business issues. Advanced computer skills include Hyperion, SQL, MS Office, and Crystal Reports.

> **Financial Analyst of the Year, 2004**
>
> *Recipient of prestigious national award from the Association for Investment Management and Research (AIMR)*

Areas of Expertise

- Financial Analysis & Planning
- Forecasting & Trend Projection
- Trend/Variance Analysis
- Comparative Analysis
- Expense Analysis
- Strategic Planning
- SEC & Financial Reporting
- Risk Assessment

Career Progression

KERFHEIMER CORPORATION–Philadelphia, PA   1998 to Present

Senior Financial Analyst, June 2001 to Present
Financial Analyst, November 1998 to June 2001

Rapidly promoted to lead team of 15 analysts in the management of financial/SEC reporting and analysis for publicly traded, $2.3 billion company. Develop financial/statistical models used to project and maximize corporate financial performance. Support nationwide sales team by providing financial metrics, trends, and forecasts.

Key Accomplishments:

- **Developed long-range funding requirements crucial to firm's subsequent capture of $1 billion** in government and military contracts.
- **Facilitated a 45% decrease in company's long-term debt** during several major building expansions through personally developed computer models for capital acquisition.
- **Jointly led large-scale systems conversion to Hyperion,** including personal upload of database in Essbase. Completed conversion without interrupting business operations.

FIGURE 7–12. Advanced Résumé (Combining Functional and Chronological Elements). Prepared by Kim Isaacs, Advanced Career Systems, Inc.

CAROL ANN WALKER
Résumé • Page Two

Career Progression (*continued*)

FIRST BANK, INC.–Bloomington, IN   1993 to 1998
Planning Analyst, September 1993 to November 1998
Compiled and distributed weekly, monthly, quarterly, and annual closings/financial reports, analyzing information for presentation to senior management. Prepared depreciation forecasts, actual-vs.-projected financial statements, key-matrix reports, tax-reporting packages, auditor packages, and balance-sheet reviews.

Key Accomplishments:

• **Devised strategies to acquire over $1 billion at 3% below market rate.**
• **Analyzed financial performance for consistency to plans and forecasts,** investigated trends and variances, and alerted senior management to areas requiring action.
• **Achieved an average 23% return on all personally recommended investments.** Applied critical thinking and sound financial and strategic analysis in all funding options research.

Education

THE WHARTON SCHOOL of the UNIVERSITY OF PENNSYLVANIA–
Philadelphia, PA
Ph.D. in Finance Candidate, Expected June 2005

UNIVERSITY OF WISCONSIN–Milwaukee, WI
M.S. in Business Administration, May 1997

INDIANA UNIVERSITY–Bloomington, IN
B.S. in Business Administration, Emphasis in Finance
(*magna cum laude*), May 1993

Affiliations

• Association for Investment Management and Research (AIMR), Member, 2000 to Present
• Association for Corporate Financial Planning (ACFP), Senior Member, 1998 to Present

Portfolio of Financial Plans Available on Request
(717) 399-2712 • caw@yahoo.com

FIGURE 7–12. Advanced Résumé (Combining Functional and Chronological Elements). Prepared by Kim Isaacs, Advanced Career Systems, Inc. (*continued*)

7

Job Search and Application

DAVID B. EDWARDS
6819 Locustview Drive
Topeka, Kansas 66614
(913) 233-1552
dedwards@cpu.fairview.edu

JOB OBJECTIVE
Programmer with writing, editing, and training responsibilities,
leading to a career in information design management.

KEYWORDS
Programmer, Operating Systems, Unipro, Newsletter, Graphics,
Listserv, Professional Writer, Editor, Trainer, Instructor,
Technical Writer, Tutor, Designer, Manager, Information Design.

EDUCATION
** Fairview Community College, Topeka, Kansas
** Associate's Degree, Computer Science, June 2003
** Dean's Honor List Award (six quarters)

RELEVANT COURSE WORK
** Operating Systems Design
** Database Management
** Introduction to Cybernetics
** Technical Writing

EMPLOYMENT EXPERIENCE
** Computer Consultant: September 2003 to Present
Fairview Community College Computer Center: Advised and trained novice
users; wrote and maintained Unipro operating system documentation.
** Tutor: January 2002 to June 2003
Fairview Community College: Assisted students in mathematics and
computer programming.

SKILLS AND ACTIVITIES
** Unipro Operating System: Thorough knowledge of word-processing,
text-editing, and file-formatting programs.
** Writing and Editing Skills: Experience in documenting computer
programs for beginning programmers and users.
** Fairview Community Microcomputer Users Group: Cofounder and
editor of monthly newsletter ("Compuclub"); listserv manager.

FURTHER INFORMATION
** References, college transcripts, a portfolio of computer programs,
and writing samples available upon request.

FIGURE 7–13. Electronic Résumé (in ASCII Format)

- Jobs you have held, your principal and secondary duties in each job, when and how long you held each job, promotions, skills you developed in your jobs that potential employers value and seek in ideal job candidates, projects or accomplishments that reflect your important contributions
- Other experiences and skills you have developed that would be of value in the kind of job you are seeking; extracurricular activities that have contributed to your learning experience; leadership, interpersonal, and communication skills you have developed; any collaborative work you have performed; computer skills you have acquired

Use this information to brainstorm any further key details. Then, based on all the details, decide which to include in your résumé and how you can most effectively present your qualifications.

Organizing Your Résumé

A number of different organizational patterns can be used effectively. The following categories are typical—which you choose should depend on your experience, goals, employer's needs, and any standard practices in your profession.

- Heading (name and contact information)
- Job Objective
- Qualifications Summary
- Education
- Employment Experience
- Related Skills and Abilities
- Honors and Activities
- References

Whether you place education or employment experience first depends on the job you are seeking and on which credentials would strengthen your résumé the most. If you are a recent graduate without much work experience, you would list education first. If you have years of job experience, including jobs directly related to the kind of position you are seeking, you would list employment experience first. In your education and employment sections, use a reverse chronological sequence: list the most recent experience first, the next most recent experience second, and so on.

Heading.   At the top of your résumé, include your name, address, telephone number (home or cell), and e-mail address. Make sure that your name stands out on the page. If you have both a school address and a permanent home address, place your school address on the left side of the page and your permanent home address on the right side of

7

Job Search and
Application

the page. Place both underneath your name, as shown in Figure 7–7. Indicate the dates you can be reached at each address (but do not date the résumé itself).

Job Objective.   Some potential employers prefer to see a clear employment objective in résumés. An objective introduces the material in a résumé and helps the reader quickly understand your goal. If you decide to include an objective, use a heading such as "Objective," "Employment Objective," "Career Objective," or "Job Objective." State your immediate goal and, if you know that it will give you an advantage, the direction you hope your career will take. Try to write your objective in no more than three lines, and tailor it to the specific job for which you are applying, as illustrated in the following examples.

- A full-time computer-science position aimed at solving engineering problems and contributing to a management team.

- A position involving meeting the concerns of women, such as family planning, career counseling, or crisis management.

- Full-time management of a high-quality, local restaurant.

- A summer research or programming position providing opportunities to use problem-solving skills.

Qualifications Summary.   You may wish to include a brief summary of your qualifications to persuade hiring managers to select you for an interview. Sometimes called a *summary statement* or *career summary*, a qualifications summary can include skills, achievements, experience, or personal qualities that make you especially well-suited to the position. You may wish to give this section a heading such as "Profile," "Career Highlights," or, simply, "Qualifications." Or you may use a headline, as in Figure 7–12 ("Award-Winning Senior Financial Analyst").

Education.   List the school(s) you have attended, the degrees you received and the dates you received them, your major field(s) of study, and any academic honors you have earned. Include your grade point average only if it is 3.0 or higher—or include your average in your major if that is more impressive. List courses only if they are unusually impressive or if your résumé is otherwise sparse (see Figure 7–8). Mention your high school only if you want to call attention to special high school achievements, awards, projects, programs, internships, or study abroad.

Employment Experience.   Organize your employment experience in reverse chronological order, starting with your most recent job and working backward under a single major heading called "Experience," "Employment," "Professional Experience," or the like. You could also organize your experience functionally by clustering similar types of jobs into one or several sections with specific headings such as "Management Experience" or "Major Accomplishments."

One type of arrangement might be more persuasive than the other, depending on the situation. For example, if you are applying for an accounting job but have no specific background in accounting, you would probably do best to list past and present jobs in chronological order, from most to least recent. If you are applying for a supervisory position and have had three supervisory jobs in addition to two nonsupervisory positions, you might choose to create a single section called "Supervisory Experience" and list only your three supervisory jobs. Or you could create two sections — "Supervisory Experience" and "Other Experience" — and include the three supervisory jobs in the first section and your nonsupervisory jobs in the second section.

The functional résumé groups work experience by types of workplace activities or skills rather than by jobs in chronological order. However, many employers are suspicious of functional résumés because they can be used to hide a poor work history, such as excessive job hopping or extended employment gaps. Functional elements can be combined with a chronological arrangement by using a qualifications summary or skills category, as shown in Figure 7–12.

In general, follow these conventions when working on the "Experience" section of your résumé.

- Include jobs or internships when they relate directly to the position you are seeking. Although some applicants choose to omit internships and temporary or part-time jobs, including such experiences can make a résumé more persuasive if they have helped you develop specific related skills.
- Include extracurricular experiences, such as taking on a leadership position in a college organization or directing a community-service project, if they demonstrate that you have developed skills valued by potential employers.
- List military service as a job; give the dates served, the duty specialty, and the rank at discharge. Discuss military duties if they relate to the job you are seeking.
- For each job or experience, list both the job and company titles. Throughout each section, consistently begin with either the job or the company title, depending on which will likely be more impressive to potential employers.
- Under each job or experience, provide a concise description of your primary and secondary duties. If a job is not directly relevant, provide only a job title and a brief description of duties that helped you develop skills valued in the position you are seeking. For example, if you were a lifeguard and now seek a management position, focus on supervisory experience or even experience in averting disaster to highlight your management, decision-making, and crisis-control skills.

7

Job Search and Application

- Use action verbs (for example, "managed" rather than "was the manager") and state ideas succinctly, as shown in Figure 7–10. Even though the résumé is about you, do not use "I" (for example, instead of "I was promoted to Section Leader," use "Promoted to Section Leader").
- Focus as much as possible on your achievements in your work history ("Increased employee retention rate by 16% by developing a training program . . ."). Employers want to hire doers and achievers.

Related Skills and Abilities.   Employers are interested in hiring applicants with knowledge of a variety of skills or the ability to learn new ones fairly quickly. Depending on the position, you might list in this section items such as fluency in foreign languages; writing and editing abilities; specialized technical knowledge; or computer skills, including knowledge of specific languages, software, and hardware.

Honors and Activities.   If you have room on your résumé, list any honors and unique activities near the end. Include items such as student or community activities, professional or club memberships, awards received, and published works. Be selective: do not duplicate information given in other categories, and include only information that supports your employment objective. Provide a heading for this section that fits its contents, such as "Activities," "Honors," "Professional Affiliations," or "Publications and Memberships."

References.   Avoid listing references unless that is standard practice in your profession or your résumé is sparse. You might include a phrase such as "References available upon request" to signal the end of a long résumé, or write "Available upon request" after the heading "References" as a design element to balance a page. In any case, you should have a separate list of references to give to prospective employers after interviews; your list should include the main heading "References for [your name]."

Special Advice for Résumé Preparation

⬛ ETHICS NOTE Be truthful. The consequences of giving false information in your résumé are serious. In fact, the truthfulness of your résumé reflects not only on your own ethical stance but also on the integrity with which you would represent the organization. See also ethics in writing (Tab 1).

Salary.   Avoid listing the salary you desire in the résumé. On the one hand, you may price yourself out of a job you want if the salary you list is higher than a potential employer is willing to pay. On the other hand, if you list a low salary, you may not get the best possible offer. See <u>salary negotiations</u>.

Returning Job Seekers.   If you are returning to the workplace after an absence, most career experts say that it is important to acknowledge the gap in your career. That is particularly true if, for example, you are re-entering the workforce because you have devoted a full-time period to care for children or dependent adults. Do not undervalue such work. Although unpaid, it often provides experience that develops important time-management, problem-solving, organizational, and interpersonal skills. Although gaps in employment can be explained in the <u>application letter</u>, the following examples illustrate how you might reflect such experiences in a résumé. They would be especially appropriate for an applicant seeking employment in a field related to child or health care.

- **Primary Child-Care Provider, 2003 to 2005**
  Provided full-time care to three preschool children at home. Instructed in beginning scholastic skills, time management, basics of nutrition, arts, and swimming. Organized activities, managed household, and served as neighborhood-watch captain.

- **Home Caregiver, 2003 to 2005**
  Provided 60 hours per week in-home care to Alzheimer's patient. Coordinated medical care, developed exercise programs, completed and processed complex medical forms, administered medications, organized budget, and managed home environment.

If you have participated in volunteer work during such a period, list that experience. Volunteer work often results in the same experience as does full-time, paid work, a fact that your résumé should reflect, as in the following example.

- **School Association Coordinator, 2003 to 2005**
  Managed special activities of the Briarwood High School Parent-Teacher Association. Planned and coordinated meetings, scheduled events, and supervised fund-drive operations. Raised $70,000 toward refurbishing the school auditorium.

Electronic Résumés

In addition to the traditional paper résumé, you can post a Web-based résumé. You may also need to submit a résumé on disk or through e-mail to a potential employer to be included in an organization's database. As Internet and database technologies converge, remain current with the forms and protocols that employers prefer by reviewing popular job-search sites, such as Monster.com at <www.monster.com/> and others.

Web Résumés.   If you plan to post your résumé on your own Web site, keep the following points in mind.

• Follow the general advice for <u>Web design</u> (Tab 5), such as viewing your résumé on several browsers to see how it looks.
• Just below your name, you may wish to provide a series of internal page links to such important categories as "experience" and "education."
• Consider building a multipage site for displaying a work portfolio, publications, reference letters, and the like.
• If privacy is an issue, include an e-mail link ("mailto") at the top of the résumé rather than your home address and phone number.

The disadvantage of posting a résumé at your own Web site is that you must attract the attention of employers on your own. As discussed in the entry <u>job search</u>, commercial services can attract recruiters with their large databases.

Scannable and Plain-Text Résumés.   A scannable résumé is normally mailed to an employer in paper form, scanned, and downloaded into a company's searchable database. Such a résumé can be well formatted, but it should not contain decorative fonts, underlining, shading, letters that touch each other, and other features that will not scan easily. Scan such a résumé yourself to make sure there are no problems.

Many employers today request ASCII or plain-text résumés via e-mail, which can be added directly into the résumé database without scanning. ASCII résumés also allow employers to read the file regardless of the type of software they are using. You can copy and paste such a résumé directly into the body of the e-mail message.

DIGITAL TIP   **PREPARING AN ASCII RÉSUMÉ**

When preparing an ASCII (American Standard Code for Information Interchange) document, proper formatting is critical. For example, you need to insert manual line breaks at 65 characters to prevent long, single lines when they are opened in various systems. Further, many word-processing elements such as bullets, underlining, and boldface are incompatible with ASCII, which is limited to letters, numbers, and basic punctuation. For more on this topic, see <bedfordstmartins.com/alred> and select *Digital Tips*, "Preparing an ASCII Résumé."

For résumés that will be downloaded into databases, it is good to use nouns rather than verbs to describe experience and skills (*designer* and *management* rather than *designed* and *managed*). You may also include a section in such a résumé titled "Keywords" (or perhaps give a descriptive name, such as "Areas of Expertise"). Keywords, also called *descriptors*, allow potential employers to search the database for qualified candidates. So, be sure to use keywords that are the same as those used in the employer's descriptions of the jobs that best match your interests and qualifications. This section can follow the main heading of your résumé or appear near the end of your résumé. Figure 7–13 is a sample of an electronic résumé that demonstrates the use of keywords.

E-mail-Attached Résumés.   An employer may request or you may prefer to submit a résumé as an e-mail attachment to be printed out by the employer. If so, consider using a relatively plain design and sending the résumé as a rich text format (.rtf) document. Or, if precise design is important, send the résumé as a PDF file that will preserve the fonts, images, graphics, and layout. You can attach this file to an e-mail message that will then serve as your <u>application letter</u>.

WEB LINK ANNOTATED SAMPLE RÉSUMÉS

For more examples of résumés with helpful annotations, see <bedford stmartins.com/alred> and select *Model Documents Gallery.*

---

salary negotiations

Salary negotiations usually take place either at the end of an interview or after a formal job offer has been made. If possible, delay discussing salary until after you receive a formal written job offer because you will have more negotiating power at that point.

Before <u>interviewing for a job</u>, prepare for possible salary negotiations by researching the following:

- The current range of salaries for the work you hope to do at your level (entry? intermediate? advanced?) in your region of the country. Check trade journals and organizations in your field, or ask a reference librarian for help in finding this information. Job listings that include salary can also be helpful.
- Salaries made by last year's graduates from your college or university at your level and in your line of work. Your campus career development office should have these figures.
- Salaries made by people you know at your level and in your line of work. Attend local organizational meetings in your field or contact officers of local organizations who might have this information or steer you to useful contacts.
- The company's range of salaries for the position you are seeking. Call the company and ask to talk with the human resources

manager. Explain that you will be interviewing for a particular position and ask if they can give you the salary range for that job.

If a potential employer requests your salary requirements with a résumé, consider your options carefully. If you provide a salary that is too high, the company might never interview you; if you provide a salary that is too low, you may have no opportunity later in the hiring process to negotiate for a higher salary. However, if you fail to follow the potential employer's directions and omit the requested information, an employer may disqualify you on principle. If you choose to provide salary requirements, always do so in a range (for example, $35,000 to $40,000).

> **WEB LINK SALARY INFORMATION RESOURCES**
>
> For links to Web sites offering useful resources for salary negotiations, see <bedfordstmartins.com/alred> and select *Links for Business Writing*.

If an interviewer asks your salary requirements toward the end of the job interview, you can try these strategies to delay salary negotiations.

- Say something like "I am sure that this company always pays a fair salary for a person with my level of experience and qualifications" or "I am ready to consider your best offer."
- Indicate that you would like to learn more details about the position before discussing salary; point out that your primary goal is to work in a stimulating environment with growth potential, not to earn a specific salary.
- Express generally a strong interest in the position and the organization without referring to the salary.
- Emphasize your unique qualifications (or combination of skills) for the job and what you can do for the company that other candidates cannot.

If the interviewer or company demands to know your salary requirements during a job interview, provide a wide salary range that you know would be reasonable for someone at your level in your line of work in that region of the country. For example, you could say, "I would hope for a salary somewhere between $28,000 and $38,000, but of course this is negotiable."

Once salary negotiations begin, resist the temptation to accept, immediately, the first salary offer you receive. If you have done thorough research, you'll know if the first salary offer is at the low, middle, or high end of the salary range for your level of experience in your line of work. If you have little or no experience and receive an offer for a salary at the low end of the range, you will realize that the offer probably is fair and reasonable. Yet, if you receive the same low-end offer but bring considerable experience to the job, you can negotiate for a higher salary that is more reasonable for someone with your background and credentials in your line of work in your region of the country.

Never say that you are unable to accept a salary below a particular figure. To keep negotiations going, simply indicate that you would have trouble accepting the first offer because it was smaller than you had expected.

Remember that you are negotiating a package and not just a starting salary. For example, benefits can offer you substantial value. If the starting salary seems low, consider negotiating for some of these possible job perks:

- The chance for an early promotion, thus higher salary within a few years
- A particular job title or special job responsibilities that would provide you with impressive chances for career growth
- Tuition credits for continued education
- Payment of relocation costs
- Paid personal leave or paid vacations
- Personal or sick days
- Overtime potential
- Flexible hours
- Health, dental, eye-care, disability, and life insurance
- Retirement plans, such as 401(k) and pension plans
- Profit sharing; investment or stock options
- Bonuses or cost-of-living adjustments
- Commuting or parking-cost reimbursement
- Child or elder care
- Discounts on company products and services

You might find it most comfortable to respond to an initial offer in writing and then meet later with the potential employer for further negotiation. If possible, indicate all of your preferences and requirements at one time instead of continually asking for new and different benefits as you negotiate. Throughout this process, focus on what is most important to you (which might differ from what is most important to your friends) and on what you would find acceptable and comfortable.

7

Job Search and
Application

8

Presentations
and Meetings

Preview

Although writing is important, <u>listening</u> and <u>presentations</u> are crucial to success in the workplace. This section contains entries on these essential subjects as well as entries on conducting <u>meetings</u> and recording <u>minutes of meetings</u>. Because preparing an oral presentation is much like preparing to write, review Tab 1, "The Writing Process," noting in particular the entries on <u>audience</u>, <u>purpose</u>, and <u>organization</u>.

8

Presentations
and Meetings

listening

Effective listening is essential. It enables the listener to understand the directions of an instructor, the message in a speaker's <u>presentation</u>, the goals of a manager, and the needs and wants of customers. Above all, it lays the foundation for cooperation. Productive communication occurs when both the speaker and the listener focus clearly on the content of the message and attempt to eliminate as much interference as possible.

Fallacies About Listening

Most people assume that because they can hear they know how to listen. In fact, *hearing* is passive, whereas *listening* is active. Hearing voices in a crowd or a ringing telephone requires no analysis and no active involvement. We hear such sounds without choosing to listen to them—we have no choice but to hear them. Listening, however, requires taking action, interpreting the message, and assessing its worth.

Many people believe that words have absolute meanings; however, words can have multiple meanings that are determined by the context in which they are used. Differences in meaning may be the result of differences in the speaker's and the listener's occupation, education, culture, sex, race, or other factors. The use of <u>idioms</u> (Tab 9) can result in misunderstanding. See also <u>global communication</u> (Tab 1), <u>international correspondence</u> (Tab 6), <u>biased language</u> (Tab 9), <u>jargon</u> (Tab 9), and <u>English as a second language</u> (Tab 11).

Active Listening

To listen actively, you should (1) make a conscious decision to listen actively, (2) define your purpose for listening, (3) take specific actions to listen more efficiently, and (4) adapt to the situation.

Step 1: Make a Conscious Decision. The first step to active listening is simply making up your mind to do so. Active listening requires a conscious effort, something that does not come naturally. To listen actively, seek first to understand and then to be understood.

Step 2: Define Your Purpose. Knowing why you are listening can go a long way toward managing the most common listening problems: drifting attention, formulating your response while the speaker is still talking, and interrupting the speaker. To help you define your purpose for listening, ask yourself these questions:

• What kind of information do I hope to get from this exchange, and how will I use it?

- What kind of message do I want to send while I am listening? (Do I want to portray understanding, determination, flexibility, competence, or patience?)
- What might interfere with listening during the interaction— boredom, daydreaming, anger, impatience? How can I keep these factors from placing a barrier between the speaker and me?

Step 3: Take Specific Actions.   Becoming an active listener requires a willingness to become a responder rather than a reactor. A *responder* is a listener who slows down the communication to be certain that he or she is accurately receiving the message sent by the speaker. A *reactor* simply says the first thing that comes to mind without checking to make sure that he or she accurately understands the message. Take the following actions to help you become a responder and not a reactor.

- Make a conscious effort to be impartial when evaluating a message. For example, do not dismiss a message because you dislike the speaker or are distracted by the speaker's appearance or mannerisms.
- Slow down the communication by asking for more information or by paraphrasing the message received before you offer your thoughts. Paraphrasing (Tab 2) lets the speaker know you are listening, gives the speaker an opportunity to clear up any misunderstanding, and keeps you focused.
- Listen with empathy by putting yourself in the speaker's position. When people feel they are being listened to empathetically, they tend to respond with appreciation and cooperation, thereby improving the communication.
- To help you stay focused on what the speaker is saying, take notes while you are listening. Note-taking (Tab 2) not only communicates your attentiveness to the speaker, it also reinforces the message and helps you remember it.

Step 4: Adapt to the Situation.   The requirements of active listening differ from one situation to another. For example, when you are listening to a lecture, you may be listening only for specific information. However, if you are on a team project that depends on everyone's contribution, you need to listen at the highest level so that you can gather information as well as pick up on nuances the other speakers may be communicating. See also collaborative writing (Tab 1).

meetings

Meetings allow people to share information and collaborate to produce better results than exchanges of e-mail messages or other means would allow. (See also selecting the medium, Tab 1.) Like a presentation, a successful meeting requires planning and preparation.

Planning a Meeting

For a meeting to be successful, determine the focus of the meeting, decide who should attend, and choose the best time and place to hold it. Prepare an agenda for the meeting and determine who should take the minutes. See also minutes of meetings.

Determine the Purpose of the Meeting.   The first step in planning a meeting is to focus on the desired outcome. Ask yourself the following question to help you determine the purpose of the meeting: What should participants know, believe, do, or be able to do as a result of attending the meeting?

Once you have focused your desired outcome, use the information to write a purpose statement for the meeting that answers the questions *what* and *why*. (See also purpose, Tab 1.)

* The purpose of this meeting is to gather ideas from the sales force [*what*] to create a successful sales campaign for our new scanner [*why*].

Decide Who Should Attend.   Schedule a meeting for a time when all or most of the key people can be present. If a meeting must be held without some key participants, e-mail those people prior to the meeting for their contributions. Of course, the meeting minutes should be distributed to everyone, including significant nonattendees.

Choose the Meeting Time.   The time of day and the length of the meeting can influence its outcome. Consider the following when you are planning a meeting:

* People need Monday morning to focus on the week's work after the weekend.
* People need Friday afternoon to complete tasks that must be finished before the weekend.
* Long meetings should include adequate breaks to allow participants to check their messages, make phone calls, and refresh themselves.
* A meeting held during the last 15 minutes of the day will be quick, but few people will remember what happened.

Choose the Meeting Location.   Having a meeting on your own premises can give you an advantage: You feel more comfortable, which, along with your guests' newness to their surroundings, may help you get an edge. Holding the meeting on others' premises, however, can signal cooperation. For balance, especially when people are meeting for the first time or are discussing sensitive issues, having a meeting at a neutral site may be the best solution. No one gains an advantage in off-site meetings, and attendees often feel freer to participate.

8

Presentations
and Meetings

Establish the Agenda.   A tool for focusing the group, the *agenda* is an outline of what the meeting will address. Always prepare an agenda for a meeting, even if it is only a handwritten list of topics. Ideally, the agenda should be distributed to attendees a day or two before the meeting. For a longer meeting in which participants are required to make a presentation, try to distribute the agenda a week or more in advance.

The agenda should list the attendees, the meeting time and place, and the topics you plan to discuss. If the meeting includes presentations, list the time allotted for each speaker. Finally, indicate an approximate length for the meeting so that participants can plan the rest of their day. Figure 8–1 shows a typical agenda.

Sales Meeting Agenda

Purpose:	To get input for a sales campaign for the new scanner
Date:	May 12, 2005
Place:	Conference Room E
Time:	9:30 a.m.–11:00 a.m.
Attendees:	New Products Advertising Manager, Equipment Sales Reps, Customer-Service Staff, and Service Managers

Topic	Presenter	Time
The Scanner	Bob Arbuckle	Presentation, 9:30–9:45
The Campaign	Maria Lopez	Presentation, 9:45–10:00
The Sales Strategy	Mary Winifred	Presentation, 10:00–10:15
Discussion	Led by Dave Grimes	Discussion, 10:15–11:00

FIGURE 8–1. Meeting Agenda

If the agenda is distributed in advance of the meeting, it should be accompanied by a memo or an e-mail informing people of the following:

- The purpose of the meeting
- The date and place
- The meeting start and stop times
- The names of the people invited
- Instructions on how to prepare for the meeting

Figure 8–2 shows a cover e-mail to accompany an agenda.

Assign the Minute-Taking.   Delegate the minute-taking to someone other than the leader. The minute-taker should record major decisions made and tasks assigned. To avoid misunderstandings, the minute-taker must record each assignment, the person responsible for it, and the date on which it is due.

Subject: Planning Meeting
Date: Thur, 05 May 2005 13:30:12 EST
From: Susan McLaughlin <smclaughlin@millenniumscanners.com>
To: **New Products Advertising Manager; Equipment Sales
              Representatives; Customer-Service Staff; Service Managers**
Attachments: 📎 Sales Meeting Agenda.doc (29 KB)

Purpose of the Meeting

The purpose of this meeting is to get your ideas for the upcoming introduction and sales campaign for our new scanner.

Date, Time, and Location

Date: May 12, 2005
Time: 9:30 a.m.–11:00 a.m.
Place: Conference Room E (go to the ground floor, take a right off the
       elevator, third door on the left)

Attendees

The groups addressed above

Meeting Preparation

Everyone should be prepared to offer suggestions on the following items:

• Sales features of the new scanner
• Techniques for selling the scanner
• Customer profile for potential business
• FAQs — questions customers may ask
• Anticipated service needs

Agenda

Please see the attached document.

FIGURE 8–2. E-mail to Accompany an Agenda

For a standing committee, it is best to rotate the responsibility of
taking minutes. See also <u>note-taking</u> (Tab 2).

Conducting the Meeting

Assign someone to write on a flip chart or project a computer image of
information that needs to be viewed by everyone present.

During the meeting, keep to your agenda; however, allow room for
differing views and foster an environment in which participants listen
respectfully to one another. (See also <u>listening</u>.) Create a productive environment.

• Consider the feelings, thoughts, ideas, and needs of others—do
  not let your own agenda blind you to other points of view.

8

Presentations
and Meetings

- Help other participants feel valued and respected by listening to them and responding to what they say.
- Respond positively to the comments of others as best you can.
- Consider ways of doing things that are different from your own, particularly those from other cultures. See also <u>global communication</u> (Tab 1).

Deal with Conflict.   Despite your best efforts, conflict is inevitable. However, conflict is potentially valuable; when managed positively, it can stimulate creative thinking by challenging complacency and showing ways to achieve goals more efficiently or economically. See also <u>collaborative writing</u> (Tab 1).

Members of any group are likely to vary greatly in their personalities and attitudes, and you may encounter people who approach meetings differently. Consider the following tactics for the interruptive, negative, rambling, overly quiet, and territorial personality types.

- The *interruptive person* rarely lets anyone finish a sentence and intimidates the group's quieter members. Tell that person in a firm but nonhostile tone to let the others finish in the interest of getting everyone's input. By addressing the issue directly, you signal to the group the importance of putting common goals first.
- The *negative person* has difficulty accepting change and often considers a new idea or project from a negative point of view. Such negativity, if left unchecked, can demoralize the group and deflate enthusiasm for new ideas. If the negative person brings up a valid point, ask for the group's suggestions to remedy the issue being raised. If the negative person's reactions are not valid or are outside the agenda, state the necessity of staying focused on the agenda and perhaps recommend a separate meeting to address those issues.
- The *rambling person* cannot collect his or her thoughts quickly enough to verbalize them succinctly. Restate or clarify this person's ideas. Try to strike a balance between providing your own interpretation and drawing out the person's intended meaning.
- The *overly quiet person* may be timid or may just be deep in thought. Ask for this person's thoughts, being careful not to embarrass the person. In some cases, you can have a quiet person jot down his or her thoughts and give them to you later.
- The *territorial person* fiercely defends his or her group against real or perceived threats and may refuse to cooperate with members of other departments, companies, and so on. Point out that although such concerns may be valid, everyone is working toward the same overall goal and that goal takes precedence.

Close the Meeting.   Just before closing the meeting, review all decisions and assignments. Paraphrase each to help the group focus on what they have agreed to do and to confirm the accuracy of the minutes.

Now is the time to raise questions and clarify any misunderstandings. Set a date by which everyone at the meeting can expect to receive copies of the minutes. Finally, thank everyone for participating, and close the meeting on a positive note.

minutes of meetings

Organizations and committees keep official records of their <u>meetings</u>; such records are known as *minutes*. Because minutes are often used to settle disputes, they must be accurate, complete, and clear. When approved, minutes of meetings are official and can be used as evidence in legal proceedings. An example of minutes is shown in Figure 8–3.

NORTH TAMPA MEDICAL CENTER

Minutes of the Monthly Meeting
Medical Audit Committee

DATE: July 25, 2005

PRESENT: G. Miller (Chair), C. Bloom, J. Dades, K. Gilley,
                   D. Ingoglia (Secretary), S. Ramirez
ABSENT: D. Rowan, C. Tsien, C. Voronski, R. Fautier, R. Wolf

Dr. Gail Miller called the meeting to order at 12:45 p.m. Dr. David Ingoglia made a motion that the June 2, 2005, minutes be approved as distributed. The motion was seconded and passed.

    The committee discussed and took action on the following topics.

(1) TOPIC: Meeting Time

    <u>Discussion</u>: The most convenient time for the committee to meet.
    <u>Action taken</u>: The committee decided to meet on the fourth Tuesday of every month, at 12:30 p.m.

FIGURE 8–3. Minutes of a Meeting

    Keep your minutes brief and to the point. Except for recording motions, which must be transcribed word for word, summarize what occurs and paraphrase discussions. To keep the minutes concise, follow a set format and use headings for each major point discussed. See also <u>note-taking</u> (Tab 2).

    Avoid abstractions and generalities; always be specific. Refer to everyone in the same way—a lack of consistency in titles or names may suggest a deference to one person at the expense of another. Avoid

8
Presentations
and Meetings

adjectives and adverbs that suggest good or bad qualities, as in "Mr. Sturgess's *capable* assistant read the *comprehensive* report to the subcommittee." Minutes should be objective and impartial.

If a member of the committee is to follow up on something and report back to the committee at its next meeting, clearly state the person's name and the responsibility he or she has accepted.

Writer's Checklist: Preparing Minutes of Meetings

Include the following in meeting minutes:

- ☑ The name of the group or committee holding the meeting
- ☑ The topic of the meeting
- ☑ The kind of meeting (a regular meeting or a special meeting called to discuss a specific subject or problem)
- ☑ The number of members present and, for committees or boards of ten or fewer members, their names
- ☑ The place, time, and date of the meeting
- ☑ A statement that the chair and the secretary were present or the names of any substitutes
- ☑ A statement that the minutes of the previous meeting were approved or revised
- ☑ A list of any reports that were read and approved
- ☑ All the main motions that were made, with statements as to whether they were carried, defeated, or tabled (vote postponed), and the names of those who made and seconded the motions (motions that were withdrawn are not mentioned)
- ☑ A full description of resolutions that were adopted and a simple statement of any that were rejected
- ☑ A record of all ballots with the number of votes cast for and against resolutions
- ☑ The time the meeting was adjourned (officially ended) and the place, time, and date of the next meeting
- ☑ The recording secretary's signature and typed name and, if desired, the signature of the chairperson

8

Presentations and Meetings

presentations

DIRECTORY

The steps required to prepare an effective presentation parallel the steps you follow to write a document. As with writing a document, determine your purpose and analyze your audience. Then gather the facts that will support your point of view and proposal and logically organize that information. Presentations do, however, differ from written documents in a number of important ways. They are intended for listeners, not readers. Because you are speaking, your manner of delivery, the way you organize the material, and your supporting visuals require as much attention as your content.

Determining Your Purpose

Every presentation is given for a <u>purpose</u> (Tab 1), even if it is only to share information. To determine the primary purpose of your presentation, use the following question as a guide: What do I want the audience to know, to believe, and to do when I have finished the presentation? Based on the answer to that question, write a purpose statement that answers the *what* and *why* questions.

- The purpose of my presentation is to convince my company's chief information officer of the need to improve the appearance, content, and customer use of our company's Web site [*what*] so that she will be persuaded to allocate additional funds for site-development work in the next fiscal year [*why*].

Analyzing Your Audience

Once you have determined the desired end result of the presentation, you need to analyze your audience so that you can tailor your presentation to their needs. (See also <u>readers</u>, Tab 1.) Ask yourself these questions about your audience:

- What is your audience's level of experience or knowledge about your topic?
- What is the general educational level and age of your audience?
- What is your audience's attitude toward the topic you are speaking about, and—based on that attitude—what concerns, fears, or objections might your audience have?
- Do any subgroups in the audience have different concerns or needs?
- What questions might your audience ask about this topic?

Gathering Information

Once you have focused the presentation, you need to find the facts that support your point of view or the action you propose. As you gather information, keep in mind that you should give the audience only the facts necessary to accomplish your goals; too much will overwhelm them and too little will not adequately inform your listeners or support

8

Presentations and Meetings

your recommendations. For detailed guidance about gathering information, see <u>research</u> (Tab 2).

Structuring the Presentation

When structuring the presentation, focus on your audience. Listeners are freshest at the outset and refocus their attention near the end. Take advantage of that pattern. Give your audience a brief overview of your presentation at the beginning, use the body to develop your ideas, and end with a summary of what you covered and, if appropriate, a call to action. See also <u>organization</u> (Tab 1).

The Introduction.   Include in the introduction an opening that focuses your audience's attention, such as in the following examples.

- You have to write an important report, but you'd like to incorporate lengthy sections of an old report into your new one. The problem is that you don't have an electronic version of the old report. You will have to rekey many pages. You groan because that seems an incredible waste of time. Have I got a solution for you! [*Definition of a problem*]

- As many as 50 million Americans have high blood pressure. [*An attention-getting statement*]

- Would you be interested in a full-sized computer keyboard that is waterproof and noiseless, and can be rolled up like a rubber mat? [*A rhetorical question*]

- As I sat at my computer one morning, deleting my eighth spam message of the day, I decided that it was time to take action to eliminate this time-waster. [*A personal experience*]

- According to researchers at the Massachusetts Institute of Technology, "Garlic and its cousin, the onion, confer major health benefits — including fighting cancer, infections, and heart disease." [*An appropriate quotation*]

Following your opening, use the introduction to set the stage for your audience by providing an overview of the presentation, which can include general or background information that will be needed to understand any more detailed information in the body of your presentation. It can also show how you have organized the material.

- This presentation analyzes three different scanner models for us to consider purchasing. Based on a comparison of all three, I will recommend the one I believe best meets our needs. To do so, I'll discuss the following five points:
  1. Why we need a scanner [*the problem*]
  2. The basics of scanner technology [*general information*]

3. The criteria I used to compare the three scanner models [*comparison*]
4. The scanner models I compared and why [*possible solutions*]
5. The scanner I propose we buy [*proposed solution*]

The Body.   If applicable, present the evidence that will persuade the audience to agree with your conclusions and act on them. (See <u>persuasion</u>, Tab 1.) If there is a problem, demonstrate that it exists and offer a solution or range of possible solutions. For example, if your introduction stated that the problem is low profits, high costs, outdated technology, or high employee absenteeism, you could use the following approach.

1. Prove your point.
   a. Marshal the facts and data you need.
   b. Present the information using easy-to-understand visuals.
2. Offer solutions.
   a. "Increase profits by lowering production costs."
   b. "Cut overhead to reduce costs or abolish specific programs or product lines."
   c. "Replace outdated technology or upgrade existing technology."
   d. "Offer employees more flexibility in their work schedules or other incentives."
3. Anticipate questions ("How much will it cost?") and objections ("We're too busy now—when would we have time to learn the new software?") and incorporate the answers into your presentation.

The Closing.   Fulfill the goals of your presentation in the closing. If your purpose is to motivate the listeners to take action, ask them to do what you want them to do; if your purpose is to get your audience to think about something, summarize what you want them to think about. Many presenters make the mistake of not actually closing—they simply quit talking, shuffle papers, and then walk away.

Because your closing is what your audience is most likely to remember, it is the time to be strong and persuasive. Consider the following possible closing.

- Based on all the data, I believe that the Worthington scanner best suits our needs. It produces 3,000 units a month more than its closest competitor and creates electronic files we can use on our Web site and on paper. The Worthington is also compatible with our current computer network and includes staff training at our site. Although the initial cost is higher than that for the other two models, the additional capabilities, longer life cycle for replacement parts, and lower maintenance costs make it a better value. I recommend we allocate the funds necessary for this scanner by the 15th of this month in order to be well prepared for next quarter's customer presentations.

8

Presentations and Meetings

The closing brings the presentation full circle and asks the audience to fulfill the purpose of the presentation — exactly what a closing should do. See also <u>conclusions</u> (Tab 1).

Transitions.   Planned <u>transitions</u> (Tab 9) should appear between the introduction and the body, between points in the body, and between the body and the closing. Transitions are simply a sentence or two to let the audience know that you are moving from one topic to the next. They also prevent a choppy presentation and provide the audience with assurance that you know where you are going and how to get there.

- Before getting into the specifics of each scanner I compared, I'd like to demonstrate how scanners work in general. That information will provide you with the background you'll need to compare the differences among the scanners and their capabilities discussed in this presentation.

It is also a good idea to pause for a moment after you have delivered a transition between topics to let your listeners shift gears with you. Remember, they do not know your plan.

Using Visuals

Well-planned <u>visuals</u> (Tab 5) not only add interest and emphasis to your presentation, they also clarify and simplify your message because they communicate clearly, quickly, and vividly. Charts, graphs, and illustrations greatly increase audience understanding and retention of information, especially for complex issues and technical information that could otherwise be misunderstood or overlooked.

You can create and present the visual components of your presentation by using a variety of media — flip charts, whiteboard or chalkboard, overhead transparencies, slides, or computer presentation software.

Flip Charts.   Flip charts are ideal for smaller groups in a conference room or classroom and are also ideal for brainstorming with your audience.

Whiteboard or Chalkboard.   The whiteboard or chalkboard common to classrooms is convenient for creating sketches and for jotting notes during your presentation. If your presentation requires extensive notes or complex drawings, create them before the presentation to minimize audience restlessness.

Overhead Transparencies.   With transparencies you can create a series of overlays to explain a complex device or system, adding (or removing) the overlays one at a time. You can also lay a sheet of paper over a list of items on a transparency, uncovering one item at a time as you discuss it, to focus audience attention on each point in the sequence.

Presentation Software. Presentation software, such as PowerPoint, Corel Presentations, and Freelance Graphics, lets you create your presentation on your computer. You can develop charts and graphs with data from spreadsheet software or locate visuals on the Web, and then import those files into your presentation. This software also offers standard templates and other features that help you design effective visuals and integrated text. Enhancements include a selection of typefaces, highlighting devices, background textures and colors, and clip-art images. Avoid using too many enhancements, which may distract viewers from your message. Images can also be printed out for use as overhead transparencies or handouts.

Rehearse your presentation using your electronic slides, and practice your transitions from slide to slide. Also practice loading your presentation and anticipate any technical difficulties that might arise. Should you encounter a technical snag during the presentation, stay calm and give yourself time to solve the problem. If you cannot solve the problem, move on without the technology. As a backup, carry a printout of your electronic presentation as well as an extra copy on diskette. Figure 8–4 shows slides for a brief presentation.

Writer's Checklist: Using Visuals in a Presentation

☑ Use text sparingly. Use bulleted or numbered lists, keeping them parallel in content and in grammatical form. Use numbers if the sequence is important and bullets if it is not. See lists (Tab 5) and **parallel structure** (Tab 9).

☑ Limit the number of bulleted or numbered items to five or six per visual. Each visual should contain no more than forty to forty-five words. Any more will clutter the visual and force you to use a smaller font that could impair the audience's ability to read it.

☑ Make your visuals consistent in type style, size, and spacing.

☑ Use a type size visible to members of the audience in the back of the room. Type should be boldface and no smaller than thirty points. For headings, forty-five- or fifty-point type works even better.

☑ Use graphs and charts to show data trends. Use only one or two illustrations per visual to avoid clutter and confusion.

☑ Make the contrast between your text and the background sharp. Use light backgrounds with dark lettering and avoid textured or decorated backgrounds.

☑ Use no more than twelve visuals per presentation. Any more will tax the audience's concentration.

☑ Match your delivery of the content to your visuals. Do not put one set of words or images on the screen and talk about the previous visual or, even worse, the next one.

☑ Do not read the text on your visual word for word. Your audience can read the visuals; they look to you to cover the salient points in detail.

8
Presentations and Meetings

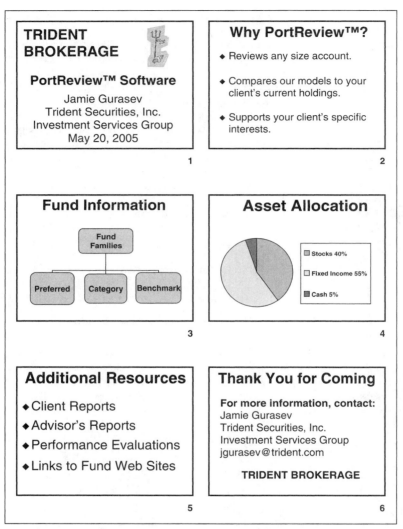

FIGURE 8–4. Slides for a Brief Presentation

Delivering a Presentation

Once you have outlined and drafted your presentation and prepared your visuals, you are ready to practice your presentation and delivery techniques.

Practice.   Familiarize yourself with the sequence of the material— major topics, notes, and visuals—in your outline. Once you feel comfortable with the content, you are ready to practice the presentation itself.

> ### WEB LINK PREPARING PRESENTATION SLIDES
>
> A number of sites on the Web offer useful information and tutorials for using software for making presentations. For a helpful tutorial, see <bedfordstmartins.com/alred> and select *Tutorials*, "Preparing Presentation Slides." For links to additional useful sites, select *Links for Business Writing.*

PRACTICE ON YOUR FEET AND OUT LOUD.   Try to practice in the room where you will give the presentation. Practicing on-site helps you get the feel of the room: the acoustics, the lighting, the arrangement of the chairs, the position of electrical outlets and switches, and so forth. Practice out loud to make clear exactly how long your presentation will take, highlight problems such as awkward transitions, and help eliminate verbal tics, such as "um," "you know," and "like."

PRACTICE WITH YOUR VISUALS AND TEXT.   Integrate your visuals into your practice sessions to help your presentation go more smoothly. Operate the equipment (computer, slide projector, or overhead projector) until you are comfortable with it. Decide if you want to use a remote control or to have someone else advance your slides. Even if things go wrong, being prepared and practiced will give you the confidence and poise to continue.

Delivery Techniques That Work.   Your delivery is both audible and visual. In addition to your words and message, your nonverbal communication affects your audience. Be animated — your words will make an impression and have more staying power when they are delivered with physical and vocal animation. If you want listeners to share your point of view, show enthusiasm for your topic. The most common delivery techniques include making eye contact; using movement and gestures; and varying voice inflection, pace, and projection.

EYE CONTACT.   The best way to establish rapport with your audience is through eye contact. In a large audience, directly address those people who seem most responsive to you in different parts of the room. Doing that helps you establish rapport with your listeners by holding their attention and gives you important visual cues that let you know how your message is being received. Are people engaged and actively listening? Or are they looking around or staring at the floor? Such cues tell you that you may need to speed up or slow down the pace of your presentation.

MOVEMENT.   Animate the presentation with physical movement. Take a step or two to one side after you have been talking for a minute or so. That type of movement is most effective at transitional points in your presentation between major topics or after pauses or emphases. Too much movement, however, can be distracting, so try not to pace.

Another way to integrate movement into your presentation is to walk to the screen and point to the visual as you discuss it. Touch the screen with the pointer and then turn back to the audience before beginning to speak (remember the three *t*'s: touch, turn, and talk).

GESTURES.   Gestures both animate your presentation and help communicate your message. Most people gesture naturally when they talk; nervousness, however, can inhibit gesturing during a presentation. Keep one hand free and use that hand to gesture.

VOICE.   Your voice can be an effective tool in communicating your sincerity, enthusiasm, and command of your topic. Use it to your advantage to project your credibility. Vocal inflection is the rise and fall of your voice at different times, such as the way your voice naturally rises at the end of a question ("You want it *when?*"). A conversational delivery and eye contact promote the feeling among members of the audience that you are addressing each one directly. Use vocal inflection to highlight differences between key and subordinate points in your presentation.

PACE.   Be aware of the speed at which you deliver your presentation. If you speak too fast, your words will run together, making it difficult for your audience to follow. If you speak too slowly, your listeners will become impatient and distracted.

PROJECTION.   Most speakers think they are projecting more loudly than they are. Remember that your presentation is ineffective for anyone in the audience who cannot hear you. If listeners must strain to hear you, they may give up trying to listen. Correct projection problems by practicing out loud with someone listening from the back of the room.

Presentation Anxiety.   Everyone experiences nervousness before a presentation. Survey after survey reveals that for most people dread of public speaking ranks among their top five fears. Instead of letting fear inhibit you, focus on channeling your nervous energy into a helpful stimulant. The best way to master anxiety is to know your topic thoroughly—knowing what you are going to say and how you are going to say it will help you gain confidence and reduce anxiety as you become immersed in your subject.

Writer's Checklist: Preparing for and Delivering a Presentation

☑ Practice your presentation with visuals; practice in front of listeners, if possible.

☑ Visit the location of the presentation ahead of time to familiarize yourself with the surroundings.

☑ Prepare a set of notes that will trigger your memory during the presentation.

Writer's Checklist: Preparing for and Delivering a Presentation (continued)

☑ Make as much eye contact as possible with your audience to establish rapport and maximize opportunities for audience feedback.

☑ Animate your delivery by integrating movement, gestures, and vocal inflection into your presentation. However, keep your movements and speech patterns natural.

☑ Speak loudly and slowly enough to be heard and understood.

☑ Do not read the text on your visuals word for word; explain the salient points in detail.

For information and tips on communicating with cross-cultural audiences, see <u>global communication</u> (Tab 1), <u>global graphics</u> (Tab 5) and <u>international correspondence</u> (Tab 6).

Style
and Clarity

Preview

The entries in this section are intended to help you develop a style that is clear and effective — and that follows the conventions of standard English. For a number of related entries, see Tab 1, "The Writing Process"; Tab 10, "Usage"; and Tab 11, "Grammar."

Some entries in this section — **awkwardness**, **coherence**, **parallel structure**, and **sentence variety** — will help you construct clear sentences and paragraphs. Other entries discuss such **word choice** issues as **abstract/ concrete words**, **idioms**, and **jargon**. Finally, this section covers the important subjects of **biased language**, **business writing style**, and **"you" viewpoint**.

absolute words

Absolute words (such as *round, unique, exact,* and *perfect*) are not logically subject to comparison, especially in business writing, where accuracy and precision are often crucial. See also <u>adjectives</u> (Tab 11).

- We modified our mission statement to more ~~exactly~~ *closely* reflect our long-term goals.

abstract / concrete words

Abstract words refer to general ideas, qualities, conditions, acts, or relationships — intangible things that cannot be detected by the five senses (sight, hearing, touch, taste, and smell), such as *learning, courage,* and *technology.* Concrete words identify things that can be perceived by the five senses, such as *diploma, soldier,* and *keyboard.*

Abstract words must frequently be further defined or described.

- The investigative team needs freedom. *to interview the maintenance technicians.*

Abstract words are best used with concrete words because concrete words help make intangible concepts more specific and vivid.

- *Transportation* [abstract] was limited to the *subway* [concrete] and *buses* [concrete].

See also <u>word choice</u>.

affectation

Affectation is the use of language that is more formal, technical, or showy than necessary to communicate information to the reader. Affectation is a widespread writing problem in the workplace because many people feel that affectation lends a degree of authority to their writing. In fact, affectation can alienate customers, clients, and colleagues.

Affected writing forces <u>readers</u> (Tab 1) to work harder to understand the writer's meaning. It typically contains abstract, highly technical, or foreign words and is often liberally sprinkled with trendy <u>buzzwords</u>.

⚡ ETHICS NOTE <u>Jargon</u> and <u>euphemisms</u> can become affectation, especially if their purpose is to hide relevant facts or give a false impression of competence. See <u>ethics in writing</u> (Tab 1).

Writers are easily lured into affectation through the use of long variants—words created by adding prefixes and suffixes to simpler words (*analyzation* for *analysis*; *utilization* for *use*). Unnecessarily formal words (such as *penultimate* for *next to last*) and outdated words (such as *herewith*) can produce affectation. Elegant variation—attempting to avoid repeating a word within a paragraph by substituting a pretentious synonym—is also a form of affectation. Another type of affectation is gobbledygook, which is wordy, roundabout writing with many pseudo-legal and pseudoscientific terms. See also <u>cliches</u>, <u>conciseness</u>, and <u>nominalizations</u>.

awkwardness

Any writing that strikes the reader as awkward—that is, as forced or unnatural—impedes the reader's understanding. The following guidelines will help you smooth out most awkward passages.

Writer's Checklist: Eliminating Awkwardness

- ☑ Strive for clarity and <u>coherence</u> during <u>revision</u> (Tab 1).
- ☑ Check for <u>organization</u> (Tab 1) to ensure your writing develops logically.
- ☑ Keep <u>sentence construction</u> (Tab 11) as direct and simple as possible.
- ☑ Use <u>subordination</u>; avoid needless <u>repetition</u>.
- ☑ Correct any <u>logic errors</u> within your sentences.
- ☑ Revise for <u>conciseness</u> and avoid <u>expletives</u>.
- ☑ Use the active <u>voice</u> (Tab 11) wherever possible.
- ☑ Eliminate any jammed <u>modifiers</u> (Tab 11) and, for particularly awkward constructions, apply the tactics in the entry <u>garbled sentences</u>.

biased language

Biased language refers to words and expressions that offend because they make inappropriate assumptions or stereotypes about gender, ethnicity, physical or mental disability, age, or sexual orientation.

⬛ ETHICS NOTE The easiest way to avoid bias is simply not to mention differences among people unless the differences are relevant to the discussion. Keep current with accepted usage and, if you are unsure of the appropriateness of an expression or the tone of a passage, have several colleagues review the material and give you their honest assessment.

Sexist Language

Sexist language can be an outgrowth of sexism, the arbitrary stereotyping of men and women in their roles in life. Sexism, a form of biased language, can breed and reinforce inequality. To avoid sexism in your writing, treat men and women equally, and do not make assumptions about traditional or occupational roles. Accordingly, use nonsexist occupational descriptions in your writing.

INSTEAD OF	CONSIDER
chairman, chairwoman	chair, chairperson
foreman	supervisor, manager
man-hour	staff hours, worker hours
policeman, policewoman	police officer
salesman, saleswoman	salesperson

Use parallel terms to describe men and women.

INSTEAD OF	USE
man and wife	husband and wife
Ms. Jones and Bernard Weiss	Ms. Jones and Mr. Weiss; Mary Jones and Bernard Weiss
ladies and men	ladies and gentlemen; women and men

Sexism can creep into your writing by the unthinking use of male or female pronouns where a reference could apply equally to a man or a woman. One way to avoid such usage is to rewrite the sentence in the plural.

- *All employees* ~~Every employee~~ will have ~~his manager~~ *their managers* sign ~~his travel voucher.~~ *their travel vouchers.*

Other possible solutions are to use *his or her* instead of *his* alone or to omit the pronoun completely if it is not essential to the meaning of the sentence.

- Everyone must submit ~~his~~ *an* expense report by Monday.

See also <u>he/she</u> (Tab 10) and <u>pronouns</u> (Tab 11).

Other Types of Biased Language

Identifying people by racial, ethnic, or religious categories is simply not relevant in most workplace writing. Telling readers that an engineer is Native American or that a professor is African American almost never conveys useful information. It also reinforces stereotypes, implying that it is rare for a person of a certain background to have achieved such a position. It also is inappropriate stereotyping to link a profession or some characteristic to race or ethnicity: a Jewish lawyer, an African-American jazz musician, an Asian-American mathematics prodigy.

Consider how you refer to people with disabilities. If you refer to "a disabled employee," you imply that the part (*disabled*) is as significant as the whole (*employee*). Use "an employee with a disability" instead. Similarly, the preferred usage is "a person who uses a wheelchair" rather than "a wheelchair-bound person," an expression that inappropriately equates the wheelchair with the person.

Terms that refer to a person's age are also open to inappropriate stereotyping. Referring to older colleagues as "geezers" and to younger colleagues as "kids" is derogatory, at the least.

In most workplace writing, such issues are simply not relevant. Of course, there are contexts in which race, ethnicity, or religion should be identified. For example, if you are writing an Equal Employment Opportunity Commission report about your firm's hiring practices, the racial composition of the workforce is relevant. In such cases, you need to present the issues in ways that respect and do not demean the individuals or groups to which you refer. See also <u>ethics in writing</u> (Tab 1).

business writing style

Business writing has evolved from a very formal and elaborate style to one that is more personal and direct. Yet, even though business writing style is less formal today, it must adhere to the conventions of standard English with the use of conventional spelling and standard grammatical forms.

Business writing legitimately varies from the conversational style you might use in a note sent as an <u>e-mail</u> (Tab 6) to the formal, legalistic style found in contracts. In most e-mail messages, letters, and <u>memos</u> (Tab 6), a style between those two extremes generally is appropriate. Writing that is too formal can alienate readers, and an overly obvious attempt to be casual and informal may seem insincere or unprofessional.

- Dear Jane,

  Your proposal arrived today, and it looks great.
  ~~Just got your proposal. It's awesome!~~

In business writing, as in all writing, know your <u>readers</u> (Tab 1).

The use of personal <u>pronouns</u> (Tab 11) is important in letters and memos. In fact, one way you can make your business writing persuasive is through the use of the <u>"you" viewpoint</u>, which often, but not always, uses the pronoun *you* to place the readers' interest foremost.

✪ ETHICS NOTE Be careful when you use the pronoun *we* in a business letter that is written on company stationery because it commits your company to what you have written. In general, when a statement is your opinion, use *I*; when it is company policy, use *we*. Do not refer to yourself in the third person by using *one* or *the writer*. It is perfectly natural and appropriate to refer to yourself as *I* and to the reader as *you*. In a report, however, you may be writing to more than one reader and may not necessarily want to refer to collective readers as *you*. See also ethics in writing (Tab 1), persuasion (Tab 1), and point of view (Tab 1).

The best writers strive to write in a style that is so clear that their message cannot be misunderstood. In fact, you cannot be persuasive unless you are clear. One way to achieve a clear style, especially during revision (Tab 1), is to eliminate overuse of the passive voice (Tab 11), which plagues most poor business writing. Although the passive voice is sometimes necessary, often it makes your writing not only dull but also ambiguous, uninformative, or overly impersonal.

You can also achieve clarity with conciseness. Proceed cautiously here, however, because business writing should not be an endless series of short, choppy sentences. (See also sentence variety and telegraphic style.) Don't be so concise that you become blunt or deliver too little information to be helpful to the readers. Appropriate and effective word choice is also essential to clarity. Finally, you can achieve clarity through the wise use of punctuation, as discussed in Tab 12, "Punctuation and Mechanics." A misplaced comma or other punctuation mark can cause misunderstanding and confusion. See also the "Five Steps to Successful Writing" (page xxi).

buzzwords

Buzzwords are words that suddenly become popular and, because of an intense period of overuse, lose their freshness and preciseness. They may become popular through their association with technology, popular culture, or even sports. We include them in our vocabulary because they *seem* to give force and vitality to our language. Actually, buzzwords sound pretentious in business writing. (See also word choice.)

interface [as a verb]	deliverables	dialogue [as a verb]
impact [as a verb]	24/7	bleeding edge
skill sets	dot-com	cash cow

Obviously, some buzzwords are appropriate in the right context or in casual conversation. It is when writers needlessly shift the normal function of a word that imprecision becomes a problem.

9

Style and Clarity

- We must establish an *interface* between the computer and the satellite hardware.

  [*Interface* is appropriately used as a noun.]

- We must ~~interface~~ *cooperate* with the Human Resources Department.

  [*Interface* is inappropriately used as a verb; *cooperate* is more precise.]

clichés

Clichés are expressions that have been used for so long that they are no longer fresh but come to mind easily because they are so familiar. Clichés are often wordy as well as vague and can be confusing, especially to nonnative speakers of English. Each of the following clichés is followed by a better, more direct word or phrase.

INSTEAD OF	USE
all over the map	scattered; unfocused
run it up the flagpole	see what others think
last but not least	last; finally

Some writers use clichés in a misguided attempt to appear casual or spontaneous, just as other writers try to impress readers with <u>buzzwords</u>. Although clichés may come to mind easily while you are writing a draft, eliminate them during revision. See also <u>international correspondence</u> (Tab 6), <u>affectation</u>, and <u>conciseness</u>.

coherence

Writing is coherent when the relationships among ideas are clear to the reader. The major components of coherent writing are a logical sequence of related ideas and clear <u>transitions</u> between these ideas. See also <u>organization</u> (Tab 1).

Presenting ideas in a logical sequence is the most important requirement in achieving coherence. The key to achieving a logical sequence is the use of a good outline (see <u>outlining</u>, Tab 1). An outline forces you to establish a beginning, a middle (body), and an end. That structure contributes greatly to coherence by enabling you to experiment with sequences and to lay out the most direct route to your purpose without digressing.

Thoughtful transition is also essential; without it, your writing cannot achieve the smooth flow from sentence to sentence and from paragraph to paragraph that is required for coherence.

Check your draft carefully for coherence during <u>revision</u> (Tab 1). If possible, have someone else review your draft for how well it expresses the relationships between ideas. Such help is especially important in <u>collaborative writing</u> (Tab 1), where coherence is often a challenge. See also <u>unity</u>.

compound words

A compound word is made from two or more words that function as a single concept. A compound may be hyphenated, written as one word, or written as separate words.

- editor-in-chief, high-energy, low-level, courthouse, nevertheless, online, home page, post office, Web site

If you are not certain whether a compound word should be hyphenated, check a dictionary. See also <u>hyphens</u> (Tab 12).

Be careful to distinguish between compound words (*greenhouse*) and words that simply appear together but do not constitute compound words (*green house*). For plurals of compound words, generally add *s* to the last letter (*bookcases* and *Web sites*). However, when the first word of the compound is more important to its meaning than the last, the first word takes the *s* (*editors-in-chief*). Possessives are formed by adding *'s* to the end of the compound word (the *editor-in-chief's* desk, the *pipeline's* diameter, the *post office's* hours). See also <u>possessive case</u> (Tab 11).

conciseness

Conciseness means that extraneous words, phrases, clauses, and sentences have been removed from writing without sacrificing clarity or appropriate detail. Conciseness is not a synonym for brevity; a long report may be concise, while its <u>abstract</u> (Tab 4) may be both brief and concise. Conciseness is always desirable, but brevity may or may not be desirable in a given passage, depending on the writer's purpose. Although concise sentences are not guaranteed to be effective, wordy sentences always sacrifice some of their readability and coherence.

Causes of Wordiness

<u>Modifiers</u> (Tab 11) that repeat an idea implicit or present in the word being modified contribute to wordiness by being redundant.

basic essentials   *completely* finished
final outcome   *present* status

Coordinated synonyms that merely repeat the same meaning contribute to wordiness.

each and every   *basic and fundamental*
finally and for good   *first and foremost*

Excess qualification also contributes to wordiness.

perfectly clear   *completely* accurate

Expletives, relative pronouns, and relative adjectives, although they have legitimate purposes, often result in wordiness.

WORDY   *There are* [expletive] many Web designers *who* [relative pronoun] are planning to attend the conference, *which* [relative adjective] is scheduled for May 13–15.

CONCISE   Many Web designers plan to attend the conference scheduled for May 13–15.

Circumlocution (a long, indirect way of expressing things) is a leading cause of wordiness and often occurs in rambling sentences.

WORDY   The payment to which a subcontractor is entitled should be made promptly so that in the event of a subsequent contractual dispute we, as general contractors, may not be held in default of our contract by virtue of nonpayment.

CONCISE   Pay subcontractors promptly. Then if a contractual dispute occurs, we cannot be held in default of our contract because of nonpayment.

When conciseness is overdone, writing can become choppy and ambiguous. (See also telegraphic style.) Too much conciseness can produce a style that is not only too brief but also blunt, especially in correspondence (Tab 6).

Writer's Checklist: Achieving Conciseness

Wordiness is understandable when you are writing a draft (Tab 1), but it should not survive revision (Tab 1).

☑ Use subordination to achieve conciseness.

• The financial report was carefully documented, and it covered five pages. *(five-page ... documented.)*

Writer's Checklist: Achieving Conciseness (continued)

☑ Use simple words and phrases.

WORDY	It is the policy of the company to provide Web access to enable employees to conduct the online communication necessary to discharge their responsibilities; such should not be utilized for personal communications or nonbusiness activities.
CONCISE	Employee Web access should be used only for appropriate company business.

☑ Eliminate redundancy.

WORDY	Postinstallation testing, which is offered to all our customers at no further cost to them whatsoever, is available with each Line Scan System One purchased from this company.
CONCISE	Free postinstallation testing is offered with each Line Scan System One.

☑ Change the passive <u>voice</u> (Tab 11) to the active voice and the indicative <u>mood</u> (Tab 11) to the imperative mood wherever possible.

WORDY	Bar codes normally are used when an order is intended to be displayed on a computer, and inventory numbers normally are used when an order is to be placed with the manufacturer.
CONCISE	Use bar codes to display the order on a computer, and use inventory numbers to place the order with the manufacturer.

☑ Eliminate or replace wordy introductory phrases or pretentious words and phrases (*it may be said that, it appears that, in the case of, needless to say*). See <u>affectation</u>.

REPLACE	WITH
in order to; with a view to	to
due to the fact that; for the reason that; owing to the fact that; the reason for	because
by means of; by using; in connection with; through the use of	by; with
at this time; at this point in time; at present; at the present	now

☑ Do not overuse modifiers, such as *very, more, most, best, quite, great, really, especially*. Instead, provide useful and specific details. See also <u>intensifiers</u>.

9
Style and Clarity

connotation / denotation

The denotations of a word are its literal meanings, as defined in a dictionary. The connotations of a word are its meanings and associations beyond its literal, dictionary definitions. For example, the denotations of *Hollywood* are "a district of Los Angeles" and "the U.S. movie industry as a whole"; its connotations are "romance, glittering success, and superficiality." Use words with both the most accurate denotations and the most appropriate connotations. See also defining terms (Tab 1) and word choice.

emphasis

Emphasis is the principle of stressing the most important ideas in writing. It can be achieved with the careful use of position, sentence length, repetition, sentence type, climactic order, intensifiers, the long dash, mechanical devices, direct statement, and active voice.

Achieving Emphasis

Position.   Place the idea in a particular position. The first and last words of a sentence, paragraph, or document stand out in readers' minds.

- Moon craters are important to understanding the earth's history because they reflect geological history.

This sentence emphasizes *moon craters* simply because the term appears at the beginning of the sentence and *geological history* because it is at the end of the sentence. See also subordination.

Sentence Length.   Vary sentence length strategically. A very short sentence that follows a very long sentence or a series of long sentences stands out in the reader's mind, as in the short sentence ("We must cut costs") that ends the following paragraph. See sentence construction (Tab 11).

- We have already reviewed the problem the accounting department has experienced during the past year. We could continue to examine the causes of our problems and point an accusing finger at all the culprits beyond our control, but in the end it all leads to one simple conclusion. We must cut costs.

Repetition.   Repeat keywords and key phrases, as in the use of the word *remains* and the phrase *come and go* in the following sentence.

- Similarly, atoms *come and go* in a molecule, but the molecule *remains*; molecules *come and go* in a cell, but the cell *remains*; cells *come and go* in a body, but the body *remains*; persons *come and go* in an organization, but the organization *remains*.
  —Kenneth Boulding, *Beyond Economics*

Sentence Type.   Vary sentences by using a compound sentence, a complex sentence, or a simple sentence. See <u>sentence variety</u>.

- The report submitted by the committee was carefully illustrated, and it covered five pages of single-spaced copy.
  [This compound sentence carries no special emphasis because it contains two coordinate independent clauses.]
- The committee's report, which was carefully illustrated, covered five pages of single-spaced copy.
  [This complex sentence emphasizes the size of the report.]
- The carefully illustrated report submitted by the committee covered five pages of single-spaced copy.
  [This simple sentence emphasizes that the report was carefully illustrated.]

Climactic Order.   List the ideas or facts within a sentence in sequence from least to most important. See also <u>lists</u> (Tab 5).

- Over subsequent weeks the Human Resources Department worked diligently, management showed tact and patience, and the employees demonstrated remarkable support for the policy changes.

Intensifiers.   Although you can use <u>intensifiers</u> (*most, much, very*), this technique is so easily abused that it should be used with caution.

- The final proposal is much more persuasive than the first.

Long Dash.   Use a <u>dash</u> (Tab 12) to call attention to a particular word or statement.

- The job will be done—after we are under contract.

Mechanical Devices.   Use *italics*, **bold type**, <u>underlining</u>, and CAPITAL LETTERS, but use them sparingly because overuse can create visual clutter. See also <u>layout and design</u> (Tab 5), <u>capitalization</u> (Tab 12), and <u>italics</u> (Tab 12).

Direct Statement.   Use direct statements of emphasis such as "most important," "foremost," or someone's name in a direct address.

- Most important, keep in mind that everything you do affects the company's bottom line.
- John, I believe we should rethink our plans.

Active Voice.   Use the active <u>voice</u> (Tab 11) to emphasize the performer of an action: Make the performer the subject of the verb.

- Our department designed the new system.
  [The performer, *our department*, is the subject of the verb, *designed*.]

euphemisms

A euphemism is an inoffensive substitute for a word or phrase that could be distasteful, offensive, or too blunt: *passed away* for *died*; *previously owned* or *preowned* for *used*; *layoff* or *downsize* for *terminate* or *fire*.

  ⬧ ETHICS NOTE Euphemisms must be used judiciously. Although they can help you avoid embarrassing or offending someone, euphemisms can also hide the facts of a situation (*incident* or *event* for *accident*) or be a form of <u>affectation</u> if used carelessly. See also <u>ethics in writing</u> (Tab 1).

expletives

An expletive is a word that fills the position of another word, phrase, or clause. *It* and *there* are common expletives.

- *It* is certain that he will be promoted.

In the example, the expletive *it* occupies the position of subject in place of the real subject, *that he will be promoted*. Expletives are sometimes necessary to avoid <u>awkwardness</u>, but they are commonly overused, and most sentences can be better stated without them.

- *Many* ~~There were many~~ orders *were* lost because of a software error.

In addition to its usage as a grammatical term, the word *expletive* means an exclamation or oath, especially one that is obscene.

figures of speech

A figure of speech is an imaginative expression that often compares two things that are basically not alike but have at least one thing in common. For example, if a device is cone-shaped and has an opening at the narrow end, you might say that it looks like a volcano.

Figures of speech can clarify the unfamiliar by relating a new concept to one with which readers are familiar. In that respect, figures of speech help establish understanding between the specialist and the nonspecialist. Figures of speech can also help translate the abstract into the concrete; in the process of doing so, figures of speech can also make writing more colorful and graphic. (See also <u>abstract/concrete words</u>.) A figure of speech must make sense, however, to achieve the desired effect.

> **ILLOGICAL**   Without the fuel of tax incentives, our economic
> engine would operate less efficiently.
> [Without fuel, it would not operate at all.]

Figures of speech also must be consistent to be effective.

- We must get our sales program *back on track*, and we are

  counting on you to ~~carry the ball.~~ *steer the effort.*
  ^

A figure of speech should not overshadow the point the writer is trying to make. In addition, it is better to use no figure of speech at all than to use a trite one. A surprise that comes "like a bolt out of the blue" seems stale and not much of a surprise. See also <u>clichés</u>.

garbled sentences

A garbled sentence is one that is so tangled with structural and grammatical problems that it cannot be repaired. Garbled sentences often result from an attempt to squeeze too many ideas into one sentence.

- My job objectives are accomplished by my having a diversified background which enables me to operate effectively and efficiently, consisting of a degree in computer science, along with twelve years of experience, including three years in Staff Engineering-

Packaging sets a foundation for a strong background in areas of analyzing problems and assessing economical and reasonable solutions.

Do not try to patch such a sentence; rather, analyze the ideas it contains, list them in a logical sequence, and then construct one or more entirely new sentences.

An analysis of the preceding example yields the following five ideas:

- My job requires that I analyze problems to find economical and workable solutions.
  My diversified background helps me accomplish my job.
  I have a computer-science degree.
  I have twelve years of job experience.
  Three of these years have been in Staff Engineering-Packaging.

Using those five ideas—together with parallel structure, sentence variety, subordination, and transition—the writer might have described the job as follows:

- My job requires that I analyze problems to find economical and workable solutions. Both my education and experience help me achieve this goal. Specifically, I have a computer-science degree and twelve years of job experience, three of which have been in the Staff Engineering-Packaging Department.

See also mixed constructions (Tab 11) and sentence construction (Tab 11).

idioms

An idiom is a group of words that has a special meaning apart from its literal meaning. Someone who "runs for office" in the United States, for example, need not be an athlete. The same candidate would "stand for office" in the United Kingdom. Because such expressions are specific to a culture, nonnative speakers must memorize them. The following are typical idioms that give nonnative speakers trouble.

call off [cancel]	get through with [finish]
call on [visit a client]	give up [quit]
cross out [draw a line through]	hand in [submit]
do over [repeat task]	hand out [distribute]
drop in on [visit unexpectedly]	keep on [continue]
figure out [solve a problem]	leave out [omit]
find out [discover information]	look up [seek in reference]

put off [postpone]   run out of [deplete supply]
run into [meet by chance]   watch out for [be careful]

Idioms often provide helpful shortcuts. In fact, they can make writing more natural and vigorous. Avoid them, however, if your writing is to be translated into another language or read in other English-speaking countries.

Idiom also refers to the practice of using certain prepositions following some adjectives (*similar to*), nouns (*need for*), and verbs (*approve of*). Because there is no sure system to explain such usages, the best advice is to check a dictionary. See also <u>international correspondence</u> (Tab 6) and <u>English as a second language</u> (Tab 11).

 WEB LINK PREPOSITIONAL IDIOMS

For links to helpful lists of common pairings of prepositions with nouns, verbs, and adjectives, see <bedfordstmartins.com/alred> and select *Links for Business Writing.*

---

intensifiers

Intensifiers are adverbs that emphasize degree, such as *very, quite, rather, such,* and *too.* Although they serve a legitimate and necessary function, unnecessary intensifiers can weaken your writing. Eliminate those that do not make an obvious contribution or replace them with specific details.

- *learn*
  The team was quite happy to ~~receive the very good news~~ that it
                              ^
  $5,000
  had been awarded a ~~rather substantial monetary~~ prize for its design.
                     ^

Some words (such as *perfect, impossible,* and *final*) do not logically permit intensification because, by definition, they do not allow degrees of comparison. Although usage often ignores that logical restriction, to ignore it is, strictly speaking, to defy the basic meanings of such words. See also <u>absolute words</u> and <u>conciseness</u>.

jargon

Jargon is a highly specialized slang that is unique to an occupational or a professional group. Jargon is at first understood only by insiders; over time, it may become known more widely. For example, human resources professionals adopted the term *head-hunting* to describe the recruitment of executive personnel. If all your readers are members of a particular occupational group, jargon may provide an efficient means of communicating. However, if you have any doubt that your entire reading <u>audience</u> (Tab 1) is part of such a group, avoid using jargon. See also <u>affectation</u>.

logic errors

Logic is essential to convincing readers that your conclusions are valid. Errors in logic can undermine the point you are trying to communicate and your credibility. Typical causes of logic errors include *lack of reason, sweeping generalizations, non sequiturs, false cause, biased or suppressed evidence, fact versus opinion,* and *loaded arguments.* See also <u>persuasion</u> (Tab 1).

Lack of Reason

When a statement is contrary to the reader's common sense, that statement is not reasonable. If, for example, you stated "New York is a small town," your reader might immediately question your logic. If, however, you stated "Although New York's population is over eight million, it is composed of neighborhoods that function as small towns," your reader could probably accept the statement as reasonable.

Sweeping Generalizations

Sweeping generalizations are statements that are too broad or all-inclusive to be supportable; they generally enlarge an observation about a small group to refer to an entire population. A flat statement, such as "Management is never concerned about employees," ignores any examples of management that show concern for employees. Using such generalizations weakens your credibility.

Non Sequiturs

A non sequitur is a statement that does not logically follow a previous statement.

- I cleared off my desk and the report is due today.

The missing link in this statement is that the writer cleared his or her desk to make space for materials to help finish the report today. In your own writing, be careful that you do not allow logical gaps that produce non sequiturs.

False Cause

A false cause (also called *post hoc, ergo propter hoc*) refers to the logical fallacy that because one event followed another event, the first somehow caused the second.

* I didn't bring my umbrella today. No wonder it is now raining.

In on-the-job writing, such an error in reasoning can happen when the writer hastily concludes that two events are related without examining the logical connection between them.

Biased or Suppressed Evidence

A conclusion reached as a result of self-serving data, questionable sources, suppressed evidence, or incomplete facts is both illogical and unethical. Suppose you are preparing a report on the acceptance of a new policy among employees. If you distribute questionnaires only to those who think the policy is effective, the resulting evidence will be biased.

    ⚡ ETHICS NOTE If you purposely ignore employees who do not believe the policy is effective, you will be suppressing evidence. Intentionally ignoring relevant data that might not support your position not only produces inaccurate results but is unethical. See also ethics in writing (Tab 1).

Fact versus Opinion

Distinguish between fact and opinion. *Facts* include verifiable data or statements, whereas *opinions* are personal conclusions that may or may not be based on facts. For example, it is verifiable that distilled water boils at 100 degrees centigrade; that it tastes better than tap water is an opinion. Distinguish the facts from your opinions in your writing so that your readers can draw their own conclusions.

Loaded Arguments

When you include an opinion in a statement and then reach conclusions that are based on that statement, you are loading the argument. Consider the following opening for a memo:

* I have several suggestions to improve the poorly written policy manual. First, we should change . . .

Unless everyone agrees that the manual is poorly written, readers may reject a writer's entire message because they disagree with this loaded premise. Do not load arguments in your writing; conclusions reached with loaded statements are weak and can produce negative reactions in readers who detect the loading.

nominalizations

A nominalization is a weak verb (*make, do, conduct, perform*) combined with a noun, when the verb form of the noun would communicate the same idea more effectively and concisely.

- The quality assurance team will ~~perform an evaluation of~~ the new software.

  evaluate

If you use nominalizations to make your writing sound more formal, the result will be <u>affectation</u>. You may occasionally have a legitimate use for a nominalization. For example, you might use a nominalization to slow the pace of your writing. See also <u>business writing style</u> and <u>conciseness</u>.

parallel structure

Parallel sentence structure requires that sentence elements that are alike in function be alike in grammatical form as well. This structure achieves an economy of words, clarifies meaning, expresses the equality of the ideas, and achieves <u>emphasis</u>. Parallel structure assists readers because it allows them to anticipate the meaning of a sentence element on the basis of its construction.

Parallel structure can be achieved with words, phrases, or clauses.

- If you want to earn a satisfactory grade in the training program, you must be *punctual, courteous,* and *conscientious.* [parallel words]

- If you want to earn a satisfactory grade in the training program, you must recognize the importance *of punctuality, of courtesy,* and *of conscientiousness.* [parallel phrases]

- If you want to earn a satisfactory grade in the training program, *you must arrive punctually, you must behave courteously,* and *you must study conscientiously.* [parallel clauses]

Correlative conjunctions (*either . . . or, neither . . . nor, not only . . . but also*) should always use parallel structure. Both parts of the pairs should be followed immediately by the same grammatical form: two similar words, two similar phrases, or two similar clauses.

- Viruses carry either *DNA* or *RNA,* never both. [parallel words]

- We have improved not only *our competitive position* but also *our financial rating.* [parallel phrases]

- Either *we must increase our production efficiency* or *we must decrease our production goals.* [parallel clauses]

To make a parallel construction clear and effective, it is often best to repeat an article, a pronoun, a helping verb, a preposition, a subordinating conjunction, or the mark of an infinitive (*to*).

- The association has *a* mission statement and *a* code of ethics.

- He was promoted *because* he was industrious, *because* he was inventive, and *because* he was an effective team leader.

Parallel structure is especially important in creating <u>lists</u> (Tab 5), outlines, <u>tables of contents</u> (Tab 4), and <u>headings</u> (Tab 5), because it lets readers know the relative value of each item in a table of contents and each heading in the body of a document. See also <u>outlining</u> (Tab 1).

Faulty Parallelism

Faulty parallelism results when joined elements are intended to serve equal grammatical functions but do not have equal grammatical form. Faulty parallelism sometimes occurs because a writer tries to compare items that are not comparable.

> **NOT PARALLEL**   The company offers special college training to help nonexempt employees move into professional careers like engineering management, software development, service technicians, and sales trainees.
> [Notice that occupations—*engineering management* and *software development*—are being compared to people—*service technicians* and *sales trainees*.]

To avoid faulty parallelism, make certain that each element in a series is similar in form and structure to all others in the same series.

> **PARALLEL**   The company offers special college training to help nonexempt employees move into professional careers like *engineering management, software development, technical services,* and *sales.*

positive writing

Presenting positive information as though it were negative is confusing to readers.

> **NEGATIVE**   If the error does *not* involve data transmission, the backup function will *not* be used.

In this sentence, the reader must reverse two negatives to understand the exception that is being stated. The following sentence presents the exception in a positive and straightforward manner.

Style and Clarity

9

| POSITIVE | The backup function is used only when the error involves data transmission. |

⚡ ETHICS NOTE Negative facts or conclusions, however, should be stated negatively; stating a negative fact or conclusion positively is deceptive because it can mislead the reader. (See also <u>ethics in writing</u>, Tab 1.)

| DECEPTIVE | In the first quarter of this year, employee exposure to airborne lead was within 10 percent of acceptable state health standards. |
| ACCURATE | In the first quarter of this year, employee exposure to airborne lead was 10 percent below acceptable state health standards. |

Even if what you are saying is negative, do not use more negative words than necessary.

| NEGATIVE | We are withholding your shipment until we receive your payment. |
| POSITIVE | We will forward your shipment as soon as we receive your payment. |

See also <u>correspondence</u> (Tab 6) and <u>"you" viewpoint</u>.

repetition

The deliberate use of repetition to build a sustained effect or to emphasize a feeling or an idea can be a powerful device. See also <u>emphasis</u>.

- Similarly, atoms *come and go* in a molecule, but the molecule *remains*; molecules *come and go* in a cell, but the cell *remains*; cells *come and go* in a body, but the body *remains*; persons *come and go* in an organization, but the organization *remains*.
  –Kenneth Boulding, *Beyond Economics*

Repeating keywords from a previous sentence or paragraph can also be used effectively to achieve <u>transition</u>.

- For many years, *oil* has been a major industrial energy source. However, *oil* supplies are limited, and other sources of energy must be developed.

Be consistent in the word or phrase you use to refer to something. In business writing, it is generally better to repeat a word (so there will be no question in the reader's mind that you mean the same thing) than to use synonyms to avoid repetition.

| SYNONYMS | Several recent *analyses* support our conclusion. These *studies* cast doubt on the feasibility of long-range forecasting. The *reports*, however, are strictly theoretical. |
| CONSISTENT TERMS | Several recent theoretical *studies* support our conclusion. These *studies* cast doubt on the feasibility of long-range forecasting. They are, however, strictly theoretical. |

Purposeless repetition, however, makes a sentence awkward and hides its key ideas. See also conciseness.

- She *said that* the customer ~~said that~~ he was canceling the order.

sentence variety

Sentences can vary in length, structure, and complexity. As you revise, make sure your sentences have not become tiresomely alike.

Sentence Length

A series of sentences of the same length is monotonous, so varying sentence length makes writing less tedious to the reader. For example, avoid stringing together a number of short independent clauses. Either connect them with subordinating connectives, thereby making some dependent clauses, or make some clauses into separate sentences. See also subordination.

STRING	The river is 60 miles long, and it averages 50 yards in width, and its depth averages 8 feet.
IMPROVED	The river, which is 60 miles long and averages 50 yards in width, has an average depth of 8 feet.
IMPROVED	The river is 60 miles long. It averages 50 yards in width and 8 feet in depth.

You can often effectively combine short sentences by converting verbs into adjectives.

- The digital shift indicator *failed.* ~~failed. It~~ was pulled from the market.

Although too many short sentences make your writing sound choppy and immature, a short sentence can be effective following a long one.

- During the past two decades, many changes have occurred in American life — the extent, durability, and significance of which no one has yet measured. *No one can.*

In general, short sentences are good for emphatic, memorable statements. Long sentences are good for detailed explanations and support. Nothing is inherently wrong with a long sentence, or even with a complicated one, as long as its meaning is clear and direct. Sentence length becomes an element of style when varied for <u>emphasis</u> or contrast; a conspicuously short or long sentence can be used to good effect.

Word Order

When a series of sentences all begin in exactly the same way (usually with an article and a noun), the result is likely to be monotonous. You can make your sentences more interesting by occasionally starting with a modifying word, phrase, or clause.

- *To salvage the project*, she presented alternatives when existing policies failed to produce results. [modifying phrase]

However, overuse of this technique itself can be monotonous, so use it in moderation.

Inverted sentence order can be an effective way to achieve variety, but be careful not to create an awkward construction.

EFFECTIVE	Never have sales been so good.
AWKWARD	Then occurred the event that gained us the contract.

For variety, you can alter normal sentence order by inserting a phrase or clause.

- Titanium fills the gap, *both in weight and in strength*, between aluminum and steel.

The technique of inserting a phrase or clause is good for emphasis, providing detail, breaking monotony, and regulating pace.

Loose and Periodic Sentences

A loose sentence makes its major point at the beginning and then adds subordinate phrases and clauses that develop or modify the point. A loose sentence could end at one or more points before it actually does end, as the periods in brackets illustrate in the following example.

- It went up[.], a great ball of fire about a mile in diameter[.], an elemental force freed from its bonds[.] after being chained for billions of years.

A periodic sentence delays its main idea until the end by presenting modifiers or subordinate ideas first, thus holding the readers' interest until the end.

- During the last century, the attitude of the Americans toward technology underwent a profound change.

Experiment with shifts from loose sentences to periodic sentences in your own writing, especially during revision. Avoid the singsong monotony of a long series of loose sentences, particularly a series containing coordinate clauses joined by <u>conjunctions</u> (Tab 11). Subordinating some thoughts to others makes your sentences more interesting. See also <u>sentence construction</u> (Tab 11).

subordination

Use subordination to show, by the structure of a sentence, the appropriate relationship between ideas of unequal importance. By putting less important ideas in subordinate <u>clauses</u> (Tab 11) or <u>phrases</u> (Tab 11), you emphasize your main idea.

- Pacific Enterprises now employs 500 people. It was founded just three years ago.
  [The two ideas are equally important.]

- Pacific Enterprises, *which now employs 500 people*, was founded just three years ago.
  [The number of employees is subordinated; the founding date is emphasized.]

- Pacific Enterprises, *which was founded just three years ago*, now employs 500 people.
  [The founding date is subordinated; the number of employees is emphasized.]

Effective subordination can be used to achieve <u>conciseness</u>, <u>emphasis</u>, and <u>sentence variety</u>. For example, consider the following sentences.

DEPENDENT CLAUSE	The regional manager's report, *which covered five pages,* was carefully illustrated.
PHRASE	The regional manager's report, *covering five pages,* was carefully illustrated.
SINGLE MODIFIER	The regional manager's *five-page report* was carefully illustrated.

Subordinating conjunctions (*because, if, while, when, though*) achieve subordination effectively. (An increase in local sales is unlikely *because* the local population has declined.) You may use a coordinating conjunction (*and, but, for, or, so, yet*) to concede that an opposite or balancing fact is true; however, a subordinating conjunction (*although, since, while*) can often make the point more smoothly. (*Although* their bank has a lower interest rate on loans, ours provides a wider range of essential services.) The relationship between a conditional statement and a statement of consequences is clearer if the condition is expressed

9

Style and Clarity

as a subordinate clause. (*Because* the bill was incorrect, the customer was angry.) See also <u>conjunctions</u> (Tab 11).

Relative pronouns (*who, whom, which, that*) can be used effectively to combine related ideas within sentences. (The generator, *which* is the most common source of electric current, uses mechanical energy to produce electricity.)

Avoid overlapping subordinate constructions that depend on the preceding construction. Overlapping can make the relationship between a relative pronoun and its antecedent less clear.

| OVERLAPPING | Shock, *which* often accompanies severe injuries and infections, is a failure of the circulation, which is marked by a fall in blood pressure *that* initially affects the skin (*which* explains pallor) and later the vital organs such as the kidneys and brain. |
| CLEAR | Shock often accompanies severe injuries and infections. Marked by a fall in blood pressure, it is a failure of the circulation, initially to the skin (thus producing pallor) and later to vital organs like the kidneys and the brain. |

telegraphic style

Telegraphic style condenses writing by omitting articles, pronouns, conjunctions, and transitions. Although <u>conciseness</u> is important, especially in instructions, writers sometimes try to achieve conciseness by omitting necessary words. Telegraphic style forces readers to supply the missing words mentally, thus creating the potential for misunderstandings. Compare the following two passages, and notice how much easier the revised version reads (the added words are italicized).

| TELEGRAPHIC | Per 5/21 e-mail, 12 copies of instruction sheet and questionnaire attached. Report can be complete as soon as above materials received. July filling quickly so let's set date. Please advise. |
| CLEAR | *As I promised in my May* 21 e-mail, attached *are* 12 copies of *the* instruction sheet and *the* questionnaire. *We can* complete *the* report as soon as *we* receive *the questionnaires. Our* July *calendar is* filling quickly, so *we should* set *a meeting* date *soon.* Please *suggest a date when you return the questionnaire.* |

Telegraphic style can also produce ambiguity, as the following example demonstrates.

9

AMBIGUOUS	The director wants report written by New York office.
	[Does the director want a report that the New York office *wrote in the past,* or does the director want the New York office *to write a report in the future*?]
CLEAR	The director wants the report *that was* written by the New York office.
CLEAR	The director wants the report *to be* written by the New York office.

Although you may save yourself work by writing telegraphically, your readers will have to work that much harder to decipher your meaning. See also <u>transition</u>.

tone

Tone is the writer's attitude toward the subject and his or her readers. In business writing, tone may range widely—depending on the purpose, situation, context, audience, and even the medium of a communication. For example, in an e-mail message to be read only by an associate who is also a friend, your tone might be casual.

- Your proposal to Smith and Kline is super. We'll just need to hammer out the schedule. If we get the contract, I owe you lunch!

In a memo to your manager or superior, however, your tone might be more formal and respectful.

- I think your proposal to Smith and Kline is excellent. I have marked a couple of places where I'm concerned that we are committing ourselves to a schedule that we might not be able to keep. If I can help in any other way, please let me know.

In a message that serves as a report to numerous readers, the tone would be professional, without casual language that could be misinterpreted.

- The Smith and Kline proposal appears complete and thorough, based on our department's evaluation. Several small revisions, however, would ensure that the company is not committing itself to an unrealistic schedule. These are marked on the copy of the report being circulated.

The choice of words, the introduction, and even the title contribute to the overall tone of your document. For instance, a title such as "Ecological Consequences of Diminishing Water Resources in California" clearly sets a different tone from "What Happens When We've

Drained California Dry?" The first title would be appropriate for a report; the second title could be appropriate for a newsletter or popular magazine article. See also <u>titles</u> (Tab 3), <u>correspondence</u> (Tab 6), <u>e-mail</u> (Tab 6), and <u>business writing style</u>.

transition

Transition is the means of achieving a smooth flow of ideas from sentence to sentence, paragraph to paragraph, and subject to subject. Transition is a two-way indicator of what has been said and what will be said; it provides readers with guideposts for linking ideas and clarifying the relationship between them.

Transition can be obvious.

- *Having considered* the benefits of a new facility, *we move next* to the question of adequate staffing.

Transition can be subtle.

- *Even if* this facility can be built at a reasonable cost, there *still remains* the problem of adequate staffing.

Either way, you now have your readers' attention fastened on the problem of adequate staffing, exactly what you set out to do.

Methods of Transition

Transition can be achieved in many ways: (1) using transitional words and phrases, (2) repeating keywords or key ideas, (3) using pronouns with clear antecedents, (4) numbering with enumeration, (5) summarizing a previous paragraph, (6) asking a question, and (7) using a transitional paragraph.

Certain words and phrases are inherently transitional. Consider the following terms and their functions:

FUNCTION	TERMS
Result	*therefore, as a result, consequently, thus, hence*
Example	*for example, for instance, specifically, as an illustration*
Comparison	*similarly, likewise, in comparison*
Contrast	*but, yet, still, however, nevertheless, on the other hand*
Addition	*moreover, furthermore, also, too, besides, in addition*
Time	*now, later, meanwhile, since then, after that, before that time*
Sequence	*first, second, third, initially, then, next, finally*

Within a paragraph, such transitional expressions clarify and smooth the movement from idea to idea. Conversely, the lack of transitional devices can make for disjointed reading.

Transition between Sentences

You can achieve effective transition between sentences by repeating keywords or key ideas from preceding sentences and by using pronouns that refer to antecedents in previous sentences. Consider the following short paragraph, which uses both of those means.

- Representative of many American university towns is Middletown. *This midwestern town*, formerly a *sleepy farming community*, is today the home of a large and vibrant *academic community*. Attracting students from all over the Midwest, *this university town* has grown very rapidly in the last ten years.

Enumeration is another device for achieving transition.

- The recommendation rests on *two conditions*. *First*, the department staff must be expanded to handle the increased workload. *Second*, sufficient time must be provided for the training of the new staff.

Transition between Paragraphs

The means discussed so far for achieving transition between sentences can also be effective for achieving transition between paragraphs. For paragraphs, however, longer transitional elements are often required. One technique is to use an opening sentence that summarizes the preceding paragraph and then moves on to a new paragraph, as in the following example.

- One property of material considered for manufacturing processes is hardness. Hardness is the internal resistance of the material to the forcing apart or closing together of its molecules. Another property is ductility, the characteristic of material that permits it to be drawn into a wire. Material also may possess malleability, the property that makes it capable of being rolled or hammered into thin sheets of various shapes. Engineers must consider these properties before selecting manufacturing materials for use in production.

  The requirements of hardness, ductility, and malleability account for the high cost of such materials. . . .

Another technique is to ask a question at the end of one paragraph and answer it at the beginning of the next.

- New technology has always been feared because it has at times displaced some jobs. However, it invariably creates many more jobs than it eliminates. Almost always, the jobs eliminated by technological advances have been menial, unskilled jobs, and workers who have been displaced have been forced to increase their skills, which resulted in better and higher-paying jobs for them. *In view of these facts, is new technology really bad?*

Certainly technology has given us an unparalleled access to information and created many new roles for employees. . . .

A purely transitional paragraph may be inserted to aid readability.

- The problem of poor management was a key factor that has caused the weak performance of the company.

    Two other setbacks to the company's fortunes also marked the company's decline: the loss of many skilled workers through the early retirement program and the intensification of the rate of employee turnover.

    The early retirement program caused the failure . . .

If you provide logical organization and you have prepared an outline, your transitional needs will easily be satisfied and your writing will have unity and coherence. During revision, look for places where transition is missing, and add it. Look for places where it is weak, and strengthen it. See also organization (Tab 1) and paragraphs (Tab 1).

unity

Unity is singleness of purpose (Tab 1) and treatment; a unified paragraph or document has a central idea and does not digress into unrelated topics. See paragraphs (Tab 1).

The logical sequence provided through outlining (Tab 1) is essential to achieving unity. An outline enables you to lay out the most direct route from introduction to conclusion, and it enables you to build each paragraph around a topic sentence that expresses a single idea.

Effective transition helps build unity, as well as coherence, because transitional terms clarify the relationship of each part to what precedes it.

vague words

A vague word is one that is imprecise in the context in which it is used. Some words encompass such a broad range of meanings that there is no focus for their definition. Words such as *real, nice, important, good, bad, contact, thing,* and *fine* are often called *omnibus words* because they can mean everything to everybody. In speech, our vocal inflections help make the meanings of such words clear. Because you cannot rely on vocal inflections when you are writing, avoid using vague words. Be concrete and specific. See also abstract/concrete words and word choice.

| VAGUE | It was a *good* meeting. [Why was it good?] |
| SPECIFIC | The meeting resolved three questions: pay scales, fringe benefits, and workloads. |

word choice

Mark Twain once said, "The difference between the right word and almost the right word is the difference between 'lightning' and 'lightning bug.'" The most important goal in choosing the right word in business writing is the preciseness implied by Twain's comment. Vague words and abstract words defeat preciseness because they do not convey the writer's meaning directly and clearly.

| VAGUE | It was a *productive* meeting. |
| PRECISE | The meeting resulted in the approval of the health-care benefits package. |

In the first sentence, *productive* sounds specific but conveys little; the revised sentence says specifically what made the meeting "productive." Although abstract words may at times be appropriate to your topic, using them unnecessarily will make your writing difficult to understand.

Being aware of the connotations and denotations of words will help you anticipate the reactions of your readers (Tab 1) to the words you choose. Understanding antonyms (*fresh/stale*) and synonyms (*notorious/infamous*) will increase your ability to choose the proper word. For help with some common usage decisions, see Tab 10, "Usage."

Although many of the entries throughout this book will help you improve your word choices and avoid impreciseness, the following entries in this tab should be particularly helpful:

abstract/concrete words	connotation/denotation
affectation	euphemisms
biased language	idioms
buzzwords	jargon
clichés	tone
conciseness	vague words

A key to choosing the correct and precise word is to keep current in your reading and to be aware of new words in your profession and in the language. In your quest for the right word, remember that there is no substitute for a good dictionary. See also English as a second language (Tab 11).

9

Style and Clarity

"you" viewpoint

The "you" viewpoint places your readers' interest and perspective foremost. It is based on the principle that your readers are naturally more concerned about their own needs than they are about those of the writer or organization. The "you" viewpoint often, but not always, means using the words *you* and *your* rather than *we, our, I,* and *mine.* Consider the following sentence that focuses on the needs of the writer and organization ("we") rather than on those of the reader.

- *We must receive* your receipt with the merchandise before *we can process* your refund.

Even though the sentence uses *your* twice, the words in italics suggest that the point of view centers on the writer's need to receive the receipt in order to process the refund. Consider the following revision, written with the "you" viewpoint.

- So you can receive your refund promptly, please enclose the sales receipt with the returned merchandise.

Because the benefit to the reader is stressed, the writer is more likely to motivate the reader to act. See also <u>persuasion</u> (Tab 1).

The "you" viewpoint, as suggested earlier, means more than simply using *you* and *your.* In some instances, you may even need to avoid using those pronouns to build or maintain goodwill. Notice how the first of the following examples—with *your*—seems to accuse the reader, while the second—without *your*—achieves the goals of the "you" viewpoint with <u>positive writing</u>.

| ACCUSATORY | *Your* budget makes no allowance for set-up costs. |
| POSITIVE | The budget should include an allowance for set-up costs to meet all the concerns of our client. |

The "you" viewpoint can be extended beyond the sentence level to include building goodwill, establishing a positive <u>tone,</u> and handling bad news tactfully, as discussed in <u>correspondence</u> (Tab 6).

Usage

Preview

Usage describes the choices we make among the various words and constructions available in our language. The line between standard and nonstandard English, or between formal and informal English, is determined by these choices. (See Tab 9, "Style and Clarity.") Your choices in any writing situation should be guided by appropriateness: Is the word or expression appropriate to your audience and subject? When it is, you are practicing good usage.

The entries in this section are designed to help you sort out the appropriate from the inappropriate. Just look up the word or term in question here or in the index. A good dictionary is also an invaluable aid in helping you select the right word.

10

Usage

a lot

A lot is often incorrectly written as one word (*alot*). The phrase *a lot* is informal and normally should not be used in business writing. Use *many* or *numerous* for estimates, or give a specific number or amount.

- The staff raised a lot of objections to the policy.
  many

above

Avoid using *above* to refer to a preceding passage or visual. Its reference is often vague. The same is true of *aforesaid* and *aforementioned*. (See also <u>former/latter</u>.) To refer to something previously mentioned, repeat the noun or pronoun, or revise your paragraph.

- Please fill out and submit the above by March 1.
  your travel voucher

accept / except

Accept is a verb meaning "consent to," "agree to take," or "admit willingly." (I *accept* the responsibility.) *Except* is normally used as a preposition meaning "other than" or "excluding." (We agreed on everything *except* the schedule.)

affect / effect

Affect is a verb that means "influence." (The corporate decisions *affect* every department.) *Effect* can function either as a noun that means "result" (The new policy had a good *effect*) or as a verb that means "to bring about" (Only the director can *effect* such a change). Avoid *effect* as a verb, however, when you can replace it with a less formal word, such as *make* or *produce*.

all right

All right means "all correct." (The answers were *all right*.) In formal writing, it should not be used to mean "good" or "acceptable." It is always written as two words, with no hyphen; *alright* is nonstandard.

also

Also is an adverb that means "additionally." (Two 5,000-gallon tanks are on-site, and several 2,500-gallon tanks are *also* available.) *Also* should not be used as a connective in the sense of "and."

- He brought the reports, the letters, ~~also~~ *and* the section supervisor's recommendations.

Avoid opening sentences with *also*. It is a weak transitional word that suggests an afterthought rather than planned writing.

- ~~Also,~~ *In addition,* he brought statistical data to support his proposal.
- ~~Also, he~~ *He also* brought statistical data to support his proposal.

amount / number

Amount is used with things that are thought of in bulk and that cannot be counted (mass nouns), as in "the *amount* of electricity." *Number* is used with things that can be counted as individual items (count nouns), as in "the *number* of employees." See also <u>nouns</u> (Tab 11).

and / or

And/or means that either both circumstances are possible or only one of two circumstances is possible. This term is awkward and confusing because it makes the reader stop to puzzle over your distinction.

AWKWARD	Use A *and/or* B.
IMPROVED	Use A or B or both.

as / because / since

As, *because*, and *since* are commonly used to mean "because." To express cause, *because* is the strongest and most specific connective; *because* is unequivocal in stating a causal relationship. (*Because* she did not have an MBA, she was not offered the job.)

Since is a weak substitute for *because* as a connective to express cause. However, *since* is an appropriate connective when the emphasis is on circumstance, condition, or time rather than on cause and effect. (*Since* it went public, the company has earned a profit every year.)

As is the least definite connective to indicate cause; its use for that purpose is best avoided. See also <u>subordination</u> (Tab 9).

as such

The phrase *as such* is seldom useful and should be omitted.

- Templates, as such, are useful in designing Web pages.

as well as

Do not use *as well as* with *both*. The two expressions have similar meanings; use one or the other and adjust the verb as needed.

and
- Both General Motors ~~as well as~~ Ford ~~is~~ marketing hybrid vehicles.
  are

- ~~Both~~ General Motors as well as Ford is marketing hybrid vehicles.

augment / supplement

Augment means to increase or magnify in size, degree, or effect. (Many employees *augment* their incomes by freelancing.) *Supplement* means to add something to make up for a deficiency. (He will *supplement* his diet with vitamins.)

average / median / mean

The *average* is determined by adding two or more quantities and dividing the sum by the number of items totaled. For example, if one report is 10 pages, another is 30 pages, and a third is 20 pages, their *average* length is 20 pages. It is incorrect to say that "each report averages 20 pages" because each report is a specific length.

The three reports average
- ~~Each report averages~~ 20 pages.

A *median* is the middle number in a sequence of numbers. For example, the *median* of the series 1, 3, 4, 7, 8, is 4. The word *mean* ("something midway between extremes") can apply to either the average or the median.

bad / badly

Bad is the adjective form that follows such linking verbs as *feel* and *look*. (We don't want to look *bad* at the meeting.) *Badly* is an adverb. (The applicant performed *badly* during the interview.) To say "I feel *badly*" would mean, literally, that your sense of touch is impaired. See also good/well.

between / among

Between is normally used to relate two items or persons. (Preferred stock offers a middle ground *between* bonds and common stock.) *Among* is used to relate more than two. (The subcontracting was distributed *among* the three firms.)

bi- / semi-

When used with periods of time, *bi-* means "two" or "every two," as in *bimonthly*, which means "once in two months." When used with periods of time, *semi-* means "half of" or "occurring twice within a period of time." *Semimonthly* means "twice a month." Both *bi-* and *semi-* normally are joined with the following element without a space or a hyphen.

can / may

In writing, *can* refers to capability (I *can* have the project finished today). *May* refers to possibility (I *may* be in Boston on Monday) or permission (*May* I leave early?).

compose / constitute / comprise

Compose and *constitute* both mean "make up the whole." The parts *compose* or *constitute* the whole. (The thirteen offices *compose* the division. Unethical activities *constitute* cause for dismissal.) *Comprise* means "include," "contain," or "consist of." The whole *comprises* the parts. (The division *comprises* thirteen offices.)

criteria / criterion

Criterion is a singular noun meaning "an established standard for judging or testing." *Criteria* and *criterions* are both acceptable plural forms of *criterion*, but *criteria* is generally preferred.

data / datum

In much informal writing, *data* is considered a collective singular noun. In formal and scholarly writing, however, *data* is generally used as a plural, with *datum* as the singular form. Base your decision on whether your readers should consider the data as a single collection or as a group of individual facts. Whatever you decide, be sure that your pronouns and verbs agree in number with the selected usage. See also <u>agreement</u> (Tab 11).

different from / different than

In formal writing, the preposition *from* is used with *different.* (The Quantum PC is *different from* the Macintosh computer.) *Different than* is used when it is followed by a clause. (The job cost was *different than* we had estimated it.)

each

When *each* is used as a subject, it takes a singular verb or pronoun. (*Each* of the reports *is* to be submitted ten weeks after *it* is assigned.) When *each* refers to a plural subject, it takes a plural verb or pronoun. (The reports *each have* company logos on *their* covers.) See also <u>agreement</u> (Tab 11).

e.g. / i.e.

The abbreviation *e.g.* stands for the Latin *exempli gratia,* meaning "for example"; *i.e.* stands for the Latin *id est,* meaning "that is." Because the English expressions (*for example* and *that is*) serve a similar purpose, there is no need to use the Latin expressions or abbreviations except to save space in notes and visuals.

If you must use *i.e.* or *e.g.,* do not italicize either and punctuate them as follows. If *i.e.* or *e.g.* connects two independent clauses, a semicolon should precede it and a comma should follow it. If *i.e.* or *e.g.* connects a noun and an appositive, a comma should precede it and follow it. (The conference included speakers from five countries, *i.e.,* Germany, Italy, Japan, Pakistan, and the United States.)

etc.

Etc. is an abbreviation for the Latin *et cetera,* meaning "and others" or "and so on." Therefore, do not use the redundant phrase *and etc.* Likewise, do not use *etc.* at the end of a series introduced by the phrases *such as* and *for example*—those phrases already indicate unnamed items of the same category. Use *etc.* with a logical progression (1, 2, 3, *etc.*) and when at least two items are named.

- The sorting machine processes coins (~~for example~~ pennies, nickels, ~~and~~ *etc.*), and then packages them for redistribution.

Otherwise, avoid *etc.* because the reader may not be able to infer what other items a list might include.

> **VAGUE**   He will bring legal pads, paper clips, *etc.*, to the trade show. [Note *etc.* is preceded and followed by a comma within a sentence.]
>
> **CLEAR**   He will bring legal pads, paper clips, and other office supplies to the trade show.

explicit / implicit

10

Usage

An *explicit* statement is one expressed directly, with precision and clarity.

* He gave us *explicit* directions to the Wausau facility.

An *implicit* meaning is one that is not directly expressed.

* Although the CEO did not mention the lawsuit directly, the company's commitment to ethical practices was *implicit* in her speech.

fact

Expressions containing the word *fact* ("due to the *fact* that," "except for the *fact* that," "as a matter of *fact*," or "because of the *fact* that") are often wordy substitutes for more accurate terms.

* *Because*
  ~~Due to the fact that~~ the sales force has a high turnover rate,
  ^

  profits have declined.

Do not use the word *fact* to refer to matters of judgment or opinion.

* *In my opinion,*
  ~~It is a fact that~~ sales are poor in the Midwest because of
  ^

  insufficient market research.

The word *fact* is, of course, valid when facts are what is meant.

* Our tests uncovered numerous *facts* to support your conclusion.

See also <u>conciseness</u> (Tab 9) and <u>logic errors</u> (Tab 9).

few / a few

In certain contexts, *few* carries more negative overtones than does the phrase *a few*.

> **POSITIVE**   There are *a few* helpful ideas in the report.
>
> **NEGATIVE**   There are *few* helpful ideas in the report.

fewer / less

Fewer refers to items that can be counted (count nouns). (*Fewer* employees retired than we expected.) *Less* refers to mass quantities or amounts (mass nouns). (Because we had *less* rain this year, the crop yield decreased.) See also <u>nouns</u> (Tab 11).

first / firstly

First and *firstly* are both adverbs. Avoid *firstly* in favor of *first*, which sounds less stiff than *firstly*. The same is true of other ordinal numbers, such as *second*, *third*, and so on.

former / latter

Former and *latter* should be used to refer to only two items in a sentence or paragraph.

- The president and his aide emerged from the conference, the *former* looking nervous and the *latter* looking glum.

Because these terms make the reader look to previous material to identify the reference, they complicate reading and are best avoided.

good / well

Good is an adjective, and *well* is an adverb.

> **ADJECTIVE**   Janet presented a *good* plan.
>
> **ADVERB**   The plan was presented *well*.

Well also can be used as an adjective to describe health (a *well* child, *wellness* programs). See also <u>bad/badly</u>, <u>adjectives</u> (Tab 11), and <u>adverbs</u> (Tab 11).

he / she

The use of either *he* or *she* to refer to both sexes excludes half of the population. To avoid this problem, you could use the phrases *he or she* and *his or her.* (Whoever is appointed will find *his or her* task difficult.) However, *he or she* and *his or her* are clumsy when used repeatedly, as are *he/she* and similar constructions. One solution is to reword the sentence to use a plural pronoun; if you do, change the noun to which the pronoun refers to its plural form.

- *Administrators* ~~The administrator~~ cannot do ~~his or her job~~ *their jobs* until ~~he or she~~ *they understand* ~~understands~~ the organization's culture.

In other cases, you may be able to avoid using a pronoun altogether.

- Whoever is appointed will find ~~his or her~~ *the* task difficult.

Of course, a pronoun cannot always be omitted without changing the meaning of a sentence. Another solution is to omit troublesome pronouns by using the imperative mood whenever possible.

- *Submit all* ~~Everyone must submit his or her~~ expense report*s* by Monday.

See also <u>biased language</u> (Tab 9).

imply / infer

If you *imply* something, you hint or suggest it. (Her e-mail *implied* that the project would be delayed.) If you *infer* something, you reach a conclusion based on evidence or interpretation. (The manager *inferred* from the e-mail that the project would be delayed.)

in / into

In means "inside of"; *into* implies movement from the outside to the inside. (The equipment was *in* the test chamber, so she reached *into* the chamber to repair it.)

its / it's

Its is a possessive pronoun and does not use an apostrophe. *It's* is a contraction of *it is*.

- *It's* important that the sales department meet *its* quota.

See also <u>possessive case</u> (Tab 11) and <u>contractions</u> (Tab 12).

kind of / sort of

In writing, *kind of* and *sort of* should be used only to refer to a class or type of things. (They used a special *kind of* metal in the process.) Do not use *kind of* or *sort of* to mean "rather," "somewhat," or "somehow."

lay / lie

Lay is a transitive verb—a verb that requires a direct object to complete its meaning—that means "place" or "put."

- We will *lay* the foundation of the building one section at a time.

The past-tense form of *lay* is *laid*.

- We *laid* the first section of the foundation on the 27th of June.

The perfect-tense form of *lay* is also *laid*.

- Since June, we *have laid* all but two sections of the foundation.

Lay is frequently confused with *lie*, which is an intransitive verb—a verb that does not require an object to complete its meaning—that means "recline" or "remain."

- Injured employees should *lie* down and remain still until a doctor arrives.

The past-tense form of *lie* is *lay*. This form causes the confusion between *lie* and *lay*.

- The injured employee *lay* still for approximately five minutes.

The perfect-tense form of *lie* is *lain*.

- The injured employee *had lain* still for approximately five minutes before a doctor arrived.

See also <u>verbs</u> (Tab 11).

like / as

To avoid confusion between *like* and *as*, remember that *like* is a preposition and *as* (or *as if*) is a conjunction. Use *like* with a noun or pronoun that is not followed by a verb.

- The new supervisor behaves *like* a novice.

Use *as* before clauses, which contain verbs.

- He responded *as* we expected he would.
- It seemed *as if* the presentation would never end.

Like and *as* are used in comparisons: *like* is used in elliptical constructions that omit the verb, and *as* is used when the verb is retained.

- He adapted to the new system *like* a duck to water.
- He adapted to the new system *as* a duck adapts to water.

media / medium

Media is the plural of *medium* and should always be used with a plural verb.

- Many communication *media are* available today.
- The Internet *is* a multifaceted *medium*.

Ms. / Miss / Mrs.

Ms. is widely used in business and public life to address or refer to a woman, especially if her marital status is either unknown or irrelevant to the context. Traditionally, *Miss* is used to refer to an unmarried woman, and *Mrs.* is used to refer to a married woman. Some women may indicate a preference for *Ms.*, *Miss*, or *Mrs.*, which you should

10

Usage

honor. If a woman has an academic or a professional title, use the appropriate form of address (*Doctor*, *Professor*, *Captain*) instead of *Ms.*, *Miss*, or *Mrs.* See also <u>biased language</u> (Tab 9).

nature

Nature, when used to mean "kind" or "sort," is vague. Avoid this usage in your writing. Say exactly what you mean.

- The ~~nature of~~ *exclusionary clause in* the contract caused the problem.

OK / okay

The expression *okay* (also spelled *OK*) is common in informal writing, but it should be avoided in more formal business writing.

- Mr. Sturgess ~~gave his okay to~~ *approved* the project.

on / onto / upon

On is normally used as a preposition meaning "attached to" or "located at." (Install the shelf *on* the north wall.) *Onto* implies movement to a position or movement up and on. (The commuters surged *onto* the platform.)

Similarly, *on* stresses a position of rest (A book lay *on* the table), and *upon* emphasizes movement or a condition (Final payment will be made *upon* completion).

only

The word *only* should be placed immediately before the word or phrase it modifies. See also <u>modifiers</u>, Tab 11.

- We ~~only~~ lack *only* financial backing.

Be careful with the placement of *only* because it can change the meaning of a sentence.

- *Only* he said that he was tired.
  [He alone said that he was tired.]

- He *only* said that he was tired.
  [He actually was not tired, although he said he was.]

- He said *only* that he was tired.
  [He said nothing except that he was tired.]

- He said that he was *only* tired.
  [He said that he was nothing except tired.]

per

When *per* is used to mean "for each," "by means of," "through," or "on account of," it is appropriate (*per* annum, *per* capita, *per* diem, *per* head). When used to mean "according to" (*per* your request, *per* your order), the expression is jargon and should be avoided. Equally incorrect is the phrase *as per.*

percent / percentage

Percent is normally used instead of the symbol % (only 15 *percent*), except in tables, where space is at a premium. *Percentage*, which is never used with numbers, indicates a general size (only a small *percentage*).

phenomenon / phenomena

A *phenomenon* is an observable thing, a fact, or an occurrence (a natural *phenomenon*). Its plural form is *phenomena.*

reason is [because]

Replace the redundant phrase *the reason is because* with *the reason is that* or simply *because*. See also <u>conciseness</u> (Tab 9).

regardless

Always use *regardless* instead of *irregardless,* which expresses a double negative and is nonstandard. The prefix *ir-* renders the base word negative, but *regardless* is already negative, meaning "unmindful."

shall / will

Although traditionally *shall* was used to express the future tense with *I* and *we*, *will* is generally accepted with all persons. *Shall* is commonly used today only in questions requesting an opinion or a preference (*Shall* we go?) rather than a prediction (*Will* we go?). It is also used in statements expressing determination (I *shall* return!) or in formal regulations (Applicants *shall* provide a proof of certification).

10

Usage

that / which / who

The word *that* is often overused.

- You will note that~~, as you assume greater responsibility, that~~ your
  as you assume greater responsibility.
  benefits will increase ~~accordingly.~~
  ^

However, include *that* in a sentence if it avoids ambiguity or it improves the pace. (See also <u>conciseness</u>, Tab 9.)

                                                    that
- Some designers fail to appreciate the workers who operate
                                                  ^

  equipment constitute an important safety system.

Use *which*, not *that*, with nonrestrictive clauses (clauses that do not change the meaning of the basic sentence). See also <u>restrictive and non-restrictive elements</u> (Tab 11).

NONRESTRICTIVE	After John left the law firm, *which* is the largest in the region, he started a private practice.
RESTRICTIVE	Companies *that* diversify usually succeed.

That and *which* should refer to animals and things; *who* should refer to people.

- Companies *that* fund basic research must not expect immediate results.
- The jet stream, *which* flows west to east, usually travels in excess of sixty-seven miles per hour.
- Diane Stoltzfus, *who* retires tomorrow, worked 23 years for the company.

there / their / they're

There is an expletive (a word that fills the position of another word, phrase, or clause) or an adverb.

EXPLETIVE *There* were more than 1,500 people at the conference.

ADVERB More than 1,500 people were *there*.

Their is the possessive form of *they*. (Managers should check *their* e-mail regularly.) *They're* is a contraction of *they are*. (Clients tell us *they're* pleased with our services.) See also <u>possessive case</u> (Tab 11) and <u>contractions</u> (Tab 12).

to / too / two

To, *too*, and *two* are confused only because they sound alike. *To* is used as a preposition or to mark an infinitive.

- Send the report *to* the district manager. [preposition]
- I do not wish *to* attend. [mark of the infinitive]

Too is an adverb meaning "excessively" or "also."

- The price was *too* high. [excessively]
- I, *too*, thought it was high. [also]

Two is a number (*two* buildings; *two* concepts).

utilize

Do not use *utilize* as a long variant of *use*, which is the general word for "employ for some purpose." *Use* will almost always be clearer and less pretentious. See <u>affectation</u> (Tab 9).

via

Via is Latin for "by way of." Use *via* only in routing instructions.

- The package was shipped *via* FedEx.
- Her project was funded ~~via~~ *as a result of* the recent legislation.

10

Usage

when / where / that

When and if (or *if and when*) is a colloquial expression that should not be used in writing.

- When ~~and if~~ funding is approved, you will get the position.

- *If*
  ~~When and if~~ funding is approved, you will get the position.

In phrases using the *where . . . at* construction, *at* is unnecessary and should be omitted.

- Where is his office ~~at~~?

Do not substitute *where* for *that* to anticipate an idea or fact to follow.

- *that*
  I read in the newsletter ~~where~~ sales have increased this quarter.

whether

Whether communicates the notion of a choice. When *whether or not* is used to indicate a choice between alternatives, omit *or not*; it is redundant.

- The client asked whether ~~or not~~ the proposal was finished.

while

While, meaning "during an interval of time," is sometimes substituted for connectives like *and, but, although,* and *whereas.* Used as a connective in that way, *while* often causes ambiguity.

- *and*
  Ian Evans is sales manager, ~~while~~ Joan Thomas is director of research.

Do not use *while* to mean *although* or *whereas.*

- *Although*
  ~~While~~ Ryan Patterson wants the job of financial services

  manager, he has not yet applied for it.

Restrict *while* to its meaning of "during the time that."

- I'll have to catch up on my reading *while* I am on vacation.

who / whom

Writers are often unsure whether to use *who* or *whom*. *Who* is the subjective case form, whereas *whom* is the objective case form. When in doubt about which form to use, substitute a personal pronoun to see which one fits. If *he*, *she*, or *they* fits, use *who*.

- *Who* is the training coordinator?
  [You would say, "*She* is the training coordinator."]

If *him*, *her*, or *them* fits, use *whom*.

- It depends on *whom*?
  [You would say, "It depends on *them*."]

who's / whose / of which

Who's is the contraction of *who is*. (*Who's* scheduled today?) *Whose* is the possessive case of *who*. (Consider *whose* budget should be cut.)

Normally, *whose* is used with persons, and *of which* is used with inanimate objects.

- The employee *whose* car had been towed away was angry.

- Completing the EMBA program is an achievement *of which* to be proud.

If *of which* causes a sentence to sound awkward, *whose* may be used with inanimate objects. (Compare "The business *whose* profits steadily declined" with "The business the profits *of which* steadily declined.")

your / you're

Your is a possessive pronoun (*your* wallet); *you're* is the contraction of *you are* (*You're* late for the meeting). If you tend to confuse *your* with *you're*, use the search function of your word processor to review both terms during <u>proofreading</u> (Tab 1).

10

Usage

Grammar

Preview

Grammar is the systematic description of the way words work together to form a coherent language. *Parts of speech* is a term used to describe the class of words to which a particular word belongs, according to its function in a sentence. For example, <u>**nouns**</u> and <u>**pronouns**</u> name things; <u>**verbs**</u> express action; <u>**adjectives**</u> and <u>**adverbs**</u> describe and modify; and <u>**conjunctions**</u> and <u>**prepositions**</u> join elements of sentences. The entries in this section are intended to help you understand grammar and parts of speech in order to diagnose and correct problems that may occur in your writing.

However, to be an effective writer, you also need to know the conventions of usage that help writers select the appropriate word or expression as well as the principles of effective business writing style. Therefore, you may wish to consult Tab 9, "Style and Clarity"; Tab 10, "Usage"; and Tab 12, "Punctuation and Mechanics."

✺ WEB LINK GETTING HELP WITH GRAMMAR

For helpful Web sites providing handouts and other grammar resources, including resources for speakers of English as a second language, see <bedfordstmartins.com/alred> and select *Links for Business Writing*. For electronic grammar exercises, select *Exercise Central*.

adjectives

An adjective is any word that modifies a <u>noun</u> or <u>pronoun</u>. Descriptive adjectives identify a quality of a noun or pronoun. Limiting adjectives impose boundaries on the noun or pronoun.

- a *hot* surface [descriptive]
- *his three* phone lines [limiting]

Limiting Adjectives

Limiting adjectives include these categories:

- Articles (*a, an, the*)
- Demonstrative adjectives (*this, that, these, those*)
- Possessive adjectives (*my, your, his, her, its, our, their*)
- Numeral adjectives (*two, first*)
- Indefinite adjectives (*all, none, some, any*)

Articles.   Articles (*a, an, the*) are traditionally classified as adjectives because they modify nouns by either limiting them or making them more specific. See also <u>articles</u> and <u>English as a second language</u>.

Demonstrative Adjectives.   A demonstrative adjective points to the thing it modifies, specifying the object's position in space or time. *This* and *these* specify a closer position; *that* and *those* specify a more re-mote position.

- *This* report is more current than *that* report, which human resources distributed last month.
- *These* sales figures are more recent than *those* figures reported last week.

Demonstrative adjectives often cause problems when they modify the nouns *kind, type,* and *sort.* Demonstrative adjectives used with those nouns should agree with them in number.

- *this* kind / *these* kinds; *that* type / *those* types

Confusion often develops when the preposition *of* is added (*this kind of, these kinds of*) and the object of the preposition does not conform in number to the demonstrative adjective and its noun. See also <u>agreement</u> and <u>prepositions</u>.

- *This kind of* human resources ~~policies~~ *policy* is standard.
- *These kinds of* human resources ~~policy is~~ *policies are* standard.

11

Grammar

ESL TIPS FOR USING ADJECTIVES

Do not add -s or -es to an adjective to make it plural.

- the *long* trip
- the *long* trips

Capitalize adjectives of origin (city, state, nation, continent).

- the *Venetian* canals
- the *Texan* hat
- the *French* government
- the *African* deserts

In English, verbs of feeling (for example, *bore, interest, surprise*) have two adjectival forms: the present participle (-*ing*) and the past participle (-*ed*). Use the present participle to describe what causes the feeling. Use the past participle to describe the person who experiences the feeling.

- We heard the *surprising* election results.
  [The *election results* cause the feeling of surprise.]
- Only the losing candidate was *surprised* by the election results.
  [The *candidate* experienced the feeling of surprise.]

Adjectives follow nouns in English in only two cases: when the adjective functions as a subjective complement

- That project is not *finished*.

and when an adjective phrase or clause modifies the noun

- The project *that was suspended temporarily* . . . .

In all other cases, adjectives are placed before the noun.

When there are multiple adjectives, it is often difficult to know the right order. The guidelines illustrated in the following example would apply in most circumstances, but there are exceptions. (Normally do not use a phrase with so many stacked <u>modifiers</u>.) See also <u>articles</u>.

The six extra-large rectangular brown cardboard take-out containers

	number		size		color		qualifier	
determiner	comment			shape		material		noun

Avoid using demonstrative adjectives with words like *kind*, *type*, and *sort* because doing so can easily lead to vagueness. Instead, be more specific. See also kind of/sort of (Tab 10).

Possessive Adjectives.   Because possessive adjectives (*my, your, his, her, its, our, their*) directly modify nouns, they function as adjectives, even though they are pronoun forms (*my* idea, *her* plans, *their* projects).

Numeral Adjectives.   Numeral adjectives identify quantity, degree, or place in a sequence. They always modify count nouns. Numeral adjectives are divided into two subclasses: cardinal and ordinal. A *cardinal adjective* expresses an exact quantity (*one* pencil, *two* computers); an *ordinal adjective* expresses degree or sequence (*first* quarter, *second* edition).

In most writing, an ordinal adjective should be spelled out if it is a single word (*tenth*) and written in figures if it is more than one word (*312th*). Ordinal numbers can also function as adverbs (John arrived *first*). See also first/firstly (Tab 10) and numbers (Tab 12).

Indefinite Adjectives.   Indefinite adjectives do not designate anything specific about the nouns they modify (*some* CD-ROMs, *all* designers). The articles *a* and *an* are included among the indefinite adjectives (*a* chair, *an* application).

Comparison of Adjectives

Most adjectives in the positive form show the comparative form with the suffix *-er* for two items and the superlative form with the suffix *-est* for three or more items.

- The first report is *long*. [positive form]
- The second report is *longer*. [comparative form]
- The third report is *longest*. [superlative form]

Many two-syllable adjectives and most three-syllable adjectives are preceded by the word *more* or *most* to form the comparative or the superlative.

- The new library is *more* impressive than the old one. It is the *most* impressive in the county.

A few adjectives have irregular forms of comparison (*much, more, most; little, less, least*).

Some adjectives (*round, unique, exact, accurate*) are not logically subject to comparison. See also absolute words (Tab 9).

Placement of Adjectives

When limiting and descriptive adjectives appear together, the limiting adjectives precede the descriptive adjectives, with the articles usually in the first position.

- *The ten red* cars were parked in a row.
  [article (*The*), limiting adjective (*ten*), descriptive adjective (*red*)]

Within a sentence, adjectives may appear before the nouns they modify (the attributive position) or after the nouns they modify (the predicative position).

- *The small* jobs are given priority. [attributive position]
- The exposure is *brief*. [predicative position]

Use of Adjectives

Because of the need for precise description, it is often necessary to use nouns as adjectives.

- The *accident* report resulted in a *product* redesign.

When adjectives modifying the same noun can be reversed and still make sense or when they can be separated by *and* or *or*, they should be separated by commas.

- The company seeks a *bright, energetic, creative* management team.

Notice that there is no comma after *creative*. Never use a comma between a final adjective and the noun it modifies. When an adjective modifies a phrase, no comma is required.

- We need an *updated Web-page design*.
  [Updated modifies the phrase *Web-page design*.]

Writers sometimes string together a series of nouns used as adjectives to form a unit modifier, thereby creating stacked (jammed) <u>modifiers</u>. See also <u>word choice</u> (Tab 9).

11

Grammar

---

adverbs

An adverb modifies the action or condition expressed by a <u>verb</u>.

- The wrecking ball hit the side of the building *hard*.
  [The adverb tells *how* the wrecking ball hit the building.]

An adverb also can modify an <u>adjective</u>, another adverb, or a <u>clause</u>.

- The brochure design used *extremely* bright colors.
  [*Extremely* modifies the adjective *bright.*]

- The redesigned brake pad lasted *much* longer.
  [*Much* modifies the adverb *longer.*]

- *Surprisingly*, the engine failed.
  [*Surprisingly* modifies the clause *the engine failed.*]

An adverb answers one of the following questions:

Where? (adverb of place)

- Move the display *forward* slightly.

When? or *How often?* (adverb of time)

- Replace the thermostat *immediately.*

- I worked overtime *twice* this week.

How? (adverb of manner)

- Add the solvent *cautiously.*

How much? (adverb of degree)

- The *nearly* completed report was deleted from his disk.

An adverb can ask a question (*where, when, why, how*).

- *How* many hours did you work last week?
- *Why* was the disk reformatted?

Conjunctive Adverbs

A *conjunctive adverb* modifies the clause that it introduces; it operates as a conjunction because it joins two independent clauses. The most common conjunctive adverbs are *however, nevertheless, moreover, therefore, further, then, consequently, besides, accordingly, also,* and *thus.*

- I rarely work on weekends; *however*, this weekend will be an exception.

In this example, note that a semicolon precedes and a comma follows *however.* The conjunctive adverb (*however*) introduces the independent clause (*this weekend will be an exception*) and indicates its relationship to the preceding independent clause (*I rarely work on weekends*). See also semicolons (Tab 12).

Comparison of Adverbs

With most one-syllable adverbs, the suffix *-er* is added to show comparison with one other item, and the suffix *-est* is added to show comparison with two or more items.

- This copier is *fast*. [positive form]
- This copier is *faster* than the old one. [comparative form]
- This copier is the *fastest* of the three tested. [superlative form]

Most adverbs with two or more syllables end in *-ly*, and most adverbs ending in *-ly* are compared by inserting the comparative *more* or *less* or the superlative *most* or *least* in front of them.

- She moved *more quickly* than any other company's sales representative.
- *Most surprisingly*, the engine failed during the final test phase.

A few irregular adverbs require a change in form to indicate comparison (*well, better, best; badly, worse, worst; far, farther, farthest*).

- The training program functions *well*.
- Our training program functions *better* than most others in the industry.
- Many consider our training program the *best* in the industry.

Placement of Adverbs

An adverb usually should be placed in front of the verb it modifies.

- The pilot *methodically* performed the preflight check.

An adverb may, however, follow the verb (or the verb and its object) that it modifies.

- The system failed *unexpectedly*.
- They replaced the hard drive *quickly*.

An adverb may be placed between a helping verb and a main verb.

- In this temperature range, the pressure will *quickly* drop.

Adverbs such as *only, nearly, almost, just,* and *hardly* should be placed immediately before the words they limit. See also <u>only</u> (Tab 10) and <u>modifiers</u>.

agreement

Grammatical agreement is the correspondence in form between different elements of a sentence to indicate number, person, gender, and case.

A subject and its verb must agree in number.

- The *design is* acceptable.
  [The singular subject, *design*, requires the singular verb, *is*.]
- The new *products are* going into production soon.
  [The plural subject, *products*, requires the plural verb, *are*.]

A subject and its verb must agree in person.

- *I am* the designer.
  [The first-person singular subject, *I*, requires the first-person singular verb, *am*.]
- *They are* the designers.
  [The third-person plural subject, *they*, requires the third-person plural verb, *are*.]

A pronoun and its antecedent must agree in person, number, gender, and case.

- The *employees* report that *they* are more efficient in the new facility.
  [The third-person plural subject, *employees*, requires the third-person plural pronoun, *they*.]
- *Kaye McGuire* will meet with the staff on Friday, when *she* will assign duties.
  [The third-person singular subject, *Kaye McGuire*, requires the third-person feminine pronoun, *she*, in the subjective case.]

See also pronouns, sentence construction, and verbs.

articles

Articles (*a, an, the*) function as adjectives because they modify the items they designate by either limiting them or making them more specific. The two kinds of articles are indefinite and definite.
The indefinite articles, *a* and *an*, denote an unspecified item.

- *A* package was delivered yesterday.
  [This is not a specific package but an unspecified package.]

The choice between *a* and *an* depends on the sound rather than on the letter following the article. Use *a* before words or abbreviations beginning with a consonant or consonant sound, including *y* or *w* (*a* person, *a* historic event, *a* year's salary, *a* one-page report, *a* DNR order).

> ⒺⓈⓁ TIPS FOR USING ARTICLES
>
> Whether to use a definite or an indefinite article is determined by what you can safely assume about your audience's knowledge. In each of these sentences, you can safely assume that the reader can clearly identify the noun. Therefore, use a definite article.
>
> - *The* sun rises in the east.
>   [The Earth has only one *sun*.]
>
> - Did you know that yesterday was *the* coldest day of the year so far?
>   [The modified noun refers to *yesterday*.]
>
> - *The* man who left his briefcase in the conference room was in a hurry.
>   [The relative phrase *who left his briefcase in the conference room* restricts and, therefore, identifies the meaning of *man*.]
>
> In the following sentence, however, you cannot assume that the reader can clearly identify the noun.
>
> - *A* package is on the way.
>   [It is impossible to identify specifically what package is meant.]
>
> A more important question for some nonnative speakers of English is when *not* to use articles. These generalizations will help. Do not use articles with the following:
>
> singular proper nouns
>
> - Utah, Main Street, Harvard University, Mount Hood
>
> plural nonspecific countable nouns (when making generalizations)
>
> - Helicopters are the new choice of transportation for the rich and famous.
>
> singular uncountable nouns
>
> - She loves chocolate.
>
> plural countable nouns used as complements
>
> - Those women are physicians.
>
> See also <u>English as a second language</u>.

- The project manager felt that it was *a* unique situation.
  [The *u* in *unique* is the consonant sound of *y*, as in *you*.]

Use *an* before words or abbreviations beginning with a vowel or vowel sound (*an* order, *an* hour).

- We purchased *an* SLR camera.
  [The *s* in *SLR* is the vowel sound of *e*, as in *escape*.]

The definite article, *the*, denotes a particular item.

- *The* package was delivered yesterday.
  [This is not just any package but one specific package.]

Do not omit all articles from your writing. Including articles costs nothing; eliminating them makes reading more difficult. (See also telegraphic style, Tab 9.) However, do not overdo it. An article can be superfluous.

- I'll meet you in *a* half *an* hour.
  [Choose one article and eliminate the other.]

Do not capitalize articles in titles except when they are the first word (*The Economist* reviewed *Winning the Talent Wars*). See also capitalization (Tab 12).

clauses

A clause is a group of words that contains a subject and a predicate and that functions as a sentence or as part of a sentence. (See sentence construction.) Every subject-predicate word group in a sentence is a clause, and every sentence must contain at least one independent clause; otherwise, it is a sentence fragment.

A clause that could stand alone as a simple sentence is an *independent clause*. (*The scaffolding fell* when the rope broke.) A clause that could not stand alone if the rest of the sentence were deleted is a *dependent (or subordinate) clause*. (I was at the St. Louis branch *when the decision was made*.)

Dependent clauses are useful in making the relationship between thoughts clearer and more succinct than if the ideas were presented in a series of simple sentences or compound sentences.

FRAGMENTED	The recycling facility is located between Millville and Darrtown. Both villages use it. [two thoughts of approximately equal importance]
SUBORDINATED	The recycling facility, *which is located between Millville and Darrtown*, is used by both villages. [one thought subordinated to the other]

Subordinate clauses are especially effective for expressing thoughts that describe or explain another statement. Too much subordination (Tab 9), however, can be confusing and produce wordiness.

- He selected instructors whose classes ~~had a slant that was~~ *were* *at accounting students.* specifically directed ~~toward students who intended to go into~~ ~~accounting.~~

11

Grammar

A clause can be connected with the rest of its sentence by a coordinating conjunction, a subordinating conjunction, a relative pronoun, or a conjunctive adverb.

- It was 500 miles to the facility, *so* we made arrangements to fly. [coordinating conjunction]

- Mission control will have to be alert *because* at launch the space laboratory will contain a highly flammable fuel. [subordinating conjunction]

- It was Robert M. Fano *who* designed and developed the earliest multiple-access computer system at MIT. [relative pronoun]

- It was dark when we arrived; *nevertheless*, we began the tour of the facility. [conjunctive adverb]

See also <u>adverbs</u>, <u>conjunctions</u>, and <u>pronouns</u>.

complements

A complement is a word, phrase, or clause used in the predicate of a sentence to complete the meaning of the sentence.

- Pilots fly *airplanes*. [word]
- To live is *to risk death*. [phrase]
- John knew *that he would be late*. [clause]

Four kinds of complements are generally recognized: direct object, indirect object, objective complement, and subjective complement.

A *direct object* is a noun or noun equivalent that receives the action of a transitive verb; it answers the question *What?* or *Whom?* after the verb.

- I designed *a Web page*. [noun]
- I like *to work*. [verbal]
- I like *it*. [pronoun]
- I like *what I saw*. [noun clause]

An *indirect object* is a noun or noun equivalent that occurs with a direct object after certain kinds of transitive verbs such as *give, wish, cause*, and *tell*. It answers the question *To whom or what?* or *For whom or what?*

- We should buy *the Milwaukee office* a color copier.
  [*Color copier* is the direct object and *the Milwaukee office* is the indirect object.]

An *objective complement* completes the meaning of a sentence by revealing something about the object of its transitive verb. An objective complement may be either a noun or an adjective.

- They call him *a genius.* [noun phrase]
- We painted the building *white.* [adjective]

A *subjective complement,* which follows a linking verb rather than a transitive verb, describes the subject. A subjective complement may be either a noun or an adjective.

- Her sister is *a consultant.* [noun phrase]
- His brother is *ill.* [adjective]

See also <u>sentence construction</u> and <u>verbs</u>.

conjunctions

A conjunction connects words, phrases, or clauses and can also indicate the relationship between the elements it connects.

A *coordinating conjunction* joins two sentence elements that have identical functions. The coordinating conjunctions are *and, but, or, for, nor, yet,* and *so.*

- Nature *and* technology affect petroleum prices. [joins two nouns]
- To hear *and* to listen are two different things. [joins two phrases]
- I would like to include the survey, *but* that would make the report too long. [joins two clauses]

Correlative conjunctions are used in pairs. The correlative conjunctions are *either . . . or, neither . . . nor, not only . . . but also, both . . . and,* and *whether . . . or.*

- The auditor will arrive *either* on Wednesday *or* on Thursday.

A *subordinating conjunction* connects sentence elements of different relative importance, normally independent and dependent clauses. The most frequently used subordinating conjunctions are *so, although, after, because, if, where, than, since, as, unless, before, that, though,* and *when.*

- I left the office *after* finishing the report.

A *conjunctive adverb* has the force of a conjunction because it joins two independent clauses. The most common conjunctive adverbs are *however, moreover, therefore, further, then, consequently, besides, accordingly, also,* and *thus.* See also <u>adverbs</u>.

11

Grammar

- The engine performed well in the laboratory; *however*, it failed under road conditions.

Coordinating conjunctions in the titles of books, articles, plays, and movies should not be capitalized unless they are the first or last word in the title.

- Our library contains *Consulting and Financial Independence* as well as *So You Want to Improve Your Bottom Line?*

Occasionally, a conjunction may begin a sentence; in fact, conjunctions can be strong transitional words and at times can provide empha-sis (Tab 9). See also transition (Tab 9).

- I realize that the project is more difficult than expected and that you have encountered personnel problems. *But* we must meet our deadline.

dangling modifiers

Phrases that do not clearly and logically refer to the correct noun or pronoun are called *dangling modifiers.* Dangling modifiers usually appear at the beginning of a sentence as an introductory phrase.

DANGLING	*While eating lunch in the cafeteria,* the computer malfunctioned. [*Who* was eating lunch in the cafeteria?]
CORRECT	While *I* was eating lunch in the cafeteria, the computer malfunctioned.

Dangling modifiers can appear at the end of the sentence as well.

DANGLING	The program gains efficiency by *eliminating the superfluous instructions.* [*Who* eliminates the superfluous instructions?]
CORRECT	The program gains efficiency *when you* eliminate the superfluous instructions.

To test whether a phrase is a dangling modifier, turn it into a clause with a subject and a verb. If the expanded phrase and the independent clause do not have the same subject, the phrase is dangling.

DANGLING	After finishing the research, the proposal was easy to write. [The implied subject of the phrase is *I*, but the subject of the independent clause is *the proposal.*]

CORRECT   After finishing the research, *I found that* the proposal
          was easy to write.
          [Now the subject of the independent clause agrees
          with the implied subject of the introductory phrase.]

CORRECT   After *I* finished the research, the proposal was easy to
          write.
          [Here the phrase is a dependent clause with the
          explicit subject *I*.]

For a discussion of misplaced modifiers, see <u>modifiers</u>.

English as a second language

DIRECTORY

Learning to write well in a second language takes a great deal of effort and practice. The most effective way to improve your command of written English is to read widely beyond the reports and professional articles your job requires, such as magazines, newspapers, articles, novels, biographies, and any other writing that interests you. In addition, listen carefully to native speakers on television, on radio, and in person. Do not hesitate to consult a native speaker of English, especially for important writing tasks, such as <u>reports</u> (Tab 3), <u>e-mails</u> (Tab 6), and <u>memos</u> (Tab 6).

Focus on areas of English that typically give nonnative speakers trouble, such as those discussed in this entry and referred to under the subsection ESL Entries on page 326. See also <u>global communication</u> (Tab 1).

11

Grammar

Count and Mass Nouns

Count nouns refer to things that can be counted (*tables, pencils, projects, reports*). Mass nouns (also called *noncount nouns*) identify things that cannot be counted (*electricity, water, air, loyalty, information*). This distinction can be confusing with words like *electricity* and *water*. Although we can count kilowatt hours of electricity and bottles of water, counting becomes inappropriate when we use the words *electricity* and *water* in a general sense, as in "Water is an essential resource." Following is a list of common mass nouns.

acid	education	knowledge	research
advice	electricity	loyalty	technology
air	equipment	machinery	transportation
anger	furniture	money	uranium
biology	health	news	water
clothing	honesty	oil	weather
coffee	information	precision	work

The distinction between whether something can or cannot be counted determines the form of the noun to use (singular or plural), the kind of article that precedes it (*a*, *an*, *the*, or no article), and the kind of limiting adjective it requires (such as *fewer* or *less* and *much* or *many*). See also fewer/less (Tab 10).

Articles

This discussion of articles applies only to common nouns (not to proper nouns, such as the names of people) because count and mass nouns are always common nouns.

The general rule is that every count noun must be preceded by an article (*a*, *an*, or *the*), a demonstrative adjective (*this*, *that*, *these*, *those*), a possessive adjective (*my*, *your*, *her*, *his*, *its*, *their*), or some expression of quantity (such as *one*, *two*, *several*, *many*, *a few*, *a lot of*, *some*, or *no*). The article, adjective, or expression of quantity appears either directly in front of the noun or in front of the whole noun phrase.

- Beth read *a* report last week. [article]

- *Those* reports Beth read were long. [demonstrative adjective]

- *Their* report was long. [possessive adjective]

- *Some* reports Beth read were long. [indefinite adjective]

The articles *a* and *an* are used with count nouns that refer to one item of the whole class of like items.

- Matthew has *a* pen.
  [Matthew could have *any* pen.]

The article *the* is used with nouns that refer to a specific item that both the reader and the writer can identify.

- Matthew has *the* pen.
  [Matthew has a *specific* pen that is known to both the reader and the writer.]

When making generalizations with count nouns, writers can either use *a* or *an* with a singular count noun or use no article with a plural count noun. Consider the following generalization using an article.

- An egg is a good source of protein.
  [*any egg, all eggs, eggs in general*]

However, the following generalization uses a plural count noun with no article.

- Eggs are good sources of protein.
  [*any egg, all eggs, eggs in general*]

When you are making a generalization with a mass noun, do not use an article in front of the mass noun.

- Sugar is bad for your teeth.

See also the discussion of articles in the entry <u>adjectives</u>.

Gerunds and Infinitives

Nonnative writers of English are often puzzled by which form of a *verbal* (a verb used as another part of speech) to use when it functions as the direct object of a <u>verb</u>. No structural rule exists for distinguishing between the use of an infinitive and a gerund as the object of a verb. Any specific verb may take an infinitive as its object, others may take a gerund, and yet others take either an infinitive or a gerund. At times, even the base form of the verb is used.

- He enjoys *working.* [gerund as a complement]
- She promised *to fulfill* her part of the contract.
  [infinitive as a complement]
- The president had the manager *assign* her staff to another project.
  [basic verb form as a complement]

To make such distinctions accurately, rely on what you hear native speakers use or what you read. You might also consult a reference book for ESL students.

Adjective Clauses

Because of the variety of ways adjective clauses are constructed in different languages, they can be particularly troublesome for nonnative writers of English. The following guidelines will help you form adjective clauses correctly.

Place an adjective clause directly after the noun it modifies.

- The tall woman *who is standing across the room* is a vice president of the company ~~who is standing across the room.~~

The adjective clause *who is standing across the room* modifies *woman*, not *company*, and thus comes directly after *woman*.

11

Grammar

Avoid using a relative pronoun with another pronoun in an adjective clause.

* The man who ~~he~~ sits at that desk is my boss.

Present-Perfect Verb Tense

As a general rule, use the present perfect tense to refer to events completed in the past that have some implication for the present. When a specific time is mentioned, however, use the simple past.

PRESENT	I *have written* the letter and I am waiting for an answer.
PERFECT	[The action, *have written*, affects the present and no specific time is mentioned.]
SIMPLE	I *wrote* the letter yesterday morning.
PAST	[The action, *wrote*, does not affect the present.]

Use the present perfect with a *since* or *for* phrase to describe actions that began in the past and continue in or affect the present.

* She *has revised* the report three times *since* the last meeting.
* This company *has been* in business *for* seven years.

Present-Progressive Verb Tense

The present progressive tense is especially difficult for those whose native language does not use this tense. The present progressive tense is used to describe some action or condition that is ongoing (or in progress) in the present and may continue into the future.

* I *am searching* for an error in the document.
  [The search is occurring now and may continue.]

In contrast, the simple present tense more often relates to habitual actions.

* I *search* for errors in my documents.
  [I regularly search for errors, but I am not necessarily searching now.]

See "ESL Tips for Using the Progressive Form" on page 351.

ESL Entries

Most of the entries in Tabs 9 through 12 may interest writers of English as a second language; however, the specific entries in the following list address issues that often cause problems. Those entries with an asterisk (*) also include ESL Tips boxes with useful information for nonnative speakers.

mixed constructions

A mixed construction is a sentence in which the elements do not sensibly fit together. The problem may be a grammar error, a logic error, or both.

- Because the copier wouldn't start ~~explains why~~ we had to call a technician.

The original sentence mixes a subordinate clause (*Because the copier wouldn't start*) with a verb (*explains*) that attempts to incorrectly use the subordinate clause as its subject. The revision correctly uses the pronoun *we* as the subject of the main clause. See also **sentence construction**.

11

Grammar

modifiers

Modifiers are words, phrases, or clauses that expand, limit, or make otherwise more specific the meaning of other elements in a sentence. Although we can create sentences without modifiers, we often need the detail and clarification they provide.

WITHOUT MODIFIERS   Production decreased.

WITH MODIFIERS   *Automobile* production decreased *rapidly*.

Modifiers generally function as **adjectives** or **adverbs**. Adjectives describe qualities or impose boundaries on the words they modify.

- *noisy* machinery; *ten* automobiles; *this* printer; *an* animal

An adverb modifies an adjective, another adverb, a verb, or an entire clause.

- Under test conditions, the brake pad showed *much* less wear than it did under actual conditions.
  [The adverb *much* modifies the adjective *less.*]

- The redesigned brake pad lasted *much* longer.
  [The adverb *much* modifies another adverb, *longer.*]

- The wrecking ball hit the wall of the building *hard.*
  [The adverb *hard* modifies the verb *hit.*]

- *Surprisingly*, the motor failed even after all the durability and performance tests it had passed.
  [The adverb *surprisingly* modifies an entire clause: *the motor failed.*]

Adverbs are <u>intensifiers</u> (Tab 9) when they increase the impact of adjectives (*very* fine, *too* high) or adverbs (*very* slowly, *rather* quickly). Be cautious using intensifiers; their overuse can lead to exaggeration and hence to inaccuracies.

Stacked (Jammed) Modifiers

Stacked modifiers are strings of modifiers preceding nouns that make writing unclear or difficult to read.

- Your *staffing-level authorization reassessment* plan should result in a major improvement.

The noun *plan* is preceded by three long modifiers, a string that forces the reader to slow down to interpret its meaning. Stacked modifiers are often the result of an overuse of <u>buzzwords</u> (Tab 9) or <u>jargon</u> (Tab 9). See how breaking up the stacked modifiers makes the sentence easier to read.

- Your plan for reassessing the staffing-level authorizations should result in a major improvement.

Misplaced Modifiers

A modifier is misplaced when it modifies the wrong word or phrase. A misplaced modifier can cause ambiguity.

- We *almost* lost all of the parts.
  [The parts were *almost* lost but were not.]

- We lost *almost* all of the parts.
  [Most of the parts were in fact lost.]

To avoid ambiguity, place modifiers as close as possible to the words they are intended to modify. Likewise, place phrases near the words they modify. Note the two meanings possible when the phrase is shifted in the following sentences:

- The equipment *without the accessories* sold the best.
  [Different types of equipment were available, some with and some without accessories.]

- The equipment sold the best *without the accessories.*
  [One type of equipment was available, and the accessories were optional.]

Place clauses as close as possible to the words they modify.

REMOTE	We sent the brochure to four local firms *that had four-color art.*
CLOSE	We sent the brochure *that had four-color art* to four local firms.

Squinting Modifiers

A modifier squints when it can be interpreted as modifying either of two sentence elements simultaneously, thereby confusing readers about which is intended. See also <u>dangling modifiers</u>.

- We agreed *on the next day* to make the adjustments.
  [Did they agree *to make the adjustments on the next day*?
  Or *on the next day*, did they agree to make the adjustments?]

A squinting modifier can sometimes be corrected simply by changing its position, but often it is better to rewrite the sentence.

- We agreed that *on the next day* we would make the adjustments.
  [The adjustments were to be made on the next day.]

- *On the next day*, we agreed that we would make the adjustments.
  [The agreement was made on the next day.]

mood

Mood in grammar identifies the <u>verb</u> functions that indicate whether the verb is intended to make a statement or ask a question, give a command, or express a hypothetical possibility.

The *indicative mood* states a fact, gives an opinion, or asks a question.

- The setting *is* correct.

- *Is* the setting correct?

The *imperative mood* expresses a command, suggestion, request, or plea. In the imperative mood, the implied subject *you* is not expressed. (*Install* the system today.)

The *subjunctive mood* expresses something that is contrary to fact, conditional, hypothetical, or purely imaginative; it can also express a wish, a doubt, or a possibility. In the subjunctive mood, *were* is used instead of *was* in clauses that speculate about the present or future, and the base form (*be*) is used following certain verbs, such as *propose*, *request*, or *insist*. See also progressive <u>tense</u>.

- If we *were* to close the sale today, we would meet our monthly quota.

- The senior partner insisted that she [I, you, we, they] *be* in charge of the project.

The most common use of the subjunctive mood is to express clearly that the writer considers a condition to be contrary to fact. If the condition is not considered to be contrary to fact, use the indicative mood.

SUBJUNCTIVE   If I *were* president of the firm, I would change several hiring policies.

INDICATIVE   Although I *am* president of the firm, I don't feel that I control every aspect of its policies.

ESL TIPS FOR DETERMINING MOOD

In written and especially in spoken English, the tendency increasingly is to use the indicative mood where the subjunctive traditionally has been used. Note the differences between traditional and contemporary usage in the following examples.

Traditional (formal) use of the subjunctive mood

- I wish he *were* here now.

- If I *were* going to the conference, I would room with him.

- I requested that she *show* up on time.

Contemporary (informal) use of the indicative mood

- I wish he *was* here now.

- If I *was* going to the conference, I would room with him.

- I requested that she *shows* up on time.

As a nonnative speaker of English, you are faced with a choice: Do you use the subjunctive and, consequently, in some circles sound sophisticated, intellectual, or even weird? Or do you use the indicative and in other circles sound uneducated? The answer might be to master both uses and be able to move freely between the different circles. In formal business and technical writing, however, it is best to use the more traditional expressions.

11

Grammar

nouns

A noun names a person, place, thing, concept, action, or quality.

Types of Nouns

The two basic types of nouns are proper nouns and common nouns. *Proper nouns*, which are capitalized, name specific people, places, and things (H. G. Wells, Boston, United Nations, Nobel Prize). See also capitalization (Tab 12).

Common nouns, which are not capitalized unless they begin sentences, name general classes or categories of persons, places, things, concepts, actions, and qualities (writer, city, organization, award). Common nouns include collective nouns, concrete nouns, abstract nouns, count nouns, and mass nouns.

Collective nouns are common nouns that indicate a group or collection. They are plural in meaning but singular in form (audience, jury, brigade, staff, committee). (See the subsection Collective Nouns on page 332 for advice on using singular or plural verb forms with collective nouns.)

Concrete nouns are common nouns used to identify those things that can be discerned by the five senses (paper, keyboard, glue, nail, grease).

Abstract nouns are common nouns that refer to things that cannot be discerned by the five senses (loyalty, pride, valor, peace, devotion).

Count nouns are concrete nouns that identify things that can be separated into countable units (desks, envelopes, printers, pencils, books).

Mass nouns are concrete nouns that identify things that are a mass rather than individual units and that cannot be easily separated into countable units (water, air, electricity, oil, cement).

Noun Functions

Nouns function as subjects of verbs, direct and indirect objects of verbs and prepositions, subjective and objective complements, or appositives.

- The *metal* failed during the test. [subject]
- The bricklayer cemented the *blocks* efficiently. [direct object of a verb]
- The state presented our *department* a safety award. [indirect object]
- The event occurred within the *year*. [object of a preposition]
- A dynamo is a *generator*. [subjective complement]
- The regional manager was appointed *chairperson*. [objective complement]
- George Thomas, the *treasurer*, gave his report last. [appositive]

11
Grammar

Words normally used as nouns can also be used as <u>adjectives</u> and <u>adverbs</u>.

- It is *company* policy. [adjective]
- He went *home*. [adverb]

Collective Nouns

When a collective noun refers to a group as a whole, it takes a singular verb and pronoun.

- The staff *was* divided on the issue and could not reach *its* decision until May 15.

When a collective noun refers to individuals within a group, it takes a plural verb and pronoun.

- The staff *returned* to *their* offices after the conference.

A better way to emphasize the individuals on the staff would be to use the phrase *the staff members*.

- The staff members *returned* to *their* offices after the conference.

Treat organization names and titles as singular.

- LRM Associates *has* grown 30 percent in the last three years; *it* will move to a new facility in January.

Forming Plurals

Most nouns form the plural by adding -*s* (dolphin/dolphins, pencil/pencils). Nouns ending in *ch*, *s*, *sh*, *x*, and *z* form the plural by adding -*es* (search/searches, glass/glasses, wish/wishes, six/sixes, buzz/buzzes). Nouns that end in a consonant plus *y* form the plural by changing the *y* to *ies* (delivery/deliveries). Some nouns ending in *o* add -*es* to form the plural, but others add only -*s* (tomato/tomatoes, dynamo/dynamos). Some nouns ending in *f* or *fe*, add -*s* to form the plural; others change the *f* or *fe* to *ves* (cliff/cliffs, fife/fifes, hoof/hooves, knife/knives). Some nouns require an internal change to form the plural (woman/women, man/men, mouse/mice, goose/geese). Some nouns do not change in the plural form (many *fish*, several *deer*, fifty *sheep*). Hyphenated and open compound nouns form the plural in the main word (sons-in-law, high schools, editors-in-chief). Compound nouns written as one word add -*s* to the end (two *tablespoonfuls*). If you are unsure of the proper usage, check a dictionary. See <u>possessive case</u> for a discussion of how nouns form possessives.

objects

The three kinds of objects are direct objects, indirect objects, and objects of prepositions. All objects are nouns or noun equivalents: pronouns, verbals, and noun phrases or clauses. See also complements, nouns, pronouns, and verbs.

A *direct object* answers the question *What?* or *Whom?* about a verb and its subject.

- We sent a *full report.* [We sent *what?*]
- Bill telephoned the *client.* [Bill telephoned *whom?*]

An *indirect object* is a noun or noun equivalent that occurs with a direct object after certain kinds of transitive verbs, such as *give, wish, cause,* and *tell.* The indirect object answers the question *To whom or what?* or *For whom or what?* The indirect object always precedes the direct object.

- We sent the *general manager* a full report.
  [*Report* is the direct object; the indirect object, *general manager,* answers the question, "We sent a full report *to whom?*"]

The *object of a preposition* is a noun or pronoun that is introduced by a preposition, forming a prepositional phrase.

- *At the meeting,* the district managers approved the contract.
  [*Meeting* is the object and *at the meeting* is the prepositional phrase.]

person

11

Grammar

Person is the form of a personal pronoun that indicates whether the pronoun represents the speaker, the person spoken to, or the person or thing spoken about. A pronoun representing the speaker is in the *first person.* (*I* could not find the answer in the manual.) A pronoun that represents the person or people spoken to is in the *second person.* (*You* will be a good manager.) A pronoun that represents the person or people spoken about is in the *third person.* (*They* received the news quietly.) The following list shows first-, second-, and third-person pronouns.

PERSON	SINGULAR	PLURAL
First	I, me, my, mine	we, us, our, ours
Second	you, your, yours	you, your, yours
Third	he, him, his, she, her, hers, it, its	they, them, their, theirs

phrases

Phrases are groups of words that are based on nouns, nonfinite verb forms, or verb combinations without subjects. See also <u>clauses</u> and <u>sentence construction</u>.

- She encouraged her staff *by her calm confidence.* [phrase]

A phrase may function as an <u>adjective</u>, an <u>adverb</u>, a <u>noun</u>, or a <u>verb</u>.

- The subjects *on the agenda* were all discussed. [adjective]
- We discussed the project *with great enthusiasm.* [adverb]
- *Working hard* is her way of life. [noun]
- The chief engineer *should have been notified.* [verb]

Even though phrases function as adjectives, adverbs, nouns, or verbs, they are normally named for the kind of word around which they are constructed—preposition, participle, infinitive, gerund, verb, or noun. A phrase that begins with a preposition is a *prepositional phrase*, a phrase that begins with a participle is a *participial phrase*, and so on. See also <u>prepositions</u>.

possessive case

A <u>noun</u> or <u>pronoun</u> is in the possessive case when it represents a person, place, or thing that possesses something. Possession is generally expressed with *'s* (the *report's* title), with a prepositional phrase using *of* (the title *of the report*), or with the possessive form of a pronoun (*our* report). See also <u>apostrophes</u> (Tab 12).

Practices vary for some possessive forms, but the following guidelines are widely used in business writing. Above all, be consistent.

Singular and Proper Nouns

Most singular nouns show the possessive case with *'s.*

- a *manager's* office; an *employee's* job satisfaction; the *company's* stock value; the *witness's* testimony; the *bus's* schedule

When pronunciation is difficult or when a multisyllable noun ends in a *z* sound, you may use only an apostrophe.

- *New Orleans'* convention hotels

Plural Nouns

Plural nouns that end in *-s* or *-es* show the possessive case with only an apostrophe.

- the *managers'* reports; the *employees'* paychecks; the *companies'* joint project; the *witnesses'* reports; the *buses'* schedules

Plural nouns that do not end in *-s* show the possessive with *'s*.

- *children's* clothing; *women's* resources; *men's* room

Apostrophes are not used in official names (*Consumers Union*) or for words that may appear to be possessive nouns but function as <u>adjectives</u> (*a computer peripherals supplier*).

Compound Nouns

Compound nouns form the possessive with *'s* following the final letter.

- the *vice president's* proposal; the *editor-in-chief's* desk

Plurals of some compound expressions are often best expressed with a prepositional phrase (presentations *of the editors-in-chief*).

Coordinate Nouns

Coordinate nouns show joint possession with *'s* following the last noun.

- *Fischer and Goulet's* partnership was the foundation of their business.

Coordinate nouns show individual possession with *'s* following each noun.

- The difference between *Barker's* and *Washburne's* test results was statistically insignificant.

Possessive Pronouns

The possessive pronouns (*its, whose, his, her, our, your, their*) are also used to show possession and do not require apostrophes. (Even good systems have *their* flaws.) Only the possessive form of a pronoun should be used with a gerund (a noun formed from an *-ing* <u>verb</u>).

- The safety officer insisted on *our* wearing protective clothing. [*Wearing* is the gerund.]

Possessive pronouns are also used to replace nouns. (The responsibility was *theirs*.) See also <u>its/it's</u> (Tab 10).

11

Grammar

Indefinite Pronouns

Some indefinite pronouns (*all, any, each, few, most, none, some*) form the possessive case with the <u>preposition</u> *of.*

- Both desks were stored in the warehouse, but water ruined the surface *of each.*

Other indefinite pronouns (*everyone, someone, anyone, no one*), however, use *'s.*

- *Everyone's* contribution is welcome.

prepositions

A preposition is a word that links a <u>noun</u> or <u>pronoun</u> (the preposition's object) to another sentence element by expressing such relationships as direction (*to, into, across, toward*), location (*at, in, on, under, over, beside, among, by, between, through*), time (*before, after, during, until, since*), or position (*for, against, with*). Together, the preposition, its object, and the object's <u>modifiers</u> form a prepositional <u>phrase</u> that acts as a modifier.

- Answer customers' questions *in a courteous manner.*
  [The prepositional phrase *in a courteous manner* modifies the verb *answer.*]

The object of a preposition (the word or phrase following the preposition) is always in the objective case. When the object is a compound noun, both nouns should be in the objective case. For example, the phrase "between you and *me*" is frequently and incorrectly written as "between you and *I.*" *Me* is the objective form of the pronoun, and *I* is the subjective form.

Many words that function as prepositions also function as <u>adverbs</u>. If the word takes an object and functions as a connective, it is a preposition; if it has no object and functions as a modifier, it is an adverb.

PREPOSITIONS	The manager sat *behind* the desk *in* her office.
ADVERBS	The customer lagged *behind*; then he came *in* and sat down.

Certain <u>verbs</u>, adverbs, and <u>adjectives</u> are used with certain prepositions (interested *in*, aware *of*, equated *with*, adhere *to*, capable *of*, object *to*, infer *from*). A more detailed list of such usages appears in the entry <u>idioms</u> (Tab 9).

11
Grammar

Prepositions at the End of a Sentence

A preposition at the end of a sentence can be an indication that the sentence is awkwardly constructed.

- *She was at the*
  ~~The~~ branch office ~~is where she was at.~~

However, if a preposition falls naturally at the end of a sentence, leave it there. (I don't remember which file name I saved it *under*.)

Prepositions in Titles

Capitalize prepositions in titles when they are the first or last words or when they contain more than four letters, unless you are following a style that recommends otherwise. See also <u>capitalization</u> (Tab 12).

- The article "New Concerns About Distance Education" was reviewed recently in the newspaper column "In My Opinion."

Preposition Errors

Do not use redundant prepositions, such as "off *of*," "in back *of*," "inside *of*," and "at *about*." See also <u>conciseness</u> (Tab 9).

EXACT	The client arrived at ~~about~~ four o'clock.
APPROXIMATE	The client arrived ~~at~~ about four o'clock.

Avoid unnecessarily adding the preposition *up* to verbs.

- *to*
  Call ~~up and~~ see if he is in his office.

Do not omit necessary prepositions.

- *to*
  He was oblivious and not distracted by the view from his office window.

11

Grammar

pronoun reference

A <u>pronoun</u> should refer clearly to a specific antecedent. Avoid vague and uncertain references.

- *, which was a big one,*
  We got the account after we wrote the proposal. ~~It was a big one.~~

For the sake of <u>coherence</u> (Tab 9), place pronouns as close as possible to their antecedents.

- The office building next to City Hall ~~was praised for its architectural design.~~

  , praised for its architectural design, is

A general (or broad) reference or one that has no real antecedent is a problem that often occurs when the word *this* is used by itself.

- He deals with personnel problems in his work. This helps him in his personal life.

  experience

Another problem is a hidden reference, which has only an implied antecedent.

- A high-lipid, low-carbohydrate diet is "ketogenic" because it favors ~~their~~ formation.

  the   *of ketone bodies*

Do not repeat an antecedent in parentheses following the pronoun. If you feel you must identify the pronoun's antecedent in that way, rewrite the sentence.

AWKWARD   The senior partner first met Bob Evans when he (Evans) was a trainee.

IMPROVED   Bob Evans was a trainee when the senior partner first met him.

For advice on avoiding pronoun reference problems with gender, see biased language (Tab 9).

pronouns

A pronoun is a word that is used as a substitute for a noun (the noun for which a pronoun substitutes is called the *antecedent*). Using pronouns in place of nouns relieves the monotony of repeating the same noun over and over. See also pronoun reference.

Personal pronouns refer to the person or people speaking (*I, me, my, mine; we, us, our, ours*); the person or people spoken to (*you, your, yours*); or the person, people, or thing(s) spoken of (*he, him, his; she, her, hers; it, its; they, them, their, theirs*). See also point of view (Tab 1) and person.

- If *their* figures are correct, *ours* must be in error.

Demonstrative pronouns (*this, these, that, those*) indicate or point out the thing being referred to.

- *This* is my desk. *These* are my coworkers. *That* will be a difficult job. *Those* are incorrect figures.

Relative pronouns (*who*, *whom*, *which*, *that*) perform a dual function: (1) they take the place of nouns and (2) they connect and establish the relationship between a dependent <u>clause</u> and its main clause.

- The department manager decided *who* would be hired.

Interrogative pronouns (*who*, *whom*, *what*, *which*) are used to ask questions.

- *What* is the trouble?

Indefinite pronouns specify a class or group of persons or things rather than a particular person or thing (*all, another, any, anyone, anything, both, each, either, everybody, few, many, most, much, neither, nobody, none, several, some,* and *such*).

- Not *everyone* liked the new procedures; *some* even refused to follow them.

A *reflexive pronoun*, which always ends with the suffix *self* or *selves*, indicates that the subject of the sentence acts upon itself. See also <u>sentence construction</u>.

- The electrician accidentally shocked *herself*.

The reflexive pronouns are *myself, yourself, himself, herself, itself, oneself, ourselves, yourselves,* and *themselves*. *Myself* is not a substitute for *I* or *me* as a personal pronoun.

- Victor and ~~myself~~ ^I^ completed the report on time.

- The assignment was given to Ingrid and ~~myself.~~ ^me.^

Intensive pronouns are identical in form to the reflexive pronouns, but they perform a different function: intensive pronouns emphasize their antecedents.

- I *myself* asked the same question.

Reciprocal pronouns (*one another, each other*) indicate the relationship of one item to another. *Each other* is commonly used when referring to two persons or things and *one another* when referring to more than two.

- Salih and Kara work well with *each other*.
- The crew members work well with *one another*.

Case

Pronouns have forms to show the subjective, objective, and possessive cases.

11

Grammar

SINGULAR	SUBJECTIVE	OBJECTIVE	POSSESSIVE
First person	I	me	my, mine
Second person	you	you	your, yours
Third person	he, she, it	him, her, it	his, her, hers, its

PLURAL	SUBJECTIVE	OBJECTIVE	POSSESSIVE
First person	we	us	our, ours
Second person	you	you	your, yours
Third person	they	them	their, theirs

> **(ESL) TIPS FOR USING POSSESSIVE PRONOUNS**
>
> In many languages, possessive pronouns agree in number and gender with the nouns they modify. In English, however, possessive pronouns agree in number and gender with their antecedents. Check your writing carefully for agreement between a possessive pronoun and the word, phrase, or clause that it refers to.
>
> - The *woman* brought *her* brother a cup of soup.
> - *Robert* sent *his* mother flowers on Mother's Day.

A pronoun that is used as the subject of a clause or sentence is in the subjective case (*I, we, he, she, it, you, they, who*). The subjective case is also used when the pronoun follows a linking verb.

- *She* is my boss.
- My boss is *she*.

A pronoun that is used as the object of a verb or preposition is in the objective case (*me, us, him, her, it, you, them, whom*).

- Ms. Davis hired Tom and *me*. [object of verb]
- Between *you* and *me*, she's wrong. [object of preposition]

A pronoun that is used to express ownership is in the possessive case (*my, mine, our, ours, his, her, hers, its, your, yours, their, theirs, whose*).

- He took *his* notes with him on the business trip.
- We took *our* notes with us on the business trip.

A pronoun appositive takes the case of its antecedents.

- Two systems analysts, Joe and *I*, were selected to represent the company.
[*Joe and I* is in apposition to the subject, *systems analysts*, and must therefore be in the subjective case.]

- The systems analysts selected two members—Joe and *me*.
  [*Joe and me* is in apposition to *two members*, which is the object of the verb, *selected*, and therefore must be in the objective case.]

If you have difficulty determining the case of a compound pronoun, try using the pronoun singly.

- In his letter, Eldon mentioned *him* and *me*.
  In his letter, Eldon mentioned *him*.
  In his letter, Eldon mentioned *me*.

- *They* and *we* must discuss the terms of the merger.
  They must discuss the terms of the merger.
  We must discuss the terms of the merger.

When a pronoun modifies a noun, try it without the noun to determine its case.

- [*We/Us*] pilots fly our own planes.
  We fly our own planes.
  [You would not write, "*Us* fly our own planes."]

- He addressed his remarks directly to [*we/us*] technicians.
  He addressed his remarks directly to *us*.
  [You would not write, "He addressed his remarks directly to *we*."]

Gender

A pronoun must agree in gender with its antecedent. Traditionally, the masculine pronoun has been used to refer to both sexes. To avoid the sexual bias implied in such usage, use *he or she* or the plural form of the pronoun, *they*.

- ~~Each~~ All may stay or go as ~~he chooses.~~ they choose.

If you use the plural form of the pronoun, be sure to change the indefinite pronoun *each* to its plural form, *all*. See also <u>biased language</u> (Tab 9).

Number

Number is a frequent problem with only a few indefinite pronouns (*each, either, neither,* and those ending with *-body* or *-one,* such as *anybody, anyone, everybody, everyone, nobody, no one, somebody, someone*) that are normally singular and so require singular verbs and are referred to by singular pronouns.

- As *each member arrives* for the meeting, please hand *him or her* a copy of the confidential report. *Everyone* must return the copy before *he or she* leaves. *Everybody* on the committee *understands* that *neither* of our major competitors *is* aware of the new process we have developed.

Person

Third-person personal pronouns usually have antecedents.

- Gina presented the report to the members of the board of directors. *She* [Gina] first summarized *it* [the report] for *them* [the directors] and then asked for questions.

First- and second-person personal pronouns do not normally require antecedents.

- *I* like my job.
- *You* were there at the time.
- *We* all worked hard on the project.

restrictive and nonrestrictive elements

Modifying <u>phrases</u> and <u>clauses</u> may be either restrictive or nonrestrictive. A *nonrestrictive phrase or clause* provides additional information about what it modifies, but it does not restrict the meaning of what it modifies. The nonrestrictive phrase or clause can be removed without changing the essential meaning of the sentence. It is a parenthetical element that is set off by commas to show its loose relationship with the rest of the sentence.

> NONRESTRICTIVE   The annual report, *which was distributed today*, shows a sales increase of 20 percent last year.

A *restrictive phrase or clause* limits, or restricts, the meaning of what it modifies. If it were removed, the essential meaning of the sentence would change. Because a restrictive phrase or clause is essential to the meaning of the sentence, it is never set off by commas.

> RESTRICTIVE   All employees *wishing to donate blood* may take Thursday afternoon off.

It is important for writers to distinguish between nonrestrictive and restrictive elements. The same sentence can take on two entirely different meanings, depending on whether a modifying element is set off by commas (because it is nonrestrictive) or not (because it is restrictive). A slip by the writer can not only mislead readers but also embarrass the writer.

> MISLEADING   He gave a poor performance evaluation to the staff members who protested to the Human Resources Department.
> [This suggests that he gave the poor evaluation because the staff members had protested.]

| ACCURATE | He gave a poor performance evaluation to the staff members, who protested to the Human Resources Department. [This suggests that the staff members protested because of the poor evaluations.] |

Use *which* to introduce nonrestrictive clauses and *that* to introduce restrictive clauses.

| NONRESTRICTIVE | After John left the restaurant, *which* is one of the finest in New York, he came directly to my office. |
| RESTRICTIVE | Companies *that* diversify usually succeed. |

sentence construction

A sentence is the most fundamental and versatile tool available to writers. Sentences generally flow from a subject to a <u>verb</u> to any <u>objects</u>, <u>complements</u>, or <u>modifiers</u>, but they can be ordered in a variety of ways to achieve <u>emphasis</u> (Tab 9). When shifting word order for emphasis, however, be aware that word order can make a great difference in the meaning of a sentence.

- He was *only* the accountant.
- He was the *only* accountant.

Subjects

The most basic components of sentences are subjects and predicates. The subject of a sentence is a <u>noun</u> or <u>pronoun</u> (and its modifiers) about which the predicate of the sentence makes a statement. Although a subject may appear anywhere in a sentence, it most often appears at the beginning. (*To increase sales* is our goal.) Grammatically, a subject must agree with its verb in number.

- These *departments have* much in common.
- This *department has* several functions.

The subject is the actor in sentences using the active <u>voice</u>.

- The *Webmaster* reported an increase in site visits for May.

A compound subject has two or more substantives (nouns or equivalents) as the subject of one verb.

- *The president* and *the treasurer* agreed to begin the audit.

11

Grammar

> **(ESL)** TIPS FOR UNDERSTANDING THE SUBJECT OF A SENTENCE
>
> In English, every sentence, except commands, must have an explicit subject.
>
> *He established*
> - Paul worked fast. ~~Established~~ the parameters for the project.
>   ^
>
> In commands, the subject *you* is understood and is used only for emphasis.
>
> - (*You*) Show up at the airport at 6:30 tomorrow morning.
> - (*You*) Do your homework, young man. [parent to child]
>
> If you move the subject from its normal position (subject-verb-object), English often requires you to replace the subject with an expletive (*there, it*). In this construction, the verb agrees with the subject that follows it.
>
> - *There are* two files on the desk. [The subject is *files.*]
> - *It is* presumptuous for me to speak for Jim.
>   [The subject is *to speak for Jim.*]
>
> Time, distance, weather, temperature, and environmental expressions use *it* as their subject.
>
> - *It* is ten o'clock.
> - *It* is ten miles down the road.
> - *It* seldom snows in Florida.
> - *It* is very hot in Jorge's office.

Predicates

The predicate is the part of a sentence that makes an assertion about the subject and completes the thought of the sentence.

- Bill *has piloted the corporate jet.*

The *simple predicate* is the verb as well as any helping verbs (*has piloted*). The *complete predicate* is the verb and any modifiers, objects, or complements (*piloted the corporate jet*). A *compound predicate* consists of two or more verbs with the same subject.

- The company *tried* but *did not succeed* in that field.

Such constructions help achieve conciseness in writing. A *predicate nominative* is a noun construction that follows a linking verb and renames the subject.

- She is my *attorney.* [noun]
- His excuse was *that he had been sick.* [noun clause]

Sentence Types

Sentences may be classified according to *structure* (simple, compound, complex, compound-complex); *intention* (declarative, interrogative, imperative, exclamatory); and *stylistic use* (loose, periodic, minor).

Structure.   A *simple sentence* consists of one independent clause. At its most basic, the simple sentence contains only a subject and a predicate.

- Profits [subject] rose [predicate].

A *compound sentence* consists of two or more independent clauses connected by a comma and a coordinating <u>conjunction</u>, by a <u>semicolon</u> (Tab 12), or by a semicolon and a conjunctive <u>adverb</u>.

- Drilling is the only way to collect samples of the layers of sediment below the ocean floor, *but* it is not the only way to gather information about these strata. [comma and coordinating conjunction]

- The chemical composition of sea water bears little resemblance to that of river water; the various elements are present in entirely different proportions. [semicolon]

- It was 500 miles to the site; *therefore*, we made arrangements to fly. [semicolon and conjunctive adverb]

A *complex sentence* contains one independent clause and at least one dependent clause that expresses a subordinate idea.

- The generator will shut off automatically [independent clause] if the temperature rises above a specified point [dependent clause].

A *compound-complex sentence* consists of two or more independent clauses plus at least one dependent clause.

- Productivity is central to controlling inflation [independent clause]; when productivity rises [dependent clause], employers can raise wages without raising prices [independent clause].

Intention.   A *declarative sentence* conveys information or makes a factual statement. (The motor powers the conveyor belt.) An *interrogative sentence* asks a direct question. (Does the conveyor belt run constantly?) An *imperative sentence* issues a command. (Restart in MS-DOS mode.) An *exclamatory sentence* is an emphatic expression of feeling, fact, or opinion. It is a declarative sentence that is stated with great feeling. (The files were deleted!)

Stylistic Use.   A *loose sentence* makes its major point at the beginning and then adds subordinate phrases and clauses that develop or modify that major point. A loose sentence might seem to end at one or more

11

Grammar

> **(ESL) TIPS FOR UNDERSTANDING THE REQUIREMENTS OF A SENTENCE**
>
> - A sentence must start with a capital letter.
> - A sentence must end with a period, a question mark, or an exclamation point.
> - A sentence must have a subject.
> - A sentence must have a verb.
> - A sentence must conform to subject-verb-object word order (or inverted word order for questions or emphasis).
> - A sentence must express an idea that can stand on its own (called the main or independent clause).

points before it actually does end, as the periods in brackets illustrate in the following sentence.

- It went up[.], a great ball of fire about a mile in diameter[.], an elemental force freed from its bonds[.] after being chained for billions of years.

A *periodic sentence* delays its main ideas until the end by presenting subordinate ideas or modifiers first.

- During the last century, the attitude of the American citizen toward automation underwent a profound change.

A *minor sentence* is an incomplete sentence. It makes sense in its context because the missing element is clearly implied by the preceding sentence.

- In view of these facts, is the service contract really useful? *Or economical?*

Constructing Effective Sentences

The subject-verb-object pattern is effective because it is most familiar to readers. In "The company increased profits," we know the subject (*company*) and the object (*profits*) by their positions relative to the verb (*increased*).

An *inverted sentence* places the elements in unexpected order, thus emphasizing the point by attracting the readers' attention.

- A better job I never had. [direct object-subject-verb]
- More optimistic I have never been. [subjective complement-subject-linking verb]
- A poor image we presented. [complement-subject-verb]

Use uncomplicated sentences to state complex ideas. If readers have to cope with a complicated sentence in addition to a complex idea, they are likely to become confused. Just as simpler sentences make complex ideas more digestible, a complex sentence construction makes a series of simple ideas more smooth and less choppy.

Avoid loading sentences with a number of thoughts carelessly tacked together. Such sentences are monotonous and hard to read because all ideas seem to be of equal importance. Rather, distinguish the relative importance of sentence elements with <u>subordination</u> (Tab 9).

LOADED   We started the program three years ago, there were only three members on the staff, and each member was responsible for a separate state, but it was not an efficient operation.

IMPROVED   When we started the program three years ago, there were only three members on the staff, each having responsibility for a separate state; however, that arrangement was not efficient.

Express coordinate or equivalent ideas in similar form. The very construction of the sentence helps the reader grasp the similarity of its components, as illustrated in <u>parallel structure</u> (Tab 9). See also <u>garbled sentences</u> (Tab 9).

sentence faults

A number of problems can create sentence faults, including faulty <u>subordination</u> (Tab 9), <u>clauses</u> with no subjects, rambling sentences, omitted <u>verbs</u>, and illogical assertions.

Faulty subordination occurs when a grammatically subordinate element actually contains the main idea of the sentence or when a subordinate element is so long or detailed that it obscures the main idea. Both of the following sentences are logical, depending on what the writer intends as the main idea and as the subordinate element.

- Although the new filing system saves money, many of the staff are unhappy with it.
  [If the main point is that *many of the staff are unhappy*, this sentence is correct.]

- The new filing system saves money, although many of the staff are unhappy with it.
  [If the writer's main point is that *the new filing system saves money*, this sentence is correct.]

In the following example, the subordinate element overwhelms the main point.

11

Grammar

FAULTY   Because the noise level in the assembly area on a
             typical shift is as loud as a smoke detector's alarm
             ten feet away, employees often develop hearing
             problems.

IMPROVED   Employees in the assembly area often develop
             hearing problems because the noise level on a
             typical shift is as loud as a smoke detector's alarm
             ten feet away.

Clauses with no subjects occur when writers inappropriately assume a
subject that they do not state in the clause.

INCOMPLETE   Your application program can request to end the
             session after the next command. [request *who* or
             what to end the session?]

COMPLETE   Your application program can request *the host
             program* to end the session after the next command.

Rambling sentences contain more information than the reader can
comfortably absorb. The obvious remedy for a rambling sentence is to
divide it into two or more sentences. When you do that, put the main
message of the rambling sentence into the first of the revised sentences.

RAMBLING   The payment to which a subcontractor is entitled
             should be made promptly in order that in the event
             of a subsequent contractual dispute we, as general
             contractors, may not be held in default of our
             contract by virtue of nonpayment.

DIRECT   Pay subcontractors promptly. Then if a contractual
             dispute occurs, we cannot be held in default of our
             contract because of nonpayment.

Some sentence faults are created when writers omit a verb.

written
• I never have and probably never will write the annual report.

Finally, a sentence is faulty if its predicate makes an illogical assertion
about its subject. "Mr. Wilson's *job* is a sales representative" is not logical, but "*Mr. Wilson* is a sales representative" is. "Jim's *height* is six feet
tall" is not logical, but "*Jim* is six feet tall" is. See also <u>logic errors</u> (Tab 9),
<u>sentence fragments</u>, and <u>comma splice</u> (Tab 12).

sentence fragments

A sentence fragment is an incomplete grammatical unit that is punctuated as a sentence.

FRAGMENT	And quit his job.
SENTENCE	He quit his job.

A sentence fragment lacks either a subject or a <u>verb</u> or is a subordinate <u>clause</u> or <u>phrase</u>. Sentence fragments are often introduced by relative pronouns (*who, whom, which, that*) or subordinating conjunctions (such as *although, because, if, when,* and *while*).

- The new manager instituted several new procedures. ~~Although~~ *, although*

  she didn't clear them with the Human Resources Department.

A sentence must contain a finite verb; verbals (nonfinite) do not function as verbs. The following sentence fragments use verbals (*providing, to work*) that cannot function as finite verbs.

FRAGMENT	*Providing* all employees with disability insurance.
SENTENCE	The company *must provide* all employees with disability insurance.
FRAGMENT	*To work* a 40-hour week.
SENTENCE	Most of our employees *are expected* to *work* a 40-hour week.

Explanatory phrases beginning with *such as, for example,* and similar terms often lead writers to create sentence fragments.

- The staff wants additional benefits. ~~For example,~~ the use of *, such as* company cars.

A hopelessly snarled fragment must be rewritten. To rewrite such a fragment, pull the main points out of the fragment, list them in the proper sequence, and then rewrite the sentence as illustrated in <u>garbled sentences</u> (Tab 9). See also <u>sentence construction</u> and <u>sentence faults</u>.

11

Grammar

tense

Tense is the grammatical term for verb forms that indicate time distinctions. There are six tenses in English: past, past perfect, present, present perfect, future, and future perfect. Each tense also has a corresponding progressive form.

TENSE	BASIC FORM	PROGRESSIVE FORM
Past	I began	I was beginning
Past perfect	I had begun	I had been beginning
Present	I begin	I am beginning

TENSE	BASIC FORM	PROGRESSIVE FORM
Present perfect	I have begun	I have been beginning
Future	I will begin	I will be beginning
Future perfect	I will have begun	I will have been beginning

Perfect tenses allow you to express a prior action or condition that continues in a present, past, or future time.

PRESENT PERFECT   *I have begun* to write the annual report and will continue for the rest of the month.

PAST PERFECT   *I had begun* to read the manual when the lights went out.

FUTURE PERFECT   *I will have begun* this project by the time funds are allocated.

Progressive tenses allow you to describe some ongoing action or condition in the present, past, or future.

PRESENT PROGRESSIVE   *I am beginning* to be concerned that we will not meet the deadline.

PAST PROGRESSIVE   *I was beginning* to think we would not finish by the deadline.

FUTURE PROGRESSIVE   *I will be requesting* a leave of absence when this project is finished.

Past Tense

The simple past tense indicates that an action took place in its entirety in the past. The past tense is usually formed by adding -d or -ed to the root form of the verb. (We *closed* the office early yesterday.)

Past-Perfect Tense

The past-perfect tense (also called *pluperfect*) indicates that one past event preceded another. It is formed by combining the helping verb *had* with the past-participle form of the main verb. (He *had finished* by the time I arrived.)

Present Tense

The simple present tense represents action occurring in the present, without any indication of time duration. (I *ride* the train.)

A general truth is always expressed in the present tense. ("Time *heals* all wounds.") The present tense can be used to present actions or conditions that have no time restrictions. (Water *boils* at 212 degrees Fahrenheit.) Similarly, the present tense can be used to indicate habitual action. (I *pass* the coffee shop every day.) In addition, the present tense can be used as a "historical present" to make things that occurred in the past more vivid.

- "Dow Jones *Reaches* a High for the Year"
  [In this news headline, *Reaches* is in the present tense.]

Present-Perfect Tense

The present-perfect tense describes something from the recent past that has a bearing on the present—a period of time before the present but after the simple past. The present-perfect tense is formed by combining a form of the helping verb *have* with the past-participle form of the main verb. (We *have finished* the draft and can now revise it.)

Future Tense

The simple future tense indicates a time that will occur after the present. It uses the helping verb *will* (or *shall*) plus the main verb. (I *will*

ESL TIPS FOR USING THE PROGRESSIVE FORM

The progressive form of the verb is composed of two features: a form of the helping verb *be* and the *-ing* form of the base verb.

PRESENT PROGRESSIVE	I *am updating* the Web site.
PAST PROGRESSIVE	I *was updating* the Web site last week.
FUTURE PROGRESSIVE	I *will be updating* the Web site regularly.

The present progressive is used in three ways:

1. To refer to an action that is in progress at the moment of speaking or writing:
   - The parliamentarian *is taking* the meeting minutes.
2. To highlight that a state or an action is not permanent:
   - The office temp *is helping* us for a few weeks.
3. To express future plans:
   - The summer intern *is leaving* to return to school this Friday.

The past progressive is used to refer to a continuing action or condition in the past, usually with specified limits.

- I *was failing* calculus until I got a tutor.

The future progressive is used to refer to a continuous action or condition in the future.

- We *will be monitoring* his condition all night.

Verbs that express mental activity (*believe, know, see,* and so on) are generally not used in the progressive.

believe
- I ~~am believing~~ the defendant's testimony.
   ^

11

Grammar

finish the job tomorrow.) Do not use the future tense needlessly; doing so merely adds complexity.

- This system ~~will be~~ *is* explained on page 3.

- When you press this button, the feeder ~~will move~~ *moves* the paper into position.

Future-Perfect Tense

The future-perfect tense indicates an action that will be completed at the time of or before another future action. It combines *will have* and the past participle of the main verb. (She *will have driven* 1,400 miles by the time she returns.)

Shift in Tense

Be consistent in your use of tense. The only legitimate shift in tense records a real change in time. Illogical shifts in tense will only confuse your readers.

- Before he visited the facility, the manager ~~meets~~ *met* with the staff.

verbs

A verb is a word or group of words that describes an action ("The copier *jammed* at the beginning of the job"), states the way in which something or someone is affected by an action ("He *was disappointed* that the proposal was rejected"), or affirms a state of existence ("She *is* a district manager now").

Types of Verbs

Verbs are either transitive or intransitive. A *transitive verb* requires a direct <u>object</u> to complete its meaning.

- They *laid* the foundation on October 24.
  [*Foundation* is the direct object of the transitive verb *laid*.]

- Rosalie Anderson *wrote* the treasurer a letter.
  [*Letter* is the direct object of the transitive verb *wrote*.]

An *intransitive verb* does not require an object to complete its meaning. It makes a full assertion about the subject without assistance (although it may have <u>modifiers</u>).

- The engine *ran*.
- The engine *ran* smoothly and quietly.

A *linking verb* is an intransitive verb that links a <u>complement</u> to the subject. When the complement is a <u>noun</u> or <u>pronoun</u>, it refers to the same person or thing as the noun or pronoun that is the subject.

- The carpet *is* stained.
  [*Is* is a linking verb; *stained* is an adjective modifying *carpet*.]

Some intransitive verbs, such as *be, become, seem,* and *appear,* are almost always linking verbs. A number of others, such as *look, sound, taste, smell,* and *feel,* can function as either linking verbs or simple intransitive verbs. If you are unsure about whether one of those verbs is a linking verb, try substituting *seem*; if the sentence still makes sense, the verb is probably a linking verb.

- Their antennae *feel* delicate.
  [*Seem* can be substituted for *feel*—thus *feel* is a linking verb.]
- Their antennae *feel* delicately for their prey.
  [*Seem* cannot be substituted for *feel*; in this case, *feel* is a simple intransitive verb.]

Forms of Verbs

Verbs are described as being either finite or nonfinite.

Finite Verbs. A finite verb is the main verb of a <u>clause</u> or sentence. It makes an assertion about its subject and often serves as the only verb in its clause or sentence. (The telephone *rang* and the receptionist *answered* it.)

A helping verb (sometimes called an *auxiliary verb*) is used in a verb <u>phrase</u> to help indicate <u>mood</u>, <u>tense</u>, and <u>voice</u>. (The phone *had* rung.) Phrases that function as helping verbs are often made up of combinations with the sign of the infinitive, *to* (for example, *am going to, is about to, has to,* and *ought to*). The helping verb always precedes the main verb, although other words may intervene. (Machines *will* never completely *replace* people.)

Nonfinite Verbs. Nonfinite verbs are *verbals*—verb forms that function as nouns, <u>adjectives</u>, or <u>adverbs</u>.

A *gerund* is a noun that is derived from the *-ing* form of a verb. (*Seeing* is *believing*.) An *infinitive*, which uses the root form of a verb (usually preceded by *to*), can function as a noun, an adverb, or an adjective.

- He hates *to complain*.
  [noun, direct object of *hates*]
- The valve closes *to stop* the flow.
  [adverb, modifies *closes*]

- This is the proposal *to consider.*
  [adjective, modifies *proposal*]

A *participle* is a verb form that can function as an adjective.

- The *rejected* proposal was ours.
  [*Rejected* is a verb form that is used as an adjective modifying *proposal*.]

Properties of Verbs

Verbs must (1) agree in <u>person</u> with personal pronouns functioning as subjects, (2) agree in tense and number with their subjects, and (3) be in the appropriate voice.

Person is the term for the form of a personal pronoun that indicates whether the pronoun refers to the speaker, the person spoken to, or the person (or thing) spoken about. Verbs change their forms to agree in person with their subjects.

- I *see* [first person] a yellow tint, but she *sees* [third person] a yellow-green hue.

ESL TIPS FOR AVOIDING SHIFTS IN VOICE, MOOD, OR TENSE

To achieve clarity in your writing, you must maintain consistency and avoid shifts. A shift occurs when there is an abrupt change in voice, mood, or tense. Pay special attention when you edit your writing to check for the following types of shifts.

Voice

- The captain permits his crew to go ashore, but ~~they are not~~ *he does not permit them* ~~permitted~~ to go downtown.
  [The entire sentence is now in the active voice.]

Mood

- Reboot your computer,/ and ~~you should~~ empty the cache.
  [The entire sentence is now in the imperative mood.]

Tense

- I was working quickly, and suddenly a box ~~falls~~ *fell* off the conveyor belt and ~~breaks~~ *broke* my foot.
  [The entire sentence is now in the past tense.]

Tense refers to verb forms that indicate time distinctions. There are six tenses: past, past perfect, present, present perfect, future, and future perfect.

Number refers to the two forms of a verb that indicate whether the subject of a verb is singular (the copier *was* repaired) or plural (the copiers *were* repaired).

Most verbs show the singular of the third-person, present-tense, indicative mood by adding *-s* or *-es* (he *stands*, she *works*, it *goes*). To indicate the plural form, the verb *to be* normally changes from singular (I *am* ready) to plural (we *are* ready).

Voice refers to the two forms of a verb that indicate whether the subject of the verb acts or receives the action. The verb is in the *active voice* if the subject of the verb acts (The bacteria *grow*); the verb is in the passive voice if it receives the action (The bacteria *are grown* in a petri dish).

Conjugation of Verbs

The conjugation of a verb arranges all forms of the verb so that the differences caused by the changing of the tense, number, person, and voice are readily apparent. Figure 11–1 shows the conjugation of the verb *drive*.

TENSE	NUMBER	PERSON	ACTIVE VOICE	PASSIVE VOICE
Present	Singular	1st	I drive	I am driven
		2nd	You drive	You are driven
		3rd	He drives	He is driven
	Plural	1st	We drive	We are driven
		2nd	You drive	You are driven
		3rd	They drive	They are driven
Progressive present	Singular	1st	I am driving	I am being driven
		2nd	You are driving	You are being driven
		3rd	He is driving	He is being driven
	Plural	1st	We are driving	We are being driven
		2nd	You are driving	You are being driven
		3rd	They are driving	They are being driven
Past	Singular	1st	I drove	I was driven
		2nd	You drove	You were driven
		3rd	He drove	He was driven
	Plural	1st	We drove	We were driven
		2nd	You drove	You were driven
		3rd	They drove	They were driven

(continued)

FIGURE 11–1.   Verb-Conjugation Chart

11

Grammar

TENSE	NUMBER	PERSON	ACTIVE VOICE	PASSIVE VOICE
Progressive past	Singular	1st	I was driving	I was being driven
		2nd	You were driving	You were being driven
		3rd	He was driving	He was being driven
	Plural	1st	We were driving	We were being driven
		2nd	You were driving	You were being driven
		3rd	They were driving	They were being driven
Future	Singular	1st	I will drive	I will be being driven
		2nd	You will drive	You will be being driven
		3rd	He will drive	He will be being driven
	Plural	1st	We will drive	We will be being driven
		2nd	You will drive	You will be being driven
		3rd	They will drive	They will be being driven
Progressive future	Singular	1st	I will be driving	I will have been driven
		2nd	You will be driving	You will have been driven
		3rd	He will be driving	He will have been driven
	Plural	1st	We will be driving	We will have been driven
		2nd	You will be driving	You will have been driven
		3rd	They will be driving	They will have been driven
Present perfect	Singular	1st	I have driven	I have been driven
		2nd	You have driven	You have been driven
		3rd	He has driven	He has been driven
	Plural	1st	We have driven	We have been driven
		2nd	You have driven	You have been driven
		3rd	They have driven	They have been driven
Past perfect	Singular	1st	I had driven	I had been driven
		2nd	You had driven	You had been driven
		3rd	He had driven	He had been driven
	Plural	1st	We had driven	We had been driven
		2nd	You had driven	You had been driven
		3rd	They had driven	They had been driven
Future perfect	Singular	1st	I will have driven	I will have been driven
		2nd	You will have driven	You will have been driven
		3rd	He will have driven	He will have been driven
	Plural	1st	We will have driven	We will have been driven
		2nd	You will have driven	You will have been driven
		3rd	They will have driven	They will have been driven

FIGURE 11–1.   Verb-Conjugation Chart (*continued*)

voice

In grammar, *voice* indicates the relation of the subject to the action of the verb. When the verb is in the *active voice*, the subject acts; when it is in the *passive voice*, the subject is acted upon.

ACTIVE　David Cohen *wrote* the newsletter article.
[The subject, *David Cohen*, performs the action; the verb *wrote* describes the action.]

PASSIVE　The newsletter article *was written* by David Cohen.
[The subject, the *newsletter article*, is acted upon; the verb *was written* describes the action.]

The two sentences say the same thing, but each has a different emphasis: the first emphasizes *David Cohen*; the second emphasizes *the newsletter article*. In business writing, it is often important to emphasize who or what performs an action. Further, the passive-voice version is indirect because it places the performer of the action behind the verb instead of in front of it. Because the active voice is generally more direct, more concise, and easier for readers to understand, use the active voice unless the passive voice is more appropriate, as described on page 358. Whether you use the active voice or the passive voice, be careful not to shift voices in a sentence.

* David Cohen corrected the inaccuracy as soon as ~~it was identified~~
identified it
~~by~~ the editor.
∧

(ESL) **TIPS FOR CHOOSING VOICE**

Different languages place different values on active-voice and passive-voice constructions. In some languages, the passive is used frequently; in others, hardly at all. As a nonnative speaker of English, you may have a tendency to follow the pattern of your native language. But remember, even though business writing may sometimes require the passive voice, active verbs are highly valued in English.

Using the Active Voice

Improving Clarity.　The active voice improves clarity and avoids confusion, especially in instructions and policies and procedures (Tab 3).

PASSIVE　Sections B and C *should be checked* for errors.
[Are they already checked?]

ACTIVE　*Check* sections B and C for errors.
[The performer of the action, *you*, is understood: (You) *Check* the sections.]

Active voice can also help avoid <u>dangling modifiers</u>.

> **PASSIVE** Hurrying to complete the work, the cables *were connected* improperly.
> [*Who* was hurrying? The implication is the cables were hurrying!]

> **ACTIVE** Hurrying to complete the work, the technician *connected* the cables improperly.
> [Here, *hurrying to complete the work* properly modifies the performer of the action: *the technician.*]

Highlighting Subjects.   One difficulty with passive sentences is that they can bury the performer of the action in expletives and prepositional phrases.

> **PASSIVE** It *was reported by* the agency that the new model is defective.

> **ACTIVE** The agency *reported* that the new model is defective.

Sometimes writers using the passive voice fail to name the performer—information that might be missed.

> **PASSIVE** The problem *was discovered* yesterday.

> **ACTIVE** The Maintenance Department *discovered* the problem yesterday.

Achieving Conciseness.   The active voice helps achieve <u>conciseness</u> (Tab 9) because it eliminates the need for an additional helping verb as well as an extra preposition to identify the performer of the action.

> **PASSIVE** Arbitrary changes in policy *are resented by* employees.

> **ACTIVE** Employees *resent* arbitrary changes in policy.

The active-voice version takes one verb (*resent*); the passive-voice version takes two verbs (*are resented*) and an extra preposition (*by*).

Using the Passive Voice

The passive voice is sometimes effective or even necessary. Indeed, for reasons of tact and diplomacy, you might need to use the passive voice to avoid accusing others.

> **ACTIVE** Your staff did not meet the quota last month.

> **PASSIVE** The quota was not met last month.

■ ETHICS NOTE Do not use the passive voice to evade responsibility or obscure an issue. See also <u>ethics in writing</u> (Tab 1).

- Several mistakes were made. [*Who* made the mistakes?]
- It has been decided. [*Who* has decided?]

When the performer of the action is either unknown or unimportant, of course, use the passive voice. (The copper mine *was discovered* in 1929.) When the performer of the action is less important than the receiver of that action, the passive voice is sometimes more appropriate. (Ann Bryant *was presented* with an award by the president.)

When you are explaining an operation in which the reader is not actively involved or when you are explaining a process or a procedure, the passive voice may be more appropriate. In the following example, anyone—it really does not matter who—could be the performer of the action.

- Area strip mining *is used* in regions of flat to gently rolling terrain, like that found in the Midwest. Depending on applicable reclamation laws, the topsoil *may be removed* from the area *to be mined*, *stored*, and later *reapplied* as surface material during reclamation of the mined land. After the removal of the topsoil, a trench *is cut* through the overburden to expose the upper surface of the coal to be mined. The overburden from the first cut *is placed* on the unmined land adjacent to the cut. After the first cut *has been completed*, the coal *is removed*.

Do not, however, simply assume that any such explanation should be in the passive voice; in fact, as in the following example, the active voice is often more effective.

- In the operation of an internal combustion engine, an explosion in the combustion chamber *forces* the pistons down in the cylinders. The movement of the pistons in the cylinders *turns* the crankshaft.

Ask yourself, "Would it be of any advantage to the reader to know the performer of the action?" If the answer is yes, use the active voice, as in the previous example.

11

Grammar

12

Punctuation
and Mechanics

Preview

Understanding punctuation and mechanics is essential to you as a writer because it enables you to communicate clearly and precisely. Punctuation is a system of symbols that helps readers understand the structural relationship within a sentence. The use of punctuation is determined by grammatical convention and a writer's intention.

Marks of punctuation may link, separate, enclose, indicate omissions, terminate, and classify. This section provides detailed information on each of the thirteen marks of punctuation as well as entries on the mechanics of writing, including the use of <u>abbreviations</u>, <u>capitalization</u>, <u>contractions</u>, <u>dates</u>, <u>ellipses</u>, <u>italics</u>, and <u>numbers</u>.

abbreviations

Abbreviations are shortened versions of words or combinations of the first letters of words (Avenue/Ave., Corporation/Corp., hypertext markup language/HTML). Abbreviations formed by combining the first letter or letters of several words are called *acronyms*. Acronyms are pronounced as words and are written without periods (*d*isk *o*perating *s*ystem/ DOS, *l*ocal *a*rea *n*etwork/LAN, *s*elf-contained *u*nderwater *b*reathing *a*pparatus/scuba). Abbreviations that are formed by combining the initial letter of each word in a multiword term are called *initialisms*. Initialisms are pronounced as separate letters (*f*or *y*our *i*nformation/FYI, *p*ost *m*eridiem/p.m.).

Abbreviations, if used appropriately, can be convenient for both the reader and the writer. Like symbols, they can be important space savers in business writing because it is often necessary to provide the maximum amount of information in a limited amount of space.

Using Abbreviations

The most important consideration in the use of abbreviations is whether they will be understood by your <u>readers</u> (Tab 1). In business, industry, and government, specialists and people working together on particular projects, for example, often use abbreviations. Like <u>jargon</u> (Tab 9), shortened forms will be easily understood within a group of specialists— outside of the group, however, they might be incomprehensible. In fact, abbreviations can be easily overused, either as an <u>affectation</u> (Tab 9) or in a misguided attempt to make writing concise, especially in <u>e-mail</u> (Tab 6). Remember that memos, e-mail, or reports addressed to specific people may be read by other people—you must consider those secondary readers as well. A good rule to follow: when in doubt, spell it out.

Writer's Checklist: Using Abbreviations

☑ Except for commonly used abbreviations (U.S., a.m.), spell out a term to be abbreviated the first time it is used, followed by the abbreviation in parentheses. Thereafter, the abbreviation may be used alone.

☑ In long documents, repeat the full term in parentheses after the abbreviation at regular intervals to remind readers of the abbreviation's meaning, as in "Remember to submit the CAR (Capital Appropriations Request) by . . ."

☑ Do not add an additional period at the end of a sentence that ends with an abbreviation. (The official name of the company is DataBase, Inc.)

12

Punctuation
and Mechanics

Writer's Checklist: Using Abbreviations (continued)

☑ For abbreviations specific to your profession or discipline, use a style guide provided by your professional organization or company. (A list of style guides appears at the end of <u>documenting sources</u>, Tab 2.)

☑ Write acronyms in capital letters without periods. The only exceptions are acronyms that have become accepted as common nouns, which are written in lowercase letters, such as *laser* (*light amplification by stimulated emission of radiation*).

☑ Generally, use periods for lowercase initialisms (a.k.a., e.d.p., p.m.) but not for uppercase ones (GDP, IRA, UFO). Two exceptions are geographic names (U.S., U.K., E.U.) and formal expressions of academic degrees (B.A., M.B.A., Ph.D.).

☑ Form the plural of an acronym or initialism by adding a lowercase *s*. Do not use an <u>apostrophe</u> (CARs, DVDs).

☑ Do not make up your own abbreviations; they will confuse readers.

Forming Abbreviations

Names of Organizations.   A company may include in its name a term such as *Brothers, Incorporated, Corporation,* or *Company.* If the term is abbreviated in the official company name that appears on letterhead stationery or on its Web site, use the abbreviated form: *Bros., Inc., Corp.,* or *Co.* If the term is not abbreviated in the official name, spell it out in writing, except with addresses, footnotes, <u>bibliographies</u> (Tab 2), and <u>lists</u> (Tab 5) where abbreviations may be used. A similar guideline applies for use of an ampersand (&); that symbol should be used only if it appears in the official company name. For names of divisions within organizations, terms such as *Department* and *Division* should be abbreviated (*Dept.* and *Div.*) only when space is limited.

Measurements.   The following list contains some common abbreviations that are used with units of measurement. Notice that, except for abbreviations that may be confused with words (*in.* for *inch*), abbreviations of measurement do not require periods.

cal, calorie	min, minute
cm, centimeter	oz, ounce
doz or dz, dozen	ppm, parts per million
F, Fahrenheit	pt, pint
ft, foot (or feet)	qt, quart
gal., gallon	sec, second or secant
hr, hour	yd, yard
km, kilometer	yr, year
lb, pound	

Abbreviations of units of measure are identical in the singular and plural: 1 cm and 15 cm (not 15 *cms*).

Personal Names and Titles.   Personal names generally should not be abbreviated: Thomas (*not* Thos.) and William (*not* Wm.). An academic, civil, religious, or military title should be spelled out and in lowercase when it does not precede a name. (The *captain* wanted to check the orders.) When they precede names, some titles are customarily abbreviated (Dr. Smith, Mr. Mills, Ms. Katz). See also <u>Ms./Miss/Mrs.</u> (Tab 10).

An abbreviation of a title may follow the name; however, be certain that it does not duplicate a title before the name (Angeline Martinez, Ph.D., *or* Dr. Angeline Martinez). When addressing correspondence and including names in other documents, you normally should spell out titles (The Honorable Mary J. Holt; Professor Charles Matlin). (See also <u>correspondence</u>, Tab 6.) The following is a list of common abbreviations for personal and professional titles.

Atty.	Attorney
Dr.	Doctor (used for anyone with a doctorate)
Drs.	Plural of Dr.
Ed.D.	Doctor of Education
Jr.	Junior (used when a father with the same name is living)
M.A.	Master of Arts
M.B.A.	Master of Business Administration
M.D.	Doctor of Medicine
Messrs.	Plural of Mr.
M.S.	Master of Science
Ph.D.	Doctor of Philosophy (for many disciplines)
Rev.	Reverend
Sr.	Senior (used when a son with the same name is living)

Common Scholarly Abbreviations.   The following is a partial list of abbreviations commonly used in reference books and for documenting sources in research papers and reports. Other than in formal scholarly work, generally avoid such abbreviations.

anon.	anonymous
bibliog.	bibliography, bibliographer, bibliographic
ca., c.	*circa*, "about" (used with approximate dates: ca. 1756)
cf.	*confer*, "compare"
chap.	chapter
diss.	dissertation
ed., eds.	edited by, editor(s), edition(s)
e.g.	*exempli gratia*, "for example" (see <u>e.g./i.e.</u>, Tab 10)
esp.	especially
et al.	*et alii*, "and others"
etc.	*et cetera*, "and so forth" (see <u>etc.</u>, Tab 10)
ff.	and the following page(s) or line(s)

GPO	Government Printing Office, Washington, D.C.
i.e.	*id est,* "that is" (see e.g./i.e., Tab 10)
l., ll.	line, lines
MS, MSS	manuscript, manuscripts
n., nn.	note, notes (used immediately after page number: 56n., 56n.3, 56nn.3–5)
N.B., n.b.	*nota bene,* "take notice, mark well"
n.d.	no date (of publication)
n.p.	no place (of publication); no publisher; no page
p., pp.	page, pages
proc.	proceedings
pseud.	pseudonym
pub.	published by, publisher, publication
rev.	revised by, revised, revision; review, reviewed by (spell out "review" where "rev." might be ambiguous)
rpt.	reprinted by, reprint
sec., secs.	section, sections
sic	inserted in brackets ([*sic*]) after a misspelled or wrongly used word
supp., suppl.	supplement
trans.	translated by, translator, translation
UP	University Press (used in MLA style of documenting sources, Tab 2, as in Oxford UP)
viz.	*videlicet,* "namely"
vol., vols.	volume, volumes
vs., v.	*versus,* "against" (v. preferred in titles of legal cases)

☀ WEB LINK USING POSTAL ABBREVIATIONS

The U.S. Postal Service Web site specifies abbreviations for states and protectorates as well as streets and other geographical names. See <bedford stmartins.com/alred> and select *Links for Business Writing.*

12

apostrophes

An apostrophe (') is used to show possession, to indicate the omission of letters, and sometimes to indicate plurals.

Showing Possession

An apostrophe is used with an *s* to form the possessive case of some nouns (the *report's* title). For advice on using apostrophes to show possession, see possessive case (Tab 11).

Indicating Omission

An apostrophe is used to mark the omission of letters or numbers in a <u>contraction</u> or a date (can't, I'm, I'll; the class of '05).

Forming Plurals

The trend for indicating the plural forms of words mentioned as words, of numbers used as nouns, and of <u>abbreviations</u> shown as single or multiple letters is currently to add only *s* rather than using *'s*.

When a word (or letter) mentioned as a word is italicized, it is current usage to add *s* in roman type. (There were five *and*s in his first sentence.) Rather than using italics, you may place a word in quotation marks. If you choose this option, use an apostrophe and *s*. (There were five "and's" in his first sentence.) To indicate the plural of a number, add *s* (7s, the late 1990s). If the letter and the *s* form a word, you may want to consider using an apostrophe to avoid confusion (A's). Use *s* to pluralize an abbreviation that is in all capital letters or that ends with a capital letter (IOUs). However, if the abbreviated term contains periods, some writers use an apostrophe to prevent confusion. (The university awarded 34 Ph.D.'s last year.) Whatever practice you follow, be consistent.

---

brackets

The primary use of brackets ([ ]) is to enclose a word or words inserted by the writer or an editor into a quotation.

- The text stated, "Hypertext systems can be categorized as either modest [not modifiable] or robust [modifiable]."

Brackets are used to set off a parenthetical item within parentheses.

- We should be sure to give Emanuel Foose (and his brother Emilio [1812–1882]) credit for his role in founding the institute.

Brackets are also used to insert the Latin word *sic*, which is a scholarly <u>abbreviation</u> that indicates a writer has quoted material exactly as it appears in the original, even though it contains a misspelled or wrongly used word.

- Dr. Smith wrote that "the earth does not revolve around the son [*sic*] at a constant rate."

See also <u>quotations</u> (Tab 2).

capitalization

The use of capital, or uppercase, letters is determined by custom. Capital letters are used to call attention to certain words, such as proper nouns and the first word of a sentence. Use them carefully, especially when they affect a word's meaning (march/March, china/China, turkey/Turkey) and because a spell checker would fail to identify an error.

Proper Nouns

Proper nouns name specific persons, places, things, concepts, or qualities and are capitalized (Business Writing 205, Microsoft, Pat Wilde, Peru).

Common Nouns

Common nouns name general classes or categories of people, places, things, concepts, or qualities rather than specific ones and are not capitalized (business writing class, company, person, country).

First Words

The first letter of the first word in a sentence is always capitalized. (Of the plans submitted, ours is best.) The first word after a colon is capitalized when the colon introduces two or more complete sentences or if the colon precedes a statement requiring special emphasis. (The meeting will address only one issue: What is the firm's role in environmental protection?) If a subordinate element follows the colon or if the thought is closely related, use a lowercase letter following the colon. (We kept working for one reason: the approaching deadline.) The first word of a complete sentence in quotation marks is capitalized. (Albert Einstein stated, "Imagination is more important than knowledge.") The first word in the salutation (Dear Mr. Smith:) and complimentary close (Sincerely yours,) is capitalized. See also <u>correspondence</u> (Tab 6).

Specific Groups

Capitalize the names of ethnic groups, religions, and nationalities (Native American, Jewish, Italian). Do not capitalize the names of social and economic groups (middle class, working class, unemployed).

Specific Places

Capitalize the names of all political divisions (Ward Six, Chicago, Cook County, Illinois). Capitalize the names of geographic divisions (Europe, Asia, North America, the Middle East). Do not capitalize geographic features unless they are part of a proper name.

* The mountains in some areas, such as the *Great Smoky Mountains*, make television transmission difficult.

The words *north, south, east,* and *west* are capitalized when they refer to sections of the country. They are not capitalized when they refer to directions. (I may travel *north* when I relocate, but my family will remain in the *South.*)

Specific Institutions, Events, and Concepts

Capitalize the names of institutions, organizations, and associations (U.S. Department of Health and Human Services). An organization usually capitalizes the names of its internal divisions and departments (Aeronautics Division, Human Resources Department). Types of organizations are not capitalized unless they are part of an official name (a business communication association, the Association for Business Communication). Capitalize historical events (the Great Depression of the 1930s). Capitalize words that designate holidays, specific periods of time, months, or days of the week (Labor Day, the Renaissance, January, Monday). Do not capitalize seasons of the year (spring, autumn, winter, summer).

Capitalize the scientific names of classes, families, and orders but not the names of species or English derivatives of scientific names (Mammalia/mammal, Carnivora/carnivorous).

Titles of Works

Capitalize the initial letters of the first and last words of the title of a book, an article, a play, or a film, as well as all major words in the title. Do not capitalize articles (*a, an, the*), coordinating conjunctions (*and, but*), or prepositions unless they begin or end the title (*The Lives of a Cell*). Capitalize prepositions in titles when they contain more than four letters (*Between, Within, Until, After*), unless you are following a style that recommends otherwise. The same rules apply to the subject line of an e-mail (Tab 6) or a memo (Tab 6).

Personal, Professional, and Job Titles

Titles preceding proper names are capitalized (Ms. March, Senator Schumer). Appositives following proper names normally are not capitalized (Charles Schumer, *senator* from New York). However, the word *President* usually is capitalized when it refers to the chief executive of a national government.

Job titles used with personal names are capitalized (Ho-shik Kim, *Division Manager*). Job titles used without personal names are not capitalized. (The *division manager* will meet us tomorrow.) Use capital letters to designate family relationships only when they occur before a name or substitute for a name (my uncle, Uncle Fred).

Abbreviations

Capitalize <u>abbreviations</u> if the words they stand for would be capitalized, such as NYU (New York University).

Letters

Capitalize letters that serve as names or indicate shapes (vitamin B, T-square, U-turn, I-beam).

colons

The colon (:) is a mark of introduction that alerts readers to the close connection between the preceding statement and what follows.

Colons in Sentences

A colon links independent <u>clauses</u> (Tab 11) to words, phrases, clauses, or lists that identify, rename, explain, emphasize, amplify, or illustrate the sentence that precedes the colon.

- Two topics will be discussed: *the new accounting system and the new bookkeeping procedures.* [phrases that identify]

- Only one thing will satisfy Mr. Sturgess: *our finished report.* [appositive (renaming) phrase for emphasis]

- Any organization is confronted with two separate, though related, information problems: *it must maintain an effective internal communication system and an effective external communication system.* [clause to amplify and explain]

- Heart patients should make key lifestyle changes: *stop smoking, exercise regularly, eat a low-fat diet, and reduce stress.* [list to identify and illustrate]

Colons in Salutations, Titles, Citations, and Numbers

A colon follows the salutation in business <u>correspondence</u> (Tab 6), even when the salutation refers to a person by first name.

- Dear Professor Jeffers: *or* Dear Georgia:

Colons separate titles from subtitles and separate sections of works in citations. See also <u>documenting sources</u> (Tab 2).

- " 'We Regret to Inform You': Toward a New Theory of Negative Messages"

- Genesis 10:16 [chapter 10, verse 16]

Colons separate numbers in time references and indicate numerical ratios.

- 9:30 a.m. [9 hours and 30 minutes]
- The cement is mixed with water and sand at 5:3:1.
  [The colon is read as the word *to*.]

Punctuation and Capitalization with Colons

A colon always goes outside <u>quotation marks</u>.

- This was the real meaning of the CEO's "suggestion": the division must show a profit by the end of the year.

As this example shows, the first word after a colon may be capitalized if the statement following the colon is a complete sentence and functions as a formal resolution or question. If the element following the colon is subordinate, however, use a lowercase letter to begin that element. See also <u>capitalization</u>.

- We have only one way to stay within our present budget: to reduce expenditures for research and development.

Unnecessary Colons

Do not place a colon between a <u>verb</u> (Tab 11) and its objects.

- Three fluids that clean pipettes are: water, alcohol, and acetone.

Likewise, do not use a colon between a <u>preposition</u> (Tab 11) and its object.

- I may be transferred to: Tucson, Boston, or Miami.

Do not insert a colon between *including, such as*, or *for example* and a simple list.

- Office computers should not be used for activities such as: personal e-mail, Web surfing, Internet shopping, and playing computer games.

One common exception is made when a <u>verb</u> (Tab 11) or <u>preposition</u> (Tab 11) is followed by a stacked <u>list</u> (Tab 5); however, it may be possible to introduce the list with a complete sentence instead.

- *The following corporations* ~~Corporations that~~ manufacture computers ~~include~~:

| Apple | Compaq | Dell |
| Gateway | IBM | Micron |

comma splice

A comma splice is a grammatical error in which two independent clauses (Tab 11) are joined by only a comma.

INCORRECT   It was 500 miles to the facility, we arranged to fly.

A comma splice can be corrected in several ways.

1. Substitute a semicolon, a semicolon and a conjunctive adverb (Tab 11), or a coordinating conjunction (Tab 11).

   ● It was 500 miles to the facility; we arranged to fly.

   ● It was 500 miles to the facility; *therefore*, we arranged to fly.

   ● It was 500 miles to the facility, *so* we arranged to fly.

2. Create two sentences.

   ● It was 500 miles to the facility. *We* arranged to fly.

3. Subordinate one clause to the other. (See subordination, Tab 9.)

   ● *Because* it was 500 miles to the facility, we arranged to fly.

See also sentence construction (Tab 11) and sentence faults (Tab 11).

commas

Like all punctuation, the comma (,) helps readers understand the writer's meaning and prevents ambiguity. Notice how the comma helps make the meaning clear in the second example.

AMBIGUOUS   To be successful managers with MBAs must continue to learn.

CLEAR   To be successful, managers with MBAs must continue to learn.
[The comma makes clear where the main part of the sentence begins.]

Do not follow the old myth that you should insert a comma wherever you would pause if you were speaking. Although you would pause wherever you encounter a comma, you should not insert a comma wherever you might pause. Effective use of commas depends on an understanding of <u>sentence construction</u> (Tab 11).

Linking Independent Clauses

Use a comma before a coordinating conjunction (*and, but, or, nor,* and sometimes *so, yet,* and *for*) that links independent <u>clauses</u> (Tab 11).

- The new microwave disinfection system was delivered, *but* the installation will require an additional week.

However, if two independent clauses are short and closely related—and there is no danger of confusing the reader—the comma may be omitted. Both of the following examples are correct.

- The cable snapped and the power failed.
- The cable snapped, and the power failed.

Enclosing Elements

Commas are used to enclose nonessential information in nonrestrictive clauses, phrases, and parenthetical elements. See also <u>restrictive and nonrestrictive elements</u> (Tab 11).

- Our new factory, *which began operations last month,* should add 25 percent to total output. [nonrestrictive clause]
- The accountant, *working quickly and efficiently,* finished early. [nonrestrictive phrase]
- We can, *of course,* expect their lawyer to call us. [parenthetical element]

Yes and *no* are set off by commas in such uses as the following:

- I agree with you, *yes.*
- *No,* I do not think we can finish as soon as we would like.

A direct address should be enclosed in commas.

- You will note, *Mark,* that the surface of the brake shoe complies with the specification.

An appositive phrase (which re-identifies another expression in the sentence) is enclosed in commas.

- Our company, *Envirex Medical Systems,* won several awards last year.

Interrupting parenthetical and transitional words or phrases are usually set off with commas. See also <u>transition</u> (Tab 9).

- The report, *therefore,* needs to be revised.

Commas are omitted when the word or phrase does not interrupt the continuity of thought.

- I *therefore* suggest that we begin construction.

For other means of punctuating parenthetical elements, see <u>dashes</u> and <u>parentheses</u>.

Introducing Elements

Clauses and Phrases.   Generally, place a comma after an introductory clause or phrase, especially if it is long, to identify where the introductory element ends and where the main part of the sentence begins.

- *Because we have not yet contained the new strain of influenza,* we recommend vaccination for high-risk patients.

A long modifying phrase that precedes the main clause should always be followed by a comma.

- *During the first series of field-performance tests at our Colorado proving ground,* the new engine failed to meet our expectations.

When an introductory phrase is short and closely related to the main clause, the comma may be omitted.

- *In two seconds* a 5°C temperature rise occurs in the test tube.

A comma should always follow an absolute phrase, which modifies the whole sentence.

- *The tests completed,* we organized the data for the final report.

Words and Quotations.   Certain types of introductory words are followed by a comma. One example is a transitional word or phrase (*however, in addition*) that connects the preceding clause or sentence with the thought that follows.

- *Furthermore,* steel can withstand a humidity of 99 percent, provided that there is no chloride or sulfur dioxide in the atmosphere.

- *For example,* this change will make us more competitive in the global marketplace.

When <u>adverbs</u> (Tab 11) closely modify the verb or the entire sentence, they should not be followed by a comma.

- *Perhaps* we can still solve the turnover problem. *Certainly* we should try. [*Perhaps* and *certainly* closely modify each statement.]

A proper noun used in an introductory direct address is followed by a comma, as is an interjection (such as *oh, well, why, indeed, yes,* and *no*).

- *Nancy,* enclosed is the article you asked me to review. [direct address]

- *Indeed,* I will ensure that your request is forwarded. [interjection]

Use a comma to separate a direct quotation from its introduction.

- Morton and Lucia White said, "People live in cities but dream of the countryside."

Do not use a comma when giving an indirect quotation. See also <u>quotations</u> (Tab 2).

- Morton and Lucia White said that people dream of the countryside, even though they live in cities.

Separating Items in a Series

Although the comma before the last item in a series is sometimes omitted, it is generally clearer to include it.

- Random House, Bantam, Doubleday, and Dell were individual publishing companies.
  [Without the final comma, "Doubleday and Dell" might refer to one company or two.]

Phrases and clauses in coordinate series are also punctuated with commas.

- Plants absorb noxious gases, act as receptors of dirt particles, and cleanse the air of other impurities.

When phrases or clauses in a series contain commas, use semicolons rather than commas to separate each item.

- Our new products include amitriptyline, which has sold very well; dipyridamole, which has not sold well; and cholestyramine, which was just introduced.

When <u>adjectives</u> (Tab 11) modifying the same noun can be reversed and make sense, or when they can be separated by *and* or *or*, they should be separated by commas.

- The drawing was of a *modern, sleek, swept-wing* airplane.

When an adjective modifies a phrase, no comma is required.

- She was investigating the *damaged inventory-control system.*
  [The adjective *damaged* modifies the phrase *inventory-control system.*]

Never separate a final adjective from its noun.

- He is a conscientious, honest, reliable, worker.

Clarifying and Contrasting

Use a comma to separate two contrasting thoughts or ideas.

- The project was finished on time, but not within the budget.

Use a comma after an independent clause that is only loosely related to the dependent clause that follows it or that could be misread without the comma.

- I should be able to finish the plan by July, even though I lost time because of illness.

Showing Omissions

A comma sometimes replaces a verb in certain elliptical constructions.

- Some were punctual; *others, late.* [The comma replaces *were.*]

It is better, however, to avoid such constructions in business writing.

Using with Numbers and Names

Commas are conventionally used to separate distinct items. Use commas between the elements of an address written on the same line (but not between the state and the zip code).

- Kristen James, 4119 Mill Road, Dayton, Ohio 45401

A full date that is written in the month-day-year format uses a comma preceding and following the year.

- November 30, 2015, is the payoff date.

Do not use commas for dates in the day-month-year format, which is used in many parts of the world and by the U.S. military. See also <u>international correspondence</u> (Tab 6).

- Note that 30 November 2015 is the payoff date.

Do not use commas if only the day or year is included. See also <u>dates</u>.

- The target date of May 2006 is optimistic, so I would like to meet on March 4 to discuss our options.

Use commas to separate the elements of Arabic numbers.

- 1,528,200 feet

However, because many countries use the comma as the decimal marker, use spaces or periods rather than commas in international documents.

- 1.528.200 meters *or* 1 528 200 meters

A comma may be substituted for the colon in the salutation of a personal letter or <u>e-mail</u> (Tab 6). Do not, however, use a comma in the salutation of a business letter or e-mail, even if you use the person's first name.

- Dear Marie, [personal letter or e-mail]
- Dear Marie: [business letter or e-mail]

Use commas to separate the elements of geographic names.

- Toronto, Ontario, Canada

Use a comma to separate names that are reversed or that are followed by an abbreviation.

- Smith, Alvin
- Jane Rogers, Ph.D.

Using with Other Punctuation

Conjunctive adverbs (*however, nevertheless, consequently, for example, on the other hand*) that join independent clauses are preceded by a <u>semicolon</u> and followed by a comma. Such adverbs function both as <u>modifiers</u> (Tab 11) and as connectives.

- The idea is good; *however,* our budget is not sufficient.

As shown earlier in this entry, use semicolons rather than commas to separate items in a series when the items themselves contain commas.

When a comma should follow a phrase or clause that ends with words in <u>parentheses</u>, the comma always appears outside the closing parenthesis.

- Although we left late (at 7:30 p.m.), we arrived in time for the keynote address.

Commas always go inside <u>quotation marks</u>.

- The operator placed the discharge bypass switch at "normal," which triggered a second discharge.

Except with <u>abbreviations</u>, a comma should not be used with a <u>dash</u>, an <u>exclamation mark</u>, a <u>period</u>, or a <u>question mark</u>.

- "Have you finished the project?/" I asked.

Avoiding Unnecessary Commas

A number of common writing errors involve placing commas where they do not belong. As stated earlier, such errors often occur because writers assume that a pause in a sentence should be indicated by a comma.

Do not place a comma between a subject and verb or between a verb and its <u>object</u> (Tab 11).

- The conditions at the test site in the Arctic,/ made accurate readings difficult.
- She has often said,/ that one company's failure is another's opportunity.

Do not use a comma between the elements of a compound subject or a compound predicate consisting of only two elements.

- The director of the design department,/ and the supervisor of the quality-control section were opposed to the new schedules.
- The design director listed five major objections,/ and asked that the new schedule be reconsidered.

Do not include a comma after a coordinating conjunction such as *and* or *but*.

- The chairperson formally adjourned the meeting, but,/ the members of the committee continued to argue.

Do not place a comma before the first item or after the last item of a series.

- The new products we are considering include,/ calculators, scanners, and cameras.
- It was a fast, simple, inexpensive,/ process.

Do not use a comma to separate a prepositional phrase from the rest of the sentence unnecessarily.

- We discussed the final report,/ on the new project.

contractions

A contraction is a shortened spelling of a word or phrase with an <u>apostrophe</u> substituting for the missing letter or letters (cannot/can't; have not/ haven't; will not/won't; it is/it's). Contractions are often used in speech and informal writing; they are generally not appropriate in reports, proposals, and formal correspondence. See also business writing style (Tab 9).

dashes

The dash (—) can perform all the punctuation duties of linking, separating, and enclosing. The dash, sometimes indicated by two consecutive hyphens, can also indicate the omission of letters (Mr. A— admitted his error).

Use the dash cautiously to indicate more emphasis (Tab 9), informality, or abruptness than the other punctuation marks would show.

A dash can emphasize a sharp turn in thought.

* The project will end May 15—unless we receive additional funding.

A dash can indicate an emphatic pause.

* The project will begin—after we are under contract.

Sometimes, to emphasize contrast, a dash is used with *but*.

* We completed the survey quickly—but the results were not accurate.

A dash can be used before a final summarizing statement or before repetition that has the effect of an afterthought.

* It was hot near the ovens—steaming hot.

Such a statement may also complete the meaning of the clause preceding the dash.

* We try to speak as we write—or so we believe.

Dashes set off parenthetical elements more sharply and emphatically than commas. Unlike dashes, parentheses tend to reduce the importance of what they enclose. Compare the following sentences:

* Only one person—the president—can authorize such activity.
* Only one person, the president, can authorize such activity.
* Only one person (the president) can authorize such activity.

Dashes can be used to set off parenthetical elements that contain commas.

* Three of the applicants—John Evans, Rosalita Fontiana, and Kyong-Shik Choi—seem well qualified for the job.

The first word after a dash is capitalized only if it is a proper noun (Tab 11).

dates

In the United States, full dates are generally written in the month-day-year format, with a comma preceding and following the year. But commas are not used for dates in the day-month-year format, which is used in many parts of the world and by the U.S. military.

- November 30, 2015, is the payoff date.
- Note that 30 November 2015 is the payoff date.

No commas are used if only the day or year is included.

- The target date of May 2006 is optimistic, so I would like to meet on March 4 to discuss our options.

When writing days of the month without the year, use the cardinal number (March 4) rather than the ordinal number (March 4th). Of course, in speech or <u>presentations</u> (Tab 8), use the ordinal number ("March fourth").

Never use the strictly numerical form for dates (11/30/06) in business writing because the date is not always immediately clear, especially in <u>international correspondence</u> (Tab 6). Writing out the name of the month makes the date immediately clear to all readers.

Centuries often cause confusion with numbers because their spelled-out forms, which are not capitalized, do not correspond with their numeral designations. The twentieth century, for example, is the 1900s: 1900–1999.

When the century is written as a noun, do not use a <u>hyphen</u>.

- During the twentieth century, technology transformed business practices.

When the centuries are written as adjectives, however, use hyphens.

- Twenty-first-century technology relies on dependable power sources.

ellipses

An ellipsis is the omission of words from quoted material; it is indicated by three spaced periods called *ellipsis points* (. . .). When you use ellipsis points, omit marks of internal punctuation at the point of omission, unless they are necessary for clarity or the omitted material comes at the end of a quoted sentence.

ORIGINAL TEXT	"Promotional material is sometimes charged for, particularly in high volume distribution to schools, although prices for these publications are much lower than the development costs when all factors are considered."
WITH OMISSION AND ELLIPSIS POINTS	"Promotional material is sometimes charged for . . . although prices for these publications are much lower than the development costs. . . ."

Notice that the final period is retained and what remains of the quotation is grammatically complete. When the omitted part of the quotation is preceded by a period, retain the period and add the three ellipsis points after it.

ORIGINAL TEXT	"Of the 172 major ethics cases reported, 57 percent were found to involve unsubstantiated concerns. Misinformation was the cause of unfounded concerns of misconduct in 72 cases. Forty-four cases, or 26 percent of the total cases reported, involved incidents partly substantiated by ethics officers as serious misconduct."
WITH OMISSION AND ELLIPSIS POINTS	"Of the 172 major ethics cases reported, 57 percent were found to involve unsubstantiated concerns. . . . Forty-four cases, or 26 percent of the total cases reported, involved incidents partly substantiated by ethics officers as serious misconduct."

Do not use ellipsis points when the beginning of a quoted sentence is omitted. Notice the comma is dropped to prevent a grammatical error. See also quotations (Tab 2).

- The ethics report states that "26 percent of the total cases reported involved incidents partly substantiated by ethics officers as serious misconduct."

exclamation marks

The exclamation mark (!) indicates strong feeling, urgency, elation, or surprise (*Hurry! Great! Wow!*). However, it cannot make an argument more convincing, lend force to a weak statement, or call attention to an intended irony.

An exclamation mark can be used after a whole sentence or an element of a sentence.

- This meeting—please note it well!—concerns our budget deficit.

When used with quotation marks, the exclamation mark goes outside, unless what is quoted is an exclamation.

- The manager yelled, "Get in here!" Then Ben, according to Ray, "jumped like a kangaroo"!

In instructional writing, the exclamation mark is often used in cautions and warnings (*Danger! Stop!*).

hyphens

The hyphen (-) serves both to link and to separate words. The hyphen, for example, joins compound words (able-bodied; self-contained; self-esteem) and forms compound numbers from twenty-one through ninety-nine and fractions when they are written out (three-quarters). Two consecutive hyphens indicate a <u>dash</u>.

Hyphens Used with Modifiers

Two- and three-word <u>modifiers</u> (Tab 11) that express a single thought are hyphenated when they precede a <u>noun</u> (Tab 11). (It was a *well-written* report.) However, a modifying phrase is not hyphenated when it follows the noun it modifies. (The report was *well written*.) If each of the words can modify the noun without the aid of the other modifying word or words, do not use a hyphen (a *new laser* printer). If the first word is an <u>adverb</u> (Tab 11) ending in -*ly*, do not use a hyphen (a *privately* held company). A hyphen is always used as part of a letter or number modifier (9-inch; A-frame). In a series of unit modifiers that all have the same term following the hyphen, the term following the hyphen need not be repeated throughout the series; for greater smoothness and brevity, use the term only at the end of the series. (The third-, fourth-, and fifth-floor rooms were recently painted.)

Hyphens Used with Prefixes and Suffixes

A hyphen is used with a prefix when the root word is a proper noun (pre-Columbian; anti-American; post-Newtonian). A hyphen may be used when the prefix ends and the root word begins with the same vowel (anti-inflammatory). A hyphen is used when *ex*- means "former" (ex-president; ex-spouse). A hyphen may be used to emphasize a prefix. (She was anti-everything.) The suffix -*elect* is hyphenated (president-elect).

Hyphens and Clarity

The presence or absence of a hyphen can alter the meaning of a sentence.

AMBIGUOUS   We need a biological waste management system.

That sentence could mean one of two things: (1) We need a system to manage "biological waste," or (2) We need a "biological" system to manage waste.

CLEAR   We need a biological-waste management system.

CLEAR   We need a biological waste-management system.

To avoid confusion, some words and modifiers should always be hyphenated. *Re-cover* does not mean the same thing as *recover*, for example; the same is true of *re-sent* and *resent*, *re-form* and *reform*, *re-sign* and *resign*.

italics

Italics is a style of type used to denote <u>emphasis</u> (Tab 9) and to distinguish foreign expressions, book titles, and certain other elements. *This sentence is printed in italics.* Italic type is signaled by underlining in a manuscript submitted for publication or where italic font is not available (see also <u>e-mail</u>, Tab 6). You may need to italicize words that require special emphasis in a sentence. (Contrary to projections, sales have *not* improved.) Do not overuse italics for emphasis, however. (*This* will hurt *you* more than *me*.)

Foreign Words and Phrases

Foreign words and phrases that have not been assimilated into the English language are italicized (*sine qua non, coup de grâce, in re, in camera*). Foreign words that have been fully assimilated into the language need not be italicized. A word may be considered assimilated if it appears in most standard dictionaries and is familiar to most readers (cliché, etiquette, vis-à-vis, de facto, siesta).

Titles

Italicize the titles of separately published documents, such as books, periodicals, newspapers, pamphlets, brochures, legal cases, movies, and television programs.

- *Turning Workplace Conflict into Collaboration* by Joyce Richards was reviewed in the *New York Times*.

<u>Abbreviations</u> of such titles are italicized if their spelled-out forms would be italicized.

- The *NYT* is one of the nation's oldest newspapers.

12

Punctuation
and Mechanics

Italicize the titles of compact discs, videotapes, plays, long poems, paintings, sculptures, and musical works.

CD-ROM	*Computer Security Tutorial on CD-ROM*
PLAY	Arthur Miller's *Death of a Salesman*
LONG POEM	T. S. Eliot's *The Wasteland*
MUSICAL WORK	Gershwin's *Porgy and Bess*

Use <u>quotation marks</u> for parts of publications, such as chapters of books and articles or sections within periodicals.

- "Bad Writing" was an article by Barbara Wallraff in the "On Language" column of the *New York Times*.

Titles of reports, short poems, musical works, and songs are also enclosed in quotation marks.

REPORT	"Analysis of Ethics Cases at CGE Corporation"
SHORT POEM	Yusef Komunyakaa's "Elegy for Thelonious"
SONG	Bob Dylan's "Like a Rolling Stone"

Exceptions are titles of holy books and legislative documents, which are not italicized or placed in quotation marks (Old Testament, Magna Carta).

Proper Names

The names of ships, trains, and aircraft (but not the companies or governments that own them) are italicized (U.S. Aircraft Carrier *Independence*; U.S. Space Shuttle *Endeavour*). Craft that are known by model or serial designations are not italicized (DC-7; Boeing 747).

Words, Letters, and Figures

Words, letters, and figures discussed as such are italicized.

- The word *inflammable* is often misinterpreted.
- The *S* and *6* keys on my keyboard do not function.

Subheads

Subheads in a report are sometimes italicized.

- *Training Managers.* We are leading the way in developing first-line managers who not only are professionally competent but. . . .

See also <u>headings</u> (Tab 5) and <u>layout and design</u> (Tab 5).

numbers

The standards for using numbers vary; however, unless you are following an organizational or professional style manual, observe the following guidelines.

Numerals or Words

Write numbers from zero to ten as words, and write numbers above ten as numerals.

- I rehearsed my presentation *three* times.
- The meeting was attended by *150* people.

Spell out numbers that begin a sentence, however, even if they would otherwise be written as figures.

- *One hundred and fifty* people attended the meeting.

If spelling out such a number seems awkward, rewrite the sentence so that the number does not appear at the beginning.

Spell out approximate numbers.

- We've had *over a thousand* requests this month.

In most writing, spell out ordinal numbers, which express degree or sequence (first, second, 27th, 42nd), when they are single words (our *third* draft) or when they modify a century (the *twenty-first* century). However,

---

ESL TIPS FOR PUNCTUATING NUMBERS

Some rules for punctuating numbers in English are summarized as follows.

Use a comma to separate numbers with four or more digits into groups of three, starting from the right (*5,289,112,001* atoms).

Do not use a comma in years, house numbers, zip codes, and page numbers.

- June *2005*
- *92401* East Alameda Drive
- The zip code is *91601*.
- Page *1204*

Use a period to represent the decimal point (*4.2* percent; *$3,742,097.43*). See also <u>global graphics</u> (Tab 5).

avoid ordinal numbers in dates on correspondence (use March 30 or 30 March, not March 30th).

When several numbers appear in the same sentence or paragraph, write them the same way, regardless of other rules and guidelines.

- The company employs *271* people, leases *7* warehouses, and owns *150* trucks.

Plurals

Indicate the plural of numerals by adding *-s* (7s, the late 1990s). Form the plural of a written number (like any noun) by adding *-s* or *-es* or by dropping *-y* and adding *-ies* (elevens, sixes, twenties). See also <u>apostrophes</u>.

Measurements

Express units of measurement as numerals (3 miles, 45 cubic feet, 9 meters). When numbers run together in the same phrase, write one as a numeral and the other as a word.

- The order was for ~~12~~ *twelve* 6-foot tables.

Generally give percentages as numerals and write out the word *percent*, except when the number is in a table. (Approximately *85 percent* of the land has been sold.)

Fractions

Express fractions as numerals when they are written with whole numbers (27½ inches, 4¼ miles). Spell out fractions when they are expressed without a whole number (one-fourth, seven-eighths). Always write decimal numbers as numerals (5.21 meters).

Money

In general, use numerals to express exact or approximate amounts of money.

- We need to charge $28.95 per unit.
- The new system costs $60,000.

Use words to express indefinite amounts of money.

- The printing system may cost several thousand dollars.

Use numbers and words for rounded amounts of money over one million dollars.

- The contract is worth $6.8 million.

Use numbers for more complex or exact amounts.

- The corporation paid $2,452,500 in taxes last year.

For amounts under a dollar, ordinarily use numerals and the word *cents* (The pens cost 50 cents each), unless other figures that require dollar signs appear in the same sentence.

- The business-card holders cost $10.49 each, the pens cost $.50 each, and the pencil-cup holders cost $6.49 each.

Time

Express hours and minutes as numerals when a.m. or p.m. follows (11:30 a.m., 7:30 p.m.). Spell out time that is not followed by a.m. or p.m. (four o'clock, eleven o'clock).

Dates

In the United States <u>dates</u> are usually written in a month-day-year sequence (August 26, 2006). Never use the strictly numerical form for dates (8/26/06) in business writing because the date is not always immediately clear, especially in <u>international correspondence</u> (Tab 6).

Addresses

Spell out numbered streets from one to ten unless space is at a premium (East Tenth Street). Write building numbers as numerals. The only exception is the building number *one* (4862 East Monument Street; One East Monument Street). Write highway numbers as numerals (U.S. 40, Ohio 271, I-94).

Documents

In manuscripts, page numbers are written as numerals, but chapter and volume numbers may appear as numerals or words (page 37, Chapter 2 or Chapter Two, Volume 1 or Volume One). Express figure and table numbers as numerals (Figure 4 and Table 3). Do not follow a word representing a number with a numeral in parentheses that represents the same number. Doing so is redundant.

- Send five (5) copies of the report.

parentheses

Parentheses are used to enclose explanatory or digressive words, phrases, or sentences. Material in parentheses often clarifies or defines the preceding text without altering its meaning.

- She severely bruised her shin (or *tibia*) in the accident.

Parenthetical information may not be essential to a sentence — in fact, parentheses deemphasize the enclosed material — but it may be interesting or helpful to some readers.

Parenthetical material does not affect the punctuation of a sentence. If a parenthesis appears at the end of a sentence, the ending punctuation should appear after the parenthesis. Likewise, a <u>comma</u> following a parenthetical word, phrase, or clause appears outside the closing parenthesis.

- She severely bruised her shin (or *tibia*), and he tore the cartilage (or *meniscus*) in his knee.

When a complete sentence within parentheses stands independently, however, the ending punctuation goes inside the final parenthesis.

- The project director listed the problems her staff faced. (This was the third time she had complained to the board.)

Parentheses also are used to enclose numerals or letters that indicate sequence.

- The following sections deal with (1) preparation, (2) research, (3) organization, (4) writing, and (5) revision.

Use <u>brackets</u> to set off a parenthetical item that is already within parentheses.

- We should be sure to give Emanuel Foose (and his brother Emilio [1812–1882]) credit for his part in founding the institute.

See also <u>documenting sources</u> (Tab 2) and <u>numbers</u>.

periods

A period usually indicates the end of a declarative or an imperative sentence. Periods also link when used as leaders (for example, in a table of contents) and indicate omissions when used in <u>ellipses</u>. Periods may also end questions that are actually polite requests and questions to which an affirmative response is assumed. (Will you please send me the financial statement.) See also <u>sentence construction</u> (Tab 11).

Periods in Quotations

Use a <u>comma</u>, not a period, after a declarative sentence that is quoted in the context of another sentence.

- "There is every chance of success," she stated.

A period is conventionally placed inside <u>quotation marks</u>. See also <u>quotations</u> (Tab 2).

- He stated clearly, "My vote is yes."

Periods with Parentheses

If a sentence ends with a parenthesis, the period should follow the parenthesis.

- The institute was founded by Harry Denman (1902–1972).

When a complete sentence within <u>parentheses</u> stands independently, the period (or other ending punctuation) goes inside the final parenthesis.

- The project director listed the problems her staff faced. (This was the third time she had complained to the board.)

Other Uses of Periods

Use periods after initials in names (Wilma T. Grant, J. P. Morgan). Use periods as decimal points with <u>numbers</u> (27.3 degrees Celsius, $540.26, 6.9 percent). Use periods to indicate <u>abbreviations</u> (Ms., Dr., Inc.). When a sentence ends with an abbreviation that ends with a period, do not add another period. (Please meet me at 3:30 p.m.) Use periods following the numerals in a numbered list.

- 1. Enter your name.
  2. Enter your address.
  3. Enter your telephone number.

Period Faults

The incorrect use of a period is sometimes referred to as a *period fault*. When a period is inserted prematurely, the result is a <u>sentence fragment</u> (Tab 11).

FRAGMENT	After a long day at the office during which we finished the quarterly report. We left hurriedly for home.
SENTENCE	After a long day at the office, during which we finished the quarterly report, we left hurriedly for home.

When two independent clauses are joined without any punctuation, the result is a *fused* or *run-on* sentence. Adding a period between the clauses is one way to correct a run-on sentence.

RUN-ON	Bill was late for ten days in a row Ms. Sturgess had to fire him.
CORRECT	Bill was late for ten days in a row. Ms. Sturgess had to fire him.

Other options are to add a comma and a coordinating conjunction (*and, but, for, or, nor, so, yet*) between the clauses, to add a <u>semicolon</u>, or to add a semicolon with a conjunctive <u>adverb</u> (Tab 11), such as *therefore* or *however*.

question marks

The question mark (?) has several uses. Use a question mark to end a sentence that is a direct question. (Where did you put the tax report?) However, never use a question mark to end a sentence that is an indirect question.

- He asked me whether sales had increased this year.

Use a question mark to end a statement that has an interrogative meaning — a statement that is declarative in form but asks a question. (The tax report is finished?) Use a question mark to end an interrogative clause within a declarative sentence.

- It was not until July (or was it August?) that we submitted the report.

When a directive is phrased as a question, a question mark is not necessary.

- Will you make sure that the system is operational by August 15.

A request, however, almost always requires a question mark.

- Will you e-mail me if your entire shipment does not arrive by June 10?

Question marks may follow a series of separate items within an interrogative sentence.

- Do you remember the date of the contract? Its terms? Whether you signed it?

Retain the question mark in a title that is being cited, even though the sentence in which it appears has not ended. (*Can Your Investments Be Protected?* is the title of her book.)

When used with <u>quotations</u> (Tab 2), the placement of the question mark is important. When the writer is asking a question, the question mark belongs outside the <u>quotation marks</u>. (Did she say, "I don't think the project should continue"?) If the quotation itself is a question, the question mark goes inside the quotation marks. (She asked, "When will we go?") If both cases apply — the writer is asking a question and the quotation itself is a question — use a single question mark inside the quotation marks. (Did she ask, "Will you go in my place?")

quotation marks

Quotation marks (" ") are used to enclose a direct quotation of spoken or written words. Quotation marks have other special uses, but they should not be used for <u>emphasis</u> (Tab 9).

Enclose in quotation marks anything that is quoted word for word (a direct quotation) from speech or written material. (She said clearly, "I want the progress report by three o'clock.") Do not enclose indirect quotations — usually introduced by the word *that* — in quotation marks. Indirect quotations are paraphrases of a speaker's words or ideas. (She said that she wanted the progress report by three o'clock.) See also <u>paraphrasing</u> (Tab 2).

■ ETHICS NOTE When you use quotation marks to indicate that you are quoting, do not make any changes in the quoted material unless you clearly indicate what you have done. For further information on using and incorporating quoted material, see <u>plagiarism</u> (Tab 2) and <u>quotations</u> (Tab 2).

Use single quotation marks (' ') to enclose a quotation that appears within a quotation.

- John said, "Jane told me that she was going to 'stay with the project if it takes all year.'"

Use quotation marks to set off special words or terms only to point out that the term is used in context for a unique or special purpose (that is, in the sense of the term *so-called*).

- What chain of events caused the sinking of the "unsinkable" *Titanic* on its maiden voyage?

Slang, colloquial expressions, and attempts at humor, although infrequent in business writing, should seldom be set off by quotation marks.

- Our first six months amounted to a ~~"shakedown cruise."~~ *shakedown cruise.*

Use quotation marks to enclose titles of reports, short stories, articles, essays, single episodes of radio and television programs, short musical works, paintings, and other works of art. However, do not use quotation marks for titles of books and periodicals, which should appear in <u>italics</u>.

- His report, "Effects of Government Regulations on Motorcycle Safety," cited the article "No-Fault Insurance and Motorcycles" published in *American Motorcyclist* magazine.

Use quotation marks for parts of publications, such as chapters of books and articles or sections within periodicals.

12

Punctuation
and Mechanics

- "Bad Writing" was an article by Barbara Wallraff in the "On Language" column of the *New York Times*.

Some titles, by convention, are not set off by quotation marks, underlining, or italics, although they are capitalized.

- Business Communication [college course title], the Bible, the Constitution, Lincoln's Gettysburg Address, the Lands' End Catalog

    <u>Commas</u> and <u>periods</u> always go inside closing quotation marks.

- "Reading *Computer World* gives me the insider's view," he says, adding, "It's like a conversation with the top experts."

<u>Semicolons</u> and <u>colons</u> always go outside closing quotation marks.

- He said, "I will pay the full amount"; this statement surprised us.

All other punctuation follows the logic of the context: if the punctuation is a part of the material quoted, it goes inside the quotation marks; if the punctuation is not part of the material quoted, it goes outside the quotation marks.

ESL TIPS FOR USING QUOTATION MARKS AND PUNCTUATION

When making choices about using quotation marks with other punctuation, keep the following examples in mind.

Correct use of a comma with quotation marks

- "as a last resort," (*not* "as a last resort",)

Correct use of a period with quotation marks

- "to the bitter end." (*not* "to the bitter end".)

Correct use of a semicolon or colon with quotation marks

- "there is no doubt"; (*not* "there is no doubt;")

12

semicolons

The semicolon (;) links independent <u>clauses</u> (Tab 11) or other sentence elements of equal weight and grammatical rank when they are not joined by a <u>comma</u> and a <u>conjunction</u> (Tab 11). The semicolon indicates a greater pause between clauses than a comma, but not as great a pause as a <u>period</u>.

Independent clauses joined by a semicolon should balance or contrast with each other, and the relationship between the two statements should be so clear that further explanation is not necessary. (The new Web site was a success; every division reported increased online sales.) Do not use a semicolon between a dependent clause and its main clause.

* No one applied for the ~~position;~~ *position,* even though it was heavily advertised.

With Strong Connectives

In complicated sentences, a semicolon may be used before transitional words or phrases (*that is, for example, namely*) that introduce examples or further explanation. See also <u>transition</u> (Tab 9).

* The press understands Commissioner Curran's position on the issue; that is, local funds should not be used for the highway project.

A semicolon should also be used before conjunctive adverbs (*therefore, moreover, consequently, furthermore, indeed, in fact, however*) that connect independent clauses.

* The test results are not complete; *therefore*, I cannot make a recommendation.
  [The semicolon shows that *therefore* belongs to the second clause.]

For Clarity in Long Sentences

Use a semicolon between two independent clauses connected by a coordinating conjunction (*and, but, for, or, nor, so, yet*) if the clauses are long and contain other punctuation.

* In most cases, these individuals are executives, bankers, or lawyers; *but* they do not, as the press seems to believe, simply push the button of their economic power to affect local politics.

A semicolon may also be used if any items in a series contain commas.

* Among those present were John Howard, president of the Omega Paper Company; Carol Delgado, president of Environex Corporation; and Larry Stanley, president of Stanley Papers.

Use <u>parentheses</u> or <u>dashes</u>, not semicolons, to enclose a parenthetical element that contains commas.

- All affected job classifications (receptionists, secretaries, transcriptionists, and clerks) will be upgraded this month.

Use a <u>colon</u>, not a semicolon, as a mark of anticipation or enumeration.

consideration:
- Three decontamination methods are under ~~consideration;~~ a zeolite-resin system, an evaporation system, and a filtration system.

The semicolon always appears outside closing <u>quotation marks</u>.

- The attorney said, "You must be accurate"; her client replied, "I will."

slashes

The slash (/)—called a variety of names, including *slant line, diagonal, virgule, bar,* and *solidus*—both separates and shows omission.
  The slash is often used to separate items in the URL (uniform resource locator) addresses for sites on the Internet (bedfordstmartins .com/alred). The backward slash is used to separate parts of filenames (c:\myfiles\reports\annual06.doc).
  The slash can indicate alternatives or combinations.

- David's telephone numbers are 549-2278/2235.
- Check the on/off switch before you leave.

The slash often indicates omitted words and letters.

- miles/hour (miles per hour); w/o (without)

In fractions and mathematical expressions, the slash separates the numerator from the denominator ($3/4$ for three-fourths; x/y for *x* over *y*).
  Although the slash is used informally with <u>dates</u> (5/11/06), do not use this form in business writing where it may not be immediately clear, especially in <u>international correspondence</u> (Tab 6).

spelling

Because spelling mistakes in your documents will damage your credibility, careful <u>proofreading</u> (Tab 1) is essential. The use of a spell checker is crucial; however, it will not catch all mistakes, especially those in personal and company names. It cannot detect a spelling error if the error results in a valid word; for example, if you mean *to* but inadvertently type *too*, the spell checker will not detect the error. Likewise, spell checkers will not detect errors in the names of people, places, and organizations. If you are unsure about the spelling of a word, do not rely on guesswork or a spell checker—consult a standard dictionary or style guide.

Acknowledgments (continued)

Leigh Ryan, "Four Criteria for Evaluating Sources" from *The Bedford Guide for Writing Tutors,* Third Edition. Copyright © 2002 by Bedford/St. Martin's. Reprinted with the permission of Bedford/St. Martin's.

Figure 2–5: "Library Homepage." Reprinted with the permission of Columbia University Libraries.

Figure 2–6: "Boston Regional Library System InfoTrac Search Page." Reprinted with permission.

Figure 2–7: "Advanced Google Search." Reprinted with the permission of Google, Inc.

Figure 2–8: "Google's Main Subject Directory." Reprinted with the permission of Google, Inc.

Figure 3–3: "Company Newsletter (front page)." From Ken Cook Company, *Connection* (April 2003). Copyright © 2003 by Ken Cook Co. Reprinted with the permission of Ken Cook Company.

"Sample Formal Report." Reprinted with the permission of Susan Litzinger, a student at Pennsylvania State University, Altoona.

Figure 5–2: "Cutaway Drawing (Hard Disk Drive)." From P. D. Moulton and Timothy S. Stanley, *Hard Disk Quick Reference.* Copyright © 1989 by Que Publishing. Reprinted with the permission of Pearson Computer Publishing, a division of Pearson Education.

Figure 5–18: "Photo of Aircraft Door." Reprinted with the permission of Ken Cook Company.

Figure 6–2: "Adjustment Letter (When Company Is at Fault)." Reprinted with the permission of American Airlines, AMR Corporation, Inc. All rights reserved.

Index

PROOFREADERS' MARKS

The marks illustrated on this page are commonly used by editors and proofreaders. These marks are also useful when revising your own writing when collaborating with others.

MARK/SYMBOL	MEANING	EXAMPLE	CORRECTED TYPE
ℒ	Delete	the manager's report	the report
∧	Insert	the report	the manager's report
dots (stet)	Let stand	the manager's report	the manager's report
≡ (cap)	Capitalize	the monday meeting	the Monday meeting
/ (lc)	Lowercase	the Monday Meeting	the Monday meeting
∼ (tr)	Transpose	the cover lettre	the cover letter
⊂	Close space	a loud speaker	a loudspeaker
#	Insert space	a loudspeaker	a loud speaker
¶	Paragraph	...report. The meeting...	...report. The meeting...
⌒	Run in with previous line or paragraph	...report. The meeting...	...report. The meeting...
— (ital)	Italicize	the New York Times	the *New York Times*
∼ (bf)	Boldface	Use boldface sparingly.	Use **boldface** sparingly.
⊙	Insert period	I wrote the e-mail	I wrote the e-mail.
⌃	Insert comma	However we cannot...	However, we cannot...
=	Insert hyphen	clear cut decision	clear-cut decision
⊥/M	Insert em dash	Our goal productivity	Our goal—productivity
⊙ or :/	Insert colon	We need the following	We need the following:
⊙ or ;/	Insert semicolon	we finished we achieved	we finished; we achieved
⌄ ⌄	Insert quotation marks	He said, I agree.	He said, "I agree."
⌄	Insert apostrophe	the managers report	the manager's report